GERMANY AT THE FIN DE SIÈCLE

GERMANY AT THE FIN DE SIÈCLE
 CULTURE, POLITICS, AND IDEAS

EDITED BY SUZANNE MARCHAND AND DAVID LINDENFELD

LOUISIANA STATE UNIVERSITY PRESS ⚜ BATON ROUGE

Designer: Laura Roubique Gleason
Typeface: Minion text, Eccentric display
Typesetter: Coghill Composition Co.
Printer and binder: Thomson-Shore, Inc.

Library of Congress Cataloging-in-Publication Data

Germany at the fin de siecle : culture, politics, and ideas / edited by
Suzanne Marchand and David Lindenfeld.
p.   cm.
Papers from a conference held at Louisiana State University in Baton Rouge
in September 2000.
Includes index.
ISBN 0-8071-2979-8 (hardcover : alk. paper)
1. Germany—History—1871–1918—Congresses.   2. Germany—Civilization—19th
century—Congresses.   3. Germany—Intellectual life—Congresses.   I. Marchand,
Suzanne L., 1961–   II. Lindenfeld, David F.
DD222.G47   2004
943.08′4—dc22
2004007500

The paper in this book meets the guidelines for permanence and
durability of the Committee on Production Guidelines for Book Longevity of the
Council on Library Resources. ♾

CONTENTS

Popular Culture: Divisive or Integrative?

Antimodern Thought: Pathological or Prescient?

ILLUSTRATIONS

ACKNOWLEDGMENTS

The papers in this volume are the product of a conference organized by the editors at Louisiana State University in Baton Rouge in September 2000. The conference was made possible by funding provided to the Modern History Colloquium by the College of Arts and Sciences at LSU, and by additional funds from the LSU Department of History. The editors would particularly like to thank the participants and the commentators, who included, in addition to those whose essays are printed here, Corinna Treitel, Uwe Püschner, Scott Murray, Kees Gispen, Anthony La Vopa, and George Williamson. We would also like to thank LSU Press, and especially Sylvia Rodrigue, for agreeing to publish a book that falls somewhat outside its usual purview and for treating our volume with such care and intelligence. Thanks are also due to Cornell University Press for allowing us to print a revised version of the chapter that appears as "*Algabal* and the Decadent" in Robert E. Norton's *Secret Germany: Stefan George and His Circle* (Ithaca, N.Y., 2002) and E. J. Brill, publishers of *Central European History*, for permission to print a slightly altered version of Fritz Ringer's essay, which originally appeared in *CEH* 35, no. 3 (2002). The essays by Peter Jelavich and Marline Otte originally appeared in German, Jelavich's as "Darf ich mich hier amüsieren? Bürgertum und früher Film," in *Der bürgerliche Wertehimmel. Innenansichten des 19. Jahrhunderts*, ed. Manfred Hettling and Stefan-Ludwig Hoffmann (Göttingen, 2000) and Otte's as "Eine Welt für sich? Bürger im Jargontheater, 1890–1920" in *Juden, Bürger, Deutsche: Zur Geschichte der Vielfalt und Differenz, 1800–1933*, ed. Andreas Gotzmann, Rainer Liedtke, and Till van Rahden (Tübingen, 2001). We are grateful to Vandenhoeck and Ruprecht and Mohr Verlag respectively for their willingness to allow us to print the authors' own translations of these important essays.

GERMANY AT THE FIN DE SIÈCLE

Germany at the Fin de Siècle

An Introduction

SUZANNE MARCHAND AND DAVID LINDENFELD

Why 'Fin de Siècle'?

Perhaps this introduction should begin with a question: Was there a German fin de siècle? Traditionally, the concept of fin de siècle has been reserved for the travails and transitions of two European nations, France and Austria, who were beset by similar problems—urbanization, political radicalization, degeneration-hysteria, escalating nationalism—and challenged, in different ways, by the rise of German political and military power in the second half of the nineteenth century. Interestingly, these two nations also developed extremely strong, innovative modernist movements in art and literature. A great part of the appeal of these two fin-de-siècle cultures derives precisely from the contrast between their waning influence in the constellation of European powers and their flourishing cultural life. Both carrying a strong whiff of mortality, the French and Austrian worlds seem to have anticipated, as few others did, the *'fin'* that nineteenth-century culture and politics would meet in 1914.

In the eyes of most other Europeans, Wilhelmine Germany, on the other hand, was experiencing something like a *'commencement'* rather than a *'fin.'* Given the newly united nation's increasing self-confidence, military prowess, economic power, and cultural vigor, many observers believed that they were seeing the dawn of the German century. The later Wilhelmine world was characterized by enormous ambition and optimism, booming industries and bustling new urban spaces, cultural and political activism on a new scale, and the promise, if not the immediate realization, of a 'place in the sun' on the world stage. And, although often underemphasized, literary and artistic modernism in Germany was also emerging in this era, sharing with other European 'modernisms' grand ambitions for social and cultural transformation. Yet as historians have often observed, numerous Wilhelmine intellectuals still depicted their world as one of spiritual or even physical decline, worrying at least as much about degeneration and the arrival of mass urban society as did the French and Austrians. The rise of völkisch and radical nationalist organizations like the Pan-German League may be seen as a reaction to those anxieties. But these new attempts to revitalize and unify the polis coexisted—not always peacefully—with older confessional, regional, and class discourses. Many felt that modernizing processes were silencing their voices, while others lamented the increasing fragmentation of the cultural scene. All of these crosscurrents have rendered the Wilhelmine era particularly resistant to easy encapsulation in terms of any dominant "-ism" or Zeitgeist and have prohibited the writing of a cultural history of the German fin de siècle.[1]

The editors of this volume have no wish to impose a new Zeitgeist on what will and should remain a period of high contrasts and diverse discourses. But it seemed high time to bring together some of the new work on the period and to offer students and scholars of German—and, more broadly, European—history a sense of the vibrancy of the field. In recent years, the study of Wilhelmine cultural history has blossomed in many new directions. Scholars have begun to examine this prewar world on its own terms, seeing in it both peculiarities and commonalities with other European nations. There is now less preoccupation with the nineteenth-century origins of Nazism; scholars who pursue this question have largely shifted their attention to the eras of the Great War and the Weimar Republic. Change has also come from the fruitful cross-pollination of cultural and intellectual history, from the inclusion of gender into cultural analyses, and from new work in the history of science and on popular culture. It was with a strong sense of the liveliness of the field and the exciting possibilities for mutual inspiration that the editors organized a conference on "Germany at the Fin

1. Some years ago, August Nitschke, Gerhard A. Ritter, Detlev J. K. Peukert, and Rüdiger vom Bruch produced an edited work entitled *Jahrhundertwende: Der Aufbruch in die Moderne, 1880–1930*, 2 vols. (Reinbek bei Hamburg, 1990). Its essays focused heavily on things German—though the purported intent was to characterize international (or at least pan-Western) developments. Thus, although the essays are highly informative and interesting, most of them do not reflect directly on the problem of fin-de-siècle Germany and largely skirt the *Sonderweg* debate. One exception is Peukert's important essay on the *Jugendbewegung*, "'Mit uns zieht die neue Zeit . . .': Jugend zwischen Disziplinierung und Revolte," ibid., 1:176–202.

de Siècle" at Louisiana State University in the fall of 2000, subsequently collecting for publication the papers from what turned out to be a stimulating exchange of ideas. If the essays presented here sketch a world of contrasts and contradictions, they also reflect the results of the innovative scholarship that is transforming this important field.

To characterize the fin de siècle as a world of sharpened contrasts and conflicts captures the feeling of unsettledness or even uprootedness shared by those who lived through it, not only in Germany but across Europe as well.[2] For contemporaries, the years between roughly 1885 and 1914 clearly were characterized by a different feel—and especially a different pace—from the preceding era of what one might call high liberal culture, which lasted from about 1850 to 1885. The post-1885 years saw extraordinary cultural change, as German cities underwent massive growth and the 'second industrial revolution' transformed the coal, iron, steel, and chemical industries; in these years, feminist, socialist, and Catholic political movements burgeoned, Germany entered the race for colonies in Africa and Asia, and electricity, cinema, telephones, typewriters, and motorcars were integrated into everyday life. School reforms opened the universities to non-Gymnasium-trained students after 1890 and to women after 1908; Ibsen and Nietzsche, Buddhism and vegetarianism attracted critics of the status quo. Life expectancy was increasing; so was leisure time, and with it nonelite entertainments like cabaret, film, circuses, and football. 'High' cultural pursuits, however, had not disappeared. Operas, art exhibitions, concerts, university lectures, and museums flourished, so much so that the avant-garde increasingly felt the need to wall off its art from the stultifying embrace of the parvenus. Never before had so much or so varied a print culture been available to the middling (and even lower middling) classes.

This was also, quite evidently, an age of less bridled passions, of street

2. Michael Stanislawski's recent *Zionism and the Fin de Siècle: Cosmopolitanism and Nationalism from Nordau to Jabotinsky* (Berkeley, Calif., 2001) offers a subtle and highly interesting discussion of the cosmopolitan cultural tendencies which worked their magic on Jewish intellectuals between about 1880 and 1920. His careful treatment of the careers of writers such as Max Nordau and Vladimir Jabotinsky nicely demonstrates the complexity of individual responses to this unsettling and exhilarating moment in Central European history, showing especially how Zionist fervor was born in circles quite distant from traditional Jewish life.

politics, of open discussions of homosexuality, female sexuality, and colonial violence, of occultism and of hypernationalist boosterism. It was an era of expanding participation in politics and new avenues of social mobility— although the promises of meritocratic permeability for various professions and institutions were by no means completely realized. Nor did cultural and technological change reach every inhabitant of the Reich. The urban street scene, as Detlev Peukert has noted, was characterized by the jostling of horses and bicycles, automobiles, and those too poor to travel any other way than by foot, and the beautiful images in Alter Kacyzne's *Polyn* remind us that in many parts of East Prussia, village life was largely untouched by industrialization and modernism even in the late 1920s.[3] In any event, the cultural scene, like the political scene, experienced an explosive series of confrontations between traditions and novel practices in a very short period of time. And like the political scene, it swarmed with new aspirants to power and prestige: never before had so many felt the desire to shape German culture to their own ends. As our essays will show, this circumstance led not only to the efflorescence of experimentation but also to virulent competition over the right to define true German *Geist*.

We have avoided using the term 'modernism' to capture the mood of Germany before World War I, but this is not because Wilhelmine Germany lacked the modern qualities exhibited by other western European nations. As suggested above, Germany both participated fully in the development of modernism (innovations in the arts, humanities, and social sciences) and demonstrated considerable support for modernity (broadly defined as belief in reason, science, and progress, and exemplified by technological innovation, industrialization, and urbanization). The term 'modern' was quite extensively and self-consciously used by German speakers in the 1890s, connoting the increased tempo of change and the resultant difficulty experienced by industrializing societies in arriving at coherent meaning and reestablishing community.[4] Of course there were antimodern forces operating

3. Peukert quoted in "Die Jahrhundertwende—eine Epoche? Eine Diskussion," in *Jahrhundertwende,* ed. Nitschke et al., 1:19; Kacyzne, *Polyn: Jewish Life in the Old Country* (New York, 1999).

4. William Everdell, *The First Moderns: Profiles in the Origins of Twentieth-Century Thought* (Chicago, 1997), 3, 11; Malcom Bradbury and James McFarlane, "The Name and

in Germany, and perhaps more skepticism about the possibilities for human progress there than was apparent in France, Britain, and the United States (but not in Russia!). But this is no reason to question Germany's 'modernity,' especially as the recent scholarly literature has probably overemphasized Western—and underreported German—optimism. 'Modernism,' however, has become so controversial and its definition so changeable that using it obscures rather than illuminates. Thus instead of trying to determine, for example, whether naturalism or symbolism were truly modernist or attempting to find a common modernist denominator shared by film and phenomenology, we simply acknowledge that the fin de siècle was a world in which the new and old coexisted, and in which individuals and groups pursued multiple, and often noncomplementary, paths into the future.

We believe that 'fin de siècle' preserves the possibility of locating commonalities with other European nations while underscoring the pervasive sense of incoherence and crisis—a sense that might have been stronger in Germany than elsewhere. Having achieved political union so late, German expectations for unity of purpose and sentiment were exceedingly high; indeed, in the wake of political unification many Germans found distressing the absence of unified style or meaning. To be sure, Marxism and Social Darwinism continued to flourish, providing more or less coherent world views for their followers. But many others bemoaned the nation's failures to achieve 'spiritual' unification, while those less happy about Wilhelmine imperialism (a group which included old conservatives like Jacob Burckhardt and radical Germanophiles like Paul de Lagarde, as well as Catholics, left-liberals, and socialists) lamented the shape of the new state. In these circumstances, as several recent historians—and several of the essays in this volume—have pointed out, a series of counterresponses appeared, in the form of new and more extravagant attempts at achieving spiritual wholeness and unity. Friedrich Meinecke's memoirs testify to the coincidence of this social fragmentation with the arrival of what might be called a neoromantic longing for wholeness: "In all of Germany, something new could be felt around 1890, not only politically but also culturally . . . a new and deeper

Nature of Modernism," in *Modernism, 1890–1930,* ed. Bradbury and McFarlane (Harmondsworth, 1976), 22, 37–42.

longing for the genuine and true but also a new awareness of the problematical fragmentation of modern life awoke and tried to dive down again from its civilized surface into the now eerie, now tempting depths."[5] For the participants, these were not years of modernism or antimodernism, but years of ambivalence: of great expectations and profound disappointments, of relinquishing old convictions and groping for new myths. Few were able to discern, in Robert Musil's words, what was moving forward and what was moving backward.

Yet another reason to prefer 'fin de siècle' to 'modern' is that modernism, as it is usually portrayed, does not lend itself to contextual cultural analysis. Modernists were widely acknowledged to have harbored an increasingly radical hostility to mass culture, doubtless provoked by the rapid growth of that very phenomenon.[6] This makes modernism almost by definition less sensitive to the complicated dynamics of the relationship between 'low' and 'high' cultures and to the study of how innovations spread from one group to another (*Rezeptionsgeschichte*). Many of the essays in this volume are innovative in just this respect, showing that intellectual and cultural history are not neat, airtight categories, but that cross-fertilization of elite and popular culture is an integral part of the Wilhelmine picture. By pursuing these linkages, we can gain a better understanding of the distinctive cultural politics of the Wilhelmine fin de siècle, something that would be obscured by an exclusive focus on the modernist avant-gardes.

Fin de Siècle, or Commencement du Mal?

The question of national cultural peculiarities points unavoidably to a set of issues and controversies that are very familiar to historians of Germany. Over the last forty years, many of us have been more interested in probing the relationship between the fin de siècle to the century being ushered in than to the one being ushered out. Following the precedents set by Fritz

---

5. Friedrich Meinecke, *Erlebtes und Erkanntes*, quoted in Fritz Ringer, *The Decline of the German Mandarins: The German Academic Community, 1890–1933* (Cambridge, Mass., 1969), 258.

6. E.g., Andreas Huyssen, *After the Great Divide: Modernism, Mass Culture, Postmodernism* (Bloomington, Ind., 1986), vii–viii; Patrick Brantlinger, "Mass Media and Culture in Fin-de-Siècle Europe," in *Fin de Siècle and Its Legacy*, ed. Mikulas Teich and Roy Porter (Cambridge, 1990), 98.

Fischer and Hans-Ulrich Wehler in the 1960s and early '70s, numerous historians have dated the first false steps that led down Germany's 'different path' (*Sonderweg*) to the later nineteenth century.[7] In the Bismarckian and Wilhelmine eras, according to Fischer and Wehler, the Germans failed to develop a real market economy and strong liberal institutions, and this failure set the state on its special—if not straight—path to fascism. Although this remains a popular view, since the publication of Geoff Eley and David Blackbourn's *The Peculiarities of German History* (1985), scholars have been forced to rethink the Wilhelmine period, to specify what exactly was 'unmodern' or 'illiberal' about it, and to detail which elements were truly 'peculiar' to Germany. Numerous recent books have shown that the evolution of German nationalism and German identity was by no means as straightforward or inherently toxic as Fischer and Wehler contended.[8] One group of studies has traced the development of Bismarck's remarkably modern social welfare legislation.[9] Historians of science and medicine have attempted to distinguish the perilous from the not-so-perilous trajectories of German biological thought.[10] The picture that has emerged is one of hybrid identities coexisting with the development of passionate nationalist, racist, confessional, and political loyalties, of increasing specialization alongside new calls for a holistic world view, of expanding state power but also widening opportunities for the expression of minority interests. Thanks to this new scholarship, we now possess a much more nuanced view of the political, social, and scientific dynamics of the Wilhelmine era.

Cultural and intellectual history, however, have been rather slow to take

7. Fritz Fischer, *Griff nach der Weltmacht: Die Kriegszielpolitik des kaiserlichen Deutschland 1914–18* (Düsseldorf, 1961); Hans-Ulrich Wehler, *Das deutsche Kaiserreich, 1871–1918* (Göttingen, 1973).

8. Celia Applegate, *A Nation of Provincials: The German Idea of Heimat* (Berkeley, Calif., 1990); Alon Confino, *The Nation as a Local Metaphor: Württemberg, Imperial Germany, and National Memory, 1871–1918* (Chapel Hill, N.C., 1997).

9. George Steinmetz, *Regulating the Social: The Welfare State and Local Politics in Imperial Germany* (Princeton, N.J., 1993); Greg Eghigian, *Making Security Social: Disability, Insurance, and the Birth of the Social Entitlement State in Germany* (Ann Arbor, Mich., 2000).

10. Paul Weindling, *Health, Race, and German Politics between National Unification and Nazism, 1870–1945* (New York, 1989); Anne Harrington, *Reenchanted Science: Holism in German Culture from Wilhelm II to Hitler* (Princeton, N.J., 1996).

up the challenges of this new historiographical movement. In past decades, intellectual historians tended to gravitate toward studies of non-Nazis (such as Sigmund Freud, Max Weber, Georg Lukács, and Walter Benjamin). Cultural historians, particularly émigré historians like Fritz Stern and George Mosse, excavated the cultural and sociological origins of Nazi ideology; but German cultural history remained quite marginal until the 1990s, when new studies of popular nationalism, of academic disciplines, and of ambivalent figures like Martin Heidegger, Werner Sombart, and Ernst Jünger began to appear. In Germany particularly, historians of the Wilhelmine and Weimar worlds still gravitate toward topics in political or social history, possibly feeling that modern German history was a matter for serious discussion, and that cultural history was not, in some sense, serious. But now a space seems to be opening for those seeking to understand the changing institutional structures, pivotal intellectual figures, and idiosyncratic cultural dynamics of the prewar era, without presuming it either to be perfectly 'clean' or completely complicit in laying the foundations for Nazism.[11] It is our hope that this volume will likewise open the way for cultural historians to identify the 'peculiarities' of the German fin de siècle.

Moreover, there are myriad other interesting questions about Wilhelmine culture that have rarely even been posed, and aspects of this cultural world that, because they seemed to have little bearing on the big political questions, have not interested historians as much, perhaps, as they should. In particular, historians have overemphasized 'cultural despair' and overstudied its purveyors.[12] The late Wilhelmine world was populated not only by

11. The work of Thomas Nipperdey, Jürgen Kocka, and others on nineteenth-century middle-class culture and sociability has suggested interesting new ways to deal with the 'peculiarities' problem, while newly fashionable topics such as women's history, religion, and what one might call the 'culture of politics' (e.g., Roger Chickering's *We Men Who Feel Most German: A Cultural Study of the Pan-German League, 1886–1914* [Boston, 1984]) have given historians new inclination to dabble in the cultural sphere. See, for example, Nipperdey, *Geschichte, Kultur, Theorie: Gesammelte Aufsätze zur neueren Geschichte* (Göttingen, 1976); Werner Conze and Jürgen Kocka, eds., *Bildungsbürgertum im 19. Jahrhundert*, 4 vols. (Stuttgart, 1985–92); Kathleen Canning, *Languages of Labor and Gender: Female Factory Work in Germany, 1850–1914* (Ithaca, N.Y., 1996); David Blackbourn, *Marpingen: Apparitions of the Virgin Mary in Bismarckian Germany* (Oxford, 1993).

12. One example is the state of theological discourse and its effects in shaping Wilhelmine debates about *Kultur* and personality. See Friedrich Wilhelm Graf's important but little-read essay, "Rettung der Persönlichkeit: Protestantische Theologie als Kulturwissen-

pessimists, but also by fervent optimists, and probably most densely by those who wavered between hope and despair. The merits of this view can be seen in the essays below, especially those by Richard Wetzell, Ann Taylor Allen, Peter Jelavich, and Marline Otte, and it is widely represented in the recent literature.[13] As a result, we have learned not only to recognize the diversity of Wilhelmine culture, but to be wary of blaming all of Germany's prewar citizens for a series of crimes and maladies they could not have predicted, and which some worked hard to prevent. We are also learning to see culture not merely as politics by other means, but as a sphere with its own ambitions and constraints, institutional structures, and charismatic individuals.

Yet over and against this new set of tendencies, there are still many cultural historians who resist giving the Wilhelmine world full independence from the Weimar and Nazi eras that followed it, and who continue to see it as embodying the warning signs of things to follow. As the essays of Fritz Ringer, Kevin Repp, Martin Ruehl, Robert Norton, Suzanne Marchand, and David Lindenfeld suggest, there remain worrying aspects of Wilhelmine culture—its intolerance, its taste for blood and tyrants, its institutionalized loathing for compromise, its preoccupation with the aesthetics of death on the one hand and its Nietzschean pursuit of life on the other, the resentment it voices (and the blame it liberally doles out) for the disenchantment of the world. While all of these scholars recognize that the fin de siècle in no way represented a complete rejection of the liberal values of reason, science, and progress, they caution that the denizens of the Wilhelmine world were also drawn, in Thomas Mann's words, to the language of "blood and beauty" and to the bathetic nostalgia of Arnold Böcklin's 'serious' paintings.[14] As the example of Stefan George shows, there are cultural continuities from the fin de siècle to the Nazi era; we must not forget that the generation of Max Weber was also that of Houston Stewart Chamberlain. As we learn more about, for example, the 'normal' German-Jewish relations on display in Ber-

---

schaft des Christentums," in *Kultur und Kulturwissenschaften um 1900: Krise der Moderne und Glaube an die Wissenschaft*, eds. Rüdiger vom Bruch, Friedrich Wilhelm Graf, and Gangolf Hübinger (Stuttgart, 1989), 103–32.

13. See, for example, H. Glenn Penny, *Objects of Culture: Ethnology and Ethnographic Museums in Imperial Germany* (Chapel Hill, N.C., 2002); Corinna Treitel, *A Science for the Soul: Occultism and the Genesis of the German Modern* (Baltimore, 2004).

14. Mann's comment is cited in Martin Ruehl's essay, 186, below.

lin's *Jargon* theaters (see the essay by Marline Otte), we must also note the increasing audience appeal of Renaissance tyrants (as does Martin Ruehl). There is no easy answer to the *Sonderweg* question, in cultural as in political and social history, but it is time we took it apart and tried to understand what 'peculiarities' are evident and significant in this sphere as well.

Some thirty years ago, Carl Schorske juxtaposed chapters in intellectual, cultural, and political history in order to endow Vienna with a fascinating, brilliant, and disturbing fin de siècle—but not a coherent one. And if such a great cultural historian could not paint a unified picture of the *Jahrhundert-wende* in one (albeit highly diverse) city, we cannot possibly hope to offer a fully coherent image of the German fin de siècle. But as Schorske showed, the juxtaposition of spheres and the evocation of the thought-worlds of diverse individuals is often enormously fruitful. Though we cannot claim to rival Schorske's brilliant survey, we hope to offer something of the same for the German world, juxtaposing, as it were, light and dark, high and low, backward and forward, in order to paint the Wilhelmine fin de siècle in its own vibrant colors.

Liberalism: Adversarial or Reformist?

The essays in this volume focus on cultural figures and trends; yet in almost every case, politics is inextricably involved. The first two papers address politics most directly, tackling the tangle of issues surrounding liberalism. Liberalism at the turn of the century, as Fritz Ringer and Richard Wetzell testify, was a melody that could be played in a number of keys, and one which changed its tunes significantly over time. It was a European phenomenon, but there were peculiarities to the German variants, just as Austrian, English, and Danish liberalism also exhibited unique turns of mind. In Germany, liberalism was a political movement, manifest in several national parties (though never a single one) and a variety of associations and organizations at local governmental levels. Being a liberal implied that one accepted market principles, though by no means acquiesced to full market dominance; it implied that one supported meritocratic principles—but not state funding to level all playing fields. Liberals frequently advocated gradual, legal reform to temper the powers of the churches and monarchical states, but they rarely demanded full disestablishment of the clergy and court. Sometimes internationalist but usually nationalist, German liberals both admired and resented their closest rivals at the fin de siècle, the British, who had managed to combine market principles and parliamentary sovereignty with economic and political world power. As in Britain and France, liberalism also had strong social implications. Its proponents derived chiefly from the merchant and white-collar middle classes, whose impact on German society had expanded enormously in the wake of the 1848 revolutions, but who were by the fin de siècle under threat from the reinvigorated power of conservative landowners, courtiers, and industrialists on the one hand, and a thriving working-class movement on the other.

'Liberalism' was also a philosophical term, denoting a series of positions in political theory, economics, and even epistemology (e.g., neo-Kantianism) that overlapped with the ideologies and strategies of politicians, though not totally coinciding with them. The term 'liberal' connoted a commitment to rationality in a broad sense, and the middle classes took justifiable pride in the accomplishments of German science and scholarship. This had further ramifications for a variety of cultural and aesthetic attitudes. At the outset of our period, for example, it was expected that a visual artist's imaginative portrayal of classical antiquity would be more or less constrained by what historians and philologists claimed to be 'real' for that period—a constraint that was soon to be shattered, as the essays by Suzanne Marchand and Robert Norton illustrate. Finally, on what one might call the affective level, one could also distinguish, as Thomas Mann once did, between "liberality" as a habit of mind and liberalism as an ideology (Mann identified himself as a liberal in the former sense but not the latter).[15]

None of these liberalisms remained static between 1880 and 1914. Reflecting the rapid socioeconomic and political changes of those years, liberal institutions underwent fragmentation or regrouping. As Bismarck borrowed liberal ideas and right-wing liberals acceded to his plans, the boundaries between liberalism and conservatism became smudged; similarly, as left-leaning liberals, revolted by the politics of the Catholic Center Party, sought peace with moderate socialists, the core beliefs of liberalism became increasingly difficult to define. Politically, economically, and even psychologically, liberalism was the position of those in the middle. It could prosper where compromise was possible, but it suffered during periods of national political

15. Thomas Mann, *Betrachtungen eines Unpolitischen* (Frankfurt am Main, 1956), 108.

polarization or economic crisis. Though numerous earlier studies emphasized these weaknesses (as well as liberals' lack of real political commitment),
recent ones have focused on liberalism's ongoing vitality, particularly in municipal politics.[16] These studies, combined with new scholarship on the high
level of voting and political participation in Wilhelmine Germany, have rendered the cliché of the "unpolitical German" increasingly mythical.[17] Moreover, as Mark Mazower and Eric Hobsbawm have recently reminded us,
Germany was by no means the only nation where liberalism collapsed under
the pressures of war and the dislocations of the postwar period.[18] All of this
suggests that our picture of the unique frailty of German liberalism is fad-
ing—but it indicates, too, the rich possibilities for the reexamination of this
critical world view.

In the essays below, Ringer and Wetzell describe the confrontation of
liberalism (or better, of various liberalisms) with the social and intellectual
transformations of the fin de siècle. Interestingly, their protagonists—the sociologist Max Weber and the legal reformer Franz von Liszt—exhibited
rather different liberal personae and reacted quite differently to the challenges of the period. Ringer presents a view of Max Weber as an "almost
instinctive liberal" in his commitment to diversity of opinion and cultural
individualism. In his openmindedness, manifested through his personal and
professional dealings with his colleagues, he approximated Mann's notion of
liberality. But how typical was Weber of German liberals? Placing Weber's
views in a broad European context that hearkens back to Wilhelm von

16. For example, Steinmetz, *Regulating the Social;* Jan Palmowski, *Urban Liberalism in
Imperial Germany: Frankfurt am Main, 1866–1914* (Oxford, 1999). For the decline at the
national level, see James J. Sheehan, *German Liberalism in the Nineteenth Century* (Chicago, 1978), chs. 15–17; Dieter Langewiesche, "German Liberalism in the Second Empire,
1871–1914," in *In Search of a Liberal Germany: Studies in the History of German Liberalism
from 1789 to the Present,* ed. Konrad H. Jarausch and Larry Eugene Jones (New York,
1990), 217–35.

17. Jonathan Sperber, *The Kaiser's Voters: Electors and Elections in Imperial Germany*
(Cambridge, 1997); Margaret Lavinia Anderson, *Practicing Democracy: Elections and Political Culture in Imperial Germany* (Princeton, N.J., 2000).

18. See Mark Mazower, *Dark Continent: Europe's Twentieth Century* (London, 1998);
Eric Hobsbawm, *The Age of Extremes: A History of the World, 1914–1991* (New York,
1994).

Humboldt and John Stuart Mill, Ringer contends that Weber's (and Mill's) insistence on toleration of minority viewpoints was hardly characteristic of German liberal thought, particularly at the turn of the century. On the contrary, as he demonstrated in *The Decline of the German Mandarins* (1969), insofar as liberals were part of the academic establishment, they tended to distrust interest-group politics as divisive and to favor the harmonization of views rather than their diversity.[19] In that book, Weber appears as a member of the innovative "modernist" minority, which is contrasted to the unadventurous "orthodox" majority. In the present essay, Ringer goes further, emphasizing Weber's almost isolated intellectual position—a position that was based on his conviction that disharmony rather than harmony of views is a healthy state of affairs.[20] Ringer effectively shows Weber as not only conceptualizing the need for clashes of opinion but also as acting out this imperative, both in his personal relationships with colleagues and also by participating in and encouraging real debate in the organizations to which he belonged. Weber, it seems, viewed himself at the very least as a leavening agent in the stultifying atmosphere of Wilhelmine politics—a self-image that was reinforced by his perception of the tendency of bureaucratization to promote order at the expense of individual freedoms.

Ringer rightly portrays the heroic qualities of Weber's resistance to various forms of tyranny. It should be noted, however, that Weber's deliberately adversarial stance—and his critique of mass society—is compatible not only with Millean liberalism, but also with Nietzschean heroic pessimism and Social Darwinism. Weber's rhetoric, with its focus on leadership qualities and its emphasis on struggle, often wandered into this neovitalist discursive realm.[21] But lest we hastily identify this aspect of Weber's world view as dis-

19. Ringer, *Decline of the German Mandarins,* 124–7; cf. Sheehan, *German Liberalism in the Nineteenth Century,* 272.

20. This may well reflect the influence of Pierre Bourdieu on Ringer's work since *Decline.* Bourdieu presented a schema for characterizing the interrelationships of different intellectual movements in terms of a dynamic field, in which the very clash of majority and minority opinions enabled ideas to become explicit and articulated. See Pierre Bourdieu, *Outline of a Theory of Practice,* trans. Richard Nice (Cambridge, 1977), 168–71; Fritz Ringer, *Fields of Knowledge* (Cambridge, 1992), introduction.

21. For comparisons of Weber and Mill, see Alan Ryan, "Mill and Weber on History, Freedom, and Reason," in *Max Weber and His Contemporaries,* ed. Wolfgang J. Mommsen

tinctively German, we should recall that none of the great founders of liberalism, from Humboldt to Mill to Tocqueville, were pollyannas; quite the
contrary. And among Weber's contemporaries, it is not difficult to find other
forms of liberal pessimism, from the dark progressivism of George Bernard
Shaw to the apocalyptic crowd psychology of Gustave Le Bon, from the
American liberals' passionate embrace of Herbert Spencer to their French
cousins' revanchist fatalism. For too long, German historians have assumed
that their subjects held a monopoly on pessimism—something easily refuted
by studies such as T. J. Jackson Lears's elegant study of American intellectuals' confrontation with the modern, *No Place of Grace*.[22] If Weber was not
typically German, perhaps he was more typically liberal than previously has
been suspected.

Ringer's essay concludes with an informative discussion of Weber's political writings during the First World War. While he shows that these essays
point forward to Weber's activities in the founding of the Weimar Republic,
he more accurately treats them as Weber's retrospective commentary on the
regime just ending. Weber viewed the political immaturity of the German
people as attributable to Bismarck and the emasculation of the Reichstag's
power as a parliamentary body. Here Weber anticipated the *Sonderweg* argument of the 1970s, an argument with which Ringer clearly sympathizes.
Ringer's portrayal of Weber as advocating a healthy, conflict-steeled parliamentary life thus offers a very different reading from Wolfgang Mommsen's
influential interpretation of Weber's politics, with its emphasis on "plebiscitary leadership democracy," a conception that later inspired Carl Schmitt.[23]

Richard Wetzell's essay, by contrast, highlights what one might call a
more cheerful side of liberal culture: the often successful pursuit of social

---

and Jürgen Osterhammel (London, 1987), 170–81; for Weber and Nietzsche, see Robert
Eden, "Weber and Nietzsche: Questioning the Liberation of Social Science from Historicism," ibid., 405–21. While Ryan concludes that the differences between Weber and Mill
outweighed their similarities (181), Eden argues that Weber drew back from Nietzschean
nihilism in defense of liberal institutions (416). For Nietzsche's influence on Weber's
work, see Wilhelm Hennis, "The Traces of Nietzsche in the Work of Max Weber," in *Max
Weber: Essays in Reconstruction*, trans. Keith Tribe (London, 1988), 146–62.

22. T. J. Jackson Lears, *No Place of Grace: Antimodernism and the Transformation of
American Culture, 1880–1920* (New York, 1981).

23. Cf. Wolfgang J. Mommsen, *Max Weber and German Politics, 1890–1920*, trans.
Michael S. Steinberg (Chicago, 1984), 189, 398–406, 432.

reform. This was part of the response of both established elites and future-oriented activists to the conditions of industrial society; it can be seen either as an attempt to contain the conflicts generated by these conditions (and especially to short-circuit the appeal of the Social Democratic Party) or as an honest attempt to improve the lives of those displaced by industrial society. Whatever their motives, these liberals emphasized social harmony rather than conflict. As is well known, this response was by no means a German peculiarity, but a common European one. In Germany, the names of Friedrich Naumann and Gertrud Bäumer come to mind, as do organizations like the Social Policy Association (*Verein für Sozialpolitik*) and the Society for Social Reform.[24] Once again, liberalism was not the only current in this stream. The Social Policy Association brought together liberals of many stripes, as well as conservatives and Christian socials, and fostered debates between them. These factions differed on certain issues (for example, on the proper role of trade unions), but they often were willing to compromise rather than to resign themselves to defeat. Able to point to numerous successes, this group epitomizes the fin de siècle's positive achievements and hopeful outlook.

Wetzell's discussion of penal reform neatly highlights the ambiguities of these reformist ideas. His main protagonist, the law professor Franz von Liszt, identified himself as a political liberal, yet justified his system of differentiated punishments on the basis of the good of society rather than the principle of individual responsibility. Interestingly, in abandoning the traditional notion of punishment as retribution, Lizst's conception of justice actually provided for greater individualization and more humane treatment for some malefactors. Wetzell also shows that such arguments were put forth not only by legal scholars, but by medical professionals who were developing an interest in criminology, such as the psychiatrist Emil Kraepelin. Wetzell's examples could be generalized beyond Germany: criminal anthropology, pioneered by the Italian Cesare Lombroso, attracted many followers through-

24. On these movements, see Rüdiger vom Bruch, ed., *Weder Communismus noch Kapitalismus* (Munich, 1985); David Lindenfeld, *The Practical Imagination: The German Sciences of State in the Nineteenth Century* (Chicago, 1997), chs. 5–6; Kevin Repp, *Reformers, Critics, and the Paths of German Modernity: Anti-Politics and the Search for Alternatives, 1890–1914* (Cambridge, Mass., 2000).

out Europe, many of whom thought of themselves as liberal.[25] Ironically, the liberals' very faith in the progress of medical and social science made it easier for them to jettison the principle of individual responsibility as sacrosanct. Pursuing the good of society was, for them, a means to temper conservatives' overly hasty condemnation of individuals—but it could also be invoked to justify the long-term quarantining of those Ibsen called 'enemies of the people.' Wetzell's essay thus paints a different picture of the relationship of individual autonomy to collective constraints than Weber's gloomy one of continual erosion of freedom by bureaucratization. The social reformers' view was rather one of tradeoffs, whereby changes in collective arrangements entailed losses of freedom in some areas and concomitant gains in others. It was still possible, in short, to be a liberal and not to be a cultural pessimist.

Can we reconcile the liberalisms portrayed in these two papers? One key is to note that they cover slightly different time periods within the years 1880–1914. Most of the intellectual groundwork for Lizst's work on penal reform was laid in the 1880s (although the process of implementation naturally took longer), while Ringer's portrait of Weber relies mostly on material that dates from 1905 or later. This suggests that important changes occurred within the so-called fin-de-siècle years—a view that has been reinforced by other scholars. These changes often took the form of generational clashes, and they made consensus and harmony increasingly difficult to achieve as time went on. The year 1905 marked something of a turning point in this regard.[26] This sea-change invites parallels with diplomatic and political history: just as the Moroccan crisis of that year marked a new threshold in international tensions and the revolution in Russia inspired talk of a general strike and a new radicalism within the labor movement, the divisions within the Social Policy Association reached an intensity unparalleled since 1879. Physics entered a new phase with Einstein's discovery of special relativity. The modernist avant-garde in art became noticeably more alienated from bourgeois tastes after 1905 than before. In the universities, numerous prom-

---

25. Stephen Jay Gould, *The Mismeasure of Man* (New York, 1981), 140.

26. H. Stuart Hughes, *Consciousness and Society: The Reorientation of European Social Thought, 1890–1930* (New York, 1958), 337–44; Lindenfeld, *The Practical Imagination*, 313–22.

inent liberals—Theodor Mommsen, Rudolf Virchow, Adolf Bastian—passed away, leaving their chairs to a new generation of a more conservative mien.[27] By this time, the divisions within liberalism—between the right and left liberals, between those closest to the conservative humanities and those more decisively linked to the emerging social sciences and/or social services (law, economics, urban planning), between hopeful feminists and anxious patriarchs—had become so pronounced as to seem virtually unbridgeable. In consequence, scholars would do better to abandon the analysis of Liberalism with a capital *L* and to develop some more precise terms as well as a more finely-tuned chronology. To deepen their analysis, historians might, for example, focus on the fate of individual reformers—classic liberals or not—between about 1880 and 1905, and expand the cast of characters to reach beyond the world of the mandarins. Here, the following essays offer a road into the open.

Gendered Discourse: Emancipatory or Proto-Fascist?

The papers by Ann Taylor Allen and Kevin Repp both extend the analysis of the fortunes of German liberalism by turning away from the world of the male mandarinate to quite different intellectual milieus. They also exemplify another recent trend in German historiography, of which the authors are leading exponents: the tendency to view gender not as a separate topic but as fully integrated into the thematic mainstream of cultural and intellectual history. "The polarity of male and female," writes Allen, "often stood for other great dichotomies: history and prehistory, order and disorder, *Gesellschaft* and *Gemeinschaft*." Both Allen and Repp try to understand what was at stake in defining these polarities, and why debates about gender roles often took an increasingly biological (rather than a liberal-political) turn. We thus see the world of Wilhelmine male liberalism from the standpoint of those enticed by its promises but still largely barred from its doors; and as a result, we are able to observe the ways in which these outsiders forged

27. Wolfgang J. Mommsen, *Bürgerliche Kultur und künstlerische Avantgarde* (Frankfurt am Main, 1994), 97–110, esp. 109; Peter Paret, *The Berlin Secession: Modernism and Its Enemies in Imperial Germany* (Cambridge, Mass., 1980), ch. 6; Jacques Barzun, *From Dawn to Decadence: Five Hundred Years of Western Cultural Life, 1500 to the Present* (New York, 2000), 679.

their weapons from the intellectual and social materials at hand. Inevitably, this casts a quite different light on the phenomenon of 'cultural despair' than previous treatments of the period.

Allen's essay offers a broad survey of views on the history of the family from the 1860s to the 1920s, addressing such varied movements as socialism, feminism, anthropology, sociology, and psychoanalysis. Demonstrating the ability of ideas to travel across disciplines and from the academy through the public sphere (and back), she shows how debates on the roles of matriarchy and patriarchy in the past provided a basis for questioning accepted gender roles in the present and for anticipating changes in the future. The contemporary importance of these debates can be seen in the fact that August Bebel's *Women under Socialism,* which explicitly dealt with all three of these time dimensions, was a best-seller, reaching over fifty editions between 1883 and 1913.[28]

Allen's overview reveals a landscape of fluid ideological borders. Differing views on sexuality, motherhood, and the family led to divisions within some movements (for example, between the League of German Women's Associations and the League for the Protection of Mothers) and made for strange bedfellows among others. Thus Johann Jakob Bachofen's conservative critique of patriarchal modernity served as an inspiration for Otto Gross's radical call for emancipation from sexual repression, and Nietzschean philosophy appealed both to the radical feminist Lou Andreas Salomé and to the anything-but-feminist members of the George *Kreis.* Allen's survey thus reinforces the picture of the fin de siècle as a period of fervid innovation and experimentation, when established certainties were called into question and a vast array of new possibilities were entertained. In some ways, this is an update of the picture that H. Stuart Hughes presented in his classic *Consciousness and Society* (1958). His characterization of the fin de siècle as a "revolt against positivism" was intended to highlight the same dissatisfaction with smug nineteenth-century theories of progress and to explore a similar range of innovative responses; but Allen considerably enriches this picture by adding gender issues and women writers to the mix. We might add that such openness and willingness to contemplate new possi-

28. Lewis A. Coser, "Introduction to the Paperback Edition" in August Bebel, *Women under Socialism,* trans. Daniel DeLeon (New York, 1971), vii.

bilities—at least on the part of sizeable groups within society—is generally predicated on a degree of self-confidence that economic security and political stability provide. In Allen's scenario, World War I undermined this security for women as well as men and thus had the effect of truncating intellectual innovation, reinforcing those positions which favored time-honored notions of patriarchy.

If Allen uses a wide-angle lens, Repp prefers the closeup. He explores the so-called 'sexual crisis' not from the point of view of doctors or male pessimists, but from that of female radicals. Concentrating on a few lesser-known figures, he reveals that they maintained ties to a number of different groups normally seen as distant from one another. Repp begins his essay with a discussion of *The Intellectuals* (1911), a novel written by feminist and expressionist Grete Meisel-Hess. He uses this extremely provocative text as a roman à clef in order to delineate the wide range of solutions to the "sexual crisis" (most of them, for Meisel-Hess, flawed) posited by members of the radical circles of fin-de-siècle Berlin. Remarkably, many of these solutions—including the one Meisel-Hess herself seems to have preferred—not only flew in the face of liberal feminism, but adopted what is often thought to be a conservative position: that biology is indeed destiny.[29] Repp then turns to a discussion of the important writer and socialite Lou Andreas Salomé, who he characterizes as a paradoxical figure; she appears both as the ultimate philosopher of eroticism and a defender of motherhood as the final, redemptive act of self-transcendence. Repp concludes with a few paragraphs on Lucia Dora Frost, an emancipated (but antifeminist) journalist. Although Frost was long associated with avant-garde symbolism, Repp shows that by 1910 she had adopted a clearly racialist point of view. Greatly complicating our view of fin-de-siècle culture, Repp demonstrates how biological ideas traveled across the political and stylistic spectrum, making for disquieting points of consensus.

By exploring the connections between feminism and biopolitics that intensified in the decade prior to World War I, Repp also raises the issue of the place of the fin de siècle in the larger sweep of twentieth-century German

---

29. For a number of important essays on this conundrum in the Weimar and Nazi eras, see *When Biology Became Destiny: Women in Weimar and Nazi Germany*, ed. Renate Bridenthal, Atina Grossmann, and Marion Kaplan (New York, 1984).

history, arriving at a conclusion that differs from Allen's emphasis on the discontinuities brought about by the Great War: he sees the 1900s as the beginning of a "slippery slope" that led to Nazism.[30] Here he builds on a seminal article by Detlev Peukert, "The Genesis of the 'Final Solution' from the Spirit of Science," which—in good Weberian fashion—traces the inhumanity of the Holocaust to the pretenses of the 'rational' sciences at the turn of the century to select the healthy from the unhealthy, the normal from the pathological.[31] This is a theme which has been taken up by postmodernist sociologists such as Zygmunt Bauman as part of a general critique of the Enlightenment—thus magnifying its relevance beyond the confines of Germany.[32]

Repp tackles, too, the question of the extent to which these Social Darwinist impulses were compatible with fin-de-siècle feminists' desires for emancipation (and antifeminists' longings for separate spheres). In fact, this question constitutes the focal point of his essay. He is certainly aware, as was Peukert, that the feminist agenda did not lead to Auschwitz in any causal sense, and that similar discourses can have sharply dissimilar moral consequences. The call for sexual liberation, after all, recurred throughout the twentieth century, often as part of a passionate antifascism (as in the case of Wilhelm Reich, for example). What leads Repp to opt for the "slippery slope" interpretation is not the mere fact that feminists and Nazis both embraced eugenics, but a more fundamental factor that Peukert also grasped: the redemptive, ersatz-religious spell that notions such as race, motherhood, vitalism, and the like exerted over their believers. It was the hope that these ideas engendered by irrationally joining the individual to the national collective, and the mother's body to the *Volkskörper*, that made them arguably protofascist (not just proto-Nazi).[33] To return to Ringer's formulation, this

30. For a thorough discussion of these viewpoints in current historiography, see Edward Ross Dickinson, "Reflections on Feminism and Monism in the Kaiserreich, 1900–1913," *Central European History* 34 (2001): 191–238.

31. Detlev Peukert, "The Genesis of the 'Final Solution' from the Spirit of Science," in *Nazism and German Society, 1933–1945*, ed. David F. Crew (London, 1994), 274–99. The essay was originally published in German as part of a work on Weber (*Max Webers Diagnose der Moderne* [Göttingen, 1989]).

32. Zygmunt Bauman, *Modernity and the Holocaust* (Ithaca, N.Y., 1989).

33. See Roger Griffin, *The Nature of Fascism* (New York, 1991), ch. 2. Dickinson also sees Ernst Haeckel's monism as contributing to this trend. See "Reflections on Feminism," cited in note 29.

mindset emphatically resisted heterodoxy, debate, and compromise in favor of unity, wholeness, and redemption. To understand such passions, one must go beyond explanations which focus on the personal element in collective identifications—like Weber's notion of charismatic authority or Freud's notion of group attachments to a surrogate father-figure. Repp's analysis suggests that ideas themselves—independently of personalities—can serve as such binding forces, something David Lindenfeld has also demonstrated.[34] Such ideas override analytical distinctions within discourses (e.g., between subjective erotic impulses and objective biological reproductive imperatives) as well as social distinctions among groups, enabling people on opposite sides to come together at an emotional level—as Repp depicts the rationalists and aesthetes doing in Berlin. In short, Repp's essay offers a revealing glimpse into the process of collective myth-construction.

Despite their differences of approach and interpretation, Allen's and Repp's papers both reinforce the conclusion that the fin de siècle was by no means an era of unrelieved pessimism. In fact, their focus on gender reveals something that previous historians, focusing exclusively on male and middle-class intellectuals, have missed: relatively powerful middle-class males (such as Weber, Simmel, and Tönnies) tended to be pessimists, while relatively less powerful women and nonelite men tended to be optimists. This is further confirmed by studies of working-class culture at the fin de siècle, which also uncover a strong note of future-oriented optimism.[35] But, as Repp suggests, those confident they could cure modernity's diseases were sometimes inclined to offer solutions that smacked less of old-fashioned liberalism than of newfangled racist utopianism.

Elite Culture: Decadence or Vitality?

The next set of essays moves into the world of artistic and literary production and attempts to identify the unique cultural conditions of the German fin de siècle. The essays by Suzanne Marchand, Robert Norton, and Martin Ruehl come closest to traditional Wilhelmine intellectual history, but they

34. David Lindenfeld, "On Systems and Embodiments as Categories for Intellectual History," *History and Theory* 27 (1988): 38–42; Lindenfeld, "The Prevalence of Irrational Thinking in the Third Reich," *Central European History* 30 (1997): 365–85, which seeks to correct Bauman's interpretation.

35. E.g., Vernon L. Lidtke, *The Alternative Culture: Socialist Labor in Imperial Germany* (New York, 1985).

also pose important new questions. All three treat hard-to-categorize figures, individuals who might have been modernists in formal terms but who disliked modernity and believed that its urban landscapes and banal preoccupations were detrimental to the development of true art. Though investigating subjects that spanned two (or even three) separate generations, all the essays are centrally concerned with the fate of liberal-era aesthetics in an emerging era of mass taste. While Arnold Böcklin, whose iconoclastic style was forged in the era of high liberalism, rather accidentally managed to find a broad new audience at the fin de siècle, the much younger Stefan George sought endlessly to escape the democratization of taste. Thomas Mann, by contrast, picked up what was already a central theme in middle-class culture—the beauty and violence of Renaissance politics—but did so without ratifying the secularism, individualism, and civic republicanism that liberals found so admirable. Combining traditional textual analysis with cultural and political contextualization, these essays nicely illuminate the closing down of the liberal ethos in the cultural sphere and the dawning of a new, ambivalent, and ambitious era of modernist innovation.

The first two essays focus chiefly on the transitional era of the 1880s and '90s, while the final paper revolves around Thomas Mann's play *Fiorenza*, completed in what we suggest above was something of a watershed year, 1905. In their essays, Marchand and Norton show how 'Germanness' became an ambivalent cultural issue at the same time that artists and writers were attempting to articulate what one might call a modern—or more interestingly, a postliberal—vision. 'Postliberalism' consisted of the rejection of rational knowledge and middle-class status as the foundation for the appreciation of beauty; neither Böcklin nor George believed that art should elevate public taste or educate the consumer. With one foot in the craft tradition and another in late romantic idealism, the very 'unseasonable' Böcklin took neoclassicism in what can only be called a psychological direction; similarly, the Roman protagonist of George's decadent epic *Algabal* represented the antithesis of the rational Athenian citizen so prized by mid-century liberals. That in departing from liberal culture Böcklin and George trafficked so heavily in classical texts and figures is intriguing—and suggests a strong desire on the part of the *Bildungsbürger* to hold onto traditional 'high culture' symbols, even as that culture was being subverted by popularization (as Peter Jelavich's essay also shows).

Here, precisely as a man 'out of season,' Böcklin is interesting. In breaking with neoclassical aesthetics in the 1860s and 1870s, Böcklin opened the way for a new psychological—rather than historical—understanding of antiquity, one which, as Marchand argues, first seemed shocking to the Wilhelmine cultural elite. Midcentury historicism, exemplified by works such as Theodore Mommsen's *History of Rome*, exhibited strong elective affinities with liberal, bourgeois culture. Although historicism flourished into the 1880s, the end of that decade saw the emergence of critiques of the 'banalization' of antiquity. And in this context, Böcklin's portrait of the ancients, which, like those of his fellow Baselers Jakob Burckhardt, J. J. Bachofen, and Friedrich Nietzsche, were suffused with sexual tension and/or a neoromantic aesthetics of death, gained popular appeal. Though Marchand recognizes the violence of some of Böcklin's images and his inclusion in an anti-French, nationalist canon, she also underscores ambivalences, both in his oeuvre and in his reception. Böcklin, she notes, lived a life torn between the sensual exuberance of *The Isle of Life* and the despairing mood of *The Isle of the Dead*. His paintings appealed to Max Ernst, Sigmund Freud, and Paula Modersohn-Becker as well as to Adolf Hitler; in fact, many German collectors and connoisseurs retained their taste for French impressionism and rejected the nationalists' argument that Böcklin, not Manet, represented the true form of modern art. Intending neither to make 'modern' nor 'German' art, Böcklin became for many people exemplary of both, a fact that suggests a powerful Wilhelmine drive to find father-figures, albeit one that was never unified or fully articulated in the Reich's institutions.

Like Marchand's study of the usually ignored Swiss painter, Robert Norton's essay on Stefan George engages a subject that has for much too long been sidelined or left to the hyperpartisans. Norton illuminates both the innovativeness and the disturbing morbidity of the young symbolist poet. Modeling himself heavily on Mallarmé, George might have become a French poet; the young man was for a time known as "Étienne George" until he opted, quite deliberately, to become "Stefan" and to write in German. Though, like Böcklin, George broke with past traditions in formal terms, the much younger poet was clearly more self-conscious in his attempts to create a poetry of the future and to insulate himself and his followers from the banalities of the present. His *Algabal* (1892) had numerous French sources in addition to the more distant Roman one, and George's imaginatively depraved protagonist closely resembles J. K. Huysmans's archetypal decadent, Des Esseintes. But it is significant that the poem was written and circulated in Germany, where its homoerotic qualities were by no means ignored, and that we know that George went on not to become a Trappist monk (as did Huysmans), but to found a secret circle in which he was worshipped as *Der Führer*. In short, *Algabal* represents a pivotal episode in George's career (the whole of which Norton has analyzed in an elegant new biography),[36] and this chapter wonderfully traces the sources of George's decadent master-piece, suggesting the disturbing psychopolitical implications of the poet's emphatically antiliberal world view.

Decadence is also central to Martin Ruehl's essay, which skillfully com-bines cultural history with literary analysis. Ruehl depicts the encounter be-tween one of Germany's leading representatives of high culture, Thomas Mann, and the middle-class fascination with the Renaissance in the arts, par-ticularly drama, at the turn of the century. He shows that the aestheticization of violence, so often charged to Burckhardt and Nietzsche, was by no means limited to high-cultural products, and that this theme served to break down taboos in the theater. The sexual excesses and bloodthirsty deeds of Renais-sance tyrants like Cesare Borgia were portrayed onstage and even glorified; George's obsessions in *Algabal*, it seems, were by no means those of a solitary figure (one is also reminded of the musical and dramatic transgressions of Richard Strauss in *Salomé* and *Elektra*). The middle classes at the turn of the century, Ruehl contends, read their own agendas and anxieties into the Renaissance past, creating a multiplicity of sometimes contradictory images compared to that which Burckhardt had presented forty years earlier. The themes of decadence and decline that preoccupied many minds in the 1880s and '90s were projected back onto the period that supposedly stood for re-birth—thus ironically mirroring the ambiguities of the fin de siècle itself. Moreover, as the Great War approached, more critics and writers backed away from the glorification of Renaissance Italy in favor of a reassertion of specifically German virtues and cultural accomplishments.

This overview serves as a backdrop for an in-depth study of Mann's own Renaissance drama of 1905, *Fiorenza*. Rather than focusing on the Borgia, as did many of his fellow playwrights, Mann's central figures were Lorenzo di

---

36. Robert Norton, *Secret Germany: Stefan George and His Circle* (Ithaca, N.Y., 2002).

Medici and the insurgent friar Savonarola. Lorenzo and his circle of humanists became the vehicle for Mann's vehement critique of aestheticism, which he saw as sterile (in a striking parallel to the George circle's postpublication reaction to *Algabal*); Savonarola was Mann's mouthpiece for a new, prophetic spirituality, one that sternly condemned sensual excesses while offering peace and blessedness to those who follow him. Ruehl brings out the Schopenhauerian overtones of this characterization, which will be familiar to readers of Mann's other early works (such as *Buddenbrooks*). Yet he also points forward to Mann's later work around the time of World War I and the Germanization of cultural values in which he took part. Specifically, Mann portrayed Savonarola as a proto-Luther, an avatar of German *Geist*. One may view this development as a stage in Mann's ongoing meditation on what it meant to be a bourgeois German—a preoccupation which led him to endow his Savonarola with a highly charged asceticism and a heroic channeling of powerful emotions that could easily have come from the pages of Max Weber's *Protestant Ethic and the Spirit of Capitalism,* which appeared in the same year as *Fiorenza.* In retrospect, Mann's telescoping of self-sacrificing devotion to a cause, authoritarian ambitions, and personal charisma into a single figure may be viewed as a worrisome harbinger of things to come, although Mann's own development of these themes took him in a very different—and antiauthoritarian—direction in the 1920s and '30s. Nevertheless, his flirtation with these possibilities in the prewar era was symptomatic of the widely felt perception that a new era was dawning and that new leaders were needed to shepherd the masses into it.

These three essays all show how liberal cultural forms were subverted as artists and writers rejected naturalism and historicism. If Böcklin's break with realism and with what Ludwig Justi in 1927 called *"Museumskultur"* was not a clean one, George's break with representational language was; in his poetry, mythological and historical figures floated freely. Erotic drives were not only hinted at, but explicitly depicted. George, who died only in 1933, was certainly more modernist in his intense and self-conscious cultivation of an antibourgeois stance. Böcklin, on the other hand, seceded from the salon society of his day not in order to produce avant-garde art, but simply to revive the Renaissance tradition of the artist as craftsman. Thomas Mann also thought of himself as a craftsman—but he took into his workshop the psychological, moral, and social concerns of his middle-class audiences in a way that both the mythologizing Böcklin and the consummately elitist George would have despised. But evident in all three careers is the interplay of despair and hope, of life and death, of the decline of old traditions and the birth of new visions. In paying close attention to the contexts of the creation and reception of works like George's *Algabal,* Böcklin's *The Isle of the Dead,* and Mann's *Fiorenza,* Marchand, Norton, and Ruehl bring intellectual history into the realm of cultural politics and open the way for a wider discussion of an important theme in the fin-de-siècle world: the confrontation of nineteenth-century high culture with new, unpredictable, and often irreverent audiences.

Popular Culture: Divisive or Integrative?

The next pair of essays, which deal with the popular culture of the fin de siècle, take up this theme. In these pathbreaking studies, the focus is on the world of entertainment rather than the world of elite enrichment, and a wider Wilhelmine audience comes into view; this in turn allows for the posing of new questions about the politics of culture at the fin de siècle. Here Peter Jelavich and Marline Otte quite directly show us the middle class's confrontation with modern media and urban lifestyles—a confrontation that was not uniformly an unhappy one. Using unplumbed sources and innovative methods of analysis, these essays represent the vitality of the new field of Wilhelmine cultural history.

While the essays in the previous section emphasize the darker side of Wilhelmine culture, these papers illuminate the lighter, more playful side of the world that was snuffed out by the Great War. Jelavich's "'Am I Allowed to Amuse Myself Here?' The German Bourgeoisie Confronts Early Film" identifies a crucial moment in the cultural history of the Reich, as a new form of entertainment opened up a new field of experience for all classes. Unlike Ruehl's study, Jelavich's is one in which specifically German elements play a rather limited role. The *Bildungsbürger,* who had been the great purveyors of nineteenth-century culture, initially resisted film, which they viewed as an unintelligible, frivolous, and sometimes even immoral medium. Jelavich describes how elite assaults on film's 'trashy' nature mimicked attacks on variety shows and popular novels in the 1890s; bourgeois standardbearers asserted that these new forms of mass entertainment inevitably spelled doom for the true, ennobling forms of *Kultur.* Accustomed to the traditional theater's conventions, the *Bildungbürgertum* could not easily assimilate early film's use of visual or musical snippets and its open intention to divert rather than to educate its audiences—a form of resistance to modernization that echoes the educated elite's initial rejection of Böcklin's unconventional classicism. But in the paper's most innovative turn, Jelavich also shows that not all members of the educated elite rejected the new forms. Nor did the film industry fail to accommodate the desires of its more affluent members of the audience; it opened upscale movie palaces and adopted the forms of bourgeois theater. Ultimately, the middle class found themselves successfully seduced—though, as Jelavich notes, still a bit uneasy about abandoning themselves to a cultural form which was playful, associative, and visual, rather than serious, rational, and textual. Jelavich concludes that by the 1920s, film was the exclusive product neither of 'mass' culture nor of 'high' culture. Its unique synthesis would transform the cultural landscape not only of Germany, but of Europe, America, and indeed the rest of the world in the decades to come.

While Jelavich's essay underscores the class divisions that will come as no surprise to students of German social history, Marline Otte's innovative study of *Jargon* theater in the early decades of the twentieth century shows that there were occasions in which social divisions might be relaxed. She suggests that Wilhelmine culture was not incurably tainted by ethnic hostilities; rather, she argues for the existence of something like a 'normal' range of relationships between Germans and Jews in the Reich's capital city. Focusing on two theaters that performed plays and skits in quasi-Yiddish ("*Jargon*"), Otte shows that specifically Jewish themes were woven into more universal plotlines, such as wives discovering their husbands' dalliances or fathers refusing to consent to their daughters' marital plans. In theaters like that of the Brothers Herrnfeld, mixed Jewish-gentile audiences could laugh and cry together about human problems, and the Yiddish—or Berlinisch, Bayerisch, or pseudo-Hungarian—dialects functioned simply to indicate cultural differences, not unbridgeable religious or racial ones. Demonstrating a real feel for what makes comedy work, Otte contends that differences were often invoked to give dramas color and naturalistic effects, or to allow actors to show off their skills; it was possible to portray both cultural difference and human harmony, and the Herrnfelds in particular often did so. Though based on a limited set of examples, Otte's essay shows that the possi-

bility for German-Jewish cultural accommodation did indeed exist. The stereotypes often associated with Germany tend to evaporate when one studies
how Germans behaved when they were simply having fun.

In comic theater as in feminist thought, however, the Great War played
into the hands of the cultural purists. In her extended discussion of the impact of the war, Otte shows how the cataclysm immediately and permanently
ended the comedic conventions of the prewar period. After August 1, 1914,
many things simply weren't funny anymore. The rapidness of this cultural
change should not shock those of us who experienced September 11, 2001,
in the United States; if culture often follows its own trajectories, there are
also moments in which political cataclysms disrupt business as usual—in
part, as Otte notes, precisely because of the 'business' side of modern culture. Unwilling to risk the disapproval of the censors or the distaste of the
public, producers sought (then as now) to preserve their foothold in the entertainment market by adjusting to the new atmosphere. The Herrnfelds, for
example, immediately gave up 'frivolous' plays; by late August 1914 they had
staged a patriotic tear-jerker which was a popular success, though one which
required the theater to give up many of its signature features. The Herrnfelds
did not abandon their attempt to encourage community in diversity, but by
1915 the fundamental presumption of *Jargon* theater had collapsed under
the twin weights of increasingly chauvinistic war propaganda and Zionist
pressures. Here the history of popular culture spectacularly illuminates the
collapse of a promise, the consequences of which were anything but a laughing matter.

Antimodern Thought: Pathological or Prescient?

The final essay by David Lindenfeld explicitly treats the relationship of Wil-
helmine ideas to twentieth-century developments—not only those of the
Weimar era and the Third Reich, but of the post–World War II era as well.
He addresses these issues by examining the work of two thinkers who grew
up in the fin de siècle and whose influence increased as the century wore on:
Carl Gustav Jung and Martin Heidegger.

Lindenfeld's discussion of these complex thinkers is shaped by his engagement with Fritz Ringer's *Decline of the German Mandarins.* In that book,
Ringer divided "modernists" from "orthodox" mandarins, arguing that the
latter, more conservative group rejected numerous aspects of the modern

world, including parliamentary governance, faith in progress and reason, technological innovation, industrialization, and urbanization. In so doing, this group doomed Germany to both moral and intellectual decline. Benefitting from the vast new literature and considerable cultural change since the publication of Ringer's influential volume, Lindenfeld, on the other hand, suggests that reports of the orthodox mandarins' decline—particularly their intellectual senescence—may have been premature. He also shows that some orthodox mandarins were fully able to use cutting-edge ideas to mount a fundamental critique of modernity—as Jung did with the help of psychoanalysis and Heidegger did with the help of phenomenology. In light of postmodern critiques of reason, science, imperialism, industrialism, and technology, the 'orthodox' attitudes of Jung and Heidegger may now seem less reactionary and outdated than prescient—an observation which underlines an oft-noted set of similarities between antimodernism and postmodernism. In addition, Jung's wide-ranging (if iconoclastic) explorations of non-Western religions anticipated the current trend away from eurocentric treatments of history.

Lindenfeld does not gloss over the roles that Jung and Heidegger played in the Weimar Republic and Third Reich. Indeed, he sees their personal intellectual trajectories as emblematic of the larger relationship between the fin de siècle and the troubled decades that followed. He presents both men as seeking and finding, in their younger years, a balance between their own religious impulses and the very different norms of the secular, rationalist world around them. Jung found such a balance in psychoanalysis, Heidegger in phenomenology. But as they grew older, this balance became increasingly precarious and finally collapsed. In both cases, their personal and intellectual crises paralleled and were amplified by the socioeconomic and political crises of Germany and Europe. In Jung's case, the crisis was the Great War; in Heidegger's, the Great Depression. And in both cases, their experiences led them to accentuate the irrational, poetic, and mystical aspects of their views at the expense of the rational. For Jung and especially for Heidegger, Nazism represented a moment of hope—and opportunity—in an otherwise bleak age.

From the perspective of a hundred years later, we can draw three general conclusions about the German fin de siècle. First, as regards German peculiarities and German historiography, the further in time we move from the

Third Reich and the Holocaust, the less central to our interpretations of the previous decades these peculiarities are likely to become. To be sure, the Holocaust will not disappear; it was far too enormous an atrocity to lose its central position in what Charles Maier has called the "moral narrative" of the twentieth century.[37] German history will ever resist normalization, not only because we now recognize that there was no 'normal' road into the modern age, but also because the attempt to exterminate whole peoples and the launching of the most deadly global conflict to date are not developments that reasonable citizens and responsible historians will forget. Those who seek the origins of Nazism should continue to look to the pre–World War I years of Hitler's youth (spent in Vienna, not in Berlin), to assess the effects of the rise of radical mass politics, biological anti-Semitism, hyper-imperialism, and sociopolitical fragmentation on German society. But we must remind ourselves and our readers that these are not the only features of the Wilhelmine world that deserve scrutiny. The era was too rich and creative to be reduced to a mere foreshadowing of the years 1933–45, and its other paths into the future, its resonances with the longer time-span of the twentieth century, also need to be explored. Drawing inspiration from Böcklin, it is time to seek the conditions of possibility for the coexistence of *The Isle of the Dead* and *The Isle of Life* (Figures 2 and 3).

In seeking such conditions, secondly, we might profit by paying closer attention to Detlev Peukert's indictment of German modernity. In trying to excavate the cultural origins of the twentieth century's disasters, we must not focus exclusively on pessimism. While pessimism enticed many "orthodox" mandarins to embrace National Socialism in some fashion, there are also disquieting connections to be drawn between utopian optimism and subsequent cataclysms. Some of the most future-oriented, energetic movements of the fin-de-siècle years later became implicated in dehumanization. This was true not only of the womens' movements which embraced eugenic solutions to the 'sexual crisis,' but of the modernist aesthetics of Stefan George; it could also be said of violent optimism of the KPD (*Kommunistische Partei Deutschlands*). Moreover, German imperialism (a prominent aspect of fin-de-siècle culture which regrettably the essays in this collection do not di-

---

37. Charles S. Maier, "Consigning the Twentieth Century to History: Alternative Narratives for the Modern Era," *American Historical Review* 105 (2000): 812, 826.

rectly address) was by and large conducted by individuals best described as optimists; their hopes for the creation of a new, German-centered world were of course mixed with anxiety about decadence and racial mixture, but were nonetheless strong enough to convince the Kaiser and much of the population that the game was worth the candle. And this hubristic venture, as we know, was responsible not only for massive exploitation, but even for attempted genocide (in the case of southwest Africa) against non-Europeans in the years before the Great War.[38] One would not want to go so far as to paraphrase Nietzsche's famous inversion of nineteenth-century philhellenism and suggest that perhaps the Germans were dangerous precisely because they were the great optimists; but Peukert's claims do deserve deeper scrutiny.

Thirdly, regarding the fin de siècle as part of a European and Western narrative, it strikes us that many of the optimistic intellectual, cultural, and social movements—and the horrifying atrocities that followed or accompanied them—shared one common preoccupation, perhaps a common metaphor: the positive value of struggle and the deeply unheroic image of compromise. Darwin and Marx had already lent this idea a halo of scientific legitimacy; throughout the century, one can find the appeal to struggle at the root of quests for emancipation. But at the fin de siècle, and especially in Germany, the appetite for conflict had become particularly keen, and the aimed-for result not so much emancipation or the dialectical unfolding of truth as the eradication of other contenders. When even the liberals, the proverbial compromisers, joined this game (or were overtaken by it), the stage was set for disaster. Could it be this longing for total victory, for full spiritual unification (on my group's terms) and for communal perfection—whether voiced by social reformers, political parties, art critics, or scholars—which made the fin de siècle both enormously creative and extraordinarily dangerous for outsiders?

This brings us back to Ringer's portrait of Max Weber. If anyone stood for intellectual honesty and sought to point out the dehumanizing conse-

---

38. See, for example, Sara Friedrichsmeyer, Sara Lennox, and Susanne Zantop, eds., *The Imperialist Imagination: German Colonialism and Its Legacy* (Ann Arbor, Mich., 1998), particularly the articles by Robert C. Holub on Nietzsche, Frederike Eigler on the colonial novelist Frieda von Bülow, John K. Noyes on novelist Gustav Frenssen, and Helmut Walser Smith on the Reichstag debates about the Herero uprising and genocide.

quences not only of modernity, but also of the emotional reaction to it, it was Weber. For him, utopias were no cure for disenchantment; the arguments had to go on. But would a fully disenchanted culture have produced the creative brilliance and experimentation of the fin de siècle? Would it even have produced the political stability and social liberality that Weber longed for? The question raised by Jung—whether resigning oneself to disenchantment is a valid mode of existence for a culture as a whole—continues to haunt Weber's legacy, the century, and ourselves.

LIBERALISM

ADVERSARIAL OR REFORMIST?

Max Weber's Liberalism

FRITZ RINGER

There are a variety of possible approaches to Weber's political thought. One can emphasize his class-conscious attack upon the new East Elbian agrarian capitalists, or his commitment to a politics of responsibility, in which the probable consequences of political proposals are explicitly announced and assessed. Wolfgang Mommsen has focused upon Weber's nationalism, almost to the exclusion of other aspects of his work. Jürgen Habermas has suggested that Weber tended to reduce ultimate value choices to essentially gratuitous, purely personal decisions. The emphasis in the present essay, however, is upon Weber's liberal pluralism, which anticipated a principled value pluralism and which was a profound and persistent theme in his political commentaries.[1]

Reading Weber, one is inclined to ascribe to him a distinctive intellectual personality. He had a pronounced penchant for heterodoxy and something like a passion for intellectual diversity. His character was reflected in his choice of friends. He was close to a few senior colleagues, among them the political scientist Georg Jellinek. He respected the economist Lujo Brentano, although they certainly had their disagreements as well. Among valued political allies were the Protestant social reformer Friedrich Naumann and the jurists Gustav Radbruch and Gerhard Anschütz. All of these were 'modernists' in my terminology; they voted with the liberal left or, more rarely, with the Social Democrats. But Weber also developed close relationships with many junior faculty and students, whom he encouraged and supported

---

1. See Wolfgang J. Mommsen, *Max Weber and German Politics, 1890–1920*, trans. Michael S. Steinberg (Chicago, 1984); Jürgen Habermas, *The Theory of Communicative Action*, trans. T. McCarthy (Boston, 1985). The present essay summarizes aspects of a chapter in a forthcoming book on Weber's work. Not covered are his comments on East Elbian agriculture, his inaugural address, and "Politics as a Vocation." In what follows, *MWG* refers to the *Max Weber Gesamtausgabe*, ed. Horst Baier (Tübingen, 1984–).

with great constancy, almost regardless of their views. As a matter of fact, he typically disagreed with them in important respects, but he liked them precisely because they took heterodox positions on principle, or else because they were in need of support against orthodox senior colleagues. A good many of them were Jews, but Weber also appreciated the Russian and Polish students who valued him as a teacher.[2]

Weber's voluminous correspondence testifies to his enduring support of the sociologist Robert Michels, despite their occasionally heated debates. Michels was a Social Democrat, who did not have his children baptized. In Prussia, a law had been passed to ensure that members of the Social Democratic Party could not become university instructors (*Privatdozenten*), even though that 'private' rank did not entail the status of a civil servant. When Michels tried to find a place at a non-Prussian university, he was turned away even in the absence of such a law. He therefore emigrated to Italy, where he joined the faculty of the University of Turin. In 1908, an annual conference of German university teachers (*Hochschullehrertag*) discussed the "freedom of learning and teaching," primarily in order to exclude specified religious affiliations for certain positions. In response, Weber reported on Michels's experience to a liberal newspaper, confessing himself unable "to behave as if we possessed anything like 'freedom of teaching' that someone could threaten to take away. . . . In the interest of good taste and of truth [there should be no further talk] of the 'freedom of learning and teaching' in Germany," he continued. "For the fact is that . . . the freedom of learning exists only within the limits of political and confessional acceptability—not outside it."[3] In a more extended commentary, he further insisted that faculty should not use the classroom to convey their world views or to stipulate the ultimate norms of social policy. They should confine themselves to empirical and logical analysis, while announcing their personal commitments only in the public arena, where they were subject to criticism.[4] Many German academics linked academic freedom to the idea of an abstract 'purity' of learn-

2. See Max Weber, *Briefe, 1906–1908* (*MWG* II/5), *1909–1910* (*MWG* II/6), *1911–1912* (*MWG* II/7), passim.

3. Max Weber, "Die sogenannte 'Lehrfreiheit' an den deutschen Universitäten," *Frankfurter Zeitung*, Sept. 20, 1908, 1.

4. Max Weber, "Die Lehrfreiheit der Universitäten," *Hochschul-Nachrichten* 19, no. 4 (Jan. 1909): 89–91.

ing and to an 'unpolitical' posture. Weber was not satisfied with that; he demanded the principled toleration of diversity, along with a distinction between classroom teaching and public debate.

In 1908, the Faculty of Philosophy at the University of Heidelberg had to recommend a candidate for the second senior position in philosophy to the Ministry of Culture in Karlsruhe, since Kuno Fischer had retired in 1906. Max Weber very much wanted to bring Georg Simmel to Heidelberg; but the posture of Wilhelm Windelband, the remaining senior philosopher, was deliberately ambiguous. Moreover, a negative report on Simmel reached Karlsruhe from Berlin, where Simmel taught in a junior position. We now know that the Berlin professor Dietrich Schäfer wrote a letter to Karlsruhe to testify that, though he did not know whether Simmel was baptized, he was an "Israelite through and through." Schäfer further suggested that Simmel's large lecture audiences were augmented by the "oriental world"— settled or newly arrived members of "eastern countries." Finally, he emphasized the contrast between "our German-Christian *Bildung*" and Simmel's "world view," which was characterized by "acid and negating" criticism. Windelband also had written of Simmel's "destructive" (*einreissend*) criticism. These terms were part of a hateful code intended to contrast 'Jewish' with 'Aryan' modes of thought. Weber did not know about Schäfer's letter; yet he was certain that some sort of intervention from Berlin had ruined Simmel's chances, and he found out enough about Windelband's position to feel deeply disappointed and, indeed, disgusted.[5]

In 1908, the young economist Franz Eulenburg published a solid and courageous report on the difficulties faced by poorly paid instructors (*Privatdozenten*), who made up a rapidly increasing portion of the teaching faculty at German universities. This attracted Weber's attention and caused him repeatedly to recommend Eulenburg for an associate professorship. Since Eulenburg was Jewish, Weber once again ran into the prejudices then faced by Jewish academics at German universities. In a letter to Brentano, he complained of always "having to see the least intelligent 'Aryan' preferred to the ablest Jew." This comment lends credibility to the story told by a contemporary, Paul Honigsheim, that Weber once fantasized about teaching a seminar

5. Weber, *Briefe, 1906–1908,* 467–73, 482–3, 492–6.

made up entirely of "Russians, Poles, and Jews."[6] Honigsheim also recalled Weber's sympathy for the young economist Emil Lederer, a talented and hardworking junior colleague who was in a precarious academic and economic position. More recently, and at a more scholarly level, Wolfgang Mommsen and Wolfgang Schwentker have published a collection of essays that analyze Weber's relationships not only with Robert Michels, the Protestant Social Congress, and Friedrich Naumann, but also with such pronounced outsiders as Ernst Toller, Ernst Bloch, and Georg Lukács.[7]

I dwell on these particulars because I want to portray Weber as an almost instinctive liberal. I mean to point up his cultural individualism, which echoed Wilhelm von Humboldt and which is also seen in John Stuart Mill's ideal of an open intellectual community. In such a community, radical differences in beliefs and in ways of life were preconditions of intellectual progress. As we will see, Weber admired autonomous individuals who acted upon carefully considered principles. He insisted that intellectuals had to be capable of swimming against the tide of established opinion, and he despised pliable natures who could adjust to almost anything in their environment that helped them to succeed—or at least survive. While a commitment to cultural individualism and intellectual diversity does not exhaust what we normally think of as liberalism, it is indisputably a vital element of it.

Another ingredient in Weber's liberal orientation was his commitment to the 'rights of man' or 'human rights' (*Menschenrechte*). This commitment was reflected in his comments on the Russian Revolution of 1905, which were originally intended as notes to a translation of a draft constitution produced by an alliance of Russian émigré liberals and social revolutionaries.[8] Weber transformed these notes into a lengthy essay, thereby underscoring his passionate interest in the cause of Russian constitutional or 'zemstvo'

6. Ibid., 568–71, 585–6, and esp. 644; Weber, *Briefe, 1911–1912*, 542; Paul Honigsheim, "Max Weber in Heidelberg," in *Max Weber zum Gedächtnis*, ed. René König and Johannes Winckelmann (Cologne, 1963), 167–241, esp. 172.

7. Wolfgang J. Mommsen and Wolfgang Schwentker, eds., *Max Weber und seine Zeitgenossen* (Göttingen, 1985), esp. the articles by Mommsen, Rita Aldenhoff, Peter Theiner, Dittmar Dahlmann, and Éva Karádi. On Lukács, see also Weber, *Briefe, 1911–1912*, 625.

8. Georg Jellinek, *Die Erklärung der Menschen- und Bürgerrechte: Ein Beitrag zur modernen Verfassungsgeschichte*, 2nd ed. (Leipzig, 1904), 1–64; Max Weber, "Zur Lage der bürgerlichen Demokratie in Russland," *MWG* I/10, 86–279, esp. 86–163.

liberalism. Though the zemstvos themselves were selectively and indirectly representative bodies of the estate type, the draft constitution that attracted Weber's attention envisaged a bicameral legislature (Duma) with a directly elected lower house and an indirectly elected upper house. The intention was to transform the tsarist regime into a genuine constitutional monarchy. The Russian liberals expressed none of the disdain for parliamentary institutions that had become fashionable in Germany; the central planks of their agenda were the 'four-part' (general, equal, direct, and secret) suffrage and constitutionally anchored human rights. The zemstvo liberals took it to be their duty to introduce fully equal suffrage, even though they knew that this was extremely risky, given the cultural backwardness of the Russian peasants. As a social group, the Russian liberals were middle-class intellectuals, not capitalist 'bourgeois,' and they were supported by the more radical 'third element' of officials that were attached to the zemstvos. Weber thought them comparable in their principled individualism to the members of the Frankfurt parliament of 1848.

The main point of Weber's commentary was that the fight for individual freedom in Russia faced very heavy odds, since the extended historical developments that had allowed liberal principles to emerge in Western Europe had not had time to do their work in Russia. The problem of cultural differences among nationality groups had not been resolved, and the separation of church and state had not been achieved. More important, the Russian peasants were probably interested only in a radical land redistribution, which in itself posed formidable political and technical problems. The belated advent of capitalism, moreover, created class conflicts that might well foster revolutionary violence and bureaucratic centralization rather than middle-class liberalism and gradualist social reform. The Leninists explicitly rejected the historicist thesis that the development of capitalism—and its contradictions—had to be complete before the proletarian revolution could take place. Weber even detected an affinity between the bureaucratic centralism of the anarcho-syndicalists and that of the tsarist regime: "The political 'individualism' of the West European 'rights of man' . . . insofar as it is 'ideally' conditioned, was created partly by former religious convictions . . . and [partly by] the optimistic faith in a natural harmony of interests among free individuals that has now been destroyed forever by capitalism. Thus these developmental stages cannot be made up in Russia even for purely 'ideal' reasons." The old middle-class individualism, having been abandoned by the propertied and educated strata, was unlikely to convert the lower middle class, not to mention the revolutionary masses.[9]

In the last six pages of his essay on the Revolution of 1905, Weber brought his themes together in an extraordinary sequence of tension-ridden paragraphs. Once again, he insisted upon the unique historical conditions that gave rise to modern freedom: the expansion of Europe; the distinctive economic and social structure of the early capitalist epoch in Western Europe; the rise of modern science and learning; and especially certain religious ideas and values that interacted with specific "political constellations" and "material preconditions" to form the "cultural values" of modern man. Current developments, unfortunately, were pointing away from democracy and individualism, not only in Russia but elsewhere as well. Weber was thinking mainly of bureaucratization: "Everywhere, the steel housing [*Gehäuse*] for the new bondage stands ready." The slowing down of technical and economic progress and the victory of 'rent' over 'profit,' along with the exhaustion of the remaining "free soil and free markets," might well make the masses pliable enough to enter that cage. Certainly, if everything depended only upon the "interest constellations" created by material conditions, then all the signs would point toward "unfreedom." As Weber wrote, "It is ridiculous to ascribe to high capitalism . . . an elective affinity with 'democracy' or 'freedom.' The question can only be: under its domination, how are these things 'possible' at all?" This, for Weber, was the burning question of his time—and the reason for his passionate interest in Russian affairs.[10]

The pessimistic tone of Weber's analysis, however, must not be interpreted as resignation. While acknowledging that zemstvo liberalism faced overwhelming obstacles in the short run, he thought that it might ultimately play the role of an inspiring memory, much as the liberalism of the Frankfurt parliament did in German history. For quite specific reasons, Weber expected liberalism to retain its power as an ideal. The current estrangement between the intellectuals of the propertied and educated middle class and their courageous 'proletaroid' cousins, he believed, would ultimately have to be overcome. The influence of "populist romanticism" was bound to be

9. Weber, "Zur Lage," 164–267, esp. 164.
10. Ibid., 269–71.

undermined by the further development of capitalism. It might be replaced by Marxism; but the "immense and fundamental agrarian problem" certainly could not be mastered by the intellectual means embodied in Marxism. On the contrary, it could be solved only by the "organs of self-government." This, indeed, might eventually bring the two wings of the intelligentsia back together again. "Thus it seems a life-and-death question that liberalism continue to find its vocation in fighting against bureaucratic as well Jacobin [revolutionary] centralism, and to try to infuse the masses with the old individualistic principle of the inalienable rights of man, which has become as 'trivial' to us West Europeans as rye bread is to those who have enough to eat," Weber declared. Liberals had to act while there was time, during the life span of the "next generations." The "much-maligned 'anarchy' of production and the equally maligned 'subjectivism'" might in fact offer a "last chance" to "construct 'free' cultures from the ground up," in America as in Russia. And that is why Weber believed that the "Russian war of liberation" could not possibly be regarded other than with profound sympathy, regardless of national differences and interests.[11]

National interests were important to Weber, but so was the freedom of the autonomous personality. This is clear from Weber's interventions in debates at meetings of the Social Policy Association during the decade before the First World War. In a 1905 session on working relationships in large-scale industry, for example, he explicitly identified his "value perspective" as a "characterological" one; he wanted to know what "becomes of the human beings" who were placed in specific "conditions of existence." He called attention to the language used in the disciplinary rules stipulated for workers in large German factories. In what Weber termed "police jargon," these rules spelled out punishments for various kinds of transgressions, reflecting a "philistine urge to dominate" that "distorted the character of our working population." Seconding Lujo Brentano, Weber protested the "sharp one-sidedness" of German labor law, which elaborately protected strikebreakers while allowing employers to threaten workers with dismissal if they joined unions. For laborers, however, unions were "valuable in themselves," whether or not they achieved much in their conflict with management. They alone fostered and sustained the "comradely honor" and "idealism" of the

11. Ibid., 268–9, 272–3.

working class. The Social Democratic Party, though less desirable than the trade unions, was nonetheless indispensable as a shield in the "petty war against the Prussian state and its police."[12]

In another session of the 1905 meeting, Weber confronted Gustav Schmoller on the question of whether government representatives should be added to the boards of large business combines and cartels. Schmoller had apparently spoken deprecatingly of "parliamentary chatter." In an admittedly exaggerated simplification, Weber answered that Germany's "pseudo-constitutional" regime had none of the advantages but all the disadvantages of the parliamentary system, including "party patronage." He therefore suspected that state positions on corporate boards would not attract "altruists," as Schmoller had suggested. Instead, they would serve as "benefices" for the clients of the dominant parties. Weber further believed that an alliance between heavy industry and the Prussian civil service would simply reinforce the stultifying effects of bureaucratization. He pointedly asked whether the industrialists were not actually interested in the survival of the Social Democratic Party (as a threat to the middle class), just as the Social Democrats were interested in the repression that strengthened their following among the workers.[13]

In 1909, the Social Policy Association discussed the public enterprises of municipalities. In his comment, Weber charged Adolf Wagner and other senior members of the association with an excess of enthusiasm for bureaucracy. Moreover, he explicitly included himself among a presumably younger group of members as "we who think differently." He could not agree that private entrepreneurs should be replaced, wherever possible, with public or municipal officials. He repeated his 1905 charge that to add state representatives to the boards of large corporations would tend to adjust social policy to the needs of employers. He fully acknowledged the "technical superiority of the bureaucratic mechanism" and the high moral standards of the German civil service, while also pointing out that France, the United States, and even Britain did very well without reliable officials, especially in

12. Max Weber, "Die Arbeitsverhältnisse in den privaten Riesenbetrieben," *MWG* I/8, 251, 254–7, 259.
13. Ibid., 269–71.

foreign affairs. But "many of us," Weber insisted, took the power of the nation to be our "ultimate value."[14]

Weber thus at least partly reinvoked the nationalist standpoint of his inaugural lecture of 1895. Yet his formulations seem to highlight another, equally salient concern. He called up a dark vision of the ancient Egyptian bureaucracy, which one day might be reincarnated in a technically perfected form:

> Awful as the thought may seem that the world will some day be made up of nothing but professors . . . even more dreadful is the thought that [it] will be inhabited only by those little cogwheels, those human beings . . . glued to a little post and striving for a little bigger one—a condition you will find . . . [in] today's civil service, and above all among its heirs, our students.
>
> [It is] as if we . . . [were] human beings who need 'order' and nothing but order, who become nervous and cowardly when that order is weakened for a moment. . . . That the world should know nothing but such men of order—that is the [current] development . . . in any case, and thus the central question is . . . what we have to set against this machinery, in order to preserve a remainder of humanity from this parcelling of the soul, from this total domination of bureaucratic ideals.[15]

This vision of the human cost of bureaucratization is surely more passionate than anything Weber wrote about the primacy of the national cause.

Weber's 1909 response to Adolf Wagner was a symptom of increasing tensions among divergent policy preferences within the Social Policy Association. By 1909, after all, Weber had challenged all of the most prominent senior members of the association except Lujo Brentano, who shared his commitment to trade union rights and the legal protection of collective bargaining. Weber himself was apparently worried about the impact of internal disagreements upon the association's public influence and the cause of social

---

14. Max Weber, "Die wirtschaftlichen Unternehmungen der Gemeinden," *MWG* I/8, 360–1, 363–6.

15. Ibid., 362–3.

policy itself. It did not help matters that influential industrialists and employers' associations became increasingly vocal in their complaints about the "Socialists of the Lectern"—and in their insistence that their viewpoint be represented among academic economists. In the so-called Bernhard Case of 1908, Weber publicly objected to what he took to be the Prussian Ministry of Culture's imposition of a pro-entrepreneurial economist upon the faculty of the University of Berlin, the home of Gustav Schmoller and other leading members of the Younger German Historical School of Economics.[16]

In 1909, Weber helped to organize the German Society for Sociology, which might have served as an alternate forum for the scholarly discussion of salient topics in the social sciences or in sociology, broadly defined. The new organization soon ran into procedural difficulties, which stemmed mainly from opposition to Weber's attempt to exclude value judgments from its proceedings. Discouraged by the personal positions taken by some of his colleagues, he officially resigned from the society's executive committee in 1912. More generally, 1912 was not a good year for Weber—or for the Social Policy Association. In an effort to demonstrate a degree of solidarity among spokesmen for social policy, Weber tried to organize a meeting early in that year in which younger members of the association were to express their continued support for the general objectives of their elders, thus stemming the tide of public sentiment against reform. But Brentano refused to go to Berlin to participate, and Schmoller cited health reasons to excuse himself. Weber then attempted to launch a more loosely structured joint demonstration by middle-class supporters of socially progressive policies; but substantive, procedural, and personal differences caused this initiative to fail as well. It was as if the whole tradition of academic social policy was now at risk, even as Germany was moving toward the First World War.[17]

When the war finally came, Weber fully shared the general enthusiasm for it. On the other hand, he soon joined a small minority of German uni-

16. Max Weber, "Der Fall Bernhard," *Frankfurter Zeitung*, June 18, 1909, 1; Weber, "Der 'Fall Bernhard' und Professor Delbrück," *Frankfurter Zeitung*, July 10, 1909, 1; Weber, *Briefe, 1906–1908*, 594–5.

17. Weber, *Briefe, 1909–1910*, 67–8, 107–8, 113–6, 121–3, 154–5, 212–20, 242–3, 273, 293, 298–304, 397–8, 622–4, 644–5, 647, 651–6, 659–61, 669, 671, 679–81, 687–8, 703; Weber, *Briefe, 1911–1912*, 78–9, 179, 575–7, 580–4, 587–8, 591–3, 605, 608, 621, 646, 649, 695, 709, 712, 726, 733, 748, 755, 773–4, 807–10.

versity faculty who sought to restrain the annexationist hysteria that gripped most of their colleagues, and he bitterly opposed the recourse to unlimited submarine warfare. Moreover, a new phase in his political commentary began in 1917, in which he outlined domestic reforms that needed to be completed before the end of the war. In the spring and fall of 1917, he published two brief articles on the democratization of the Prussian electoral system. Between April and June of that year, he also wrote a series of essays for the liberal *Frankfurter Zeitung* that ultimately became a treatise on "Parliament and Government in Germany under a New Political Order." In a preface to "Parliament and Government," Weber announced that his arguments would not be confined to the realm of science but would encompass value judgments, as would his attacks upon the reactionary speculations of the "academically educated." "We . . . who have stayed at home," he wrote, have no business distinguishing truly "German" political forms from "Western" alternatives, as if Germany had no politically liberal traditions. Noncombatants certainly should not tell men at the front that they will have "bled in vain" unless extensive new territories are annexed, he continued; instead, those at home must transform traditional political institutions so that after the war, returning soldiers will be able to participate fully in shaping the nation's political future. To that end, he concluded, engaged citizens must be willing to deal with "sober civic" issues of political technique in ways that may not satisfy the cultural pretensions of the "literati."[18]

The starting point of Weber's critique of the Wilhelmine sociopolitical system was an attack on the "Bismarck legend" that had been created by politically immature publicists. According to the current "literati's fashion," Bismarck's liberal collaborators and rivals in the construction of the German empire were people without talent or vision, who were unrepresentative of the "German spirit." In the face of this orthodoxy, Weber conceded the limitations inherent in the laissez-faire economic liberalism of old liberal leaders; but he fully identified with their determination to create a framework for liberal politics that could endure beyond the era of Bismarck's personal dominance. The fact that they failed in this project was due not to their lack

18. Max Weber, "Das preussische Wahlrecht," *MWG* I/15, 224–35; Weber, "Wahlrecht und Demokratie in Deutschland," *MWG* I/15, 344–96; Weber, "Parliament und Regierung im neugeordneten Deutschland," *MWG* I/15, 432–633, esp. 432–6.

of leadership qualities, but to Bismarck's profound contempt for mankind in general and to his inability to tolerate men of independent views among his competitors. To defeat his liberal rivals, Bismarck engaged in the worst sort of "demagogic" tactics, using the seven-year military budget and the anti-Socialist law (1878) not only to wrest concessions he thought he needed, but also to impose illiberal solutions that destroyed his principled opposition. In an analogous way, he refused to accept the trade unions' right to represent the legitimate interests of the workers, while unsuccessfully wooing the working class with social insurance payments from a state in which they played no role. The police and judicial harassment institutionalized by the anti-Socialist law virtually forced the Social Democratic Party into the fruitless posture of unconditional opposition, while the dramatized threat of revolution kept the middle class pliant out of sheer cowardice. A state that based its military system on honor and comradeship deprived the proletariat of comradely honor, the only possible source of working-class idealism. Thus Bismarck's heritage left a huge deficit in the political education of the nation, a powerless parliament unable to attract political talents comparable with its early leaders, and the unchecked rule of the government bureaucracy.[19]

According to Weber, the modern world was characterized by the steady advance of bureaucracy. In a modern state, the actual exercise of power lay in the hands of the civil service. Just as economic modernization was equivalent to progress toward capitalism, so the modernization of the state entailed the emergence of a bureaucracy based upon specialized training, secure salaries, pensions, and promotions, designated spheres of competence, systematic recordkeeping, and a clearly defined hierarchy of super- and subordination. Municipal government, the modern army, and private capitalist enterprise were also characterized by bureaucratic organization, and thus by the separation of the official, the officer, and the employee from the means of administration, warfare, and production or distribution. The parallel development of capitalism and bureaucracy was no accident. Modern Western capitalism rested essentially upon rational calculation, and it therefore

19. Weber, "Parliament und Regierung," 437–50; Weber, "Wahlrecht und Demokratie," 347–8.

needed a system of public administration and justice whose workings were predictable or calculable, like the operations of a machine.[20]

Modern political parties, too, were increasingly bureaucratic in structure. They had always been essentially voluntary organizations, dependent upon solicitation and advertising to maintain and increase their membership and influence. In recent times, however, they had evolved from informal associations of local and national notables to mass organizations administered by a staff of salaried officials. Parties still had to compete for votes, but the ordinary voter and party member played a less and less active role in determining party programs. Notables continued to be important, whether as financial patrons or as figureheads, but much of their former influence had passed to party secretaries, publicists, and other professionals. Modern political parties were of two main types. The first type of party primarily pursued the patronage of offices that became available after a victory at the polls. Particularly in the United States, such patronage parties adjusted their platforms in an ad hoc manner to attract as many votes as possible; party bosses traded in patronage to deliver election results, and the rank and file actually preferred the resulting corruption to the arrogance of expert officials. But even in the United States, as initially unlimited resources became scarcer, the efficiency of specialized training and discipline pointed the way toward bureaucratization. The second type of party was more characteristic of Germany. It was committed to a 'world view,' and it accordingly pursued more or less fixed substantive political ends. The Catholic Center was an example of this type, as was the Social Democratic Party; yet particularly the latter, the largest and most democratic party in the German political system, also illustrated the increasing convergence of the two types of modern political parties.[21]

Against this background sketch of bureaucratization, Weber developed a penetrating critique of the Wilhelmine political system. The fatal flaw of that system, Weber wrote, lay in the absence of responsible political leadership. Ever since Bismarck's time, the German state had been governed by men who behaved like honorable civil servants, trying to stand "above" the politi-

20. Weber, "Parliament und Regierung," 450–4.
21. Ibid., 451–5, 457–61.

cal parties in the Reichstag rather than taking responsibility in their own behalf for a deliberate political course. Emperor Wilhelm II's misguided determination to govern in person led to offensive and pointless gestures rather than to reflected policies, for the monarch was surrounded only by a self-interested courtly clique and by men who did not recognize their elementary duty to resign when egregious mistakes were made. In short, there were no responsible political leaders, no one to restrain the administrative rule of the bureaucracy, and no genuine intermediary between the government and the Reichstag. In England, by contrast, a monarch retained a measure of political influence precisely by withdrawing from day-to-day political decisions. There, a working parliament represented the citizens in the face of officialdom, and genuine political leaders guided a state that was able to attract the largely voluntary submission of much of the globe.[22]

Article 9 of the German constitution of 1871 forbade leading statesmen, who had to be members of the Federal Council, from holding or retaining their seats in the Reichstag. Thoughtlessly adapted from the English separation of Lords and Commons, this disastrous provision prevented political party leaders from taking ministerial positions without severing their parliamentary roots—thus condemning themselves to impotence. As a result, young aspirants for political leadership were shunted away from the Reichstag, which became a de facto recruiting ground for civil servants. As Weber wrote, this seemed a 'German' solution of the parliamentary problem to the literati, who "examine officials and feel themselves to be officials and the fathers of officials," and who sneer at "West European" and specifically "democratic" place hunting. He observed, however, that the conventions of the civil service hierarchy did not favor personal independence and the talent for politics, which required conflict and the ability to recruit allies and followers. Of course, there were flaws in the selection of leaders by the parties. But the authoritarian regime left the people no choice and simply gave them a functionary to obey. "Philistine moralists" harped upon the obvious fact that the "will to power" motivated aspirants to political leadership, while the "egotistic striving for office" moved their followers. Candidates for civil service posts, by contrast, were presumably never conformist "climbers" (*Streber*)—or hungry for salaries. Weber believed that a framework had to

22. Ibid., 467–72.

be created in which such all-too-human traits would serve to select political talents. That is why party leaders had to have a real chance at power and responsibility. That is why, too, a working parliament was needed, in which service on commissions and acquired expertise would be as important as good speeches. Germany needed true political leaders, not mere demagogues. Politically neutral officials could never take their place.[23]

In a characteristic contrast, Weber compared the "parliamentary system" that made England a "democracy" (*Volksstaat*) with the "negative politics" of Germany's "authoritarian state." Since the Reichstag could only grant or refuse budgetary provisions and accept or reject policies proposed to it, it was bound to confront the government as a hostile force. It could express the dissatisfaction of its constituents, but it could never be asked to participate in the formulation of positive political programs. The highest places in the monarchical regime were occupied by successful civil servants or courtiers. The struggles for neither power nor office patronage ceased under these circumstances; instead they took covert and subaltern forms, and the system consistently favored policies considered acceptable at court (*hoffähig*). The political parties consequently developed something like a "will to powerlessness," while extraparliamentary forces were encouraged to intervene in the decision-making process. In this "pseudo-constitutional" context, it was taken for granted that Prussian officials were politically conservative; that was what the claim to 'stand above the parties' really meant. The Social Democratic Party actually collaborated in this "negative politics." Its members cultivated their class solidarity and the antipolitical vision of "brotherliness." Its leaders were given no incentive to break out of the "ghetto existence" that was thus perpetuated. "Negative politics" was perfectly consistent, moreover, with blatant concessions to the material interests of government supporters. That was why the representatives of big capital stood united behind a regime that obviously benefited them.[24]

Weber's account of English parliamentary government was highly specific. The statesmen who led the nation in England had to have the confidence of the strongest political party or of a parliamentary majority. Members of the government had to answer critical questions put to them by

23. Ibid., 476–7, 481–2, 484, 486–7, esp. 482.
24. Ibid., 473–6, 500–1, 503–5.

the parliamentary opposition and had to exert control over the administrative apparatus in the sense desired by the people's representatives. To help them in that task, they had to have the right of parliamentary inquiry (*Enqueterecht*); they had to be able to compel civil servants to testify before them under oath. It was imperative that they have the ability to penetrate the specialized knowledge and the administrative records of the bureaucracy, and to override the official secrecy invoked by administrators to protect their prerogatives. The proceedings of a working parliament and its commissions should usually be public, Weber believed, so that they would contribute to the political education of the citizens. To Weber, it was ludicrous that philistine German literati should look down upon the proceedings of the British parliament from the height of their impotence.[25]

The key question for the German polity, according to Weber, was how to make the Reichstag fit to exercise power. He asserted that Article 9 and various procedural rules should be altered to meet this objective. But above all, Germany needed parliamentarians who could make politics their full-time occupation. This was the context in which Weber introduced the distinction between living from and living for politics as a vocation. The secretaries, publicists, and other officials of political parties and pressure groups should be able to earn their living from their positions. Among people in nonpolitical occupations, some were more "dispensable" (*abkömmlich*) than others, in that they could free themselves from their ordinary duties to take on political work; lawyers were the outstanding examples of this type. Party officials could no longer be dispensed with, but they might make it difficult for truly independent leaders to reach high office. The notion that the winners of political contests were typically unscrupulous demagogues was almost certainly exaggerated, but some sort of demagogic solicitation of voters was indeed inescapable. Nevertheless, the public exposure of candidates during elections was no worse a means of selection than, for example, the collegial assessment of candidates for academic appointments. In modern mass democracies, the selection of leaders was likely to take on a plebiscitary character. Yet unlike pure Caesarism, plebiscitary leadership was relatively stable and controllable, limited by legally guaranteed civil rights and by the leader's

25. Ibid., 423, 488–91.

apprenticeship in the usages of parliamentary work. Besides, the plebiscitary leader whose program failed could be peacefully replaced.[26]

Asking himself why there were democratic opponents of parliamentary government, Weber pointed to the voluntary character of party politics. The popular leader did not emerge directly from a mass constituency. Rather, he sought power and responsibility to "realize specific political ideas," and he began by seeking party support for his program. Thus the leader proposed both policy ends and political means, and the voters could only dispose of the proposal by accepting or rejecting it. The safeguard against merely demagogic leaders lay in their prior political work and in their commitment to the norms of their political system.[27]

Weber's 1917 political essays can only be understood as challenges to contemporary orthodoxies he meant to contest. We have to remember that the harmonious mood of August 1914 had been quickly dissipated by what Weber saw as a class war from the right. The campaigns in behalf of radically expansionist policies and unlimited submarine warfare deeply embittered Weber and a few of his colleagues. The division between an orthodox majority and a modernist minority among German academics deepened to the point of undisguised hostility. Weber could not help but feel that the 'unpolitical' rhetoric of his conservative and nationalist opponents, the 'ideas of 1914,' and the defense of German 'culture' against Western 'civilization' actually served to rationalize a ruthless campaign to preserve the status quo at home through conquest abroad. He was not surprised that the immediate beneficiaries of the distorted domestic balance of power should press for the total victory of a distinctively 'German' polity. What really angered him was the complicity of many German university professors in this disastrous course. Tensions ran so high within the German academic world that false rumors described the liberal *Frankfurter Zeitung* and Weber himself as recipients of English funds. Weber in turn increasingly portrayed his orthodox colleagues as either empty-headed or mendacious.[28]

One of the "soap bubbles" launched by the literati was the idea of a legislature representing "occupational estates." While this scheme exemplified

26. Ibid., 535–7, 539–40.
27. Ibid., 547, 549–51.
28. Ibid., 532.

the ingenious "electoral arithmetic" that had become fashionable, it also reflected widespread fears of democracy and was fundamentally nonsensical. Under modern conditions, as Weber pointed out, the formal occupations of individuals had little to do with their social functions. The main conflicts that had to be compromised were between employers and workers, and any attempt to evade that reality would aggravate class antagonisms to the point of "rage." The German literati might associate occupational representation with the vision of a "communal economy" based upon wartime experiences, but that simply revealed their ignorance of the spirit of modern rational capitalism. Modern individuals, Weber added, lived in private spheres that had become highly differentiated. They were divided, moreover, by socially constituted inequalities of wealth and education. All the more urgent was the demand that they be equal as citizens, just as they were equal in death, including death on the battlefield. Finally, modern men were typically members of various voluntary associations and interest groups. If an occupational representation were devised, the conflict among these associations and interest groups would certainly continue, whether inside or outside the newly created legislature. Weber declared himself unwilling to take any further interest in political speculations and nationalist slogans that either served as covers for plutocratic interests or grew out of the unreflected daydreams of politically immature literati.[29]

Another vague project that drew Weber's criticism was the plan to privilege advanced education in the assignment of individuals to the Prussian voting classes. Weber saw higher education as a major source of status advantages, as against the economic roots of class positions. As he wrote, "Differences of *Bildung* . . . are today one of the very strongest inner barriers in society. Especially in Germany, where almost all privileged positions within and without the civil service are tied not only to specialized knowledge, but also to 'general *Bildung*.' . . . All our examination diplomas also and primarily certify this important status quality." But Weber insisted that the graduates of German "doctoral factories" had no more to offer than "specialized knowledge" (*Fachwissen*). They might be suitable counselors to political leaders, or they might serve in an advisory upper house of the legislature.

29. Weber, "Das preussische Wahlrecht," 332–4; Weber, "Wahlrecht und Demokratie," 355–8, 368–72; Weber, "Parliament und Regierung," 456–7.

Beyond that, Weber could not imagine a politically less qualified stratum. The total lack of political measure demonstrated by university professors during the war left no doubt about that. The ever-increasing demand for examinations as professional qualifications was nothing more than a quest for prebends: for secure salaries and pensions that were appropriate to the status of the diploma holders. Weber was not kind in his comments upon the social pretensions of the highly educated, who habitually looked down upon modern entrepreneurs, labor leaders, politicians, and journalists. He could not think of a group less eligible for electoral privileges.[30]

In some of the darkest passages of his 1917 essay, "Parliament and Government in Germany under a New Political Order," Weber traced the links between the social interests and ideological propensities of most German university faculty, the stubborn resistance to parliamentary democracy, and the inescapable advance of bureaucratization. In what was clearly an attack on the majority of his colleagues, he denounced the "academic literati," their "resentment" of anyone not examined and certified by them, and their "fear for the prestige of their own stratum." These attitudes, he thought, were behind their repeated diatribes against democracy and "parliamentary dilettantism." Their instincts made the mass of them "forever blind" to political realities. Their "typical snobbism" caused them to dismiss the "subaltern" problems of political reform in favor of more elevated speculations about the 'ideas of 1914,' 'true socialism,' and the like. But a people that was ruled by an uncontrolled bureaucracy, that was not master of its own fate at home, should certainly not try to play the master abroad. Only a politically mature nation had the right to touch the wheel of history.[31]

More than other people, Weber thought, the Germans displayed a talent for rational administration in every kind of organization. They applauded the victorious march of bureaucratization as a "form of life"; the prebends and status claims of the "examination diploma" were their real objectives. "The fact of universal bureaucratization is really hidden behind the so-called ideas of 1914, behind what the literati euphemistically term the 'socialism of the future,' behind the slogan about 'organization,' the 'communal econ-

30. Weber, "Das preussische Wahlrecht," 229–31; and esp. Weber, "Wahlrecht und Demokratie," 350–1.

31. Weber, "Parliament und Regierung," 591–5.

omy,' and . . . behind all similar contemporary turns of phrase." In a pecu-
liarly double-edged rebuke, Weber claimed that "the old Chinese mandarin
was not a specialized official, but . . . a literarily and humanistically educated
gentleman." The modern official, by contrast, was increasingly in need of
specialized training, and thus not really a man of *Bildung*. There were literati
who believed that private capitalism could be domesticated through state
control. But instead of weakening the "steel housing" of modern industrial
work, this would have left the bureaucracy in sole command. A bureaucracy
was a human machine; like a purely mechanical one, it was "congealed
mind." Together, the animate and inanimate machines were constructing
the "housing for the new bondage," to which "future human beings . . . may
have to submit, if a technically good—that means rational—bureaucratic
administration and safety net is the ultimate and sole value that will guide
the regulation of their affairs."[32]

But if that was the fate that awaited mankind, Weber added, one had to
"smile at the fear of our literati" that people might have too much individualism or democracy, and that true freedom would arise only when the "anarchy" of contemporary production and the parliamentary jostling of our
parties were replaced by "social order" and "organic stratification." Given
the advance of bureaucratization, the questions about our political future
could only be put as follows:

1. How is it . . . still possible at all to salvage any remnants of an in some
   sense individualistic freedom of movement? For it is . . . crude self-
   deception to believe that, without the achievements of the age of the
   'rights of man' . . . we could nowadays bear to live.
2. How, in view of the increasing . . . dominance of . . . state officialdom
   . . . will there be powers to keep . . . this growing stratum . . . under
   effective control?
3. A third question, the most important of all, emerges from a consideration of what bureaucracy as such does not achieve. . . . The guiding
   spirit: the entrepreneur here, the politician there, is something other
   than an official.

These formulations have much in common with Weber's outwardly pessimistic reflections on the problems of liberalism in Russia. Again, the image

32. Ibid., 461–4, esp. 462, 464.

of the "housing for the new bondage" functioned as a prophecy of doom that cried out, against the tide of history, for whatever sources of human social vitality might yet be mobilized. The overwhelming threat in Weber's wartime article, however, was simply bureaucracy. Whereas Weber elsewhere conceded that future officials would require general *Bildung* as well as specialized training, he here contrasted the German civil servant with the humanistically educated "Chinese mandarin." We know that Weber was almost the only German academic of his time to dismiss *Bildung* as a realistic objective of German university education. His exclusive emphasis upon the technical training of the official was meant to contribute to his image of the bureaucracy as a machine, which in turn underscored the need to mobilize residual sources of individualism and liberty, in politics and elsewhere.[33]

A final element in Weber's political essays of 1917 was an interesting aesthetic critique of German culture, which reflected the modernist project of selectively appropriating elements of the national heritage. Weber argued that both in England and in France, genuine aristocracies developed "ideals of dignity" (*Vornehmheit*) that proved capable of partial democratization, affecting the aesthetic tastes and social forms of all social strata in those nations. Aristocracies were valuable to the extent that they practiced the habit of cool reflection in politics. Moreover, their canons of taste might survive as barriers to the "pseudomonumentalism" that was characteristic of "parvenu" states like Italy and Germany. The fact remained that Germany had no real aristocracy. Accordingly, there was a need for distinguished lawyers and rich rentiers to make up a political class that was "dispensable" (*abkömmlich*) from occupational commitments—and thus capable of the "distance" required for political planning. Not that the large rentier "lives in an interest-free [social] space," Weber wrote. "There is no such thing." But the large rentier was not involved in the daily struggles of his firm, and he was thus not directly a representative of "plutocratic interests."[34]

The most dangerous surrogates for the culture of an aristocracy, Weber remarked, were not so much the conventions of the German officer corps as its civilian extensions, including the mores of the student fraternities, the "braggart's gesture," and the diploma holder. In truth, the German people

33. Ibid., 465–6.
34. Weber, "Wahlrecht und Demokratie," 374–8.

were a "plebeian people" or, better, a middle-class people. Unfortunately, a "German form" suitable to the nation's socially dominant strata had not so far been found. Instead, Germans were forced to witness the antics of those who falsely claimed to represent the "old Prussian spirit." Democratization, if it were to be successful in Germany, had to prepare the way for a genuine set of middle-class civic (*bürgerlich*) "form values," based upon "distance and reserve." Such distance, however, would not be achieved by those who contrasted themselves with the "all-too-many," in a misunderstood Nietzschean sense; it was inauthentic if it required such a prop. The Weimar classicists demonstrated that the Germans had been a culturally creative people in a time of material poverty and political impotence. Their ethical ideals and philosophical insights could still stimulate reflection. But they could no longer shape cultural production. "The modern problems of parliamentarianism and of democracy, and the essential character of our modern state itself, lay entirely beyond their horizon." The aesthetic and social forms needed by the German people would have to be defined by future generations.[35]

Altogether, Weber's wartime political writings laid out a coherent and plainly liberal position. His famous 1919 essay, "Politics as a Vocation," enlarged and clarified this position in important respects, but it needs further consideration in a broader context.[36] That only leaves a sequence of five short articles in the liberal *Frankfurter Zeitung* in November and December 1918, collected in a pamphlet in January 1919 and supplemented by a note on the "Reich President" two months later. This small cluster of texts reflected Weber's changing tactical choices, but otherwise only slightly modified his wartime perspective. To be sure, the six months from November 1918 to March 1919 saw Weber more actively engaged in current political affairs than ever before. It looked for a time as if he might be elected a representative and a potential leader of the newly formed German Democratic Party. But after professional party officials had undercut that possibility— and after Weber had failed to fight for a mandate—he continued to campaign energetically for the new party, to sit on constitutional commissions,

35. Ibid., 382, 385, 388–90.
36. See chap. 8 of my *Max Weber: An Intellectual Biography* (Chicago, 2004).

and to travel to the peace conference at Versailles. In substance, Weber favored a constitutional monarchy until the behavior of Wilhelm II made that impossible. He was dismayed at the revolutionary disorders of November 1918 and appalled by German left-wing pacifists who seconded the Allied claim that Germany was solely responsible for the war. He preached dignity in defeat. As the terms of the Versailles settlement began to emerge, his outrage and his pessimism deepened. Yet he soon recovered his equilibrium and his characteristic sense of reality. He came to recommend a program of cooperation between the Social Democrats and the progressive elements within the German middle class. For a while, he even gave lip service to limited forms of "socialization." Nevertheless, he remained firmly opposed to socialist planning.[37]

The chief purpose of Weber's political articles of late 1918 was to prepare the ground for a democratically elected national assembly that would reestablish the authority of the German central government and lay the constitutional foundations for a republic. The legitimacy of the new regime, according to Weber, could only be based upon the "natural law" conception of popular sovereignty. More specifically, Weber's political plan extended the institutions of the old empire, including in particular its federal structure (although with significant changes). Yet he eventually modified his initially federalist emphasis in a unitary direction. Thus, partly in view of the need for an active social policy, he excluded anything like the extensive autonomy of the American states. With respect to primary and secondary education, moreover, Weber intended the national legislature to stipulate "norms" for the policies of the several states. The president of the German Republic, he believed, should be directly elected by the voters rather than by the Reichstag. Like the president of the United States, he would thus have an independent political mandate and position, one based upon the plebiscitary principle of popular sovereignty. He was also to be equipped with a suspensive veto, and with the right to dissolve the Reichstag and call for new elections, particularly if no prime minister succeeded in constituting a governing majority from among the political parties. Weber's longstanding interest in the education and selection of talented political leaders ultimately culminated in this call for a plebiscitary presidency. Equally interesting for us is

37. I am relying upon Wolfgang Mommsen's introduction to *MWG*, I/16, 1–37.

Weber's insistence upon the control of the bureaucracy by means of a parliamentary right of inquiry (*Enqueterecht*), and his call for a set of fundamental human rights (*Grundrechte*) to be anchored in the constitution.[38]

In addition, Weber's essays of November and December 1918 insisted upon the need for political cooperation between the working class and middle-class progressives. Since a Social Democratic majority could not be expected in the forthcoming elections to the National Assembly, Weber argued, the new regime absolutely required the support of the German bourgeoisie, or of genuinely liberal and democratic elements within it. A purely socialist government was impossible in any case; the Western governments would not accept it, and Germany needed economic credits that would not be granted unless expropriation was formally excluded. This was no time to listen to radical intellectuals, who lived from and not for the revolution, or to flirt with the fantasies of "academic literati" about a "communal economy" and the like. Above all, Weber believed, the German middle class had to abandon the "spirit of security" it had enjoyed under the protection of an authoritarian regime, as well as its fear of innovation and its "will to powerlessness." For broad segments of the German population, technically sound administration and material welfare had provided a framework (*Gehäuse*) that gradually had suppressed all "pride of citizenship, without which even the freest institutions are mere shadows." The republic would put an end to this "security." The middle class would have to learn to fend for itself, as the working class had always had to do. New political parties would have to be formed, and they could hardly draw upon politicians who had participated in the campaign against Western democracy, in the annexationist propaganda campaign, and in the campaign for unlimited submarine warfare. Indeed, Germany would have to abandon its imperialist dreams, so as peacefully to cultivate its national traditions within the League of Nations. In this and other respects, Weber's 1918 articles were an extension of his wartime position, though with modifications that reflected the new revolutionary situation.[39]

38. Max Weber, "Deutschlands künftige Staatsform," *MWG* I/16, 110–2, 116–22, 125–30, 138–40. Weber's offhand remark that the fundamental right to property might have to be modified was almost certainly tactical only.

39. Ibid., 99–109, 112–6, 145–6, esp. 103, 105–9, 116.

From Retributive Justice to Social Defense

Penal Reform in Fin-de-Siècle Germany

RICHARD F. WETZELL

In 1882 a young professor of criminal law at the University of Marburg published an article that challenged the major tenets of nineteenth-century penal philosophy and practice and called for a radical reform of imperial Germany's criminal justice system. The author's name was Franz von Liszt, and the article was titled "The Concept of Purpose in Criminal Law" ("Der Zweckgedanke im Strafrecht").[1] Liszt's article gave rise to a penal reform movement that brought about a gradual transformation of German criminal justice. This transformation manifested itself in two ways: a shift in emphasis from moral retribution to the protection of society as the primary purpose of the criminal justice system, and the gradual dissolution of the nineteenth-century system of fixed and uniform punishments in favor of a system of individualized preventive measures, a process that rendered penal sanctions increasingly similar to nonpenal forms of state intervention.

Criminal Justice in Imperial Germany

Imperial Germany's criminal justice system was the product of three main influences: the late eighteenth- and early nineteenth-century penal reforms shaped by liberal and Enlightened ideas; the nineteenth-century prison reform movement; and Hegelian retribution theory. The imperial German

---

1. The article was first published in the *Marburger Universitätsprogramm* of October 1882 and is therefore sometimes referred to as the "Marburger Programm"; it was reprinted a few months later in *Zeitschrift für die gesamte Strafrechtswissenschaft* 3 (1883): 1–47, and later reprinted in Franz von Liszt, *Strafrechtliche Aufsätze und Vorträge*, 2 vols. (Berlin, 1905), 1:126–79. The article's centenary was honored by a new edition, *Von der Rache zur Zweckstrafe: 100 Jahre Marburger Programm von Franz von Liszt*, ed. Heribert Ostendorf (Frankfurt am Main, 1982), and an exhibition in the Universitätsbibliothek Marburg in October 1982. See the mimeographed catalog, *100 Jahre Marburger Programm: Franz von Liszt*.

penal code, which took effect in the empire's first year of existence (1871), was closely modeled on the Prussian penal code of 1851. The Prussian code, in turn, had been strongly influenced by the Napoleonic *Code Pénal* and the Bavarian penal code of 1813, the latter drafted by liberal penal reformer Paul Johann Anselm Feuerbach. As a result of this genealogy, imperial Germany's penal code was a classic liberal code: it reflected the liberal concern to limit state power and protect citizens against arbitrariness by carefully defining all crimes and punishments. The code also reflected the penal philosophy of general deterrence, which held that both the penal code's delineation of punishments and the actual punishment of particular offenders served the purpose of deterring the general public from violating the law.[2]

Deterrence, however, was too negative and abstract a purpose for most prison administrators. Beginning in the late eighteenth century, Anglo-American prison reform movements inspired an indigenous German move-ment that called for the rehabilitation of criminals as the primary goal of punishment. The criminal would be prevented from committing future crimes by reshaping his habits. In its pure form the rehabilitationist vision contradicted the imperatives of deterrence: punishment should no longer be disagreeable, but educative. Its length and content could not be fixed in ad-vance, but should depend on the individual convict's response to rehabilita-tive treatment. In practice, however, prison life reflected a compromise, and rehabilitation took place within the penal code's general framework of deter-rence and fixed prison terms.[3]

While the penal code reflected the philosophy of deterrence and most prison administrators championed rehabilitation, judicial practice in the courts and the teaching of criminal law in the universities centered on the

2. On imperial Germany's criminal justice system, see Eric Johnson, *Urbanization and Crime: Germany, 1871–1914* (New York, 1995), 15–51; Eberhard Schmidt, *Einführung in die Geschichte der deutschen Strafrechtspflege*, 3rd ed. (Göttingen, 1964), 313–21, 343–5.

3. The history of German prisons remains a severely underresearched area. For a brief overview of the nineteenth century and the *Kaiserreich*, see Thomas Krause, *Geschichte des Strafvollzugs* (Darmstadt, 1999), 67–84. On the beginnings of prison reform in Prussia, see Thomas Nutz, "Gefängnisreformdiskurs und Kriminalpolitik in Preußen bis 1806," in *Kriminalität und abweichendes Verhalten: Deutschland im 18. und 19. Jahrhundert*, ed. Helmut Berding, Diethelm Klippel, and Günther Lottes (Göttingen, 1999), 39–67. On prison reform after 1850, see Thomas Berger, *Die Konstante Repression: Zur Geschichte des Strafvollzugs in Preussen nach 1850* (Frankfurt am Main, 1974).

concept of retribution as an essential component of justice. Whereas both deterrence and rehabilitation were utilitarian and forward-looking in the sense of imposing punishment to prevent future crimes, retributive justice took a moral and backward-looking approach. It relied on the past offense and the offender's degree of guilt in order to determine the proper measure of punishment, which was intended to represent the "just measure of pain." The individual offender's guilt depended on his or her motives as well as extenuating or aggravating circumstances. While Feuerbach's Bavarian code had originally featured very narrow ranges of punishment for any given offense, the judiciary soon succeeded in invoking the ideal of retributive justice to have these restrictions on judicial discretion relaxed. The Prussian and imperial penal codes of 1851 and 1871 allowed judges considerable latitude in adjusting sentences to the individual offender's degree of guilt. In addition, after the 1840s the idea of retribution also came to dominate German penal scholarship in the form of Hegelian retribution theory. Applying his dialectical method to criminal law, Hegel had argued that crime must be understood as a "negation of the law" and punishment as the negation of the negation that cancelled out the crime and restored the legal order. While the logic of this dialectic was essentially retributive, Hegel's dictum that the offender required the punishment in order to be "honored as a rational being" suggests that he was not exclusively concerned with retribution. This aspect, however, was ignored by the penal jurists, who, from the 1840s on, drew on Hegel and his dialectical method to erect a highly abstract system of Hegelian penal theory that laid exclusive stress on the retributive aspect of criminal justice.[4]

Thus, in the early years of the *Kaiserreich*, the German criminal justice system was an uneasy compromise between three potentially contradictory conceptions of punishment. The penal code prescribed a range of punishments for each offense in accordance with the principle of general deterrence; the judiciary sentenced each offender according to his or her individual degree of guilt within the framework of retributive justice; and prison officials associated with the prison reform movement attempted to rehabilitate their charges.

4. Schmidt, *Einführung*, 294–303.

Otto Mittelstädt's Legal-Positivist Critique

Throughout most of the 1870s, the latent tensions between deterrence, retribution, and rehabilitation lay dormant. In 1879, however, an attempt to introduce mandatory solitary confinement for every prisoner provoked a controversy in which these tensions broke into the open. A diverse set of critics radically challenged the logical coherence and practical efficiency of the existing criminal justice system.

Imperial Germany's prison reformers had long been calling attention to the country's substantial recidivism rate, which they blamed on the communal confinement of prisoners. Communal confinement, they argued, made any kind of rehabilitation impossible because it brought first-time offenders into contact with veteran criminals, so that the prisons actually served as schools of crime. The only solution, they argued, was single-cell prisons. In 1879 the prison reformers appeared to be on the verge of victory: the Prussian Ministry of Justice submitted a draft bill to the *Bundesrat* (the Reich's upper legislative chamber) that sought to oblige every German state to introduce solitary confinement for an initial period of imprisonment and for all short-term sentences.[5]

The prospect of seeing this bill become law provoked a high-ranking Hamburg judge, Otto Mittelstädt, who would be appointed to the newly created *Reichsgericht* (Supreme Court) in Leipzig two years later, to launch a major attack on the idea of rehabilitation.[6] Although conservative critics had occasionally grumbled about the prison reformers' "exaggerated humanitarianism," Mittelstädt was the first to attack prison reform and the principle of rehabilitation head-on. In his provocatively titled pamphlet *Against Prison Sentences* (*Gegen die Freiheitsstrafen*), published in 1879, he roundly condemned what he saw as the prison system's exclusive focus on rehabilitation and called for a return to deterrence as the sole purpose of punishment.[7]

5. The bill was submitted to the *Bundesrat*, the second legislative chamber of the Reich, which was composed of representatives of the different German states. Berger, *Konstante Repression*, 223–35.

6. For biographical information on Mittelstädt, see *Biographisches Jahrbuch und deutscher Nekrolog*, vol. 4 (1900).

7. Otto Mittelstädt, *Gegen die Freiheitsstrafen: Ein Beitrag zur Kritik des heutigen Strafensystems* (Leipzig, 1879). Mittelstädt answered some of his critics, supplementing and moderating his argument in his "Für und wider die Freiheitsstrafen," *Zeitschrift für die gesamte Strafrechtswissenschaft* 2 (1882): 419–49 (hereafter cited as *ZStW*).

At first glance, Mittelstädt's pamphlet appeared to be simply a radicalized version of standard conservative attacks on the misguided humanitarianism of rehabilitation. Mittelstädt, too, suggested that prisoners had it so good in prison that punishment had lost its deterrent effect. He thus demanded the reintroduction of corporal punishment and a more frequent use of the death penalty. He also insisted that prisons be "removed from the regime of a coddling, professional humanitarianism indulging in educational experiments and [that they be] firmly placed under the strict and merciless rule of deprivation, endurance, and pain." Predictably, this sort of talk provoked an outcry of indignation in the liberal press, while earning applause from conservative respondents such as the historian Heinrich von Treitschke.[8]

At second glance, however, Mittelstädt's argument differed from the usual conservative calls for harsher punishments. Whereas conservative critics always identified the penal code with the moral order of the Christian fatherland and invoked retributive justice as the justification for punishment, Mittelstädt denied that the penal code reflected an absolute moral order and rejected the notion that punishment had any moral meaning. Instead, he adopted the radical legal-positivist standpoint that while the criminal code might protect some of the "unchanging fundaments" of human culture, it also reflected the "changing institutions" of each society and the "ephemeral purposes of state power." As he wrote, "What is still permitted today, may be forbidden tomorrow, and what is illegal today, may be perfectly acceptable the next day."[9] In short, Mittelstädt defined crime in purely formal terms as an infraction of a given (albeit potentially arbitrary) legal order. If crimes were simply created by the law, he argued, punishment could have no moral meaning, but only the strictly utilitarian purpose of preventing the infraction of a given set of legal norms.

What made Mittelstädt's argument truly unique was that he used his radical legal-positivism simultaneously to attack retribution and rehabilitation. Since rehabilitation was an effort to improve the criminal morally, rehabilitation assumed that the criminal had done something morally wrong. And

8. Heinrich von Treitschke, "Unsere Aussichten," *Preussische Jahrbücher* 44 (1879): 559–76. Reprinted in *Im Bismarckschen Reich* (Darmstadt, 1978), ed. Hans Fenske, 239ff. (mention of Mittelstädt, 242).

9. Mittelstädt, "Für und wider die Freiheitsstrafen," 443. The same idea is present in his *Gegen die Freiheitsstrafen*, 20.

if crimes were not immoral acts but merely infractions of potentially arbitrary laws, then rehabilitation made as little sense as "just moral retribution."

Not satisfied with having undermined the raison d'être of rehabilitation, Mittelstädt proceeded to expose a number of internal inconsistencies in rehabilitationist thinking. First, he argued that the very object of rehabilitation had dissolved. The inventors of the penitentiary in Philadelphia had regarded crimes as sins against God's moral order and had therefore sought to transform punishment into penitence. But, Mittelstädt argued, in a secularized age this was no longer possible. Contemporaries were disputing whether the causes of crime lay in individual will, underdeveloped reason, physiological processes, poverty, sickness, ignorance, or accident—with no agreement in sight. If crime could be the result of any of these causes, what exactly was the object of rehabilitation?[10]

Second, Mittelstädt criticized the methods of rehabilitation. Solitary confinement made sense if one wanted to induce religious conversion, but how was it supposed to aid secular rehabilitation? How was isolation supposed to prepare people for life in freedom? Prison labor had originated as a way of inflicting additional hardship on the incarcerated. How could this same oppressive form of labor now effect rehabilitation?[11] Furthermore, Mittelstädt pointed to the disjunction between a judicial system based on deterrence and a prison system based on rehabilitation. Was there not a contradiction between the fixed prison sentences pronounced by judges and the unpredictable course of individual rehabilitative treatment? Of course there was, he asserted, and it was high time to "finally abandon the terrible misconception that legally fixed quanta of captivity [*Unfreiheit*] could educate people for freedom."[12] Finally, Mittelstädt insisted that current sentencing procedures be radically reformed. Instead of basing their sentences on the individual criminal's degree of guilt, which varied according to motives and possible extenuating circumstances, judges should impose the same punishment for a given infraction regardless of individual circumstances and motives.

In summary, Mittelstädt's critique had two main thrusts. One was di-

10. Mittelstädt, *Gegen die Freiheitsstrafen*, 26.
11. Ibid., 27–50, 62.
12. Ibid., 50–62 (quotes, 52, 58).

rected against retribution theory and its manifestations in legal scholarship and judicial sentencing practices; the other, more visible, was directed against rehabilitation as promoted by prison reformers and to some extent practiced in prisons. Yet Mittelstädt's actual reform proposals did not live up to his pamphlet's provocative title—*Against Prison Sentences*. For even though intensive prison labor and reduced food rations were intended to increase prison's deterrent effect, the prison was to remain the standard punishment in the future.

Not surprisingly, Mittelstädt's attack on rehabilitation and his demand for harsher punishments provoked outraged denunciations in the liberal press as well as testy rebuttals from prison reformers and administrators, who dismissed him as a reactionary and simply glossed over the contradictions he had pointed out. But the Prussian government's project of getting solitary confinement introduced throughout the Reich was shelved, although this was largely due to other reasons, most importantly the high cost involved.[13]

Emil Kraepelin's Vision of Medicalized Criminal Justice

The strongest defense of rehabilitation in response to Mittelstädt's attack came from a young psychiatrist, Emil Kraepelin (1856–1926), who was soon to become the most influential figure in German psychiatry.[14] Unlike most defenses of rehabilitation, Kraepelin's 1880 *The Abolition of Fixed Punishments* (*Die Abschaffung des Strafmaßes*) acknowledged Mittelstädt's point that current prison sentences reflected a debilitating compromise between retribution, deterrence, and rehabilitation. But while Mittelstädt wanted to resolve these contradictions in favor of pure deterrence, Kraepelin sought to overcome them by radicalizing the practice of rehabilitation.

13. Among the pro-rehabilitation responses, see especially Friedrich Oskar von Schwarze, *Die Freiheitsstrafe* (Leipzig, 1880); Karl Krohne, "Der gegenwärtige Stand der Gefängniswissenschaft," *ZStW* 1 (1881): 53–92. On the fate of the Prussian proposal in the Bundesrat, see Berger, *Konstante Repression*, 223–35 (on Mittelstädt's possible impact, 232).

14. On Kraepelin, see Edward Shorter, *A History of Psychiatry* (New York, 1997), 100–9; Kurt Kolle, "Emil Kraepelin," in *Große Nervenärzte*, 3 vols., ed. Kurt Kolle (Stuttgart, 1956–63), 1:175–86; Eric Engstrom, "Emil Kraepelin: Psychiatry and Public Affairs in Wilhelmine Germany," *History of Psychiatry* 2 (1991): 111–32; Emil Kraepelin, *Lebenserinnerungen* (Berlin, 1983).

Kraepelin shared Mittelstädt's position that the penal code did not reflect an absolute moral order but only changing social norms, and that the purpose of punishment could therefore not be found in moral retribution. But instead of replacing the moral definition of crime with a legal-positivist one, Kraepelin proposed a social definition of crime: crime was not an immoral act, but an antisocial one. Moreover, since the term "crime" invariably implied connotations of moral censure, Kraepelin suggested that it be replaced by the morally neutral concept of the "antisocial act." Similarly, he argued that the notion of "punishment," which connoted vindictiveness, should be replaced by the term "protective measures," that is, measures designed to protect society.[15]

If what mattered was not retribution but the protection of society against antisocial acts, Kraepelin asserted, then it was immaterial whether those acts were committed by a child, a lunatic, or a healthy adult. In other words, it was no longer necessary to determine whether or not the offender was legally responsible. This, Kraepelin suggested, was a good thing because recent developments in science and medicine had made it impossible to defend such a judgment. Whether legal responsibility was defined as free self-determination or, more specifically, as the ability to discern the illegality of one's action, the concept had been decisively undermined. Sidestepping philosophical arguments about free will, Kraepelin argued that modern medicine and criminal psychology had so broadened the range of mental illness that any sharp distinction between mental illness and "normality" had become impossible to discern. The point was not that most criminals were insane, but that there were innumerable transitional states between rationality and mental incapacity. In any event, in the eyes of the scientist, both the criminal and the lunatic were simply products of heredity and milieu, subject to the same universal laws as all other organisms.[16]

In Kraepelin's blueprint, the criminal trial would no longer ascertain the culprit's legal responsibility or the degree of his or her guilt. Instead, all who "violate[d] the conditions for the happy existence of human society" would

15. Emil Kraepelin, *Die Abschaffung des Strafmaßes. Ein Vorschlag zur Reform der heutigen Strafrechtspflege* (Stuttgart, 1880), 1–29, esp. 27–8. The booklet was Kraepelin's first published work.
16. Ibid., 9, 28, 39.

simply be categorized as "dangerous" and subjected to a treatment designed to turn them into "useful or at least innocuous members of the community." Without regard to moral or legal responsibility, "dangerous" individuals' treatment would depend only on their specific problems and needs. Their assessment would provide a new role for the medical expert. No longer needed in the courtroom to determine legal responsibility, the medical expert would now be found in the antechambers of rehabilitative and therapeutic institutions, where he would decide on the proper treatment for each individual.[17]

The extent to which Kraepelin was still in the grip of the conventional categories that he professed to explode can be seen in the fact that such treatment was to take place in three different kinds of institutions. While lunatics would enter insane asylums and minors educational institutions, the remainder, those "currently referred to as criminals"—Kraepelin was unable to coin a new term—"were in need of a special kind of education." Considering "criminals" to be the "product of perhaps abnormal heredity and demoralizing circumstances," Kraepelin suggested that their treatment should aim at the correction of their antisocial character traits by "repressing perverse passions" and "reinforcing moral notions and giving them regulatory power over natural instincts." Since the purpose of "punishment" was to be purely corrective, its length could not be fixed in advance but would depend solely on the achievement of a permanent change in the individual's character. Only this drastic reform would remove the remnants of retribution in penal practice in favor of the absolute rule of rehabilitation as the purpose of punishment.[18]

Kraepelin's new type of correctional facility was to be modeled on both educational institutions for juvenile delinquents and insane asylums. Corrective treatment would be based on the presumption that placing a patient in an institution effected two major (and beneficial) changes: the inmate's removal from familiar surroundings and his integration into a new routine. The institution's personnel would consist of professional "criminal pedagogues," whose training would be similar to that of teachers and psychiatrists.[19] But for inmates, the most important pedagogical incentive would lie

17. Ibid., 39 passim.
18. Ibid., 40.
19. Ibid., 53–67 (quotes, 59, 63).

in the indefinite duration of the internment. Given the innate human desire for liberty, the knowledge that his release depended upon his reform would powerfully motivate the inmate "to work toward his moral convalescence."[20]

Kraepelin's demands that the very idea of punishment be discarded in favor of "protective measures," that the criterion of legal responsibility be eliminated, and that the practice of fixed sentences be replaced by indefinite detention constituted far too radical a break with the fundamental principles of German criminal justice to garner any significant support in the short term. Nevertheless, his blueprint for a purely rehabilitative treatment of criminals modeled on the insane asylum anticipated the gradual medicalization of criminal justice that would become a powerful trend in reformist thinking over the course of the ensuing decades.[21]

Franz von Liszt's Penal Reform Program

While both Mittelstädt's and Kraepelin's publications generated considerable debate, it was Franz von Liszt's inaugural lecture, "The Concept of Purpose in Criminal Law," that exerted the strongest and longest-lasting influence on the development of German criminal justice. The young law professor's published lecture quickly became the programmatic founding statement of a new German penal reform movement, of which he became the recognized leader. Liszt's critique of German criminal justice shared certain commonalities with those of Mittelstädt and Kraepelin. Like them, Liszt rejected the moral conception of punishment as retribution in favor of a utilitarian and pragmatic conception of punishment as a means of protecting society. In most respects, however, Liszt's position was much closer to Kraepelin's than to Mittelstädt's. In contrast to Mittelstädt's legal positivism, Liszt shared Kraepelin's understanding of crime as an antisocial act. Furthermore, both Liszt and Kraepelin dismissed Mittelstädt's exclusive belief in general deterrence and insisted that punishment should consist of individualized "protective" or "preventive" measures (Kraepelin's *Schutzmittel*,

20. Ibid., 61–2, 68, 72.

21. On this aspect, see Richard F. Wetzell, "The Medicalization of Criminal Law Reform in Imperial Germany," in *Institutions of Confinement: Hospitals, Asylums, and Prisons in Western Europe and North America, 1500–1950,* ed. Norbert Finzsch and Robert Jütte (Cambridge, 1996), 275–84.

Liszt's *Schutzstrafe*) that were designed to prevent the individual criminal from offending again. But whereas Kraepelin identified these measures exclusively with rehabilitation, Liszt had a more comprehensive and differentiated understanding of preventive measures. He also presented his proposals in a much less radical form than Kraepelin.

Liszt began from the premise that the purpose of punishment was not to administer retribution but to protect society from crime. He pointed to the rising number of repeat offenders as evidence that the existing criminal justice system was woefully ineffective in this respect. The purpose of protecting society, he insisted, could only be achieved through individual behavioral prevention—that is, by modifying or controlling the behavior of the individual criminal in order to prevent him or her from committing further crimes. Consequently, Liszt argued that punishments should not depend on the legal offense committed (the principle of deterrence) or on the offender's individual degree of guilt (the principle of retribution), but on the future danger which the individual criminal posed.[22]

By assigning punishment the purpose of preventing convicted offenders from committing future crimes, Liszt was not only calling for the individualization of punishments; he was raising the question of the proper content of punishment. The purpose of punishment was no longer to inflict the "just measure of pain," but to modify the future behavior of the offender. Clearly, the search for the best method of individualized prevention had to be based on some knowledge of what caused individuals to commit crimes in the first place. As a result, Liszt and his followers became intensely interested in criminological research.[23]

Liszt's and his fellow penal reformers' burgeoning interest in scientific research on the causes of crime was also fueled by the decline of the classic

22. Liszt, "Der Zweckgedanke im Strafrecht," *Strafrechtliche Aufsätze und Vorträge,* 1:126–79; Liszt, "Kriminalpolitische Aufgaben" (1889–1892), ibid., 1:290–467. On Liszt, see Eberhard Schmidt, *Einführung in die Geschichte der deutschen Strafrechtspflege,* 357–86; Monika Frommel, "Internationale Reformbewegung zwischen 1880 und 1920," in *Erzählte Kriminalität,* ed. Jörg Schönert (Tübingen, 1991), 467–95. Born in Vienna in 1851, Liszt held chairs in criminal law in Gießen (1879–1882), Marburg (1882–1889), Halle (1889–1899), and finally Berlin (from 1899 until his death in 1919).

23. On the history of German criminology, see Richard F. Wetzell, *Inventing the Criminal: A History of German Criminology, 1880–1945* (Chapel Hill, N.C., 2000).

liberal image of the self. The social problems of an industrialized society and the obvious failure of general deterrence had eroded the liberal assumption that most people were autonomous and rationally calculating individuals. Unlike the early nineteenth-century generation of penal reformers, Liszt and his supporters believed that individual actions, including crimes, were significantly constrained by both environmental and biological factors.[24]

But Liszt did not put the elaboration of his reform proposals on hold until criminological research had fully elucidated the causes of crime. He had definite ideas about the major categories of criminals and the penal measures appropriate to each. He began with the proposition that punishment could serve three different purposes: rehabilitation, individualized deterrence, or incapacitation of the offender. Arguing that "there must be three categories of criminals that correspond to these three forms of punishment," he recommended rehabilitation for those criminals who were both in need of and capable of rehabilitation, deterrence for those not in need of rehabilitation, and incapacitation through incarceration—Liszt saw no need for the death penalty[25]—for those incapable of rehabilitation. Elaborating on these categories, he argued that a large proportion of repeat offenders were "incorrigibles" who could be prevented from committing future crimes only by being "incapacitated,"[26] by means of indefinite detention, most likely for life. By contrast, "habitual" repeat offenders who appeared corrigible should receive an indeterminate prison sentence of one to five years, the length of which would depend on the progress of rehabilitation. Finally, first-time offenders who appeared to be "occasional" criminals were not in need of rehabilitation but of deterrence. Since a prison term presented the danger of further criminalizing them, the best way to deter such criminals from committing further crimes was to suspend their sentences under a probation system.[27]

Liszt's conviction that penal sanctions serve the purpose of preventing recidivism thus led him to call for the replacement of the standard fixed

24. See especially Liszt, "Die Aufgaben und die Methode der Strafrechtswissenschaft," in Strafrechtliche Aufsätze und Vorträge, 2:290.

25. On the death penalty in imperial Germany, see Richard Evans, Rituals of Retribution: Capital Punishment in Germany, 1600–1987 (Oxford, 1996), 351–484.

26. Liszt's term was "unschädlichmachen."

27. Liszt, "Der Zweckgedanke im Strafrecht," 163–73.

prison sentence with a variety of alternative sanctions that were tailored to the individual offender. Moreover, even though Liszt and his followers still used the term "punishment," they proposed to strip penal sanctions of their punitive content. Here traditional punishments dissolved into a spectrum of individualized preventive measures, many of which were similar to nonpenal measures, such as education (for juvenile delinquents), medical treatment (for abnormal offenders), and administrative detention in a workhouse (for incorrigible habitual criminals).

Building a Reform Movement

Liszt's reform proposals quickly found considerable support, especially among younger professors and students of criminal law but also among reform-minded lawyers and judges. By starting a new academic journal of criminal law in 1881, setting up his own university institute (*Kriminalist-isches Seminar,* 1888), and founding in 1889 the International Union of Penal Law (*Internationale Kriminalistische Vereinigung,* or IKV, which discussed and promoted penal reform at its national and international meetings), Liszt provided his legal reform movement with a strong institutional basis. By the end of the 1880s, he had given shape to the so-called "modern school of criminal law," which led a growing movement for the reform of Germany's criminal justice system.[28]

Not surprisingly, however, the penal reformers' proposals for a radical transformation of criminal justice met with considerable resistance. A protracted debate ensued, pitting Liszt's modern school of criminal law against the so-called "classical school," which defended the retributivist status quo. The retributivists' critique of the proposed reforms focused on two main issues. First, the retributivists charged that the determinism inherent in the reformers' "scientific" approach to crime fatally undermined the notion of individual legal responsibility on which the criminal justice system was based. This criticism was often linked to the charge that the reformers were a

28. Liszt's new journal was the *Zeitschrift für die gesamte Strafrechtswissenschaft.* On the Internationale Kriminalistische Vereinigung (usually translated as International Union [or Association] of Penal Law), see Elisabeth Bellmann, *Die Internationale Kriminalistische Vereinigung* (Frankfurt, 1994); Leon Radzinowicz, *The Roots of the International Association of Criminal Law and Their Significance: A Tribute and Reassessment on Its Centenary* (Freiburg, 1991).

group of weak-kneed humanitarians whose focus on prevention rather than retribution, and on determinism rather than individual responsibility, sapped criminal justice of its moral meaning and deterrent effect. While this first line of attack might well be labeled politically conservative, the second major issue raised by Liszt's retributivist critics reflected concerns that most readers today would regard as liberal. For representatives of the classical school also charged that the reformers' call for indeterminate preventive detention based on the vague criterion of "dangerousness" would open the door to arbitrariness and thus posed a grave threat to the *Rechtsstaat* and to individual liberty.[29]

On the issue of individual legal responsibility, the reformers wavered between frankly acknowledging that their approach had indeed rendered the notion of individual responsibility untenable and trying to redefine individual responsibility in ways that would make it compatible with their determinist view of crime. For example, in a lecture at the Third International Congress of Psychology (1896), Liszt argued that the "distinction between the detention of incorrigible criminals and the institutionalization of dangerous insane persons is not only impracticable but also to be dismissed as a matter of principle." "Let the notions of crime and punishment live on in the creations of our poets as before," he concluded, "they do not stand up to the strict criticism of scientific knowledge. Thus the concept of punishment gives way to those of curative rehabilitation and preventive detention. The conceptual dividing line between crime and insanity gives way and falls—and with it . . . the concept of legal responsibility."[30]

Eliminating the notion of legal responsibility and the distinction between punishment and medical treatment did not pose a substantive problem for Liszt because he regarded the protection of society—rather than retributive justice—as the sole purpose of punishment. Since, in Liszt's scheme, offenders would be subject to whatever measures were necessary to prevent them

29. A good collection of retributivist critiques of the "modern school" is found in the series *Kritische Beiträge zur Strafrechtsreform*, 16 vols., ed. Karl Birkmeyer und Johannes Nagler (Leipzig 1908–1913); see also Karl Birkmeyer, *Was läßt Liszt vom Strafrecht übrig?* (Munich, 1907).

30. Franz von Liszt, "Die strafrechtliche Zurechnungsfähigkeit," *ZStW* 17 (1897): 70–84; reprinted in Liszt, *Strafrechtliche Aufsätze und Vorträge*, 2:214–29.

from offending again, the question of whether they were legally or morally responsible for their actions was irrelevant. From a pragmatic standpoint, however, Liszt recognized that the elimination of legal responsibility was simply not acceptable to the legal establishment or to the German public at large. Accordingly, in the same lecture, Liszt conceded that the "reigning legal-moral conceptions of the people undoubtedly demand a distinction between crime and insanity, prison and asylum."[31]

When the IKV took up the question of legal responsibility at its 1897 congress, a number of penal reformers called for the abolition of the concept. Now, however, Liszt expressed concern that the elimination of legal responsibility, which would abolish the distinction between punishment and treatment, might go "too far in giving a unified [state] organ the right to impose both administrative and judicial measures."[32] He worried that the abandonment of legal responsibility would dissolve criminal justice in a larger system of administrative sanctions without any of the safeguards that judicial procedures guaranteed. Torn between recognition of the fact that criminological research had fatally undermined the notion of legal responsibility and fear that the abolition of legal responsibility would spell the end of the criminal justice system with its procedural guarantees, German penal reformers subsequently abandoned the issue of criminology's radical challenge to legal responsibility. They opted instead for pragmatic reform proposals that focused on the sentencing and punishment stages of criminal justice.

On the issue of indefinite punishment and the threat it posed to civil liberty, the penal reformers and the classical school reached a compromise. Although the retributivists insisted that all punishments must be fixed by law in advance to protect individual freedoms, they shared the reformers' worry about incorrigible criminals and were therefore sympathetic to the demand for the indefinite detention of such malefactors. The resulting compromise proposal was to divide an habitual offender's detention into a fixed

31. Ibid., 227.

32. Proceedings of the Seventh Hauptversammlung of the Internationale Kriminalistische Vereinigung (IKV), Lisbon, 20–22 April 1897, *Mitteilungen der IKV* 6 (1896–97): 474–5.

term of punishment and a subsequent indefinite term of preventive detention that would not be considered punishment and therefore would not violate the principle that all punishments be fixed by law.[33]

Penal Reform before the Great War

This compromise reveals that the retributivist mainstream of the legal profession was beginning to yield to the reformers' call for a highly interven-
tionist strategy of crime prevention. By 1902 the Conference of German
Jurists (*Deutscher Juristentag*) was calling for a comprehensive revision of the
German penal code, and in 1906 the Reich Justice Office (*Reichs-Justizamt*)
formed an official reform commission. Against Liszt's proposal to base punishments on the potential future danger posed by the criminal, adherents of
the classical school were successful in defending the principle that punishments should depend on the offense. But the reform commission's 1909
draft code also made significant concessions to Liszt's position, introducing
a number of preventive measures that could be imposed in addition to the
regular fixed punishments. Among these were indefinite detention for dangerous habitual or degenerate criminals and detention in a workhouse for
the "work-shy" (*Arbeitsscheue*), thieves, and prostitutes. In addition, the
draft code also introduced not only the possibility of suspended sentencing
for first-time offenders but also a general aggravation of punishment for re-
cidivists.[34]

Although the effort to revise the penal code was cut short by the outbreak
of the Great War, the draft code shows that the modern school's ideas were
beginning to affect mainstream opinion in legal and governmental circles.
Moreover, several piecemeal reforms had already anticipated the school's
comprehensive program. Between 1895 and 1903, for example, most German states introduced suspended sentencing by way of administrative ordinances; these special ordinances allowed the state ministries of justice to use
the power of pardon to suspend an offender's prison sentence on probation.

33. Otto Mittelstädt, "Schuld und Strafe," *Gerichtssaal* 46 (1892): 252–60; Melchior
Stenglein, "Die IKV und ihre Zielpunkte," *Gerichtssaal* 49 (1894): 152; Karl von Birkmeyer, "Gedanken zur bevorstehenden Reform der deutschen Strafgesetzgebung," *Archiv
für Strafrecht und Strafprozeß* 48 (1901): 78.

34. *Vorentwurf zu einem deutschen Strafgesetzbuch*, 3 vols. (Berlin, 1909); Schmidt,
Einführung, 394–9.

Likewise, several German states introduced legislation that allowed juvenile offenders to be placed in correctional education instead of serving a prison term, and some states formed special juvenile courts. Finally, in 1912 the Reichstag passed a partial reform bill that downgraded certain types of theft so that such cases could be punished with fines rather than prison sentences.[35]

Penal Reform and German History

The penal reformers' abandonment of a retributivist system of punishments had profoundly ambivalent implications. On the one hand, the primacy given to individualized treatment was an attempt to liberate criminal justice from the schematism of deterrence and from the harshness of retribution. By turning the penal sanction into a preventive rather than a punitive measure, the reformers clearly paved the way for a more humane criminal justice system. On the other hand, the new approach was fraught with grave dangers. If the determination of punishment was no longer limited by the principle of retributive justice or by a system of fixed punishments, the individual would be left unprotected against society's potentially limitless self-protective needs.

Liszt himself was a left-liberal who served as a *Freisinniger* (independent liberal) delegate in the Prussian House of Deputies and later in the Reichstag, and most of his closer students and followers were liberals as well. Thus the demand for an increase in the state's punitive powers, such as the indefinite detention of repeat offenders, did not derive from a politically conservative position. Liszt himself saw his penal reform proposals as part of a move from an earlier individualist liberalism to a more collectivist and statist type of liberalism, such as could be found in the Social Policy Association (*Verein für Sozialpolitik*) in this same period. "The *Rechtsstaat*, the nothing-

---

35. Schmidt, *Einführung*, 399–401. On juvenile justice reform, see Detlev Peukert, *Grenzen der Sozialdisziplinierung. Aufstieg und Krise der deutschen Jugendfürsorge von 1878 bis 1932* (Cologne, 1986); Edward Ross Dickinson, *The Politics of German Child Welfare from the Empire to the Federal Republic* (Cambridge, Mass., 1996); Gabriel Finder, "Education, Not Punishment: Juvenile Justice in Germany, 1890–1930" (Ph.D. dissertation, University of Chicago, 1997). On the shift from short-term prison sentences to fines, see Hermann Stapenhorst, *Die Entwicklung des Verhältnisses von Geldstrafe zu Freiheitsstrafe seit 1882* (Berlin, 1993).

but-*Rechtsstaat*," he wrote, "has . . . in the course of several decades developed into the modern administrative state, which purposely interferes in the free play of forces . . . to support, on the one hand, the weak against the strong, and, on the other hand, to defend the interests of the population as a whole against the wantonness of the individual. The same great intellectual current that brought us *Sozialpolitik* has brought us *Kriminalpolitik*."[36] Because social reformers and penal reformers alike had become disillusioned with the idea that most people were autonomous and rationally calculating individuals, they became willing to entrust the state with more power to intervene in the lives of its citizens.

The politically ambivalent nature of the reform proposals explains why they met with critical responses that reflected contrasting political concerns. As we have seen, some criticisms reflected the liberal concern that the reformist system of individualized and indefinite preventive measures would establish a police state without any protection for individual rights, while others articulated the conservative charge that the reformers destroyed the principle of individual responsibility and thus undermined the very basis of the criminal justice system.

It is precisely the political ambivalence of the reform movement—the impossibility of simply labeling it "progressive" or "authoritarian"—that makes it interesting for the historian and gives it relevance to the broader debates in modern German history. Most historians, myself included, still feel the urge to categorize the ideas and actions of nineteenth- and twentieth-century Germans into a progressive, liberal, emancipatory, and modern category on the one hand, and a conservative, illiberal, reactionary, authoritarian, antimodern category on the other. As we know, the *Sonderweg* interpretation of German history, which explained the Third Reich as the product of the dominance of authoritarian ideas and institutions in modern Germany, was built on this dichotomy. Since the 1980s, critics of the Sonderweg have reassessed the relative weight of modern and premodern, liberal and authoritarian, features in imperial Germany. Even more importantly, they have challenged the normative assumptions underlying Sonderweg historiography. The latter approach was taken by Detlev Peukert, who disputed the assumption that moderniza-

36. Liszt speaking at the Fifteenth Landesversammlung of the IKV, *Mitteilungen der IKV* 19 (1912): 377–8.

tion was progressive and called attention to the "rifts and danger-zones which result from the modern civilizing process."[37] Such an analysis runs the risk of overemphasizing the dark side of modernization to the point where Nazism appears as the logical outcome of modernity itself, a danger that Peukert himself did not always escape. But if one takes care to avoid such one-sided emphasis, an awareness of the political ambivalence of many developments that are usually associated with the "modernization" of society—including the various nineteenth-century reform movements—may allow us to arrive at a better understanding not only of imperial Germany, but of the complex continuities and discontinuities of German history.

Like any historian working on the Nazi period, the legal historian must navigate a difficult path between making the Nazi regime appear as an aberration (by stressing the rupture of 1933) and presenting it as the logical outcome of a German Sonderweg (by stressing continuities). Understanding the ambivalence of the German penal reform agenda prior to 1933 enables us to recognize that key aspects of Nazi penal policy were neither complete aberrations nor the result of a German Sonderweg, but extreme manifestations of dangers that were inherent in a penal reform agenda that Germany shared with many Western countries. This is not to say that this penal reform agenda necessarily led to Nazi penal policies; as the history of other countries that shared this agenda shows, there was no such inevitability. What this approach shows, however, is that major aspects of Nazi penal policy are best understood not as a break with the past (although there were important breaks) nor as the outcome of German legal traditions that deviated from the West (although there were some), but as a process of drawing on pre-1933 reform projects that contained emancipatory and humanitarian as well as highly repressive implications. Which aspect would be emphasized, and to what extreme either would be pushed, depended on political circumstances. Because modern Germany underwent extreme changes in political circumstances, from imperial Germany to the Weimar Republic to the Nazi regime, its history reveals with unusual clarity both the emancipatory and repressive potentials inherent in many of the "modern" intellectual traditions and reform projects that emerged in the late nineteenth century and shaped the twentieth.

37. Detlev Peukert, *Volksgenossen und Gemeinschaftsfremde* (Cologne, 1982), 296. Translated by Richard Deveson as *Inside Nazi Germany: Conformity, Opposition, and Racism in Everyday Life* (New Haven, Conn., 1987), 249.

GENDERED DISCOURSE

EMANCIPATORY OR PROTO-FASCIST?

Patriarchy and Its Discontents

The Debate on the Origins of the Family in the German-Speaking World, 1860–1930

ANN TAYLOR ALLEN

To associate the cultural history of Germany and Europe at the turn of the twentieth century with some kind of crisis has become an historical cliché. The crisis is commonly attributed to rapid change in such areas as scientific methods, religious beliefs, and political ideologies, but seldom in gender relations—a theme that, though extensively discussed by historians of women or gender, is still neglected by a majority of intellectual historians.[1] Yet an awareness of what the Viennese feminist Grete Meisel-Hess called a "sexual crisis" pervaded many aspects of this era's culture: not only its intellectual life, but its literature and visual arts as well. One stimulus to this awareness was certainly the growth and visibility of feminist movements and of the sexual reform milieu described by Kevin Repp in his contribution to this volume.[2] But the preoccupation with gender and its many cultural meanings was by no means confined to these radical groups; it was of central importance to the development of mainstream intellectual movements in philosophy, sociology, anthropology, psychology, and psychoanalysis. In all these fields, gender figured as a category of analysis. The polarity of male and female often stood for other fundamental dichotomies: history and prehistory, culture and nature, order and disorder, *Gesellschaft* and *Gemeinschaft*.

One of the great controversies of the fin de siècle centered on the history

1. But there have been some recent exceptions to this pattern. See, for example, Andrew Lees, *Cities, Sin, and Social Reform in Imperial Germany* (Ann Arbor, Mich., 2002); Kevin Repp, *Reformers, Critics, and the Paths of German Modernity: Anti-Politics and the Search for Alternatives, 1890–1914* (Cambridge, Mass., 2000).

2. See Kevin Repp, "Sexualkrise und Rasse: Feminist Eugenics at the Fin de Siècle," below; Grete Meisel-Hess, *Die sexuelle Krise in ihren Beziehungen zur sozialen Frage und zum Krieg und zu Moral, Rasse, und Religion, und insbesondere zur Monogamie* (Jena, 1917). On gender and history, see Joan Wallach Scott, "Gender, a Useful Category of Social Analysis," in *Feminism and History*, ed. Joan Wallach Scott (New York, 1996), 152–80.

of the family. It is not the purpose of this essay to evaluate the scientific accuracy of any of the theories that emerged from that debate, most of which, according to the latest research, were right on some points and wrong on others.[3] Rather, this essay will contextualize the debate over the history of the family in order to trace the emergence of important theoretical paradigms—the evolutionary theories of the mid-nineteenth century, the cultural relativism of the 1890s, and functionalism and psychoanalysis, which emerged around 1910. The prominence of the history of the family as a theme of discussion in all of these movements suggests that the hopes, fears, and insights that arose from this era's crisis in gender relations exercised a formative influence on its intellectual history.[4]

As background to the turn-of-the-century debate about the history of the family, we must look at some foundational midcentury publications. Friedrich Engels stated in his enormously influential work, *The Origins of the Family, Private Property, and the State,* that the "history of the family dates from 1861, from the publication of Bachofen's *Mutterrecht.*"[5] Here, Engels meant critical history: histories of the family written before 1861, with few exceptions, had simply assumed that patriarchy was the original form of the family.[6] Johann Jakob Bachofen (whose life and work has been sensitively recounted by Lionel Gossmann)[7] intended no modernist critique of the pa-

3. A useful survey of the latest research is Cynthia Eller, *The Myth of Matriarchal Prehistory: Why an Invented Past Won't Give Women a Future* (Boston, 2000).

4. Ann Taylor Allen, "Feminism, Social Science, and the Meanings of Modernity: The Debate on the Origin of the Family in Europe and the United States, 1860–1914," *American Historical Review* 104 (October 1999): 1085–113. Many more references to sources and secondary works are given in this article.

5. Friedrich Engels, *The Origin of the Family, Private Property, and the State,* 4th ed. (New York, 1942), 8.

6. For example, Henry Sumner Maine, *Ancient Law* (1861; reprint, London, 1954); Johann Jakob Bachofen, *Das Mutterrecht: eine Untersuchung über die Gynaikokratie der alten Welt nach ihrer religiösen und rechtlichen Natur* (1861), reprinted in *Johann Jakob Bachofens Gesammelte Werke,* 8 vols., ed. Karl Meuli (Basel, 1943–48), vols. 2 and 3. A useful collection of excerpts from Bachofen's voluminous works in English translation is: Johann Jakob Bachofen, *Myth, Religion, and Mother-Right: Selected Writings of J. J. Bachofen,* trans. Ralph Manheim (Princeton, N.J., 1976).

7. Lionel Gossman, *Basel in the Age of Burckhardt: A Study in Unseasonable Ideas* (Chicago, 2000), 109–200.

triarchal family. Indeed, this deeply conservative Basel patrician, who had resigned all his public offices in 1844 and 1845 as a protest against the liberalization of that city's political life, aimed at something quite different in *Das Mutterrecht*. In his alternative account of the rise of Western civilization, he hoped to expose the arrogance of modern European culture and to show that the cost of progress was loss, discontinuity, and emotional conflict.

The source material for *Das Mutterrecht* consisted of visual and written texts from the archaic period of Greek civilization, which Bachofen, still working within the short Biblical chronology that dated the creation to 4004 BC, considered to be close to the origins of the human race. Bachofen traced the development of the family through four stages. In the first, or Aphroditean, stage, the human race lived in a state of sexual promiscuity. Fatherhood was unknown; accordingly, the first family units were matrilineal, consisting only of mothers and their dependent children. As the first social tie, the mother-child bond was the source of all ethics, altruism, and religion, and thus of culture. In the second, or Demetrian, stage, mothers used their more advanced cultural development to dominate men, imposing marriage, a matrilineal and female-headed family structure (*Mutterrecht*), and an ordered, peaceable society based on human bonds. This was the classical period of matriarchy. In the third, or Dionysian, stage, the matriarchs abused their power by returning once again to sexual license and indulging in the wild and lustful cult of Dionysus, the phallic god of male fertility. Having through this cult acknowledged the role of the male in procreation, the matriarchs subverted their own system and laid it open to its inevitable defeat by the forces of patriarchy. The fourth stage, the Apollonian, was characterized by the patriarchal and patrilineal form of the family and by the exaltation of the male principles of reason, law, and abstract thought over female emotionality.

Bachofen's story ostensibly celebrated the triumph of patriarchy, but in fact the meanings that he assigned to gender roles were more complex, for the conservative scholar admired the peaceable and nurturing world of the matriarchy and lamented its loss. In his narrative, femaleness stood for the material world, the body, and the emotions, but it could connote the compassionate order of the mother-headed family and community as well as the disorder of promiscuity and Dionysian orgies. Maleness stood for reason and law, but it too was double-edged; it could signify both the enlightened reign of justice (as in Roman law) and the life-denying detachment of reason from emotion. Moreover, Bachofen insisted that the patriarchs could not eliminate but only repress their female opponents and that submerged feminine emotionality would always threaten the stability of patriarchal society. Bachofen's methodology eschewed the positivism then in vogue in the field of classical philology and aimed at an imaginative reconstruction of the past, using mythology and symbolism as windows into human consciousness.[8]

Bachofen (like his young colleague, Nietzsche) was emphatically rejected by the dominant German school of classical philology.[9] His chief influence was on the growing field of anthropology. In the 1880s, Bachofen's thesis was espoused by anthropologists such as the American Lewis Henry Morgan, the Briton Edward Burnett Tylor, and the German Adolf Bastian, leaders of the field in their respective countries. Anthropology sought for origins of culture not, as Bachofen had, in the classical world, but among non-Western "primitive" societies, which were assumed to replicate early stages of the rise of civilization that had reached its apogee with the modern West.[10]

Largely ignoring Bachofen's own aversion to modern society, these anthropologists created a typically Victorian narrative of cultural evolution, in which Western forms of patriarchy represented the civilization's apex. Though they found no existing examples of true matriarchy (that is, the political dominance of women over men), they did find societies that were characterized by matrilineal family structures and by a greater degree of gender equality than those of the West. They concluded that the transition from mother-right to father-right was a universal aspect of human evolution. Wilhelm Wundt, the creator of the field of *Völkerpsychologie* (the psychology of peoples), traced the same pattern in the evolution of social and ethical life from maternal norms of emotion and nurture to paternal values of abstract justice and rationality.[11]

8. Cf. ibid., 158.

9. Cf. Suzanne L. Marchand, *Down from Olympus: Archaeology and Philhellenism in Germany, 1750–1970* (Princeton, N.J., 1996), 124–33.

10. Lewis Henry Morgan, *Ancient Society: or Researches in the Lines of Human Progress from Savagery through Barbarism to Civilization* (London, 1878). For a discussion of anthropology and the rise of an idea of prehistory, see Thomas Trautmann, *Lewis Henry Morgan and the Invention of Kinship* (Berkeley, Calif., 1997).

11. Wilhelm Wundt, *Ethics: An Investigation of the Moral Life,* trans. Julia Gulliver (London, 1908), 227–80.

But in the 1880s and 1890s this narrative was disrupted because of developments in political and social thought that called the prevailing belief in progress into question. Karl Marx and Friedrich Engels, who were voracious readers of anthropology, used the work of Bachofen and Morgan to attack rather than to support patriarchy. The early age of mother-right, they asserted, had also been an age of economic and social equality, while the onset of patriarchal control of women and children had initiated a long history of inequality. Engels and August Bebel, who formulated an enormously influential socialist version of the history of the family, portrayed matriarchy as a form of primitive equality and patriarchy as a form of oppression that would disappear with the destruction of capitalism and private property. Though they did not encourage feminism—women were assumed to share the interests of men of their class—the works of Engels and Bebel brought the prehistory and history of the family into political discourse.[12]

The 1890s saw an upsurge in feminist organizing, which in Germany focused on the aspirations of women to higher education, professional opportunities, and an improved legal status in marriage and the family. Two major feminist organizations were founded: the League of German Women's Associations (*Bund deutscher Frauenvereine*), an umbrella organization for many middle-class feminist groups, in 1894, and the Union of Progressive Women's Associations (*Verband fortschrittlicher Frauenvereine*), a more progressive middle-class organization, in 1899. Starting in 1899, these groups brought feminist concerns into the political arena through an aggressive and highly visible campaign for the reform of the *Code of Civil Law* (*Bürgerliches Gesetzbuch*). Among the laws they denounced were those that gave total control over legitimate children to fathers and left mothers legally powerless, thus violating what many feminists claimed was a natural bond between mother and child. Meanwhile, the Social Democratic Party's advocacy of suffrage and other rights for women had encouraged the organization of working-class women, who under the leadership of Klara Zetkin soon created by far the largest and most active socialist women's movement in Europe. The history of gender relations, as recounted by Engels and Bebel, served several generations of socialist feminists and some of their nonsocial-

---

12. Engels, *Origin of the Family*, 144–63; August Bebel, *Die Frau in der Vergangenheit, Gegenwart, und Zukunft* (Zürich, 1883). Later versions bore the title *Die Frau und der Sozialismus*.

ist colleagues as a theoretical framework for an increasingly aggressive attack on male dominance in many areas of politics and society.

The involvement of academics in these political movements brought gender relations into the center of intellectual controversies, particularly in the social-science disciplines which were then in their formative phase. Some theorists refuted the socialist and feminist challenge through a defense of the patriarchal family, now based on arguments derived from the Darwinian theories of human evolution and behavior that had become fashionable in the 1890s. The Finnish scholar Edward Westermarck, who was very influential in the German-speaking world, contended that the sexual jealousy of all—and especially of human—male primates had always prevented totally promiscuous mating, and that the patriarchal family was universal and necessary.[13] However, other well-known German anthropologists, including Josef Kohler and Franz Müller-Lyer, defended the theory of mother-right and placed it in the service of feminism. In the history of civilization, Kohler argued, motherhood was the "first and holiest" of social bonds, while fatherhood, which in early stages of human development was not even recognized as biological fact, had always been a more distant and tenuous relationship. Through the recent establishment of patrilineal inheritance and patriarchal family structure, Kohler wrote, the "position of women was entirely distorted and the mother separated from her child."[14] According to Müller-Lyer, the prehistoric defeat of the mothers had to be remedied in the present through the deserved decline of the patriarchal household and the rise of a more individualistic family system in which men and women would be "spiritually and economically free and independent personalities."[15]

But by the fin de siècle, the field of anthropology had yielded a profusion of data so daunting as to undermine the foundation of these and other evolutionary theories. The colorful diversity of human behavior hardly fit into

13. Edward Westermarck, *The History of Human Marriage* (1891; reprint, London, 1903), 117.

14. Josef Kohler, "Die Mutter im Rechte der Völker," in *Mutterschaft*, ed. Adele Schreiber (Munich, 1911), 57–67 (quotation, 59).

15. Franz Müller-Lyer, "Die Ehe: ihre Entwicklung und Reform unter dem Gesichtspunkt des wirtschaftlichen und kultürlichen Fortschritts und der Rassenhygiene," in *Mutterschaft*, ed. Schreiber, 133–55 (quotation, 148); Müller-Lyer, *Die Familie* (Munich, 1912).

the conventional hierarchy of "low" and "high" cultures, with Western civilization at the apex. Instead, cultures were increasingly seen individually, as political arrangements that had come into being (and might pass away) in response to specific historical circumstances.[16] The results of anthropological research, particularly concerning sexuality and the family, thus drove the turn to cultural relativism that would eventually transform Western thought in the early twentieth century. And the rise of cultural relativism left other conventional assumptions open to contestation—especially the Western preference for the rationality that was characterized as male over the emotionality that was stereotyped as female. The story of the problematic victory of patriarchy, as presented by Bachofen and Engels, often provided a symbolic framework for a critique of Western modernity.

Gender as a category of analysis underlay the development of the field of sociology at the turn of the twentieth century. Ferdinand Tönnies, a founder of the field in Germany, based his major work, *Gemeinschaft und Gesellschaft,* partly on the research of Bachofen and Morgan. Tönnies's diagnosis of the central problem of modern society as the tension between two forms of relationship—*Gemeinschaft,* or community, and *Gesellschaft,* or association—owed much to these two scholars. The threatened *Gemeinschaft,* which was characterized by familial bonding and traditional loyalties, was in many ways like Bachofen's matriarchal stage; Tönnies wrote that the "eternal feminine, or the principle of motherliness, is the root of all being together."[17] The ascendant *Gesellschaft,* in which contractual relationships took the place of traditional obligations, bore many of the traits of Bachofen's patriarchy; it was "cold and calculating, superficial and enlightened."[18] Responding to the decline of the evolutionary paradigm, Tönnies portrayed the struggle be-

16. George W. Stocking, *After Tylor: British Social Anthropology, 1888–1951* (Madison, Wis., 1988), 230–92; Stocking, *Victorian Anthropology* (New York, 1987), 326.

17. Ferdinand Tönnies, "The Concept of Gemeinschaft" (1925), in Tönnies, *On Sociology Pure, Applied, and Empirical,* ed. Werner J. Cahnman and Rudolf Heberle (Chicago, 1971), 67–72 (quotation, 69). For a helpful analysis of the German sociologists' views of gender, see Terry R. Kandal, *The Woman Question in Classical Sociological Theory* (Miami, Fla., 1988), 89–185 (on Tönnies, see 177–81). See also David Lindenfeld, "Tönnies, the Mandarins, and Modernism," *German Studies Review* 11 (February 1988): 60–1.

18. Ferdinand Tönnies, *Gemeinschaft und Gesellschaft: Grundbegriffe der reinen Soziologie* (1887; reprint, Darmstadt, 1964), 150.

tween these opposing forces not just as an historical phase but also as a present-day dilemma. And he denied that the growing ascendancy of *Gesellschaft* over *Gemeinschaft* meant progress: like Bachofen, he lamented the estrangement of the modern individual from the sustaining energies of *Gemeinschaft*—home, soil, and family.

Similar perceptions of gender polarity also informed the sociology of Georg Simmel, who attributed the psychic problems of the modern individual to the difficult adaptation to a culture that exalted rational objectivity and suppressed emotion and intuition. Like Bachofen and Engels, Simmel speculated that this one-sided culture had resulted from some ancient victory of patriarchy over matriarchy—at any rate, in its existing form it was "thoroughly male."[19] Furthermore, Simmel traced the subordination of women in Western societies to a distinctively female psychology in which emotion and reason were integrated. He asserted that women, though perhaps healthier than men, could not adapt to the demands of male-dominated culture. In Simmel's tragic view of the world, men were condemned to psychic conflict and women to a disadvantaged existence on the margins of society.[20]

Max Weber, too, saw the triumph of rationality and calculation over emotional spontaneity as the central problem of modern life. Monogamous marriage, that bulwark of the ascendant patriarchy, he imagined as one of the bars of the "iron cage" that blocked all life-giving drives.[21] Weber associated the emotional energies that had been suppressed by modern culture with femaleness and eroticism. For him, charisma—the gift for ecstatic leadership in religion and politics—represented (in the words of his biographer, Arthur Mitzman) the "resurrection of the long-suppressed deities of the li-

19. Georg Simmel, "Female Culture," (1911) in Georg Simmel, *On Women, Sexuality and Love*, ed. and trans. Greg Oakes (New Haven, Conn., 1984), 67; cf. Kandal, *The Woman Question*, 163.

20. See Kandal, *The Woman Question*, 156–76.

21. Max Weber, "Religious Rejections of the World and Their Directions: The Esthetic Sphere" (1915), in *From Max Weber: Essays in Sociology*, ed. H. H. Gerth and C. Wright Mills (New York, 1958), 348–50; see also Laurence Scaff, *Fleeing the Iron Cage: Culture, Politics, and Modernity in the Thought of Max Weber* (Berkeley, Calif., 1989), 88–111, and Arthur Mitzman, *The Iron Cage: A Historical Interpretation of Max Weber* (New Brunswick, N.J., 1985), 295.

bido, femininity, Eros, and community, of blind passion as well as compassion." Weber regarded the chaotic energies that he identified as female as exciting but dangerous; on the whole, he considered the maintenance of male-identified rationality necessary to social order.[22] Following H. Stuart Hughes, intellectual historians tend to regard the world view expressed by these sociologists (which Hughes characterized as "bleak in the extreme") as representative of the entire era.[23] Indeed, the editors of this volume remark that German culture at the turn of the century was marked by a "pervasive sense of incoherence and crisis."[24]

But we must not characterize an entire era through the attitudes of its male elites. As the editors of this volume admit, "The late Wilhelmine world was also populated . . . by optimists."[25] To feminist intellectuals, the breakdown of the midcentury paradigms that had justified women's subordination brought no sense of "incoherence," but instead new visions of order. Many cited anthropological research to refute the conventional equation of patriarchy with progress, enlightenment, and rationality. They asserted that the matriarchal period—sometimes invoked more as an "ideal type" than as historical reality—had been supremely rational, and that the triumph of patriarchy had been a regression to barbarity and violence. Two foreign authors who influenced German feminists, the American Charlotte Perkins Gilman and the Swedish Ellen Key, asserted that mother-love had been the first social bond and remained the most natural and enduring one; further, they proclaimed that the law of the mother was the basis of all compassion and justice. The subjection of women and the family to male control—and especially to the irresponsible male sex drive—had impeded human evolution and caused the high rates of infant and maternal mortality that had sapped the vitality of Western nations.[26]

22. Cf. Mitzman, *The Iron Cage,* 302–6 (quotation, 304); see also Kandal, *The Woman Question,* 126–55.

23. H. Stuart Hughes, *Consciousness and Society: The Reorientation of European Social Thought, 1890–1930* (New York, 1958), 332.

24. See above, 5.

25. See above, 8–9.

26. See Charlotte Perkins Gilman, *The Man-Made World, or Our Androcentric Culture* (New York, 1914); Ellen Key, *The Woman Movement,* trans. Mamah Bouton Borthwick (New York, 1912), and many other works by these authors.

The influence of these ideas was not confined to academic or intellectual circles. They were enthusiastically received by political activists, among whom were the feminists of the League for the Protection of Mothers (*Bund für Mutterschutz*). In 1904, the founder of this organization, the school-teacher Ruth Bré (her real name was Elisabeth Bonness), called for a kind of matriarchal utopia. Appalled by the fate of unmarried mothers and their children, who were often condemned by conventional law and custom to ostracism, poverty, and death, Bré called both on government and private philanthropy to support independent communities of mothers and children in the countryside. But the sexual reformers who took over the leadership of the group in 1905—among whom were prominent figures such as Helene Stöcker, Adele Schreiber, Henriette Fürth, and Lily Braun—rejected any such return to matriarchy. The development of the two-parent family, Stöcker wrote, was a positive change that should not be reversed. She added, "Our knowledge of historical development helps us to understand what we must demand today." Women's subordination was not due to nature—it was as contingent and transitory as all other historical phenomena. It was the triumph of patriarchy that had condemned women, who "until then had been on a level of approximate equality . . . to absolute instrumentalization in the service of men."[27] Leaders of the organization therefore argued that the reorganization of family life and reproduction along lines that would ensure the equality of women was not a violation of any universal natural or moral law, but instead the long-overdue remedy for millennia of injustice.

The leaders of the league advocated not only the reform of marriage laws, but also the abolition of all other laws and customs that upheld patriarchal legitimacy. They insisted that illegitimate children should be given the same rights as their legitimate siblings, that nonmarital relationships should be recognized, and that single women should be permitted to choose mother-hood, supported by maternity insurance and other state benefits. Some even took the daring position that women should have access to birth control, abortion, and sexual abstinence in order to control their own reproduc-tion.[28] As Kevin Repp explains, female reproductive power freed of the

27. Helene Stöcker, *Die Liebe und die Frauen* (Minden, 1908), 178.

28. Ann Taylor Allen, *Feminism and Motherhood in Germany, 1800–1914* (New Brunswick, N.J., 1991), 173–88. Many more sources are given in the notes to this chapter.

bonds of patriarchy was often romantically extolled as a mighty force for biological and cultural regeneration.[29] Though the league included only a small minority of all German feminists and was soon split by factional conflict, its open denunciation of patriarchal oppression in the sensitive and previously taboo areas of sexuality and reproduction attracted widespread attention in the German-speaking world and in many Western countries.

But whatever its sensational impact, this "New Ethic" found little support among the majority of German feminists, as represented by the leadership of the *Bund deutscher Frauenvereine* (BDF) and other mainstream organizations. Our fascination with the skeptical avant-garde must not lead us to overlook the religious values that still pervaded even the progressive middle-class culture of the Wilhelmine era. Some moderate feminists protested in the name of traditional religious morality; others did so in the name of motherhood, which they saw as a cultural and spiritual function that had been degraded by an overemphasis on biology. Marianne Weber, a leading member of the BDF, voiced another concern of the movement's majority. The proposals of the League for the Protection of Mothers—which her husband Max called "crude hedonism . . . an ethic that would benefit only the man . . . simply nonsense!"—might well bring more harm than good to the majority of all women who still depended on marriage for their subsistence.[30]

In 1904, Marianne Weber warned her feminist contemporaries against dreams of a matriarchal "lost Paradise" and pointed out the findings of the latest anthropological research: matrilineal family structures, in the cultures where they existed, did not ensure a high status for women.[31] In her monumental work *Wife and Mother in Legal History* (*Ehefrau und Mutter in der Rechtsentwicklung*), she argued that marriage had not enslaved but, on the contrary, had advanced Western women by guaranteeing their own status and that of their children. But although Weber by no means shared Stöcker's sexual reform agenda, she too placed the family in historical perspective. As

29. See below, 114, 117–9, 125–6.

30. Marianne Weber, *Max Weber: Ein Lebensbild* (1926; reprint, Heidelberg, 1950), 412.

31. Marianne Weber, "Die historische Entwicklung des Eherechts" (1904), in *Frauenfragen und Frauengedanken* (Tübingen, 1919), 10–9.

marriage had evolved in the past, she argued, it must continue to evolve in the future toward the equality and independence of men and women.[32]

Marianne Weber's warning against nostalgia for a lost matriarchal utopia was justified, for such seductive fantasies inspired antifeminist as well as feminist agendas. In Germany, the best-known disciples of Bachofen belonged to the Cosmic Circle, a group of academics and literary figures that met between 1897 and 1904 in Munich, led by the poet Stefan George, the philosopher Ludwig Klages, the classical scholar Karl Wolfskehl, and the poet Alfred Schuler. This group, who made *Das Mutterrecht* into a cult classic, associated the age of matriarchy with a healthy and uninhibited sexual promiscuity and contrasted it to the repressive system imposed on the West by the patriarchal theology of Judaism and Christianity. Klages declared that modern society must return to the sexual permissiveness that had characterized the age of mother-right and that had been celebrated in the Dionysian orgies (which were sometimes tamely reenacted at the group's *Fasching* [Mardi Gras] costume balls). These interpretations of Bachofen gave no support to feminism. Indeed, the Munich group regarded feminism as a soul-destroying manifestation of modern rationality and advised women to forsake masculine pursuits (such as education and professional work) and return to their original reproductive and maternal roles. Borrowing an idea from the socialist movements that they otherwise despised, the Cosmic Circle advocated collective support for motherhood and reproduction. The end of patriarchal repression in the family and in Western culture as a whole, they hoped, would release the purgative and bracing forces of sex, race, and blood, which were signified by the group's symbol, the swastika.[33]

The Cosmic Circle, however, was a manifestation of the same cultural ferment that had also produced the League for the Protection of Mothers, and its reactionary discourse could be turned to feminist purposes. Otto Gross, Sigmund Freud's most gifted pupil, was a prominent member of the Munich group; he aspired to use psychoanalysis as a justification for the

---

32. Marianne Weber, *Ehefrau und Mutter in der Rechtsentwicklung: eine Einführung* (Tübingen, 1907), 24–77.

33. Ludwig Klages, *Vom kosmogonischen Eros* (1922; reprint, Bonn, 1963), 226. See also Wolf Lepenies, *Between Literature and Science: The Rise of Sociology* (Cambridge, 1988), 258–77, on the relationships of members of this group to the founders of the field of sociology.

overthrow of patriarchy and the lifting of sexual repression. But Gross was a convinced feminist who included among his most important aims the liberation of women from patriarchy. To this end, he turned psychoanalysis on its head. Freud, Gross asserted, had shown that the patriarchal family produced inhibition and deformation of the personality, but had then timidly refused to draw the logical conclusion—that patriarchy, the product of usurpation and violence, should be abolished and replaced by the nurturing and nonrepressive mother-headed household which Gross, an ardent reader of Bachofen, considered to be "natural" to the human race.[34]

In 1908, Gross was treated for morphine addiction at the Burghölzli, a psychiatric institute in Zürich, by Carl Gustav Jung. The roles of analyst and analysand seem to have been reversed. Jung was very much drawn to Gross's vision of psychoanalysis as the basis for a new, Dionysian approach to religion and sexual morality.[35] Shortly thereafter, Jung broke with his former mentor, Freud, questioning the theory of the Oedipus complex, which Freud believed persisted in the adult subconscious but had to be repressed for fear of the father's authority. In a 1912 letter, Jung asked Freud how the Oedipus complex could possibly be part of a universal pattern of male personality development. After all, in the period when human culture originated— which Jung (following Gross and Bachofen) believed to have been matriarchally organized—fathers did not know their sons, nor sons their fathers. As Jung wrote, "In fact, there was no such thing as a father's son."[36]

Freud had already repudiated Gross, and his response to Jung showed his fear of the co-optation of psychoanalysis by a sexual radicalism that he

34. Otto Gross, "Zur Überwindung der kulturellen Krise," (1913), in Gross, *Von geschlechtlicher Not zur sozialen Katastrophe,* ed. Kurt Kreiler (Frankfurt, 1980), 13–5, and other essays in this volume. See also Martin Green, *The von Richthofen Sisters: The Triumphant and the Tragic Modes of Love: Else and Frieda von Richthofen, Otto Gross, Max Weber, and D. H. Lawrence in the Years 1870–1970* (New York, 1974); Richard Noll, *The Aryan Christ: The Secret Life of Carl Jung* (New York, 1997), 69–89.

35. Richard Noll, *The Jung Cult: The Origins of a Charismatic Movement* (Princeton, N.J., 1994), 151–76. Noll also explains the considerable influence of Bachofen on Jung, a native of Basel whose grandfather, as rector of the university, had known the famous and eccentric scholar.

36. Jung to Freud, 8 May 1912, in *The Freud-Jung Letters: The Correspondence between Sigmund Freud and C. G. Jung,* ed. William McGuire, trans. Ralph Manheim and R. F. C. Hull (Princeton, N.J., 1974), 503.

considered a threat to social order. "Most authors regard a primordial state of promiscuity as unlikely," he responded to Jung. "It seems likely that there have been father's sons at all times."[37] Between 1911 and 1913, both Freud and Jung produced works that, though not extensively citing Bachofen (whose work was no longer considered scientific), nonetheless showed his influence by importing elements of his historical narrative into their very different theories of psychological development.[38]

Jung's *Wandlung und Symbole der Libido,* published in segments from 1912 to 1913 and translated into English as *Psychology of the Unconscious* in 1916, signaled his break with Freud by providing an alternative explanation for incest fantasies centered on the mother which Freud had attributed to the Oedipus complex. Jung interpreted such fantasies not literally but symbolically. In his view, they stemmed from the longing of patients who were overwhelmed by the problems of adult life to return to the blissful irresponsibility and security of infancy, as symbolized by the mother. As evidence for such wishes, Jung cited myths of the hero's journey to the underworld (symbolic of the womb and the female earth-deities), which he claimed were common to all human cultures and therefore represented the contents of a collective subconscious.[39] Convinced that fatherhood was a later-developing and more superficial relationship, Jung allotted slight attention to the father or to patriarchy.

Like his contemporaries of the Cosmic Circle, Jung explicitly repudiated any feminist interpretations of the awe-inspiring maternal archetypes that haunted his patients' fantasies. In fact, Jung regarded female power with fear, declaring it a threat to masculinity and rationality, which he stereotyped as male. He warned that excessive attachment to the mother—whom he often personified as the "Destructive Mother"—condemned whoever was

37. Freud to Jung, 14 May 1912, in *The Freud-Jung Letters,* 504. On Jung's early development and his relationship to Freud, see John Kerr, *A Most Dangerous Method: The Story of Jung, Freud, and Sabina Spielrein* (New York, 1993), 105–348; Frank McLynn, *Carl Gustav Jung* (New York, 1996), 92–267.

38. On the influence of Bachofen on both Jung and Freud, cf. Noll, *The Jung Cult,* 169–76, and Henri F. Ellenberger, *The Discovery of the Unconscious: The History and Evolution of Dynamic Psychiatry* (New York, 1970), 727–30.

39. C. G. Jung, *Psychology of the Unconscious: A Study of the Transformations and Symbolisms of the Libido,* trans. Beatrice M. Hinkle (New York, 1916), 3–41.

too weak to resist it to permanent infantilism, weakness, and neurosis. Only liberation from this primordial attachment could enable the individual to attain adulthood, a precarious state that was constantly threatened by dangerous and regressive nostalgia for maternal love and the lost paradise of infancy. "And there is no doubt," Jung concluded, "that there is nothing that so completely enfolds us as the mother."[40]

Meanwhile, Freud, who attributed Jung's picture of a fatherless unconscious to an Oedipal wish to destroy his intellectual father, set out to assert the primordial existence of patriarchy in a collection of essays published in 1913 as *Totem and Taboo* (*Totem und Tabu*). Like Jung, Freud based his conclusions on the mythology of so-called "primitive" peoples, but he also relied on a still deeper evolutionary prehistory. He started from Darwin's theory that the human race had originally lived (like certain primates) in patriarchal hordes, where, in the absence of any incest taboo, the dominant male monopolized all the females and drove away the adolescent males. Mad with desire for the females, the adolescent males had combined to kill the father; but then, stricken with terrible remorse, they had renounced sexual access to the females and had elevated the murdered father to the status of a god, thus initiating the incest taboo and the law of exogamy.

In each individual, this "memorable crime" was replicated through the Oedipus complex and its resolution.[41] The stages of child development that Freud later identified in fact corresponded to Bachofen's stages of prehistory: a period of maternal love and permissiveness and of uninhibited sexuality (infancy) is ended through the father's imposition of the incest taboo, the first and most universal of laws. The Freudian "id" was in some sense the repressed matriarchy, and the "superego" the ascendant patriarchy.[42] Freud insisted that only the acceptance of the law of the father, as imposed by a human father, a father-god, or a patriarchal civilization, could complete the transition to adulthood.

40. Ibid., 483.

41. Sigmund Freud, *Totem and Taboo: Resemblances between the Psychic Lives of Savages and Neurotics,* trans. A. A. Brill (New York, 1918), 193. See also Kerr, *A Most Dangerous Method,* 343–5.

42. See Sigmund Freud, "The Dissection of the Psychical Personality," (1933) in Freud, *New Introductory Lectures on Psychoanalysis,* trans. James Strachey (New York, 1965), 57–80, for a fuller explanation of the structure of the unconscious.

Freudian psychoanalysis thus may be understood in part as an attempt to restabilize patriarchy by locating its origins not just in prehistory and history, but in a universal theory of human nature. But this vindication of patriarchy was beset by an ambivalence that was characteristic of the era. Neither Freud nor Jung depicted the patriarchal order as wholly natural or inevitable. Rather, both saw the acceptance of patriarchy as the outcome of a process of psychic development that was fraught with struggle and tension, and that often required the deformation of important parts of the personality. "It must be said that the revenge of the deposed and reinstated father has been very cruel," Freud concluded. "It culminated in the dominance of authority."[43]

The stabilization of patriarchy and the father-headed family was a central agenda of another highly influential theory of human behavior, functionalism, which also originated in the early twentieth century. A major proponent of functionalism, the anthropologist Bronislaw Malinowski, was born in 1884 as an Austrian subject of Polish nationality. Malinowski studied in Cracow and Leipzig before moving to Britain in 1910; thus his formative years were spent in the German-speaking world. As a student of anthropology whose mentors included Wundt and Westermarck, Malinowski soon turned his attention to the origins of the family. His frustration at the "distinctly polemical, often irritated tone" of scholarly debates on this issue contributed to his growing doubts about existing anthropological methods.[44] He concluded that fieldwork, the intensive empirical study of a single culture, was a more objective source of data than evolutionary theories that could be documented only through literary sources. However, Malinowski did not undertake fieldwork in a totally impartial spirit; before he left for the Trobriand Islands in 1914, he already doubted that either a state of total promiscuity or a mother-headed family structure had ever existed. He therefore supported the conclusion of his mentor, Westermarck, that all human civilizations had recognized fatherhood.[45]

Malinowski's research confirmed his hypothesis. In an account that is

43. Freud, *Totem and Taboo,* 190.
44. Bronislaw Malinowski, "The Sociology of the Family" (1913–14), in Malinowski, *The Early Writings of Bronislaw Malinowski,* ed. Robert J. Thornton and Peter Skalnik, trans. Ludwik Krzyzanowski (Cambridge, 1993), 247–69 (quotation, 248).
45. Ibid., 247–68.

challenged by recent anthropological research, he claimed that the Trobrianders were in much the same state as the prehistoric people imagined by
Bachofen: they had a matrilineal family structure and did not recognize the
biological role of the father. Nonetheless, they recognized both fatherhood
and male supremacy. The mother's brother was head of the family, and the
mother's husband supervised the children's development. From this and
other examples, Malinowski derived two basic premises of functionalist social theory: that human behavior arose not from biology but from culture,
and that cultural practices were designed to satisfy needs that were common
to all human societies.

Despite his irritation at the polemical uses of scholarship, Malinowski
did not hesitate to plunge into the political controversies of his era, including those concerning gender relations and family structure. Among the
needs that were universal to the human race, he asserted, was the need for
male authority in the family. Malinowski contended that the "principle of
legitimacy, which demands a male as the guardian, protector, and regent of
the family," was upheld by a universal condemnation of women who bore
children out of wedlock, thus founding mother-headed families.[46] This assertion seemed to fly in the face of the facts—the Trobrianders, for example,
permitted premarital sexual activity among both women and men. But so
eager was Malinowski to prove that the Trobrianders practiced the "principle of legitimacy" that he accepted the rather improbable assurances of his
informants that sexually active unmarried women, though they had no
knowledge of contraception, very seldom became pregnant.[47]

Malinowski explained the incest taboo functionally by asserting that it
preserved family cohesion by preventing sexual rivalry, and thus conflict,
between father and son.[48] Because functionalists rejected comparative ap-

46. Bronislaw Malinowski, *Sex and Repression in Savage Society* (London, 1927),
253–4, 212–3.

47. Bronislaw Malinowski, *The Father in Primitive Psychology* (New York, 1927), 57–
85. On the anthropological critique of these conclusions, see Eller, *Myth of Matriarchal
Prehistory*, 93–7. For another instance of an anthropologist's credulity with respect to sexual practices, see Derek Freeman, *The Fateful Hoaxing of Margaret Mead: A Historical
Analysis of Her Samoan Research* (Boulder, Colo., 1999).

48. Malinowski, *Sex and Repression*, 253. Malinowski believed that father-daughter incest, though far more common, was much less important than the mother-son variety.
"In this discussion, the daughter receives but little of our attention. . . . On the one hand,

proaches (claiming that individual customs could be understood only as part of the culture in which they were embedded), the fieldwork method limited the researcher to the present and to a few cultures. Malinowski nonetheless believed that it provided a basis for generalization, since all cultures arose from a common human nature. "Marriage and the family," he concluded, "always have been, are, and will remain the foundations of human society."[49]

Malinowski's functionalism and Freud's psychoanalysis gained hegemonic status in the 1920s. The disruption and trauma caused by the First World War and the Russian Revolution seemed to threaten all civilized norms, but none more than that of the family. In this atmosphere, the evolutionary paradigms that had emphasized the plasticity of all forms of culture, including family and gender relations, were superseded by timeless theories of human nature. Dominant interpretations of psychoanalysis and anthropology asserted the universality and necessity of patriarchy. Now living in Britain, Malinowski in 1927 attributed the horrors of the Russian Revolution partly to the pernicious theories of Engels and Bebel.[50] In 1929, Freud reflected on "civilization" and female discontent in terms that recalled Bachofen: women, who had "laid the foundations of civilization by the claims of their love," were increasingly "forced into the background by the claims of civilization," upon which they could exercise only a "retarding and restraining" influence.[51] In the 1920s, Jung incorporated the maternal archetype into a more general feminine archetype, the *anima*, which represented the female element in the male psyche (as the *animus* constituted the male side of the female). In contrast to Freud, Jung advocated not the overcoming but the recognition and integration of women and femininity. However, Jung's con-

---

as results from all that has been said above . . . incest between father and daughter is less important, while on the other, the conflicts between the mother and the daughter are not so conspicuous." Ibid.

49. M. F. Ashley Montagu, ed., *Marriage, Past and Present: A Debate between Robert Briffault and Bronislaw Malinowski* (Boston, 1956), 28. This is a transcript of a radio program broadcast in 1927.

50. Ibid., 22.

51. Sigmund Freud, *Civilization and Its Discontents,* trans. James Strachey (1929–30; reprint, New York, 1961), 50–1.

ceptions of *anima* and *animus* confirmed the conventional associations of women with emotional and relational thinking and of men with rationality, thus encouraging the gender stereotyping which was a prominent trend among psychologists of the 1920s.[52]

Though very fashionable, these positions were also contested. To give only one example, in 1923 the psychologist Mathilde Vaerting was appointed by the socialist government of Thuringia to a professorship of education in Jena (she was only the second German woman to attain such a position).[53] In 1921, she had published *A New Basis for the Psychology of Man and Woman (Neubegründung der Psychologie von Mann und Weib)*, in which she argued that gender-role division was functional rather than biological in origin and that its purpose was to structure power and authority. Most studies of gender, she asserted, were invalid because they were based on a "kind of unquestioned association of men with dominance and women with subordination."[54] However, she claimed that this assumption was not necessarily valid for all times and places; if gender hierarchy was produced by power relationships, it must be as changeable as any other political arrangement. In order to prove this argument, Vaerting referred to the same anthropological and historical data used by earlier theorists to show the immense variation of gender-role behavior over time and space. Power, she asserted, could be and had been exercised by women; under female supremacy, women showed dominant and men subordinate behavior. Although she continued to believe in the existence of prehistoric matriarchy, Vaerting encouraged no nostalgia for a "lost Paradise." The consequence of gender-based hierarchy, she wrote, was always the "suppression of individuality."[55] She looked not to

52. On the later development of Jung's thought, see Polly Young-Eisendrath, "Gender and Contrasexuality: Jung's Contribution and Beyond," in *The Cambridge Companion to Jung,* ed. Polly Young-Eisendrath and Terence Dawson (Cambridge, 1997), 223–39.

53. Theresa Wobbe, "Mathilde Vaerting (1884–1977)," in *Frauen in den Kulturwissenschaften: Von Lou-Andreas Salomé bis Hannah Arendt,* ed. Barbara Hahn (Munich, 1994), 123–35.

54. Mathilde Vaerting, *Neubegründung der Psychologie von Mann und Weib: Die weibliche Eigenart im Männerstaat und die männliche Eigenart im Frauenstaat* (1921; reprint, Berlin, 1980), 1.

55. Ibid., 136.

the past but to the future, when a more equitable social system would challenge gender stereotypes and enable men and women to develop individual talents that were not attributable to sex. She concluded that equality between the sexes would serve the needs of society better than the domination of either sex over the other.

Although Vaerting's belief in the existence of ancient matriarchies would have been considered old-fashioned by most progressive social scientists of the 1920s, other aspects of her theoretical framework, which rejected sentimental notions of the "eternal feminine" and stressed the cultural construction of gender, were modern. Indeed, her conclusions were in many ways similar to those advanced by the American anthropologists Ruth Benedict and Margaret Mead, who during the 1920s and 1930s used data from existing cultures to document the malleability of gender behavior and family structure.[56] But unlike the Americans, who were supported by the prestigious Franz Boas, Vaerting incurred little but hostility and rejection from her colleagues at Jena, who did all they could to deprive her of her professorship (she was dismissed in 1933) and who accused her of promoting "feminism in the guise of science."[57]

The high visibility of the debate on the origins of the family shows that sex, gender, and patriarchy were central concerns to many intellectuals of both genders, in many fields, and of many political persuasions at the turn of the twentieth century. As we have seen, the perception of a crisis in gender relations contributed to two major theoretical realignments in the social sciences. The first—the turn to cultural relativism—was driven by a widespread recognition that anthropological data showing the vast diversity of human behavior over time and space called all conventional notions, including the universality of patriarchy, into question. The ensuing discussion both shaped and was shaped by a widespread revolt against conventional sexual and family morality, which was not limited to intellectual debate but also included various forms of political and social activism. The disturbing impact of this crisis in gender relations can be seen in the transition, led by such figures as Freud and Malinowski, to the theories that would become hegemonic in the 1920s—psychoanalysis and functionalism. These helped

56. Ibid., 145.
57. Wobbe, "Mathilde Vaerting," 128.

to restabilize patriarchy by grounding it not in uncertain historical and anthropological data, but in timeless theories of universal human nature. But, as Mathilde Vaerting pointed out, the discussion had just begun. The universality and necessity of patriarchy could no longer be simply assumed. It had to be argued for. And the argument continues.[58]

58. For contemporary discussions of the origin of the family, see (among many other examples) Gerda Lerner, *The Creation of Patriarchy* (New York, 1986); Margaret Ehrenburg, *Women in Prehistory* (Norman, Okla., 1989); Sarah Blaffer Hrdy, *Mother Nature: A History of Mothers, Infants, and Natural Selection* (New York, 1999); Eller, *The Myth of Matriarchal Prehistory.*

"Sexualkrise und Rasse"

Feminist Eugenics at the Fin de Siècle

KEVIN REPP

A formidable presence in popular discourse throughout Europe at the fin de siècle, the 'sexual crisis' took many shapes in Wilhelmine Berlin, blending easily into that broader 'crisis of modernity' which historians have so often described as a key feature of cultural life in late imperial Germany. The literary tropes were many, and they spread across diverse social classes and professional callings. The delusions of a domestic servant, trapped in a marriage to an aging employer, then cast into the streets by her own youthful fantasies of a mysterious "lover" hardly aware of her existence. An army recruit ruined by debt, fraud, and scandal after blowing his inheritance on a weekend fling of music halls and ladies of easy pleasure. A proud single mother holding her own on the job market, but humiliated by a desperate bid to find love in the personal columns. An unbalanced poet tumbling from one love affair to another between frenzied bouts of writing and long stays at a sanatorium. Even harmless, unsuspecting, *haute bourgeois* daughters of the fashionable new district, "Berlin WW"—*Tiergärtnerinnen* and *Zoopuppen* (translated, roughly, as zoo-garden girls and zoo-dolls)—casting unabashed glances at the "Asiatic Mongols" who lurked late at night at the Café des Westens with "sweetly malevolent smiles."[1] Such stories were also common stock-in-trade in a burgeoning "scientific" literature on the sexual crisis at the turn of the century. Indeed, they might well have been drawn straight from the anonymous case files published in the Swiss psychiatrist August Forel's 1905 *Sexual Question* or, closer to home, in the Berlin physician Iwan Bloch's *Sexual Life of Our Times* (1907).[2]

The title of this essay is the title of Section VIII in Grete Meisel-Hess's *Die Sexuelle Krise* (Jena, 1909), 281.

1. Grete Meisel-Hess, *Die Intellektuellen: Roman* (Berlin, 1911), 90–106, 146–50, 197–213, 242–57, 263–5.

2. On the dangers of the "Liebesrausch," for instance, see August Forel, *Die Sexuelle Frage: Eine naturwissenschaftliche, psychologische, hygienische, und soziologische Studie für Gebildete* (Munich, 1905), 494–509; on the financial ruin and scandals resulting from the

Told by leading members of the medical profession, such stories expressed concern over the impact of venereal disease and mental derangement, moral depravity and racial miscegenation, not only on the lives of individuals, but—more emphatically—on the military and economic 'fitness' of the nation as a whole. Talk of sexual crisis reverberated in anxious discussions of 'degeneration,' a catchword that resonated across Europe and as far as America at the time. While such misgivings could and did easily give way to outbursts of 'cultural despair' and 'antimodernism' in some notable cases, for progressive reformers like Forel and Bloch this common sense of 'crisis' merely reaffirmed the vital role of modern medical science and biotechnology in protecting the health of the nation. Scorning the "superstitions" perpetuated by received religion and conventional morality, these latter-day disciples of "sexual enlightenment" demanded that their contemporaries face the harsh realities of the sexual crisis by following the 'objective' dictates of new fields like social and racial hygiene, population policy, and 'rational' reproductive politics. As Forel proclaimed, "I cherish the conviction that the introduction of the scientific spirit, of healthy inductive and philosophical thinking in the schools and in the masses of humanity in general, is the one and only means of curbing, to some degree, this thoughtless parroting behavior, this mindless routine that arises out of the mechanical repetition of imbecilic prejudices."[3]

In progressive circles, the sexual crisis thus appeared in the guise of an imperative to talk openly about sex in order to regulate its functions for the benefit of the nation. Such progressive talk appears to fit nicely into the trajectory Michel Foucault and others have described as the "biopolitics" of modern, rationalizing states, in which the most intimate aspects of personal life—and ultimately the laws of life itself—are subordinated to the Enlightenment's goals of productive efficiency, material prosperity, and technological advance. Following Foucault, Detlev Peukert has traced the "pathologies" of German modernity to the "progressive optimism" and "fantasies of om-

---

"für 'gentlemanlike' geltenden Jagd nach Vergnügungen und nach dem Weibe" in "Animierkneipen," see Iwan Bloch, *Das Sexualleben unserer Zeit in seinen Beziehungen zur modernen Kultur,* 4th–6th ed. (Berlin, 1908), 318; on "immoral newspaper advertisements" in the personal column, ibid., 786–91. Both authors published dozens of case studies to illustrate the "psychopathia sexualis" they described in these weighty tomes. See, for example, Forel, 133–48, 430–1, 502–3; Bloch, 254–9, 486, 564–9, 597–601, 628–30.

3. Forel, *Die Sexuelle Frage,* 517.

nipotence" that this biopolitical vision evoked in the circles of medical men
and reformers around Bloch and Forel. Here Peukert detected a perilous
devaluation of the fleeting lives of individual human beings, which were in-
eluctably cheapened as Wilhelmine progressives found themselves seduced
by the glittering prospect of everlasting *national* life. Unreflective faith in
science, instrumental rationality, and the relentless immanent materialism
of the progressive political culture of late imperial Germany inspired the
proliferation of fin-de-siècle plans for the efficient management of "human
material" through population policy, racial hygiene, or eugenics. Once articulated, these plans helped to give rise to what Peukert termed the "genesis
of the 'final solution' from the spirit of science."[4]

A eugenicist consensus certainly underwrote progressive responses to the
sexual crisis at the fin de siècle—but, as recent studies have shown, this
consensus was hardly an exclusively male one. The women's movement
played a key role in shaping this response and in the broader public policy
debates over reproductive rights and biopolitics that raged at the turn of the
century.[5] This was particularly true of the "moderate" wing in Wilhelmine
feminism led by Gertrud Bäumer. Sharply denouncing the subjectivist,
"neoromantic" views of the "radical" wing, which promoted women's
emancipation as a necessary guarantee of the individual's right of self-
determination, Bäumer justified emancipation in "objective," scientific

4. Detlev Peukert, "The Genesis of the 'Final Solution' from the Spirit of Science," in
Nazism and German Society, 1933–1945, ed. David F. Crew (London, 1994), 274–99.

5. For a good recent survey of the literature, see Edward Ross Dickinson, "Reflections
on Feminism and Monism in the Kaiserreich, 1900–1913," *Central European History* 34,
no. 2 (2001): 201–4. See also Barbara Greven-Aschoff, *Die bürgerliche Frauenbewegung
in Deutschland, 1894–1933* (Göttingen, 1981), 105–15; Ann Taylor Allen, *Feminism and
Motherhood in Germany, 1800–1914* (New Brunswick, N.J., 1991), 7–11, 230–3; Allen,
"The Holocaust and the Modernization of Gender: A Historiographical Essay," *Central
European History* 30, no. 3 (1997): 349–64; Kathleen Canning, *Languages of Labor and
Gender: Female Factory Work in Germany, 1850–1914* (Ithaca, N.Y., 1996), 190–214;
Christoph Sachße, *Mütterlichkeit als Beruf. Sozialarbeit, Sozialreform, und Frauenbeweg-
ung, 1871–1929* (Frankfurt, 1986), passim; Young-Sun Hong, "Gender, Citizenship, and
the Welfare State: Social Work and the Politics of Femininity in the Weimar Republic,"
Central European History 30, no. 1 (1997): 1–24; Ute Frevert, "The Civilizing Tendency of
Hygiene: Working-Class Women under Medical Control in Imperial Germany," in *German Women in the Nineteenth Century: A Social History,* ed. John Fout (New York, 1984),
320–44; Ute Gerhard, *Unerhört. Die Geschichte der deutschen Frauenbewegung* (Hamburg,
1990), 271.

terms as the release of productive social forces that might provide a substantial, material contribution to the vitality of the national economy. In what turned out to be a decisive victory for the social-scientific orientation she represented, an "overwhelming majority" at the 1908 conference of the German Women's League flatly rejected a resolution put forward by the radicals calling for the legalization of abortion. As one speaker put it, Germany needed "people, indeed many people" in order to fulfill its "mission to become the first cultural power on earth through the conquest of economic and political domains for ourselves."[6] In place of the radicals' proposal, however, the assembly passed a resolution that endorsed revisions of § 218 of the German Penal Code according to "racial hygienic concepts," thereby endorsing the legalization of abortion in cases where it could "be expected with certainty that the child will enter life severely handicapped either physically or mentally."[7]

Yet support for these and other, more aggressive, eugenicist measures in the debates over reproductive politics did not come only from Bäumer and the moderates. In fact, the "racial hygienic concepts" that paved the way for the 1908 compromise resolution actually came from the same organization that had spearheaded the radicals' campaign for free love and the "new morals" in response to the sexual crisis at the fin de siècle: the League for the Protection of Mothers and Sexual Reform.[8] The revised marriage code proposed in 1904 by Ellen Key, an influential Swedish reformer whose ideas helped to inspire the founders of the Sexual Reform League, specifically denied marriage and reproductive rights to those without a health certificate proving them free of all "inheritable and infectious disease that would be injurious to children" (though not, as Bloch pointed out, diseases that were injurious merely to one's sexual partner).[9] Two years later, Key further suggested "eliminating those lives that can never be enhanced."[10] Forel, who

6. Minutes, 1908 BDF congress, Helene-Lange-Archiv, Landesarchiv Berlin, 62-262[7] and 262[8]; Allen, *Feminism and Motherhood*, 190–7; Richard Evans, *The Feminist Movement in Germany, 1894–1933* (London, 1976), 134–6; Theresa Wobbe, *Gleichheit und Differenz. Politische Strategien von Frauenrechtlerinnen um die Jahrhundertwende* (New York, 1989), 159–77.

7. Minutes, 1908 BDF congress, 62-262[8].

8. The "concepts" were championed by Maria Lichnewska. Ibid., 262[7].

9. Bloch, *Sexualleben*, 292–3. For the details of her "New Marriage Law," see Ellen Key, *Über Liebe und Ehe: Essays*, authorized trans. Francis Maro (Berlin, 1904), 398–459.

10. Quoted in Dickinson, "Reflections," 224.

was himself a founding member of the Sexual Reform League and an ardent supporter of the women's movement, bitterly repudiated "laws that force us to keep fruit born of cretins, idiots, hydrocephalics, microcephalics, and the like . . . alive" as a "ghastly" holdover from the superstitious days of the Christian era; in *The Sexual Question,* he regretted that begetting degenerate offspring could not be made a criminal offense. In the same work, the Swiss sexologist also confessed to having ordered the "castration" of a "fourteen-year-girl, whose mother and grandmother were pimps and whores, and who was already surrendering herself out of pleasure in the street, because," he explained, "I wanted in this way to prevent the genesis of ill-fated off-spring."[11]

If the sexual crisis in fin-de-siècle Berlin thus drew moderates and radicals together in support of eugenics, it divided them in other ways, notably on the question of free love. Motivated by personal passions, aestheticism, and alienation from the rationalizing constraints of law, order, and capitalist economics, radical feminists prescribed free love as a cure for both the sexual crisis and the broader crisis of German modernity. Nevertheless, the 'irrational' eroticism of the radicals often mixed with social-scientific arguments about the instrumentality of sexual instincts for perpetuating the life of the nation, transforming the radicals' subjective eroticism into an 'objective' means to ends that might have nothing at all to do with individual rights or personal fulfillment. The leader of the League for the Protection of Mothers and Sexual Reform, Helene Stöcker, bitterly opposed the instrumentalization of erotic pleasure, which was for her an aesthetic experience to be cultivated in its own right as an end in itself. Rather than grounding her feminism in science, Stöcker preferred to look back to the age of German romanticism. She especially held up Friedrich Schlegel's novel *Lucinde* (1799) as a model of the happiness to be attained by "two people, man and woman . . . , who find one another as full equals and give themselves to each other in free agreement." Yet in the end this radical individualist—inspired also by Friedrich Nietzsche and the Young Hegelian philosopher of 'egoism,' Max Stirner—joined the socially-conscious moderates of the women's movement by endorsing the utilitarian arguments of racial hygiene and pop-

11. Forel, *Die Sexuelle Frage,* 381–2, 399–400.

ulation policy as a means to promote her own aestheticist vision of free love.[12]

How could eugenics prove so powerfully alluring precisely to those circles that were most critical of the "authoritarian nation state" and most keenly aware of the perils inherent in what a future generation would call "instrumental rationality"? Why were feminists, especially those closest to anarchism, symbolism, and leftist cultural criticism, drawn into the eugenicist consensus of late imperial Germany, at times seemingly almost against their wills? Seeking answers, this essay turns first to the radical feminist Grete Meisel-Hess and her 1911 novel, *The Intellectuals,* in which the opening tales of sexual crisis related above actually do appear. A prominent figure in Berlin's expressionist circles, Meisel-Hess depicted the tensions between science and symbolism, materialism and idealism, instrumental rationality and aestheticism, which suffused notions of feminist eugenics at the fin de siècle.

Between Manfred and Lucinda

The heroine of *The Intellectuals* is—like Meisel-Hess herself—young, Jewish, and a self-defined New Woman struggling to rise above the sexual crisis of the fin de siècle. Again like the author, Olga Diamant comes from the Slavic provinces and goes first to Vienna, where she studies national economics and philosophy before seeking the broader intellectual horizons of the "world city," Berlin. Here she joins her brother Stanislaus, who has just finished a scathing but constructive critique of modernism (reminiscent of Samuel Lublinski's 1904 *Bilanz der Moderne*), and who introduces her to the unbalanced poet Werner Hoffmann. Plunging into the world of feminist activism and social politics, Olga quickly joins the League for the Protection of Mothers and Sexual Reform and, with the help of Stanislaus and Werner,

12. Helene Stöcker, "Das Werden der sexuellen Reform seit hundert Jahren," in Hedwig Dohm et al., *Ehe? Zur Reform der sexuellen Moral* (Berlin, 1911), 63–8 (on *Lucinde,* 47–8); see also Heinrich Meyer-Benfey's "Lucinda," published by Stöcker in her journal *Die Mutterschutz* 5 (1906): 173–92. While Dickinson correctly points out that Stöcker was by no means immune to eugenicist discourse and always emphasized the social as well as the individual moment in her appeals for free love, the difference in tone between Stöcker's essay and the others by proponents of free love in *Ehe?* is striking. See especially Anita Augspurg, "Reformgedanken zur sexuellen Moral," in ibid., 19–35.

establishes a correspondence service to supply the Austrian press with news items about the women's movement in Berlin. Through a swirl of cafés, clubs, and face-to-face contact with the shattered destinies of impoverished single women struggling to survive in the city, Olga and her friends encounter numerous manifestations of the sexual crisis and experiment with many of the standard remedies of the day. Stanislaus undertakes a sociological study of the "stepfather family" as a means to rescue single mothers and their children from an otherwise grim statistical fate, while Werner (in the throes of an infatuation for Olga) tries to join the Social Democratic Party, only to be turned away as an intellectual snob by a stodgy August Bebel.[13]

In short, Olga and her friends find themselves deeply entangled in the radical fringes of the Wilhelmine reform milieu.[14] And while eugenics always lay within the horizons of that milieu, it was by no means prefigured as the ultimate destination, the ultimate solution; this world teemed with colorful solutions, including vegetarianism, nudism, free love, "modernist Buddhism," and even the neoromantic aestheticism of a salon presided over by a decadent reincarnation of Schlegel's *Lucinde*. Or was eugenics prefigured after all? "Man's destiny . . . is his body," we learn in the novel's early pages, and the problem with "the intellectuals" is that their ideals "have not yet become corporeal enough, not yet somatic, as we doctors say." Despite their best efforts, the high-minded friends seem incapable of overcoming this deficiency and languish instead in private sexual crises of their own making. Repelled by his own physical degeneracy and convinced that he has "nothing to pass on genetically," Stanislaus fights delirium brought on by denial of his sexual urges. Olga is unwillingly seduced by Werner upon his return from a sojourn at the sanatorium. She is then crushed when he leaves her for a fallen aristocrat turned cabaret singer, and she finally flees to the notorious life reform colony at Ascona.[15] None of their solutions seem to work.

Redemption appears in the form of Manfred, eldest son of the sexual reform leader in the novel, who suddenly arrives as a *deus ex machina* with

13. Meisel-Hess, *Intellektuellen*, 21–2, 85–90, 132–3, 144, 154–7, 164–76, 213, 257–61, 388–96.

14. See chap. 5, "The Wilhelmine Reform Milieu," in Kevin Repp, *Reformers, Critics, and the Paths of German Modernity: Anti-Politics and the Search for Alternatives, 1890–1914* (Cambridge, Mass., 2000); on the place of eugenics, see 300–12.

15. Meisel-Hess, *Intellektuellen*, 31, 126–8, 161, 275, 287–90, 397, 423–7, 429–49.

plans for a worldwide organization of intellectuals committed to ensuring the "production of highly valuable human beings." Returning from a ten-year study tour around the world, Manfred brings with him a "staff of dazzling names, that alone are capable of attaining the authority to help [his] organization to power." Now he is about to step into the public light and found a "Central Committee" to spearhead the daring venture of "intellectual *Weltpolitik*":

> The animating problems of the world were to be viewed from the standpoint of international knowledge. In the areas of social configuration, the organization of nations, the linking of intellects, the revision of moral laws upon which humanity could gain a footing, there was work to be done. And in the center of the entire global centralization stood a Committee for Research into the Laws of Descent and Variation, a scientific commission that would investigate the biological laws through which the production of highly valuable human beings might seem assured.[16]

While bizarre, Manfred's project and Olga's selfless victory at the end of *The Intellectuals* are not particularly surprising, given the picture of the women's movement that has emerged from the flourishing scholarship of the past few decades. As we have seen, feminists placed work and reproduction at the top of an agenda that was enunciated in the language of production and social-scientific realism (*Sachlichkeit*). Protective labor laws, factory inspections, vocational training, and new careers in social service and education would enable women's financial independence while simultaneously applying their nurturing skills beyond the home in the public sector. Maternity insurance and state subsidies would provide for women's material needs during the brief periods when they were physically incapacitated by childbirth, thus sustaining their economic independence as well as the nation's physical—human—reproduction.[17]

Yet we have seen that strident objections to the alienating impact of this productivist, materialist, rationalizing orientation were still to be heard in the women's movement, particularly at the radical fringes of the Wilhelmine

16. Ibid., 409–10.
17. See above, note 4.

reform milieu—from the same aesthetes, symbolists, and anarchists that Grete Meisel-Hess depicted in her novel. In fact, despite her own polemics against the "decadence" reigning in these circles—ire evoked by the antifeminism of writers like August Strindberg, Frank Wedekind, and Otto Weininger—Meisel-Hess was quite close to them herself.[18] An active member of the circle of Berlin expressionists around Franz Pfemfert, she often wrote feminist pieces for Pfemfert's journal, *Die Aktion,* a mouthpiece for opposition to authoritarianism and militarism that staunchly defended the revolutionary wing in German Social Democracy before the First World War.[19] It is perhaps not entirely coincidental that *Die Aktion* launched publication in 1911—the same year Meisel-Hess published Manfred's plan for a "global centralization" in *The Intellectuals*—with its own calls for an international "Organization of Intelligence" that was to coordinate the younger generation's sporadic opposition to the establishment in a sustained, "organized mass protest" through the "precision work" of a "Central Office" in Berlin.[20]

Certainly Meisel-Hess shared the expressionists' anguish over the alienation of personal culture in an era increasingly menaced by industrial capi-

18. Meisel-Hess published a book-length polemic against Weininger, *Weiberhaß und Weiberverachtung: Eine Erwiderung auf die in Dr. Otto Weiningers Buche 'Geschlecht und Charakter' geäußerten Anschauungen über 'Die Frau und ihre Frage'* (Vienna, 1904). For examples of her polemics against aestheticism after moving to Berlin in 1908, see Meisel-Hess, *Die Sexuelle Krise,* 77–9, 334–7; Meisel-Hess, "Der Aesthet und die Frauenfrage," *Die Aktion* 1, no. 25 (August 7, 1911): 779–81; and above, note 5. See also Susanne Omran, "Weib und Geist um 1900: Intellekt, Rasse, und Instinkt in den Schriften von Grete Meisel-Hess," *Philosophin: Forum für feministische Theorie und Philosophie* 19 (April 1999): 11–35; Irmgard Roebling, "Grete Meisel-Hess: Sexualreform zwischen Nietzsche-kult, Freudrezeption, und Rassenhygiene," in *Literarische Entwürfe weiblicher Sexualität,* ed. Johannes Cremerius et al. (Würzburg, 1993), 205–30; Ellinor Melander, "Toward the Sexual and Economic Emancipation of Women: The Philosophy of Grete Meisel-Hess," *History of European Ideas* 14, no. 5 (1992): 695–713.

19. Meisel-Hess wrote seventeen articles for *Die Aktion* between 1911 and 1913. On her relationship to Pfemfert's circle, see the brief biographical entry on her in the list of contributors included at the beginning of volume 1 in the reprint edition of *Die Aktion* edited by Paul Raabe (Stuttgart, 1961), 82–3.

20. K. W., "Die Organisation der Intelligenz," *Die Aktion* 1, no. 1 (February 20, 1911): 9; see also "Note," *Die Aktion* 1, no. 2 (February 20, 1911): 24; Siegfried Lederer, "Die Organisation der Intelligenz," *Die Aktion,* 1, no. 3 (March 6, 1911): 65–8.

talism and the "philosophy of money."[21] Published under the auspices of *Die Aktion* by Jena cultural critic Eugen Diederichs, her treatise *The Sexual Crisis* criticized mainstream feminism's focus on gainful employment, which she scorned as "bread-peonage."[22] Base materialist concerns, Meisel-Hess believed, were distracting attention from the "greater, the more central sun of the whole movement," that is, "liberated sexuality." Work could "never, ever be a 'surrogate' for a full, fulfilled, general life," she wrote. She agreed with Lucia Dora Frost, a sharp critic of Bäumer and the progressives with close ties to Berlin's symbolist circles, that the feminist movement's obsession with careers had produced some "exceptionally hideous types," androgynous creatures who were understandably the "terror of the aesthetically and erotically sensitive man."[23] While acknowledging the importance of providing for material needs, Meisel-Hess dismissed the "woman emancipated from sex" as a sad but necessary sacrifice. Economic rights were merely a transitory stage in a development that was leading the way to a disinterested, spiritual, and aesthetic cultivation of feminine sexuality emancipated from the compulsion of all physical necessities.

Only when love was freed from the base rule of money would such a state be possible, Meisel-Hess insisted. In bizarre, protosurrealist passages betraying an unlikely blend of Kurd Laßwitz's 1897 sci-fi novel *Two Planets* and Schiller's *Letters on the Aesthetic Education of Mankind,* she extolled the uplifting moral virtues of pure, noninstrumental "love-play" as an "educator to goodness, forbearance, and humility." This alone was the true and ultimate aim of the women's movement: "Only through recognition of this purely erotic experiential possibility, independent of the social alliance of both partners, and unleashed from all terrors of impending shame, and only

21. The work of Georg Simmel, author of *Philosophie des Geldes* (Leipzig, 1900), was often inspiring, though also controversial among the expressionists writing for both *Die Aktion* and *Der Sturm;* see Kurt Hiller, "Über Kultur I," *Der Sturm* 1, no. 24 (August 11, 1910): 187–8; Hiller, "Infolge von Simmel-Lektüre," *Die Aktion* 1, no. 14 (May 22, 1911), 430; Ludwig Rubiner, "Erwähnung zur Psychoanalyse," *Die Aktion* 3, no. 25 (June 18, 1913): 607–8.

22. Meisel-Hess, *Die Sexuelle Krise,* 272–9; Meisel-Hess, "Prostitution, Frauenbewegung, und Rasse," *Die Aktion* 1, no. 30 (September 11, 1911): 940–3.

23. Meisel-Hess, *Die Sexuelle Krise,* 247–52.

through a highly cultivated manner of bringing this possibility out into the open could there be created, little by little, a condition of erotic liberation that would release both sexes from restraining sexual tensions, allowing them every freedom, and making prostitution expendable."[24]

Meisel-Hess's solution to the sexual crisis was thus hardly an expression of unreflective, utilitarian faith in rationality, of the "progressive optimism" and "fantasies of omnipotence" that Detlev Peukert identified as most culpable in unleashing the "pathologies of modernity."[25] The Jewish feminist from the Slavic East was all too aware of the dangers lurking beneath ostensibly objective and scientific methods for the efficient management of "human material." In *The Sexual Crisis,* she accordingly devoted considerable space to confronting such dangers, engaging in lengthy polemics against Alfred Ploetz, founder of the Society for Racial Hygiene and the central figure illustrating the "dark side" of fin-de-siècle progressivism in Peukert's essay. Quoting from Ploetz's own speeches, Meisel-Hess lashed out at him for denouncing "protective social-policy organizations" as a "deleterious suspension of the struggle for survival" and sentimental "protection of the weak."[26] Rejecting the racial hygienist's diatribes against the "pampering back to health of weak constitutions," she insisted, "The urge of all higher creatures to preserve what has been produced by them, to nurture it along, even if it is weak, is far too deeply rooted ever to expect parents not to seek to preserve weak children. Once something is *there* in life, it has a claim to protection too." Indeed, "protection of the weak" was nothing less than a "test of the fitness of—society," Meisel-Hess proclaimed. "The society that is capable of healing its unfortunate, caring for its sick, supporting its weak, proves that it bears powers of regeneration within itself." She continued:

24. Ibid., 216–7.

25. Detlev Peukert, *Max Webers Diagnose der Moderne* (Göttingen, 1989), 106, 111–2.

26. Meisel-Hess, *Die Sexuelle Krise,* 283–6, 291–6, 309–15. For more on Ploetz and his turn away from social reform agendas with the victory of "hard heredity" in scientific circles around the turn of the century, see Peter Becker, *Zur Geschichte der Rassenhygiene: Wege ins Dritte Reich* (New York, 1988), 62–99; Cornelius Bickel, "Tönnies' Kritik des Sozialdarwinismus: Immunität durch Philosophie. Die Auseinandersetzung mit der Krupp-Preisfrage von 1900," in *Rassenmythos und Sozialwissenschaft in Deutschland: Ein verdrängtes Kapitel sozialwissenschaftlicher Wirkungsgeschichte,* ed. Carsten Klingemann (Opladen, 1987), 180–5; Paul Weindling, *Health, Race, and German Politics between National Unification and Nazism, 1870–1945* (New York, 1989), 121–38, 223–303.

Uncivilized nations . . . leave their invalids, cripples, and idiots without 'aid,' they drag their existence along the public street until they perish. . . . If these invalids are placed in the appropriate institution and 'cared for'—is it they alone who are being 'protected'? Isn't society above all protecting itself through its care? And doesn't it prove, if it is capable of this, that its great body is strong enough for this work of regeneration, therefore fit and 'prevailing' in the struggle for survival?[27]

And yet, for all her awareness of the perils, for all her recognition of the centrality of individual freedom and spiritual self-fulfillment beyond all material interests or constraints, Meisel-Hess went on to praise Ploetz's focus on selective reproduction as a brilliant solution to the sexual crisis. The transfer of the struggle for survival from the world of adult human beings to the harmless, microscopic level of "germ cells" was nothing less than a revolution, she enthused, a new world view that successfully brought together "humane ideals" and the "aristocratic principle of the victory of the 'strong.' "[28] Pure "sexual selection" on the basis of free choice and free love was the only way to carry out this revolution, she argued, rather than the brute force of sterilization, marriage restrictions, and euthanasia endorsed by racial hygiene, which actually tended to undermine biopolitical principles. But Meisel-Hess clearly endorsed the view of race as the true site of transcendence and eternal life, quoting with approval a passage from Ploetz that perfectly captured the "utopia of the gradual elimination of death" that Peukert discerned in progressive notions of the "eternal body of the nation."[29] She placed this utopian notion at the center of the "cult of love" she

27. Meisel-Hess, *Die Sexuelle Krise*, 292, 314. Cf. Peukert, *Max Webers Diagnose*, 92–101.

28. Meisel-Hess, *Die Sexuelle Krise*, 315–6; this despite the fact that Meisel-Hess had taken pains to repudiate Ploetz's notion of a "Hamlet conflict" between Darwinist science and humanism (309).

29. Ibid., 282. The passage, taken from a speech by Ploetz at a racial hygiene congress, reads: " 'Das heute Lebendige stammt in direkter Kontinuität ab von dem vor Äonen Lebendigen, und so wird das künftige Lebendige sich in direktem Zusammenhange ergeben aus dem heutigen. Das Leben ist also eine Bewegung bestimmter Art von ungeheurer Dauer gebunden an hochdifferenzierte Eiweißstoffe.' Unter dem eigentlich Lebendigen versteht dieser Biologe aber nicht das einzelne Individuum, sondern jenes 'Erhaltungs- und Umwandlungsorgan einer durchdauernden Lebenseinheit oder die organische Zu-

believed would one day be practiced by a "future humanity"—not as a "cult of men," she emphasized, but "no, a real cult of God."[30] In an impassioned appeal for the great "Breeding Reformation" that would usher in this new age, Meisel-Hess declared the species alone to be divine:

> Reverence unto Breeding is the religion of the future. Here is holiness, here is the root of all wholesome ethics and morality. Here too is natural constraint of the individual will (an essential moment of all religion). And here too this constraint is deeply rooted in the individual's most intimate egoistic feeling. Moral laws cannot apply to the limited life span of the individual, only to the unlimited [life span] of the species. Here is the highest holiness, here is the boundary, the categorical barrier, that is to be set against the freedom of one's own ego.[31]

Why? Why did eugenics prove so powerfully alluring to a woman like Meisel-Hess? Why did this prophet of "liberated sexuality," this radical feminist so close to the anarchism and revolutionary socialism of Berlin's expressionists, turn to "racial politics" as the holiest of holies despite her own clear recognition of its perils?

A clue to solving this puzzle is to be found, I think, in *The Intellectuals*, particularly in the unhappy marriage between Manfred, the world eugenicist, and Lucinda, the decadent mistress of a salon filled with starry-eyed poets, aesthetes, and anarchists whose name alone is an obvious referent to the enthusiasms of Helene Stöcker, the neoromantic admirer of Schlegel. Manfred and Lucinda gradually become estranged, though they had in their youth once been deeply in love. They had met studying philosophy at the

---

sammenfassung der aus ihr sprossenden und sie tragenden Individuen'." ("'The living [being] of today is descended in direct continuity from what lived eons ago, and so the living [being] of the future will issue forth in direct connection with that of today. Life is thus a movement of a certain kind, of great duration, bound to highly differentiated proteins.' The biologist does not understand what is actually living as an isolated individual, but instead as that 'organ for the preservation and transformation of a continually enduring unity of life or the organic summation of the individuals sprouting from and sustaining it.'")

30. Meisel-Hess, *Die Sexuelle Krise*, 158.
31. Ibid., 317, 323.

university, discovering a common sense of purpose in one another; then each had gone on to pursue this interest along a separate path. In doing so, they had drifted apart. While Lucinda was drawn toward radical subjectivism, mysticism, and the occult, Manfred became ever more insistent on the "setting aside of all subjective coloration" in order to arrive at a purely objective view of the improvement of the human race. Ultimately, Manfred had come to loathe the "romantic self-befoggery" of Lucinda and her symbolist following, condemning it as "that twilit self-deception, in which entire ages happily content themselves, [ages] that willingly blind themselves to the facts with a veil of obscurity."[32]

What could have drawn such disparate minds together in the first place? It was a quality they still shared: "Both believed in a meaningful plan for the world, only for Lucinda it was called 'destiny,' *fatum*—for Manfred 'necessity'; where she saw purposes, he recognized causes."[33] It was a fine line indeed that separated the "hypermodern" from the "antimodern." But that very line was also the common thread that drew them toward the erotic (seen from the inside) or reproductive politics (seen from the outside) and ever closer to the eugenicist consensus in their search for meaning, fulfillment, and redemption in the modern world.

Lou Andreas Salomé's Dialectic of Eroticism

The capacity of the erotic to bestow meaning and new life on external things was a significant element in its attraction to those who frequented Lucinda's domain, that is, to the circles of symbolists and expressionists, who described it as an almost magical—for some, a demonic—force. The "delusion-imparting effect" of the "erotic hallucination" exerted a "more binding influence than any factual dependency would ever bring about," observed Lou Andreas Salomé, an important figure in aestheticist circles in Berlin (and indeed, throughout Europe) at the fin de siècle. This is so, Andreas Salomé insisted in *Die Erotik* (1910),

> since the other remains for us 'outside' too—just barely touching the
> periphery of our essence in a fruitful way—so the entire rest of the

32. Meisel-Hess, *Intellektuellen*, 418, 434.
33. Ibid., 435 ("Beide glaubten an einen sinnvollen Weltplan, nur hieß er für Lucinda 'Bestimmung, Fatum,'—für Manfred 'Notwendigkeit'; wo sie Zwecke sah, erkannte er Ursachen").

world opens up to us from this point, it becomes for us the actual point of marriage to life, this outside of things that otherwise can never quite be incorporated: it becomes the medium through which life speaks eloquently to us, finds for our soul just the right sounds and accents. To love means in the most earnest sense: to know some- one whose color things must take on if they want to reach us, so that they stop being indifferent or terrible, cold or hollow, and even the most threatening among them, like angry beasts on entry into the Garden of Eden, lie down mollified at our feet.[34]

Like poetry and art, the erotic was a creative spiritual force, transforming the world into a place filled with meaningful symbols and the body itself into a "fleshly script of signs."[35] But it was also a physical force. Unlike purely intellectual work, Andreas Salomé believed, it pushed individuals to reach out beyond themselves to a "being-outwards above the subjective"; it forced them to leave the flighty realm of personal fancy and "return to life," with its weighty entanglements in the outer, social world.[36] In attempting to realize the most intense egotistical urges, the manic impulse of eroticism rushed willy-nilly past the individual into a moment of objectification, through which it became something alien and external to the ego (whose "self-sacrifice" desire ultimately demanded). In other words, if love was to survive, it could not remain pure, like art. But love also surpassed art, in that it could actually exert a creative physical force, changing the external world even as it became a changeling itself in the dialectical encounter of matter with spirit.[37] For women in symbolist and reformist circles, it was precisely this physical, transformative power of the erotic that seemed to vindicate the subjective realm, giving it empirically verifiable meaning and purpose in an age of materialism.

Drawing on the popular Darwinist writings of Wilhelm Bölsche, another member of Berlin's aestheticist circle, Andreas Salomé depicted evolution as a physical process driven by a spiritual force, one which was becoming ever

34. Lou Andreas Salomé, *Die Erotik*, vol. 33 in Martin Buber's documentary series *Die Gesellschaft: Sammlung sozialpsychologischer Monographien* (Frankfurt am Main, 1910), 24.
35. Ibid., 27–8 ("leibliche Zeichenschrift").
36. Ibid., 37, 62–3.
37. Ibid., 25–8.

more autonomous and investing the individual subjectivity of human beings with increasing importance. In the beginning, with single-celled organisms, the moment of objectification in the erotic impulse had quite literally meant sacrifice, Andreas Salomé wrote. It mandated the death of both sexual partners, who merged physically, devouring one another in the process of creating a new being in which elements of each—and the erotic force behind them—were transformed, but nonetheless continued to live on. With increasing differentiation and more complex organisms, however, it became possible for sexual partners to survive the act of reproduction, passing on only what had been inherited from their parents through the specialized "germ plasm," while retaining possession of all the personal characteristics they had acquired over the course of an individual life span. Here lay the seeds of egoism; for the first time, eroticism took on a purely "psychic" dimension as well. The spiritual moment of egotistical pleasure gradually came to prevail in sexual acts between human beings with a highly cultivated sense of self. And while the physical aspect always remained essential even in the most spiritually refined forms of eroticism, the social moment—the unaltered passing on of the germ plasm, which contained nothing personal from the life experience of either sexual partner—threatened to be lost altogether. Yet in striving for union with the other, the erotic impulse transcended the egotistical moment even in romantic love, reenacting at a purely spiritual level the primeval dissolution of both partners into a single whole, an "egoism for two."[38]

But what has this to do with eugenics, or, for that matter, with social reform? At this point in the argument, Andreas Salomé suddenly veered back onto the discursive terrain of biopolitics—at the moment of ultimate sublation, in which the intimacy of "egoism for two" itself is externalized, objectified in the concrete form of "the child." Like the Swedish feminist Ellen Key and her followers among the radical sexual reformers of the League for the Protection of Mothers—even like the progressives in the

---

38. Ibid., 8, 12–8, 29–31, 37–8, 42. See also Lou Andreas Salomé, "Der Mensch als Weib: Ein Bild im Umriß," *Neue Rundschau* 10, no. 1 (1899): 225–43; Andreas Salomé, "Gedanken über das Liebesproblem," *Neue Rundschau* 11, no. 2 (1900): 1009–27. It is worth noting that Andreas Salomé's views on the continuity of life through the "Keim-plasma" bears some affinities to the views on race as transcendence and eternal life voiced by Meisel-Hess, Bloch, and even Ploetz; see above, note 29.

mainstream women's movement represented by Gertrud Bäumer—Andreas Salomé discovered the true significance and legitimation of individual striving only in the social act of biological reproduction, which she portrayed as a moment of supreme self-sacrifice to the greater, "supra-subjective goal" of the erotic life force. "At least insofar as it surrenders itself with natural life primitively and of itself, the heat of passion is socialized in the brood, love in the child," she wrote. Indeed, it was only in the "crowning act of motherhood" that the "conscious shoving aside of the most personal aspects outside of oneself, as an thing alien to oneself, comes to pass—only in a last, painful, voluntary spontaneity, a most extreme ridding oneself of the self, has it brought its fruit entirely into the world at last."[39]

Reproduction as redemption? Such interpretations of the organic had the advantage of reconciling the spiritual and material, subjective and objective, individualist and socialist impulses—the paths of Lucinda and Manfred—which had fallen into conflict in the modern world. But organic thought had an additional appeal for feminists at the fin de siècle, since it placed women front and center as the redeemers of the world, as both agents and embodiments of this biological capacity for creative synthesis. "Precisely in the physiological aspect of woman lie the seeds to her superior evolution onward to a more human universality," Andreas-Salomé argued. Like feminists of all stripes, she stressed the power of motherhood as a dynamic, vital force capable of healing the wounds of modern society. Nothing could be more misguided than to view women as the passive element in procreation, she wrote for the *Neue Rundschau* in 1899. Although man was the "more aggressive, more enterprising part," his role was "only partial and momentary in the whole process." Once his task was hastily dispatched, he went on to expend his surplus energy "in a continual dissipation of all powers," while the entire work of "concentration," synthesis, and the organization of new life from elements of both partners was left to the woman, who focused all her energy inwardly to complete this task. "The feminine substance in itself has remained more uniform, rests and reposes in what it has absorbed into itself, identified with itself," Andreas Salomé declared. "It completes its work of creation not in . . . isolated and special activities directed toward an external goal, it grows together organically with what it is creating, consummates it-

39. Andreas Salomé, *Erotik*, 37–40.

self in something that can hardly be called a deed, because it consists merely of issuing forth, radiating forth from its uniformly living life uniformly living life in turn."[40]

In such visions of motherhood, reproduction, and the organic, symbolists and social reformers found common ground. This is not to minimize the antagonisms that separated them. More moderate, progressive feminists like Gertrud Bäumer certainly fought tooth and nail against the enthusiasm for eroticism that produced affinities between Andreas Salomé and radical sexual reformers like Helene Stöcker, Ellen Key, and Meisel-Hess.[41] Yet while mainstream feminists scorned the notion that "liberated sexuality" could ever exert a healing influence on modern Germany in the form of a "pure sexual selection" that was emancipated from all material concerns, they nonetheless attributed many of the same properties to a dynamic and creative "life force." And, like Meisel-Hess and Andreas Salomé, they claimed a special relationship to this force that put women in the forefront of the search for solutions to the broader "crisis of modernity" before the First World War. The "essence of organic development" was "deeply and immediately imprinted on feminine nature," Bäumer argued in 1909, echoing Andreas Salomé's views on the "physiological aspect of woman." Mothers watched "from quite near at hand how a soul forms itself, how foreign substance slowly becomes one's own, dead matter becomes organic life." Such intimate proximity to the process of human becoming endowed women with a special ability to recognize "expressions of personal will, feeling, cognition" in "works of culture," Bäumer believed. "This capacity acts like the special light sensitivity of a photographic plate, it provides a specially tinted image of the world that is the same as the masculine one in its contours, but deviates decidedly from it in its tone, its mental expression." If "modern *Zivilisation,* like the *Zivilisation* of all ages, bears the stamp of masculine psyche," the task of transforming products of human thought and action, the material of life, back into personal *Kultur,* can only be done by woman,

---

40. Ibid., 44; Andreas Salomé, "Mensch," 28–9.

41. Despite such affinities, however, Andreas Salomé sharply distanced herself from the sexual reform movement, which she dismissed as *"unsachlich"* ("unobjective"); she rejected the notion that the erotic drive was a selective force in racial evolution. Andreas Salomé, *Erotik,* 8–9, 11–2.

Bäumer proclaimed—"or, to be more circumspect, let us say it cannot be done without her."[42]

The Evolution of Lucia Dora Frost

Bäumer's skillful deployment of the discourse of *Zivilisationskritik* indicates the depth of the affinities between modernists and antimodernists, but from the other side, as it were, from Manfred's side. I have argued at length else-where that despite her enthusiastic endorsements of "racial politics" and "eugenics," the leader of the progressive consensus in the Wilhelmine wom-en's movement was by no means guilty of unreflective faith in science or rationality. On the contrary, like Meisel-Hess, she was keenly aware of the dangers inherent in such a stance, and she angrily opposed versions of eu-genics that violated the dignity of human life. From her peculiar and histori-cally situated vitalistic perspective, eugenics meant something quite different than what it does to us today. Far from sustaining assaults on human life and human dignity, it actually seemed to reinforce humanistic values in the modern world by rendering them "more corporeal, more concrete."[43] What I want to show here, however, is how powerful the tug toward eugenics was from Lucinda's side. And I can think of no better illustration of this than the disturbing slide down that same slippery slope on the part of one of the most virulent critics of instrumental rationality among the women in Ber-lin's symbolist circles at the fin de siècle: Lucia Dora Frost.

Frost wrote only one slender volume of wartime essays, *Prussian Im-prints,* and I have to confess that I have not been able to find out much about her.[44] Meisel-Hess described her as "an emancipated woman who also belongs to the 'reaction' against the women's movement, whose arguments spread their rather withered root fibers out into the meager soil of the aes-theticists' domain."[45] She lived in Charlottenburg and published occasionally

---

42. Gertrud Bäumer, "Die Frauenbewegung und die Zukunft unserer Kultur," *Die Frau* 16, no. 9 (June 1909): 520–3. '

43. See especially Kevin Repp, "'More Corporeal, More Concrete': Liberal Human-ism, Eugenics, and German Progressives at the Last Fin de Siècle," *Journal of Modern His-tory* 72, no. 3 (September 2000): 707–20; Repp, *Reformers, Critics, and the Paths of German Modernity,* 104–47.

44. Lucia Dora Frost, *Preußische Prägungen* (Berlin, 1915).

45. Meisel-Hess, *Die Sexuelle Krise,* 247.

in Maximilian Harden's *Zukunft,* but her main venue seems to have been the *Neue Rundschau,* a paper that served first as an organ for Berlin naturalists and then increasingly for symbolists and expressionists after the mid-1890s. It was there that Andreas Salomé expressed her views on the "sexual question," as the temperamental antifeminist Laura Marholm had done in the early years of the journal's existence. Lapsing into stony silence on the subject at the turn of the century, after a gap of some years the *Neue Rundschau* suddenly began publishing a series of essays by Frost, who wrote ten pieces on the women's movement between 1908 and 1914 (including a rather vicious review of Meisel-Hess's *The Sexual Crisis*),[46] effectively becoming the paper's sole voice on feminist issues in the years before the First World War. Given the wide influence of the *Neue Rundschau,* it is no wonder that someone as close to her intellectual circles as Meisel-Hess felt compelled to launch withering public assaults on Frost's aestheticist misogyny—a position often to be found among Berlin modernists in those years.

Lucia Dora Frost was a bitter enemy of the feminist movement, particularly of the progressive wing and its efforts to win economic and political rights for women. Her first essays, written in 1909–10, focused on Bäumer's campaign to reform Prussian girls' schools, which she angrily repudiated as a curricular program aimed at training women for careers in public service under the guise of "education to womanliness." Once won, the right to work would soon become a compulsion, Frost insisted. In forcing women out of the home and into the job market, Wilhelmine feminists were playing into the hands of hostile powers; in striving to oppose the patriarchal capitalist system, they had become complicit with the rationalizing forces of state and economy, which had a strong interest in such "ominous exploitation of womanly powers," or, "in the jargon of 'social feeling,' the development of the powers of woman through education."[47] Frost asserted that progressive feminists like Bäumer were not interested in education at all, but only in "creating careers, markets, demand," and in accelerating the "consumption of educated women" who were trained to think solely in terms of efficiency,

46. Lucia Dora Frost, "Die Vertreibung aus der Ehe," *Neue Rundschau* 20, no. 3 (1909): 1337–40.

47. Lucia Dora Frost, "Königlich Preußische Frauenbewegung," *Neue Rundschau* 21, no. 1 (1910): 258; Frost, "Die 'soziale' Frauenbildungsreform," *Neue Rundschau* 19, no. 3 (1908): 1382.

instrumental rationality, and "*Sachlichkeit.*"[48] The reigning powers of German militarism and industrial capitalism could have hardly asked for a better ally in their drive to make most efficient use of all available "human material," she sneered, dubbing the moderate progressive wing in Wilhelmine feminism the "Royal Prussian Women's Movement."[49]

The subjection of women to the rationalizing impulse amounted to nothing less than a destruction of the private sphere, the violation of what, for Frost, was the true domain of woman and the last refuge of autonomous aesthetic culture that throughout most of the nineteenth century had somehow managed to remain free from the compulsion of brute force and materialistic interests. "Reason was always the enemy of happiness. The immanent overbearing dominance of instrumentality destroyed stylistic cultures," she fumed. "War was the great carrier and legitimizer of rationalism; in it the dominance of reason was most violently effective, and the animosity toward what has grown up in and of itself."[50] Drawing on the same physiological distinction between men and women Andreas Salomé had used, Frost passionately insisted that rationality—with its aggressive, outward-directed compulsion to attain mastery over isolated targets, thereby cutting them off from the rich, living web of their surroundings—was a fundamentally destructive, mechanistic, masculine drive.[51] Sheer "poison" to the physical essence of woman, the dry sterility of *Sachlichkeit* was in any event beyond woman's capabilities. Trying to compete with men on this terrain was as futile as the vain "hope for equality. . . . In nothing can we become equal, not even a common semblance of education can unite us; since even our misunderstandings must be different [ones]." Instead of chasing after "equality" on masculine ground, Frost asserted, women should be striving with all their might to defend their autonomous femininity if they hoped to prevail against the hostile forces of rationalization. "The road to dominion is long, very long, and leads through a field magnetized by masculine values

48. Lucia Dora Frost, "Frauenwege," *Neue Rundschau* 22, no. 2 (1911): 531, 536; Frost, "Frauenbewegung," 256–60; Frost, "Frauenstudium," *Neue Rundschau* 22, no. 3 (1911): 1177–86.

49. Frost, "Frauenbewegung," 256–60.

50. Frost, "Frauenstudium," 1179.

51. Lucia Dora Frost, "Ich will auf Feindschaft setzen . . . ," *Neue Rundschau* 20, no. 1 (1909): 399–409.

and masculine self-assurance," Frost warned. "How will we prevent our-selves from falling into imitation and losing our way then, if we don't keep watch over the polarity, if we try to rid ourselves of our own distinctive-ness?"[52]

Frost recognized that the "classifying concept" of "race" imported from "anthropology" was a particularly key ingredient in the rationalistic dis-course on social policy that had penetrated to the core of the women's movement. The anthropological use of "race" as a term "accords with the systematic need" of the scientific discipline, she observed, and it contrasted sharply with colloquial understandings of race as "raciness" (*Rassigkeit*).[53] In late imperial Germany, the latter meaning roughly combined the sexual piquancy conveyed by modern American 'racy' with a sense of light, sporty adeptness and high-toned physical prowess that, applied to horses, might be rendered by the term 'thoroughbred.' For Frost, this represented the original meaning of race, its "natural linguistic usage," which had nothing at all to do with science, efficiency, or "adaptation" in the "struggle for survival":

> Race is nothing rational, but is instead beyond usefulness and instru-mentality, is character that rests within itself, that is, [it] is an ideal of unanimity and coyness, for which our taste wishes change least of all and permanence above all else. Most of all the individual blessed by race feels his preferential condition himself; as a lively sensation of wholeness, a light feeling of unity, the archetype of everything psychic (upon which the precise and penetrating power of heredity rests). Proud, light demeanor is the most visible expression of this feeling and [one] peculiar to race: the life that runs through the body to the tips of its extremities as a corporeal consciousness.[54]

Race as raciness was, in other words, a purely internal, subjective, aes-thetic sensation. If man had been "bred" to race, Frost declared, it was not by "natural selection," but by a sense of awe and reverence before noble qualities that had been lacking in the "pre-human and the early human, that

52. Ibid., 408–9; Lucia Dora Frost, "Die Sendung der Frau," *Neue Rundschau* 20, no. 4 (1909): 1717.

53. Lucia Dora Frost, "Züchtung," *Neue Rundschau* 21, no. 2 (1910): 778–80.

54. Ibid., 779–80.

grotesque collection of rudiments and anticipations." In an article entitled "Breeding," she traced the spiritual origins of race back to the rites of prehistoric animal cults, particularly to the "cult of the horse." Dazzled by the grace and agility of this untamed animal, early men were driven to imitate its "perfection" and "virtuosity" by feelings of humility and shame that were remote from any thought of instrumentality. In their ritual dances and masks, these lowly creatures had assumed and preserved the characteristics they most admired in the horse, gradually, through imitation, passing on a fixed set of noble qualities that finally raised them above the animal world at the dawn of humanity. "As poet and actor, as interpreter of the animal, man became a rich transcription on a primitive, very powerful theme," Frost wrote. "He danced himself pure, he danced himself together, his limbs and his soul, he danced himself lyrically, spiritually, to race."[55]

In such polemics against feminism's ominous concessions to instrumental rationality, capitalism, and the state, Frost thus posited an alternative definition of 'race' that explicitly upheld the noninstrumental, nonrational, aesthetic values cherished in Berlin's symbolist circles. Again we seem miles from the progressive milieu of Bäumer and the eugenicist consensus of late imperial Germany. And yet in adopting the discourse of biology and race to voice her critique, Frost had stepped onto common ground that gradually pushed her—it seems unwittingly and almost against her will—right back to the productivist rhetoric of feminist eugenics.

Entitled "Politics of Generation," Frost's last article in the *Neue Rundschau* before the First World War (published in early 1914) began by contrasting the peaceful life of primitive "community" that had lasted for "untold millennia" in the prehistoric world with the sudden appearance of the state and politics upon the rise of the polis in classical antiquity. From the beginning, the state represented "something essentially different from the spirit of community," which had remained vague and directionless. Only with the rise of the polis did sustained intentionality appear in the actions of men, in the great project of collecting "valuable human material," which would ultimately be completed by capitalist industry and "population policy."[56] Given her previous tirades against these rationalizing forces, one

55. Ibid., 781–7 (quote, 784).
56. Lucia Dora Frost, "Generationspolitik," *Neue Rundschau* 25, no. 1 (1914): 305–7, 310–1.

might have expected Frost to depict the rise of the modern state and the destruction of primeval "community" as a tragic loss; but instead she embraced it as a culminating "organization of the trend toward higher breeding." In a still more surprising turn, Frost now enlisted women in the state's drive for global conquest. Declaring women and family to be the foundation of the modern state, she placed biological reproduction and the protection of mothers at the very "center of political renewal."[57] In the same terms as Meisel-Hess and the other radical advocates of sexual reform, she insisted that it was vital to the nation's interests that the fittest women be allowed to procreate rather than slaving away to earn money: "The optimum would be the conjuncture of economic and biological ripeness for marriage." Echoing the progressive opponents of Stöcker and Marie Stritt in the debates over abortion at the 1908 women's league conference, Frost insisted that only reproductive politics could ensure that Europeans would prevail against the "colored races" in the struggle for world dominance. Only fresh supplies of healthy offspring could supply a "safeguard against the lower, more sensual races getting the upper hand."[58]

How had such a passionate defender of the right to spiritual self-fulfillment in the personal, private, subjective sphere of aesthetic freedom come to embrace the most reductive, destructive tendencies lurking beneath the progressives' faith in science, the market, and instrumental rationality? In "Politics of Generation," Frost was clearly beguiled by common notions of "race" and an admiration for perseverance in fostering particular physical and intellectual qualities in human beings. A common discourse on the organic was enough to blind her to the vast gulf she herself had pointed out— the gulf separating her own, subjective view of race as raciness from commercial and military agendas in which the "objective" value of "human material" was defined in terms of the state's colonialist competition in an international "struggle for survival."

The attraction of this biopolitical discourse, I have tried to argue, was that it placed women at the forefront in the Wilhelmine search for solutions to the social problem and the sexual crisis. It also seemed to vindicate nonrational, personal, spiritual forces in the concrete terms demanded by an age

57. Ibid., 311, 316.
58. Ibid., 311, 315.

of materialism, science, and reason. At once inside and outside, subjective and objective, the "life force" (whether seen as erotic or maternal or both) seemed to reconcile the scientific and humanistic impulses of the Enlightenment that clashed to produce the "crisis of modernity" in late imperial Germany. Biopolitics seemed to allow feminists to step into the modern materialist world without relinquishing their pious regard for humanity. But it also forced them to accept the categories of that world, to legitimate their positions in terms of instrumentality, rationality, capitalism, and the state. Could they have done otherwise if they wanted to be heard in that new world? Could they have tried to push social and political developments down a different path? Perhaps not. But this was the step that placed Grete Meisel-Hess, Lucia Dora Frost, and many others on the treacherous ground of feminist eugenics at the fin de siècle.

ELITE CULTURE
DECADENCE OR VITALITY?

Arnold Böcklin and the Problem of German Modernism

SUZANNE MARCHAND

Had a nationwide poll been taken in 1900, it is highly likely that Arnold Böcklin would have been named the preeminent German painter of the fin de siècle. Today, Böcklin is hardly a name to conjure with. Few museum-goers (especially outside Switzerland and Germany) have seen his work; art historians ignore him; textbooks have trouble characterizing him and explaining both the origins of his style and the effects of his work on other artists. He may occasionally be given credit for anticipating symbolism or for inspiring Giorgi di Chirico and Max Ernst, but few now recognize him, as did his contemporaries, as the German answer to Manet; fewer still rank him with Richard Wagner and Friedrich Nietzsche as one of the great German cultural innovators of the century's end. Though two recent exhibitions and their accompanying catalogs have revived interest in Böcklin in the German-speaking world,[1] Fritz Novotny's comments in the 1971 edition of *The Pelican History of Art* still sum up a general judgment on the painter: "Böcklin presented ideals which were simple and crude enough to appeal to the taste of the artistically-minded upper-middle-class society of the so-called 'Gründerzeit' or boom period of the 1870s and 1880s." Novotny concluded that Böcklin's "eclecticism left him little scope for genuine invention."[2]

Why Böcklin—who, like Wagner and Nietzsche, plumbed the psyche in new and initially unpopular ways—now looks crudely bourgeois or kitschy rather than profound is a complicated question. Part of the answer surely

1. *Arnold Böcklin* (exhibition catalog, Basel, 2001); Guido Magnaguagno and Juri Steiner, eds., *Arnold Böcklin, Giorgio di Chirico, Max Ernst: Eine Reise ins Ungewisse* (Bern, 1998). Also see the Basel Kunstmuseum's slightly older but well-done catalog, edited by Dorothea Christ and Christian Geelhaar, *Arnold Böcklin: Die Gemälde im Kunstmuseum Basel* (Basel, 1990).

2. Fritz Novotny, *Painting and Sculpture in Europe, 1780–1880* (Harmondsworth, Middlesex, 1971), 320, 319.

lies in the success of French modernism in portraying itself as modernism *tout court;* German art, from Heinrich Füssli to Max Beckmann, is little known beyond Central Europe, and even such talented painters as Max Liebermann and Adolph Menzel lack much international appeal. Another reason may be that Böcklin's art actually *was* crude and kitschy; even contemporary admirers like Thomas Mann admitted some of his paintings were bathetic and badly executed.[3] But perhaps the most formidable barrier to our appreciation of Böcklin is our inability to take seriously the mythological figures which populate his best-known images. For most members of the German educated middle classes (*Bildungsbürgertum*) at the fin de siècle, by contrast, the classical tradition was still a fundamental point of reference and its major texts were common knowledge. That Böcklin was able to modernize and democratize this tradition without destroying it was central to his relatively brief but intense period of high influence and popularity (from about 1890 to 1905); that his reputation as the 'German Manet' could not be sustained in the face of other, more radical forms of artistic modernism after 1905 is an important barometer of the changing fortunes of German neoclassicism—and an important window on the fast-moving and hotly contested world of Wilhelmine cultural politics.

At the outset, it is critical to note that, *pace* Novotny, Böcklin's popularity was not the result of market-pleasing tactics; the Swiss painter achieved fame only in his old age. Born in the last years of the romantic era, he developed his mature style and his repertoire of oversexed centaurs and otherworldly nymphs (see Figure 1) while a struggling painter in the 1860s. Attacked viciously by critics in the 1870s, his apotheosis came only after he reached his sixtieth birthday and occurred not in his real or adopted homelands (Switzerland and Italy, respectively), but rather in the post-Bismarckian *Kaiserreich.* Changes in Böcklin's style are perceptible over time, with a major break occurring around 1863; but it was not a change of style that made for his post-1885 success. It was a change in Wilhelmine culture, and particularly a change in the cultural salience of classical antiquity, that made

3. Mann described Böcklin's *Madonna Enthroned in the Clouds* as "odd, primitive and so ugly as to almost be comical; I think the old master is simply playing a joke." Mann to Paul Ehrenberg, June 29, 1900, in *Thomas Mann: Briefe, 1948–1955 und Nachlese* (Frankfurt, 1965), 424–5.

Figure 1. Böcklin, *Centaur and Nymph,* 1855.

Staatliche Museen zu Berlin—Preußischer Kulturbesitz Nationalgalerie / bpk. Photo by Joerg P. Anders.

Böcklin the German modernist par excellence for an audience that included Thomas Mann and Hugo von Hofmannsthal, the Munich Secession and Sergey Rachmaninoff, Stefan George and Max Ernst, and Paula Modersohn-Becker. And it was a further change in prewar culture, beginning around 1905, that scratched the 'modern' from Böcklin's epitaph and made the Swiss-Italian landscapist the full-blooded German painter whom Adolf Hitler adored.

It is this series of cultural changes that I want to explore, tackling the separate problems of the genesis of Böcklin's vitalistic classicism (in the 1860s and '70s), the enthusiastic reception of his work (in the 1880s and '90s), and, briefly, his post-1905 banalization as a means to understand the diverse and antagonistic nature of cultural modernism in Wilhelmine Germany. As Peter Paret has recently argued, "The war over modernism [in Germany] was not fought along a single front"; nor was it one in which the public, the political elite, or even artists and art critics themselves retained consistent attitudes toward particular works or styles of art.[4] The story of Böcklin's passage from outré iconoclast to modernist to Germanic painter nicely illustrates the contentious nature of Germany's search for a modern national style at the fin de siècle. Moreover, the painter's eclectic vision reminds us of something this volume as a whole is concerned to underscore, namely, the ambivalence toward the modern exhibited in late nineteenth- and early twentieth-century German culture. This world exhibited strong streaks of cultural pessimism, to be sure, but it also demonstrated a strong will to modernization; the two combined to form a rich and diverse culture of creative energy and bitter debate. To understand Böcklin, just as to understand the cultural history of the Wilhelmine fin de siècle as a whole, we must recall that it was possible for individuals in this era to be both mourners and modernizers, to live simultaneously on *The Isle of Life* and *The Isle of the Dead* (see Figures 2 and 3).

In a single essay, it is impossible to do justice to the whole of Böcklin's life and labors. I have therefore opted to address one central aspect of his work: the representation of classical antiquity. I chose this direction not only because it is central to Böcklin's reception, but also because I believe that examining transformations in the interpretation of classical antiquity opens a very important window on the changing self-image of those who were most influential in shaping Wilhelmine *Kultur*, the *Bildungsbürgertum*. Böcklin, I hope to show, rose to prominence on the strength of his ability to revitalize the classical tradition; but in the process, he broke all the rules of neoclassicism, abandoning the principle of *ut pictura poesis* (from the poem, or text, the picture is to be drawn), as well as Winckelmannian gravitas and

---

4. Peter Paret, *German Encounters with Modernism, 1840–1945* (Cambridge, 2001), 128.

Figure 2. Böcklin, *The Isle of Life*, 1888.

Öffentliche Kunstsammlung Basel, Kunstmuseum. Photo by Martin Bühler.

Figure 3. Böcklin, *The Isle of the Dead*, 1883 version.

Staatliche Museen zu Berlin—Preußischer Kulturbesitz Nationalgalerie / bpk. Photo by Joerg P. Anders.

Figure 4. Böcklin, *Holy Sanctuary*, 1882.

© Hamburger Kunsthalle / bpk. Photo by Elke Walford.

grandeur. He gave to his half-classicizing dreamscapes a new, less elitist, psychological depth; but he retained enough of what Ludwig Justi called the *'Museumskultur*'[5] of the nineteenth century to convince the embattled *Bildungsbürger* of the 1890s and 1900s that he was the painter who would save art from modernizing debasement on the one hand and academic obsolescence on the other. Conjuring the more psychological gods—Eros and Thanatos—rather than avatars of rationality and achievement such as Athena and Heracles, Böcklin appealed to a German middle class still proud of its classical learning, but no longer satisfied by the sunnier genre scenes and text-based history paintings of the previous era. In passion-infused paintings like *Holy Sanctuary* (see Figure 4) and *Battle of the Centaurs* (see Figure 5), this postliberal middle class, as well as many members of the avant-garde, found emotional (not social) truths with which they could identify without abandoning themselves to the urbane, cultureless world de-

5. Ludwig Justi, *Arnold Böcklin: Ein Führer zur Böcklin Sammlung der National-Galerie* (Berlin, 1927), 25.

Figure 5. Böcklin, *Battle of the Centaurs,* 1873.
Öffentliche Kunstsammlung Basel, Kunstmuseum. Photo by Martin Bühler.

picted by realists and impressionists. In Böcklin's world, they could observe raw human passions—lust, terror, grief, anger—while still believing that *Kultur* mattered and would endure.

A study of Böcklin, then, may provide an intriguing way to get at the problem—delineated long ago by Carl Schorske—of discerning what in Central European culture was moving forward and what was moving backward.[6] For art historians and critics writing in the wake of abstraction's advent, Böcklin's story is one of the persistence of classical forms and the defense of traditional *Kultur* against a cosmopolitan form of modernism that flaunted its departures from traditions of all sorts. But seen from the perspective of the 1890s, his story is also one of quite radical discontinuity. Böcklin's Gymnasium-educated fans of the fin de siècle lauded the painter precisely for breaking away from the stifling culture of the museum and making antiquity relevant by investing it with new emotional appeal. "Böcklin has jumped the tracks of tradition," wrote one fan; the Swiss genius, wrote another, "was spared the Procrustean bed of plaster-cast classicism, which was so fateful to [Winckelmann's] successors from [Asmus

6. Schorske posed the problem by quoting Robert Musil. See Carl Schorske, *Fin-de-Siècle Vienna: Politics and Culture* (New York, 1979), 116.

Jakob] Carstens to [Anselm] Feuerbach, for, unphilologically and unfactu-
ally, with a sensual energy thirsting for life, he conjured up only smiling or
sighing dreams of an ancient paradise."[7] That Böcklin, like Richard Wagner,
"jumped the tracks" while also revitalizing the world of myth is a notable
peculiarity of one moment in the complicated evolution of German modernism; it deserves scrutiny, not simple condemnation. For if Böcklin's 'escape' now appears (to our Picasso-oriented eyes) fusty and arcane, the
acceptance of his vitalistic vision of antiquity[8] marked a real turning point
in Wilhelmine culture—the moment in which liberal historicism collapsed
under pressures exerted not only by the rapid diversification of the cultural
world, but also by the onset of a deeper, darker cast of mind.

Arnold Böcklin, Swiss-Italian Eclectic

Born in 1827 and named after a character in Schiller's *Wilhelm Tell*, Böcklin
fits beautifully into the 'unseasonable' world of midcentury Basel that Lionel
Gossman sketched a few years ago in his marvelous study of the town's infa-
mous intellectuals.[9] Though Böcklin escaped from his hometown—and his
father's cloth trade—in 1845, he carried away with him the city's unique
brand of iconoclastic antimodernism and eclectic individualism. Like Jacob
Burckhardt, who played an important role in advancing the painter's early
career, Böcklin wove his way through Prussian institutions, but he came out
very much his own man. He first studied art in Düsseldorf, where he at-
tended Prussia's second largest art academy. There, before 1848, classical
painting, romantic and Nazarene styles, and Biedermeier realism coexisted,

7. Carl Neumann, "Zu Arnold Böcklin's siebzigstem Geburtstag," *Kunst für Alle* 13
(1897–98): 6; Franz Hermann Meissner, *Arnold Böcklin*, 3d ed. (Berlin, 1898), 87.

8. Vitalism is a notoriously slippery term; nonetheless, it describes what seems to have
been a real tendency in late nineteenth-century culture, a strain of thought, or better still,
a cast of mind that valued experience over erudition, healthy emotions (and action, often
for its own sake) over pallid thought, primitive drives over "civilized" manners—the un-
bourgeois, that is to say, over the bourgeois. For a subtle and engaging discussion of the
many forms of this cast of mind, see August K. Wiedmann, *The German Quest for Primal
Origins in Art, Culture, and Politics, 1900–1933; Die 'Flucht in Urzustände'* (Lewiston, N.Y.,
1995).

9. Lionel Gossman, *Basel in the Age of Burckhardt* (Chicago, 2000); Rolf Andree, ed.,
Arnold Böcklin: Die Gemälde (Basel, 1977), 16.

apparently unproblematically.[10] Böcklin stayed in Düsseldorf nearly two years, studying with the landscape painter Johann Wilhelm Schirmer and the romantic Carl Friedrich Lessing; he also would have had ample opportunity to study the work of the Nazarene J. G. Schadow, whose son Wilhelm was the director of the Düsseldorf academy. In 1847, he traveled to Belgium, where he saw early Dutch painting and was captivated by Rubens; from there, he went to Geneva, where he found Alexandre Calame's studio confining (his training there was limited to making sketches of paintings).[11] The young Böcklin's first canvases show clear debts to Schirmer, Lessing, and Calame, a trio of romantic-realist landscape painters who all more or less followed in the tradition of Caspar David Friedrich. He was not yet an original—or even an 'unseasonable'—painter.

Critical to Böcklin's development was his brief, bitter experience in Paris, where he landed in early 1848. Eking out a bohemian existence as a medical illustrator,[12] he made many visits to the Louvre, admiring especially Camille Corot's landscapes and Thomas Couture's 1847 *The Romans of the Decadence,* an enormous archaizing canvas that exemplified neoclassical history painting at its most theatrical. Drawn along with the crowds into the Tuileries in February 1848, he was horrified by the bloodshed of the June Days, during which, it seems, some of his acquaintances were executed. Franz Zelger traces Böcklin's lifelong loathing of France to the days he spent watching out of his Parisian garret window as transports of prisoners were carted away to execution.[13] Interestingly, however, Böcklin was never moved to paint the sufferings of the revolutionaries, as did Menzel and many of his Düsseldorf contemporaries. Seeing Böcklin's early landscapes in the context of such works as Menzel's *The March Casualties Lying in State* (1848) or Johann Peter Hansclever's *Workers before the Magistrates* (1848–49) points up the extent to which the Swiss artist's means of representing pain and sorrow were always psychological or mythological, not social or historical. An

10. Joachim Grossmann, *Künstler, Hof, und Bürgertum: Leben und Arbeit von Maler in Preußen, 1786–1850* (Berlin, 1994), 71.

11. Andree, ed., *Arnold Böcklin: Die Gemälde,* 18.

12. Ferdinand Runkel, ed., *Böcklin Memoiren: Tagebuchblätter von Böcklins Gattin Angela* (Berlin, 1910), 331.

13. Franz Zelger, *Arnold Böcklin: Die Toteninsel. Selbstheroisierung und Abgesang der abendländischen Kultur* (Frankfurt, 1991), 31.

1890 depiction of *Poverty and Worry,* for example, employs emblematic an-cient figures to embody his subject matter; *Plague* and *War* (1897–98) are Düreresque allegories (see Martin Ruehl's essay, Figure 14). Böcklin might have been eclectic, but the absence of attempts at history painting or social realism throughout his career is also indicative of the kinds of influence to which the artist was always immune.

Quitting Paris, the painter retreated to Basel in September 1848. But he again found the Swiss city's Biedermeier culture oppressive and elected to go, as Jacob Burckhardt advised him, to Italy. This was a wholly conven-tional thing to do; ever since the Renaissance, artists and architects had gone to Rome to finish their educations—though the great German landscapist Caspar David Friedrich and Böcklin's French contemporary, Gustave Cour-bet, had been daring enough to break with this convention. As Georg Schmidt points out, had Böcklin followed Courbet's lead and remained in Paris, he would have seen that painter's epoch-making paintings in the salons of 1849 and 1850. He missed another opportunity to experience Eu-ropean art's cutting edge when, after a sojourn in Munich and Weimar (1858–62), he returned to Rome instead of going to Paris, where the first works of Degas, Monet, and Manet (whose *Déjeuner sur l'herbe* dates to 1863) were becoming known.[14] But Böcklin was never one to rush to see the latest exhibitions, and he rarely expressed appreciation for his contemporar-ies, whether French, German, Swiss or Italian. He probably did see impres-sionist art early on, but he ignored it in favor of the old masters and the academic art that was more highly valued by most Europeans at the time. In this he resembles his otherwise wholly differently inclined contemporary Anton von Werner, whose patriotic realism became de rigueur at the court of Wilhelm II.[15] Werner, at least, wanted to make waves in the cultural his-tory of his day; it is not at all clear that Böcklin shared this aspiration. He was not a man to join a 'school,' launch a movement, or even work out a philosophy of art.[16] In this way, he was anything but a modern artist—and as a result, he frequently felt himself out of step with his times.

14. Georg Schmidt, "Böcklin heute," in *Arnold Böcklin: Die Gemälde,* ed. Andree, 54–6.

15. On Werner's visit to Paris, see Dominik Bartmann, *Anton von Werner: Zur Kunst und Kunstpolitik im Deutschen Kaiserreich* (Berlin, 1985), 22–6.

16. His classification as a member of the "Deutsch-Römer" postdates most of his oeuvre and almost certainly would have been disputed by the painter himself.

But Böcklin found love and good light in the south; in any case, he preferred the company of the Italian old masters and the vegetative exuberance of the Italian countryside to the urban culture scenes of the north. After the death of one fiancée, a rejected proposal, and a broken engagement, in 1853 he married the seventeen-year-old daughter of a Papal Guard, Angela Pascucci. If the liaison was rapidly formed, it would prove enduring; Angela became Böcklin's chief cheerleader, his nursemaid, and the stable center around which the moody artist revolved. It may well be that Angela Böcklin also provided the inspiration for her husband to see Italy through nonclassicizing eyes; there is a lovely dual portrait of the couple strolling past a vine-covered ruin which dates to 1863–64. She was his muse, as he testified in his *Portrait of Angela Böcklin as a Muse,* and it is almost certainly her grieving form that we see in moving paintings such as *Melancholia* (1871), *Vestal Virgin* (1874), *The Dying Cleopatra* (1872), and perhaps, in smaller form, in the many versions of *Villa by the Sea* and *Isle of the Dead.* The couple had much to grieve about. In the late 1850s, Angela's ultra-Catholic aunt threatened to dissolve her niece's marriage to the Protestant Böcklin, and the couple could not live in Rome until after her death in 1862; nor was his family ever particularly friendly or supportive. Financial conditions were always tight. But much worse, five of their fourteen children would die in childhood, making for a family history shot through with deep lines of sorrow. It may indeed be Angela's influence that makes the most memorable women in Böcklin's paintings the strong, passionate, serious ones; these women are not simply objects of male desire, but rather individuals whose psychological experiences comprise a central part of the image's drama (see Figures 6 and 8).

The painter spent his early years of marriage exclusively cultivating his eye for landscape. Though it lacked the grand prestige of history painting, landscape was the bread and butter of starving young artists—and Böcklin in these years both fit this romantic stereotype and suffered its unromantic realities. But landscape to the young Böcklin was much more than a mercenary form of art. His earliest paintings exhibited the neoromantic tendency to infuse nature with human passions, and in many ways his mature style was simply a blending of emotive landscapes—in the manner of Friedrich or his teachers Schirmer and Calame—with the humor and coloristic panache of the Italian baroque. Though never a *plein air* painter, Böcklin did make careful studies of rocks, seas, and foliage; his trees were particularly expressive, though often they owed much to Corot, another great anti-

Figure 6. Böcklin, *Odysseus and Calypso*, 1882
Öffentliche Kunstsammlung Basel, Kunstmuseum. Photo by Martin Bühler.

impressionist. The representation of nature was always central for Böcklin, and in images featuring mythological demigods or sacred scenes, the trees, grasses, water, and rocks often seem to absorb more of the painter's (and the viewer's) attention than the figures. That the natural details often seem out of proportion with respect to the scenes depicted (as in the enormous cypresses in *Isle of the Dead* or the towering birches in *Holy Sanctuary*) adds to the uncanny sensibility these images convey and suggests a kind of cultural pessimism that characterizes at least part of Böcklin's corpus.[17] But there are sunnier pictures as well (see Figure 7), pastoral images that celebrate love, youth, and spring. Nature, for Böcklin, served as critique and promise, a sign of endurance in times of suffering as well as an incitement to revelry—but it was never merely a backdrop. It has always been difficult to characterize clearly the genre Böcklin worked in—but he almost certainly would have preferred to be called a landscape painter than a history painter.

    17. This treatment was not, of course, invented by Böcklin; he could have learned it from C. D. Friedrich, Claude Lorraine, or Poussin, whom we know Böcklin greatly admired.

Figure 7. Böcklin, *Look, the Meadow Smiles,* 1887.
Hessisches Landesmuseum Darmstadt.

More pantheist than humanist, he spent his early years in Italy not in deepening his appreciation for European civilization's past achievements, but in perfecting his portrayal of nature's moods.

In fact, Böcklin long evinced little interest in antiquities. Unlike his younger contemporary Paul Cézanne, Böcklin created no sketchbooks of ruins, sculptures, and frescoes during his sojourns in the Italian countryside.[18] As Klaus Vierneisel has observed, there are no archaeological details in Böcklin's paintings of the '50s and early '60s—*Pan Frightens a Shepherd* (1860), *Pan amongst the Reeds* (1859), *Nymph at the Spring* (1855)[19]—and, we could add, few thereafter. Rather, his first images of nymphs and fauns seem shaped by rococo genre paintings; indeed, the semiclassical figures might have been added to landscapes to make the pictures sell.[20] They did sell, but not very well, and it is unlikely that Böcklin moved further into

18. Klaus Vierneisel, "Archäologisches bei Arnold Böcklin," in *Arnold Böcklin, Giorgio di Chirico, Max Ernst: Eine Reise ins Ungewisse,* ed. Guido Magnaguagno and Juri Steiner (Bern, 1998), 87.

19. Ibid., 89.

20. Schmidt, "Böcklin heute," 54.

the realm of myth simply to satisfy market demand. There is no evidence, moreover, that he self-consciously adopted classical themes in order to make a political point, or even to *épater l'académie*. What he and his contemporaries fought over in his first classicizing pictures was not his vision of antiquity, but his already flashy use of color, his hypernaturalist rendering of vegetation, and the potentially salacious disposition of his nymphs.[21] If, in his early work, Böcklin was developing a repertoire of favorite mythological figures, he had not yet arrived at a notably new approach—in either technical or intellectual terms—to the ancient past.

At this stage of his career—as for the next quarter-century—Böcklin remained an authentically garret-dwelling bohemian. Though he sold *Pan amongst the Reeds* to the Bavarian king in 1859 for the Neue Pinakothek, he was still virtually penniless. He had, in fact, nearly died of typhus and grief in 1858–59 (his son Robert had died during the painter's illness), and the first catalog entry for the Pinakothek described him as deceased.[22] In 1860, he landed a job as professor for landscape painting at the new art academy in Weimar—but he despised the bleakness of the weather and the stuffiness of the court. Already by the late 1850s, he had developed what would be a lifelong obsession with building a flying machine that would take him soaring through the skies like a bird—leaving behind, presumably, all his earthly cares. Characteristically, however, he would never agree to degrade his vision by incorporating into it a modern utilitarian device, and without an engine, his planes could not but fail to satisfy his avian aspirations.[23]

Still seeking a style, a home, and a steady income, Böcklin returned with his family to Rome in 1862. Here, at last, he found real inspiration—first from Raphael's Vatican murals and then, more powerfully, from the Pompeian wall paintings, which he saw for the first time in 1863. "The impres-

21. The original version of Böcklin's *Nymph and Centaur* could not be exhibited in Rome on "moral grounds" until Böcklin supplied the nymph with a veil. Andree, ed., *Arnold Böcklin: Die Gemälde*, 20. A later image (1866) was apparently rejected by the Basel Museum as "too naked." Rudolf Schick, *Tagebuch-Aufzeichnungen aus den Jahren 1866, 1868, 1869 über Arnold Böcklin*, 2nd ed., ed. Hugo von Tschudi (Berlin, 1902), 80–1.

22. Runkel, ed., *Böcklin Memorien*, 83.

23. On Böcklin's flying aspirations, see Ferdinand Runkel and Carl Böcklin, *Neben meiner Kunst: Flugstudien, Briefen, und Persönliches von and über Arnold Böcklin* (Berlin, 1909), 37.

sion was so powerful," his student Rudolf Schick recounted, "that he was driven completely out of his previous path," requiring a full year to reorient himself.[24] When he completed his transition, he emerged with a much deeper devotion to decoration, to color, and to imaginative (rather than naturalistic) painting. Impressed with Roman encaustic paintings, his colors became more vibrant, his contrasts sharper, and his will to experiment greater. Schick's diaries, which cover the years 1866 and 1868–69, show Böcklin obsessed with tints and fixatives, ceaselessly experimenting and usually failing in his attempts to recreate the beauties of ancient and Renaissance fresco painting. When we see him reading a book, it is a treatise on colors, not a volume of Greek poetry or philosophy. His friend Franz von Lenbach, who would later excel in reproducing Titian's tones, apparently learned a great deal from Böcklin's technical experiments.[25] Quite simply, the point was to delight the viewer's eye and to make his delight in brilliant coloration last. A painting, Böcklin would later tell an eager listener, "must be painted for the eye, and not for the reason [*Verstand*]."[26]

Simultaneously with this immersion in frescoes (and flying machines), Böcklin's personality began to assert itself more dramatically. His characteristic combination of saturnine melancholy and passionate zeal for life can be felt in paintings like *Faun Playing for a Blackbird* (1864–65) or *Villa by the Sea*, which went through six versions between 1864 and 1878 (see Figure 8). Perhaps frequent resettlement and adversity, in addition to his Pompeian experience, helped forge the eccentric vision which developed over the course of this decade; his infant son Maurizio died in 1866, and his beloved six-year-old daughter Lucia died after being hit by a cart in 1868. Basel, to which the family had fled in 1866, hardly had proved welcoming. Finances remained limited, but Böcklin did obtain some commissions; by 1869, his newfound confidence in his own vision had become so strong that it produced a lifelong break with Burckhardt, whose insistence that Böcklin modify the murals he had begun in the Basel Museum angered the painter.[27] Looking at these muddled and messy paintings now, many of us would

24. Schick, *Tagebuch-Aufzeichnungen,* 171.

25. Sonja von Baranow, *Franz von Lenbach: Leben und Werk* (Cologne, 1986), 59–60.

26. Böcklin quoted in Adolf Grabowsky, *Der Kampf um Böcklin* (Berlin, 1906), 148.

27. Schick, *Tagebuch-Aufzeichungen,* 265, 281; Runkel, ed., *Böcklin Memorien,* 127–32.

Figure 8. Böcklin, *Villa by the Sea,* 1878 version.

Kunstmuseum Winterthur. Presented by the heirs of Olga Reinhart-Schwarzenbach, 1970.

probably agree with Burckhardt: the murals were both poorly conceived and awkwardly executed. Neither these nor the portraits that sustained his family in Basel advanced Böcklin's vision; the time had come for the painter to free himself entirely from the world of his 'fathers.'

Abandoning Basel, Böcklin moved on to Munich, where he worked, in part, with his friend Franz Lenbach in the employ of the lawyer-poet (and translator of Persian, Arabic, and Spanish literature) Graf Adolf Friedrich von Schack. Schack, one of the aristocrats whose patronage sustained Böcklin throughout his hungry years, had begun an art collection that consisted, oddly, of copies of old masters and original works by living German artists, which he hung side by side in his personal gallery.[28] Lenbach was employed as a copyist, and Böcklin seems to have assisted him in this endeavor. But Böcklin was never a very good copyist; indeed, he disapproved

28. See Andrea Pophanken, "Graf Adolf Friedrich von Schack und seine Galerie: Anmerkungen zur Münchener Sammlungsgeschichte," in *Sammler, Stifter, und Museen: Kunstförderung in Deutschland im 19. und 20 Jahrhundert,* ed. Ekkehard Mai and Peter Paret (Cologne, 1993), 114–34.

of those who, like his erstwhile friend Anselm Feuerbach, were too concerned with painting "like the old masters" as well as of realists like Adolph Menzel, who, Böcklin claimed, simply painted nature's surfaces.[29] Nonetheless, the years in Munich would inspire Böcklin to produce two important works which would make his reputation as an iconoclastic painter of mythological scenes: *The Battle of the Centaurs* (1872–73), and *Triton and Nereid* (two versions, 1874–75).

In these two striking paintings, the imaginary animals and demigods have escaped from forest tapestries into the sunlit center of the canvas. By focusing on the figures and reducing the landscape (which took up the greatest part of images like *Pan Frightens a Shepherd*), Böcklin gave his characters new psychological power—and new audience appeal. *The Battle of the Centaurs* was widely exhibited and popularly acclaimed; it sold for 6,750 francs in 1876.[30] Schack bought the first version of *Triton*, and it seemed as if the National Gallery in Berlin would buy the second one. Impressed by the success of these two images, Böcklin quickly produced a series of more Pan pictures, which included *Nymph on Pan's Shoulders* (1874); *Two Pans Fishing* (1874); *Idyll* (1875); *Sleeping Diana, Watched by Fauns* (1877, see Figure 9); and *Centaur by the Water* (1878). Combining lessons learned from Rubens with his own love of the sea, he also began to produce a highly amusing set of Dionysian seascapes. It has been estimated that allegories and motives taken from classical antiquity make up one-half of Böcklin's paintings as a whole; a total of thirty-two works treat his favorite figures—Pan, fauns, and nymphs.[31] While there is much in his corpus that is not classical from the 1870s on, the representation of this arcadian world defined his style.

These paintings exhibit a self-confident departure from the formal serenity and high moral tone of both neoclassicism and naturalism. Böcklin formally created a sense of intense irreality by combining naturalistic exactitude and implausible characters, poses, or colors, by dwarfing figures in vast, spiritualized landscapes, and by erasing all modern elements, such as roads, houses, or figures in contemporary dress. Applying the language of romantic painters like Caspar David Friedrich to semiclassical scenes (see, for exam-

29. See his comments quoted in Grabowsky, *Der Kampf,* 187, 185.
30. Runkel, ed., *Böcklin Memorien,* 252.
31. Vierneisel, "Archäologisches bei Arnold Böcklin," 88.

Figure 9. Böcklin, *Sleeping Diana, Watched by Two Fauns*, 1877.
Stiftung museum kunst palast, Düsseldorf.

ple, *Holy Sanctuary*), Böcklin created the feel of primeval isolation and religious intensity.[32] In the absence of historicizing details, his romantic staging
of moods—not actions—turned the symbolism inward. Accordingly, the
content of images became quite clearly psychological; viewers were not referred to any particular stories, but rather were invited to think about male/
female relations in general (*Triton and Nereid*) or to partake of someone
else's classicizing dream (*The Isle of Life*). The ancient world itself was either
a source of pleasurable titillation or distressing dreams, but it was not in any
way directly accessible or morally instructive.

There has been much discussion of the sources of Böcklin's psychological, bacchanalian antiquity; in search of textual sources, many scholars have
followed Andrea Linnebach's closely argued speculations. In her excellent
study *Böcklin und die Antike,* Linnebach notes the painter's knowledge of

32. Cf. Robert Rosenblum, *Modern Painting and the Northern Romantic Tradition:
Friedrich to Rothko* (New York, 1975). Many thanks to Lionel Gossman for directing me
to this wonderful book.

Homer, Aristophanes, Ovid, and Heinrich Heine; she also adduces the possibility that the painter might have read J. J. Bachofen's *Mother Right* and/or Nietzsche's *Birth of Tragedy.* She rightly suggests that Böcklin likely heard about Burckhardt's lectures on Greek history, as he remained a close friend of the historian until the end of the 1860s, during which time Burckhardt was preparing the lectures later published as the *Cultural History of the Greeks.*[33] Böcklin's Dionysian creations surely owed something to the antiliberal preoccupations of his fellow Baselers, Bachofen, Burckhardt, and Nietzsche, and Linnebach's work does a lovely job of sketching the neoromantic undercurrents that were available to Böcklin and his iconoclastic contemporaries.

But given the paucity of first-hand testimony (as the painter's son explained, Böcklin "had something of an aversion to the written word"),[34] Linnebach's reconstructions of Böcklin's reading list remain undocumentable—and somewhat beside the point. As she herself points out, throughout his life Böcklin rarely painted major classical figures or conventional scenes (such as Achilles battling Hector or the lovemaking of Venus and Adonis); he preferred half-heathen figures, like nymphs, centaurs, and mermaids, whose antics were not described in any ancient sources. Historical figures and referents are entirely missing from his oeuvre; he did not attempt a *Death of Socrates* or a *Battle of Salamis,* which would have required archaeologically accurate props—or a full-on, Klimtian, modernism that Böcklin could hint at but could not quite envision. We know from numerous of his pronouncements that he was in no way a literary or cerebral painter; unlike the Pre-Raphaelites, he did not peruse arcane works of medieval flower symbolism or devote careful study to poetry, philosophy, or music. He wanted his viewers to feel the grief of the woman in *Villa by the Sea,* the frigid dampness of the sea in *Triton and Nereid,* and the lust and terror of the pursuing centaur and the frightened nymphs in *Playing in the Waves* (see Figure 10). Identifying the woman as Iphigenia, Triton and Nereid as characters spawned by Heine's poetry, and a libidinous centaur as Böcklin's own friend Anton Dohrn, simply does not unlock the meaning of his images, as might

33. Andrea Linnebach, *Arnold Böcklin und die Antike: Mythos, Geschichte, Gegenwart* (Munich, 1991), 21–35, 68–72.

34. Runkel and Böcklin, *Neben meiner Kunst,* 13.

Figure 10. Böcklin, *Playing in the Waves*, 1883.
Bayerische Staatsgemäldesammlungen, Neue Pinakothek, Munich.

be the case for seventeenth-century allegories. Rather naively, Böcklin had thrown a monkey wrench into the tradition of *ut pictura poesis*—and in the 1860s and '70s, that made his work seem distinctly bizarre.

This departure from conventional practice was, as suggested above, less a conscious choice than the rather accidental result of the interweaving of romantic landscape painting, Pompeian decoration, and Italian baroque grandeur in Böcklin's maturing style. Above all, the painter conceived of himself as a craftsman. As such, he was heir to an ongoing (if increasingly threatened) 'classical' tradition, one that was not narrowly (if at all) defined by literature but rather sprang from the pattern books of the old masters. Böcklin was one of the first German painters to have a full range of Italian canvases at his fingertips, and in museums and in photographic reproductions, he carefully scrutinized the old masters. His pronouncements on art show that he studied closely at least the following: Raphael, Titian, Poussin, Rubens, Corregio, Michelangelo, the Carracci, Caravaggio, Giorgione, Tintoretto, Rogier van der Weyden, Guercino, Parmiagiano, Rembrandt, and

Giotto.[35] He 'seceded' from the salons of his day not by becoming a painter of the future but by reverting to an artisanal tradition that had been left behind. In this, of course, he had precursors and companions abroad, from the Pre-Raphaelites to the German Nazarenes, from the proto-symbolist French painter Puvis de Chavannes to the arts and crafts movement in America. But there is neither need nor warrant to interpret these similarities as the result of 'influence.' Böcklin was simply responding to the same anxieties that many of his contemporaries had about the demise of the artisanal tradition, reacting to new kinds of inspiration that were offered by expanded access to the pre- and postclassical art of the past. While the Nazarenes, Pre-Raphaelites, and Puvis gravitated toward medieval Christian art, Böcklin was most powerfully influenced by Pompeian wall paintings and the Italian baroque. This gave his works their unique—and, according to men and women of the fin de siècle, their uniquely German—flavor.

The other source for Böcklin's peculiar vision of the ancient world was, unquestionably, the contradictions within his own psyche, which lent his pictures their unique and highly variable "moods." The vicissitudes of his own fortune alone might well have made him doubt the liberal philhellenist insistence on Greek balance and happiness. Böcklin was a moody man, torn between his northern patrons and his southern tastes; his life was characterized by the contrast between the repressive Basel business world of his father and the bohemian delights of Italy. He could express grief and longing or revel in nudity, humor, and sensuousness. Quite open in his acknowledgment of the erotic element in human relations, this apparently monogamous father of fourteen celebrated sensual pleasures as part of the natural landscape (as in *Spring* or *Look, the Meadow Smiles*), but he also could portray repression as a kind of tragic sublimity (as in *Odysseus and Calypso*). Böcklin's paintings, Ludwig Justi maintained, "guide one through all the peaks and valleys of life: jubilation and pain, childish romps and pensive old age, sweet love and raw force, incense and wine, music and murder, joyful dance and terrifying loneliness, spring passions and pestilences."[36] A painter of passions, Böcklin defied the liberal-bourgeois code of respectable expres-

35. See ibid., 178–88. Böcklin mentions (184–8) a number of German moderns—Menzel, Piloty, Makart, von Marées, Feuerbach, Dreber, and von Werner—all negatively.
36. Justi, *Arnold Böcklin: Ein Führer*, 22.

sion. Like Nietzsche and Burckhardt, he returned to the ancients the right to experience the full range of human emotions.

As was clear both to his critics of the 1870s and to his fans of the 1890s, Böcklin was no academic neoclassicist. In one (undated) revealing rant, the painter exclaimed: "To be Greeks! Us? Why were the Greeks Greeks? Because they created what they saw, as seemed right to them. (The ancients did not want to make antiquity, as far as I know—only we want to do that.). . . . The fresh water of life is what we want, and that is ever flowing for us, as it was for the Greeks. We will only be Greek when we grasp it in our own way."[37] In many ways, this is what the neohumanists had been saying since Humboldt. For Böcklin, however, 'grasping in our own way' meant abandoning the Winckelmannian, *wissenschaftlich* classicism of the Gymnasium and the plaster cast for a pantheistic arcadia whose existence was (and had always been) primarily psychological, not historical. And quite suddenly, around 1880, for one important sector of the population, this became the antiquity of choice.

The Discrete Charm of Mythological Modernism

If this story so far is one of the artistic genesis of an 'unseasonable' painter, the remainder is a tale of grand success—success that came to Böcklin not as a result of changes in his style but rather as a result of rapid cultural changes occurring rather to the north of his usual haunts. We pick up the story at about 1871, just as Böcklin began to emerge from poverty and obscurity. The years following the foundation of the Wilhelmine empire were happy ones for Germany's middle classes, although, as Peter Gay has recently underlined, the bourgeoisie did not speak with one voice, then or ever.[38] The moneyed elite (*Besitzbürgertum*), for example, had begun to assert its more urbane and utilitarian tastes against those of the educated elite, which nonetheless remained dominant in the bureaucracy, churches, and schools. In the 1870s, painting academies still followed neoclassicist rules: students copied plaster casts of ancient statues and aspired to work in the genre that topped

37. Quoted in Gustav Floerke, *Zehn Jahre mit Böcklin: Aufzeichnungen und Entwürfe* (Munich, 1901), 127.

38. Peter Gay, *Schnitzler's Century: The Making of Middle-Class Culture, 1815–1914* (New York, 2002).

the French Academy's hierarchy, history painting. But even for history painters, ancient and mythological scenes had become rather rare, giving way to more modern—and often specifically Germanic—canvases, like those of Carl Friedrich Lessing and Adolph Menzel. By midcentury, social realism and genre scenes had become very popular, in Germany as in France and Britain. Landscape, reviled by the seventeenth-century French Academy, had attained a new prestige, as was clear in the favorable reception given the pioneering work of Constable, Corot, and Friedrich in Europe, and Alfred Bierstadt and Thomas Cole in America. But as we have seen, in the 1850s and '60s Böcklin's combination of romantic landscape and rococo mythology did not seem to suit almost anyone's taste, not to mention any nation's self-conception. As a result, throughout the 1870s Böcklin remained an eccentric outsider rather than a Germanic genius.[39]

Interestingly, the first Germans to take an interest in Böcklin were bankers, particularly Jewish collectors who were based in Berlin.[40] Evidently, these modern-minded cosmopolitans saw something new in the maverick artist's pantheistic paganism; perhaps their outsider status with respect to the heavily Protestant cultural elite allowed them to appreciate, as others as yet could not, Böcklin's explorations of antiquity's saturnalian psyche. Yet as their admiration grew, an anti-Böcklin claque increasingly emerged as well. In the 1870s, cultural conservatives ridiculed what one called Böcklin's "truly shameless use of color" and his juxtaposition of "imaginary conception" and "hyper-realistic representation." The classically-schooled criticized the painter for departing from literary sources. The liberal-era elite were, after all, learning from scholars like Theodor Mommsen to appreciate a Roman Empire "where the wind blows and bad weather dominates, and which reminds one of today's prosaic national economy."[41] Where, they asked, did the ancients record a battle of centaurs? As Lutz Tittel has shown, these devotees of neoclassicism thought Böcklin's work 'bizarre' and overly concerned

---

39. In the Basel catalog, Thomas Gaehtgens has shown that the French did not think of Böcklin as 'German' in this period—or in the prewar era either. Thomas W. Gaehtgens, "Böcklin and Frankreich," in *Arnold Böcklin*, 89, 101–3.

40. Angelika Wesenberg, "Böcklin und die Reichshauptstadt," in *Arnold Böcklin*, 76.

41. In the hands of midcentury scholars like Ernst Curtius, ancient Greece remained much more highly aestheticized, but equally distant from Böcklin's vision. See Hermann Grimm, "E. Curtius über Kunstmuseen," *Preussische Jahrbücher* 25 (1869): 616.

with being different.[42] Nor were the painter's imaginary animals acceptable to a culture steeped in positivistic natural science. Vexed by Böcklin's rendering of mythological beasts, Berlin professor of natural history Emil Dubois-Reymond proved that the artist's sea creatures were anatomically impossible.[43] Though by the mid-1870s Böcklin had developed his mature style and had found a small following, the *Bildungsbürgertum* was not yet ready for his brand of neoromantic classicism.

Few if any of his admirers described Böcklin as a 'German' painter in the years just after unification (the painter in fact resettled in Florence in 1875); nonetheless, he had achieved enough notoriety to attract the attention of Max Jordan, director of the soon-to-open National Gallery in Berlin. Partial to Italian Renaissance and German romantic art, Jordan evidently hoped that Böcklin would marry the two styles successfully, and commissioned a work from him for the new institution. But when the Swiss painter delivered the second version of his *Triton and Nereid* in 1875, Jordan rejected it, telling the cultural minister, "His image has an unmistakable parodistic quality, and has resulted in the emancipation of ugliness, a tendency which frequently disfigures Böcklin's—always in their way interesting—images."[44] In 1876, Empress Augusta rejected Böcklin's bathetic *Lamentation beneath the Cross* (the nude, plastic Christ's eyes are open, while the two Marys evince unconvincing gestures of grief), and Böcklin himself remained unsatisfied with his new *Pieta* sketches. He offered to try a new *Triton* with more mythical mystique and less parody, but the regional art commission asked for a different subject, a landscape with many figures—perhaps hoping to keep Eros and Thanatos at bay.[45] Böcklin finally produced an image that was dubbed by Jordan *The Elysian Fields,* a dreamscape in which a faun carries a woman across a stream to a Poussinian garden party. The image was attacked as

---

42. Comments from reviews for the *Zeitschrift für bildende Kunst* (1873 and 1872 respectively) quoted in Lutz Tittel, "Die Beurteilung Arnold Böcklins in der Zeitschrift für bildende Kunst von 1866 bis 1901," in *Arnold Böcklin, 1827–1901: Gemälde, Zeichnungen, Plastiken* (exhibition catalog, Basel, 1977), 125, 124.

43. Kenworth Moffett, *Meier-Graefe as Art Critic* (Munich, 1973), 53; Linnebach, *Böcklin und die Antike,* 56.

44. Quoted in Wesenberg, "Böcklin und die Reichshauptstadt," 78.

45. Justi, *Arnold Böcklin: Ein Führer,* 17; Wesenberg, "Böcklin und die Reichshauptstadt," 78–81.

unintelligible, base, and sensational, and Wilhelm I was forced to promise not to buy any more of Böcklin's pictures.[46]

In 1880, the Catholic nationalist August Reichensperger blasted Böcklin in the Reichstag, insisting that the painter's pagan scenes, unlike real Greek and Roman nudes, exerted a deleterious effect on modern morals—and especially on women—to the detriment of German *Geist* and German identity.[47] But Reichensperger would be one of the last cultural conservatives to denounce Böcklin in this way. Soon after 1880, conservatives, as well as members of the avant-garde, began lauding the Swiss painter for precisely the sort of non-Winckelmannian penchants the previous generation had abhorred. One critic summed up this new rhetoric nicely: "Born in a world which groans under the weight of suffocating [*zudrängender*] tradition, in a world of excavations and museums, where almost every creative drive is smothered by imitation and insensitivity, [Böcklin] remains untouched. The dreary medium of knowledge seems not to obscure his eye. It is as if this man has arisen directly from the original splendor of the elements, from a paradise in which men and animals live together in brotherhood and harmony, where they understand one another and men are free of arrogance."[48]

What gave Böcklin's antiquity this primeval new vitality is a question that requires much more research, but some reflections are in order. It is surely the case that by the fin de siècle, the proponents of 'modern' education had convinced a broad section of the population—one which included the emperor himself—that neohumanist, elitist *Bildung* was no longer the appropriate sort of education for German students. Even within the *Bildungsbürgertum,* the younger generation (those whose formative experiences occurred after the founding of the Reich in 1871) now began to call for new life to be breathed into German culture, attacking the 'dry as dust' philological positivism of their fathers. Once the need for reform was recognized, plans for remaking German culture proliferated. Of course, as 'Germany' was a brand-new creation, the question of what 'German culture' actually was remained terrifically fraught. Each of the individual states had its own cultural

46. Moffett, *Meier-Graefe as Art Critic,* 52.

47. Andrea Linnebach, "Antike und Gegenwart: Zu Böcklins mythologischer Bilderwelt," in *Arnold Böcklin, Giorgio di Chirico, Max Ernst,* ed. Magnaguagno and Steiner, 196; Wesenberg, "Böcklin und die Reichshauptstadt," 82.

48. Neumann,"Zu Arnold Böcklin's siebzigstem Geburtstag," 5.

institutions and traditions; trying to fuse them all into one 'culture' without destroying some of them was an impossibility from the outset. Moreover, this quest was going on at the same time as all of Europe was experiencing what should be seen as a democratizing revolution in the cultural sphere. Not only were newspapers and magazines proliferating at a fantastic rate; booksellers and publishers also were multiplying and rapidly diversifying their wares. Travel, popular theater, sports, and museum-going all became more commonplace experiences, thanks to increased leisure time and swifter means of transport. The circulation of photographs and the advent of film further fragmented the cultural scene. Avant-gardes evolved and subdivided, and conservative cultural critics strove to force myriad genies back into antiquated bottles. In this atmosphere, longing for 'cultural unification' was deep and regularly expressed, but rarely (if ever) achieved; certainly there was no consensus in the world of artistic practice. The proliferation of galleries, patrons, associations, secessions, exhibitions, and publications made it possible for numerous artistic 'flowers' to bloom—and for numerous half-appreciated artists to cultivate grudges and/or bohemian sensibilities. This rich world of possibilities might have been experienced as exhilarating and, for some people, perhaps it was. But by and large, contemporary literary accounts testify to anxiety in the face of too much diversity. A 'styleless' age, it was agreed, could not be a great one; it could not unite national talent. In such a state of disunity, Germans could hardly hope to rival French and Italian painting—something, many felt, the nation already famous for its poetry, philosophy, science, and music should now attempt to do.

This anxiety about style was particularly rife among the *Bildungsbürger*, who were accustomed to being Central Europe's cultural providers; they were loath to give up the privileged task they had wrested from the aristocracy in the eighteenth century. This is the sociocultural context in which to understand Germans' adoption of Böcklin as a national hero: not as a simple reaction against modernization, but as the attempt of one sector of the classically-educated elite to substitute *their* form of modernism for what was being offered by the antihistorical impressionists or, worse, the socially critical naturalists. Böcklin was not the most conservative choice that could have been made, institutionally or intellectually; that was Anton von Werner, longtime director of the Berlin Academy, member of the Prussian state art commission, president of the Association of Berlin Artists, and favorite painter of Wilhelm II. Böcklin's fans were not of this type. Rather, they were men like the poet Stefan George or the painter Gustav Floerke (who came to study with Böcklin in 1881), men who did attend the classical Gymnasien, only to emerge as critics of the desiccation of the neohumanist tradition. "The aesthetic dogmas and presuppositions of our fathers," Floerke recalled, "were transmitted to us in flesh and blood, and after generations, they still shape our popular books and our Gymnasium teachers. Those who have used them to enjoy [life] or shape themselves are few." In contrast, he wrote, Böcklin's art was "sensuous, immediate, not abstract, intellectual, [the kind that] is devious in its effects."[49] Böcklin, claimed Julius Langbehn in his hugely popular *Rembrandt als Erzieher* (*Rembrandt as Educator*), was one of the few living artists to have escaped the "anal historicism" of archaeological fetishism and accepted Winckelmann's obsolescence.[50] For these cultivated young men, reared in a world in which industrial, commercial, and practical knowledge threatened to destroy the prestige of humanistic *Bildung*, it was imperative to preserve the status of their own group and the grand cultural traditions that had been entrusted to it, the most important of which was the classical one. But they were unable and unwilling to return to the comfortable conventions of academic neoclassicism, especially since professionalization and historicization seemed to be destroying the creative power of Greek culture. Feeling repressed and confined by the banal pleasantries and narrowly focused scholarship of the midcentury, they concluded that antiquity had either to take on a new vitality or be consigned to the dustbin.[51]

Without the intervention of Böcklin, the dustbin perhaps would have triumphed—but the simultaneous growing appeal of Bachofen's *Mother Right* and Nietzsche's *Birth of Tragedy*, the appearance of George's *Algabal* and Richard Strauss's *Elektra*, and the launching of new attempts to universalize classical experience (J. G. Frazer's *Golden Bough*, Freud's Oedipus

49. Floerke, *Zehn Jahre mit Böcklin*, 194, 106.

50. [Julius Langbehn], *Rembrandt als Erzieher*, 39th ed. (Leipzig, 1891), 30–5.

51. There are strong parallels here with a revolt going on within the realm of classical scholarship itself. See Suzanne Marchand, "From Liberalism to Neoromanticism: Albrecht Dieterich, Richard Reitzenstein, and the Religious Turn in Fin-de-Siècle German Classical Studies," in *Out of Arcadia: Classics and Politics in Germany in the Age of Burckhardt, Nietzsche, and Wilamowitz*, ed. Ingo Gildenhard and Martin Ruehl (London, 2003), 129–60.

complex, C. G. Jung's studies of Mithraism) all suggest that the new generation was eager to rekindle the classical tradition's fires, supplying it a torch
to carry into battle with a materialist and insufficiently heroic present. What
Böcklin provided was the equivalent in oils to what others were producing
in scholarship, music, and poetry: a subjective and psychological understanding of antiquity. His popularity was also bolstered by the fact that many
of his canvases belonged to what one commentator called the *"antike Nied-
ergangsstimmungssphäre* (the realm of ancient feelings of decline),"[52] for by
the 1890s the lament for the passing of paganism had become a familiar
topos. The sense of loss and longing—conveyed so poignantly across the English Channel by Walter Pater—was echoed by Böcklin in paintings like *Heracles' Tomb* and *Villa by the Sea,* about which Henriette Mendelssohn wrote
in 1901: "To us . . . the image has become a great elegy for the disappearance
of ancient splendor. In the waves, which strike the shore with ritual force,
the swan song of a great past resounds."[53] But the loss was not irreparable,
Böcklin taught; repeatedly, in poems dedicated to the aging painter, he was
credited with giving new life to an arcadian world that had nearly disappeared.[54] "You, alone," wrote Stefan George, "have prevented . . . this cold
age's extinguishing of the holy fire."[55] The power of Böcklin's pagan-pastoral
vision had liberated the ancients from the fetters of historicizing, philological classicism and had given German art an entrancing new authenticity.
Böcklin, the great Pan of painting, permitted his viewers to break with the
past and yet resist the unedifying and superficial culture of the present. They
could be mourners and modernizers all at once.

Though they praised him to the skies, the intellectuals of the fin de siècle
often admitted that they did not entirely understand Böcklin; it was difficult,
many confessed, to find the key to what one 1895 commentator described
as the "secret magical garden of this painter-mystic."[56] Yet what would have
been, for Böcklin's admired Renaissance greats as for nineteenth-century
neoclassicists, disaster—namely, the failure of the painter to communicate

52. Meissner, *Böcklin,* 39.
53. Quoted in Linnebach, *Böcklin und die Antike,* 132.
54. See, e.g., Schack's poem, quoted in Nikolaus Meier, "Böcklin-Gesänge," in *Arnold Böcklin, 1827–1901,* 134.
55. George quoted in ibid., 142.
56. Quoted (in another context) in Tittel, "Die Beurteilung Arnold Böcklins," 123.

his vision clearly—was now fully acceptable, indeed part of the "life" with which he infused his art. Unlike the critics of the 1870s, the viewers of the 1890s did not want to be able to identify the literary sources or exact archaeological provenance of Böcklin's scenes; his mythological figures did not need to tell a recognizable story.[57] The vitality of the vision, its ability to speak to the spectator's psyche, was more important than the viewer's ability to recognize and 'read' a traditional tale. It is not clear why Böcklin himself broke away from the literary tradition. Perhaps he simply did not think that texts should constrain the painter's vision, any more than that vision should constrain the audience's appreciation of a work of art. If some saw Iphigenia in the mourning woman in *Villa by the Sea,* the painter approved: "That is perfectly fine; everyone should think of the image in the way it speaks to him. It is not necessary that this is exactly the same as what the painter conceived. I did not think of Iphigenia in [creating] the image."[58] It was surely this sort of radical personalizing of mythological scenes that made it possible for Freud to articulate his Oedipus complex as an aspect of universal experience, and for Eugene O'Neill, several decades later, to write his own *Mourning Becomes Electra.*

By the early 1890s, then, Böcklin had an intense and expanding audience for his art. The French symbolists were enthusiastic; his German-speaking imitators—including Franz von Stuck, Max Klinger, and August Macke—were enthralled. For a brief time, he enjoyed both the endorsement of avant-garde critics like Julius Meier Graefe and great popularity among the more Germanophile *Bildungsbürger.* Three major retrospectives were held in 1897 in honor of his seventieth birthday; the Berlin exhibition drew sixty thousand visitors in one day. In Munich, a celebratory dinner attracted so many fans from so many walks of life that the card room of the royal Hofbräuhaus could hardly hold them.[59] Reproductions of his work circulated widely and were easy to obtain; *The Isle of the Dead,* it is said, hung in every bourgeois living room and had made the island of Pondiconissi (the so-called 'false' model for the painting) something of a tourist attraction already by the turn

57. Böcklin himself once argued that paintings do have something to tell, but not necessarily a story. Floerke, *Zehn Jahre mit Böcklin,* 69.

58. Runkel and Böcklin, *Neben meiner Kunst,* 144.

59. Beth Irwin Lewis, "Kunst für Alle: Das Volk als Förderer der Kunst," in *Sammler, Stifter, und Museen,* ed. Mai and Paret, 190.

of the century.[60] His paintings now sold for an average of sixteen thousand marks, four times what he had commanded in the '70s and early '80s.[61] When one of Freud's patrons hinted that a Böcklin might be secured for the Modern Gallery in Vienna, the Austrian minister of culture moved quickly to promote the psychoanalyst to a university professorship.[62] The Swiss artist became a household name, even a household necessity—and, increasingly, the man upon whom Germanophile commentators pinned their hopes for the development of a truly German modern style.

Arnold Böcklin, German Hero

The process by which this Swiss-Italian semimodernist became the iconic German painter, his name coupled with the other two great heroes of the modern-minded, fin-de-siècle *Bildungsbürgertum*, Friedrich Nietzsche and Richard Wagner, is rather complicated. It should be noted that the painter himself was no passionate Germanophile, either before or after 1890.[63] As we have seen, he revolted early against the conventions and expectations of bourgeois Basel. He married an Italian woman and apparently spoke Italian at home for the rest of his life; the couple lived in Germany as infrequently as possible. Although he perpetually looked to Germany for his market, he felt he had been swindled by German dealers and treated shabbily by Basel society, and he disliked Berlin almost as much as he disliked Paris. It has proved impossible to read into his *Battle of the Centaurs* a hurrah for Germany's victory in the Franco-Prussian war; nor can his post-1890 apocalyptic paintings *War* and *Plague*, as Andrea Linnebach notes, be seen as positive reflections on Germany's rise to world power.[64] His French symbolist fans

60. Zelger, *Arnold Böcklin: Die Toteninsel,* 54; Gerd Roos, "Giorgio di Chirico und der lange Schatten von Arnold Böcklin," in *Reise ins Ungewisse,* ed. Magnaguagno and Steiner, 208–9.

61. Robin Lenman, *Artists and Society in Germany, 1850–1914* (Manchester, 1997), 162.

62. Schorske, *Fin-de-Siècle Vienna,* 245.

63. Georg Schmidt described him as a fan of Bismarck, while Norbert Schneider called him an 'enlightened republican.' Schmidt, "Böcklin heute," 55, 57; Schneider, "Böcklins 'Toteninsel': Zur ikonologischen und sozialpsychologischen Deutung eines Motivs," in *A. Böcklin, 1827–1901* (exhibition catalog, Darmstadt, 1977), 116–7.

64. Linnebach, *Böcklin und die Antike,* 138–44.

never viewed him as a nationalist painter,[65] and even many conservative contemporaries doubted his Germanness. For lovers of military realism, like Anton von Werner and Kaiser Wilhelm II, Böcklin was just as foreign and as repulsively modernist as Monet. "Nature doesn't look like that," Wilhelm apparently jeered.[66]

But Böcklin did clearly prefer German styles to French ones. Of impressionism's claim to represent the world as the eye really sees it, he scoffed: "My houseboy 'sees' too."[67] He disliked France and the French; for a man of his generation, he traveled remarkably little beyond the triangle linking Italy, Switzerland, and southern Germany. But even though he loved the Italian countryside, Böcklin could not conceive himself as an Italian; he wanted a German education for his children and apparently formed few friendships with Italian nationals. As Gustav Floerke claimed, perhaps rather rashly, "He believed that with Italians—without exception [presumably including his own wife]—one could, at best, have the same sort of relationship one has with a lovely pet."[68] His circle of students and friends—including Franz von Lenbach, Anselm Feuerbach, and Gottfried Keller—were all German-speakers. Thus, Böcklin was not entirely resistant to Germanization. He belonged to the school of cultural pessimists who saw more creative potential in German *Kultur* than in any other national or international tradition.

But Böcklin's adoption as a German hero had nothing whatever to do with his own attitudes or initiatives; rather, this process was driven by the search for a German 'modern' style and with battles over the reception of impressionism in the later Wilhelmine cultural world.[69] By the mid-1890s, German attacks on impressionism had become habitual; in them, commentators voiced resentment of France's presumption that its artists alone defined 'modern' art, revulsion at impressionism's 'unartistic' subject matter (e.g., cities or railroads), and disdain for the style's scientific pretensions. As Peter Paret has described, polemics grew increasingly fierce after the appointment of Hugo von Tschudi to the directorship of the National Gallery

65. See Gaehtgens, "Böcklin and Frankreich," 89–111.

66. Report on the Kaiser's visit to the National Gallery in 1899 quoted in Bartmann, *Anton von Werner*, 217.

67. Böcklin quoted in Floerke, *Zehn Jahre mit Böcklin*, 115.

68. Ibid., 10.

69. Paret, *Berlin Secession*, 172.

in Berlin in 1896. A Renaissance specialist, soon after his appointment Tschudi (who was, incidentally, Swiss) became enamored of French impressionist painting and tried to collect more of it; as director of the only Prussian state museum that collected 'modern' (nineteenth-century) art, he thought it necessary to expose Germans to a wide range of contemporary artistic styles. Yet Wilhelm II, whose idea of good artistic taste was the bathetic double row of Hohenzollern sculptural portraits known as the *Siegesallee*, insistently opposed the intrusion of 'foreign' and 'tasteless' art into a museum he believed should be devoted exclusively to good, solid, German art. Tschudi would finally be forced out in 1908, but not until a grand debate had been joined over what sort of art would improve the German soul and guide German painters down the correct creative path.[70] There were at least three sides in this debate: the conservatives, including Wilhelm II and Anton von Werner, who argued for a return to patriotic, academic realism; the cosmopolitans, including Tschudi, Julius Meier-Graefe, and some of the great secessionist painters of the day (such as Max Liebermann and Lovis Corinth), who were fans of French modern art; and a group I will call the nationalist modernizers. It was this last group that championed Böcklin—especially after Meier Graefe launched an attack on the painter in 1905, causing his popularity among members of the avant-garde to plummet. Thereafter, Böcklin was left almost exclusively to the not-so-tender mercies of his Germanophile fans.

As we have seen, Böcklin's rise to late Wilhelmine fame and fortune occurred precisely in the period in which competition over the definition of 'the modern' and 'the German' was reaching its zenith. For a time, it was possible to believe he represented both. In the context of the Tschudi debates, however, Böcklin's Germanic resonances began to supersede his modern ones. Already in 1898, he had been called the "most German painter of our century"; his art, it was said, seemed "to be born from the soul of our Volk."[71] He was compared repeatedly to Richard Wagner—and also, very often, to that other German cultural prophet, Winckelmann.[72] The question

---

70. For Paret's most recent treatment of these events, see his chapter on "The Tschudi Affair" in *German Encounters with Modernism*, 92–118.

71. Friedrich Haack quoted in Paret, *Berlin Secession*, 53–4.

72. For more examples, see Moffett, *Meier-Graefe as Art Critic*, 52–60.

of his actual birthplace (and domicile) could be deflected by insisting, as Gustav Floerke did, on his "unquestionably Germanic [alemannischer] skull."[73] Naturally, in the context of the debates over impressionism, Böcklin's Germanness was not simply invoked by patriots to embellish the nation's artistic legacy; for sympathetic critics, most of whom were looking for an alternative modern art rather than rejecting modernism out of hand, he became a means to establish the nation's cultural autonomy, its modernity, and, if possible, its primacy. "Whatever Böcklin touched," wrote the influential critic Ferdinand Avenarius in a 1901 elegy for the painter, "became spiritual. Art in this sense, northern, Germanic art, is all that he created. No matter how many ideas he took from the south, even ideas concerning subject matter, he took them as a conqueror who seeks to expand Germany's possessions. If our art is to endure the fight with foreign powers, with foreigners both inside and outside our borders, it will nowhere find a weapon stronger than Böcklin's immortal work."[74] Here, the colonizing ambitions and rivalries of Wilhelmine *Weltpolitik* were mapped onto the struggle to define an independent national style, and Böcklin's paintings had become the weapons with which to fight—internally and externally—a cultural war.

One of the major ways in which Böcklin was said to demonstrate his 'Germanness,' not surprisingly, was in his unique ability to reanimate the world of the Greeks. Henry Thode said of Böcklin's work: "The covenant is fulfilled: the Germanic and the Greek have united."[75] Franz Hermann Meissner's popular biography of the painter (1898) introduced his subject with a long disquisition on Germany's exceptional ability to reconjure the magic of Greek antiquity and the "instinctive drive of the race's blood" toward the mythical.[76] Böcklin had revitalized an essential national-cultural tradition by stripping it of its pedantry, Meissner exulted. Rather than reading books, Böcklin wandered through the streets and houses of the Pompeian necropolis, experiencing the völkisch life-pulse that coursed beneath the "cold marmoreal statuary of official ancient classicism." Haunted by Roman ghosts

73. Floerke, *Zehn Jahre mit Böcklin*, 10.
74. Avenarius quoted in Paret, *Berlin Secession*, 172.
75. Thode quoted in Linnebach, *Böcklin und die Antike*, 53.
76. Meissner, *Böcklin*, 10–4 (quote, 14).

and reveling in Goethe's spiritual surroundings, Böcklin, Meissner concluded, became a 'modern Greek' during his years in Weimar and now represented the reincarnation of Faust's marriage with Helen of Troy.[77]

By the time this process of Germanization shifted into high gear, Böcklin himself was ailing, though still producing. We do not know what he thought of these patriotic tributes, but he probably disliked them; he refused even to attend the exhibition and seventieth-birthday festivities held in his honor in Basel. Had he paid careful attention to his fans, Böcklin surely would have noticed a peculiarity in his post-1895 reception. This was the increasing emphasis put on his 'serious' pictures. While they constitute the larger share of his work, by no means did they entirely reflect his world view, the humorous side of which can be seen in paintings like *Sleeping Diana Watched by Two Fauns* and *Playing in the Waves* (see Figures 8 and 10). His later admirers, it seems, strongly preferred his pessimistic pictures to his pastoral landscapes and comic scenes; only the former seemed worthy of counting as truly 'German' modern art. We have already noted the enormous popularity of *The Isle of the Dead*—a print of which hung in Georges Clemenceau's dining room; second most popular was probably *Holy Sanctuary,* which Thomas Mann exhibited over his writing desk—to draw his mind away from banal, bourgeois concerns.[78] When Avenarius produced a Böcklin-Mappe in 1901, it contained framable copies of these two images as well as *Silence of the Forest,* one of the painter's few Germanicizing paintings; it also included copies of *Maria Tending the Corpse of the Savior* (a histrionic picture disliked by Burckhardt) and two now little-discussed images, *The Attack* and *Poetry and Painting.*[79] For Avenarius, these paintings—not the light-hearted or erotic ones—represented Böcklin's best work. And it was exactly patriotic critics like Avenarius and the Heidelberg art historian Henry Thode, seeking to promote German modernism, who unintentionally gave the Swiss-Italian painter a reputation for Germanic chauvinism and bathetic seriousness. Though a few—most notably Giorgio di Chirico—were still able to recover a parodistic and playful Böcklin, his long-term reputation was greatly damaged by the post-1895 emphasis on his most melancholy canvases.

77. Ibid., 48, 114–5.
78. Linnebach, *Böcklin und die Antike,* 100.
79. Gerd Roos, "Giorgio di Chirico," 206–7.

This process of patriotic domestication surely diminished Böcklin's status as a 'modernist.' But even more important was Meier Graefe's *The Case of Böcklin (Der Fall Böcklin)* of 1905, a vituperative attack on the artist by Germany's best-known art critic and champion of modern art. The title of the book was apt, for just as Friedrich Nietzsche had renounced his early admiration for Wagner in *Der Fall Wagner* (1888), Meier Graefe rescinded his earlier appreciation for Böcklin—and accused the painter of many of the same sins Wagner had purportedly committed. The painter, Meier Graefe argued, was not only a superficial dilettante with an inexcusably wide and fanatical circle of followers: he was a danger to German *Kultur* as a whole. For Meier Graefe, Böcklin was a personality, not an artist. After 1860, his work had become anachronistic and illogical, ignoring the rules of painting in favor of a stupid, self-interested individualism. His bizarre colorations and figural placements made the inessential parts of a painting seem central; in striving for effect, he destroyed the unity of the image to such an extent that Meier Graefe was willing to concede him merely the status of a mosaicist, not that of a painter. "Böcklin's evolution is like that of the impatience of a pianist, who pounds the keys harder and harder, the more incorrectly he plays," he fulminated.[80] Moreover, the critic lamented, the cheap tricks of this 'barbarian' had worked so well that his art was obscuring all memory of the greatness of the European artistic tradition. Böcklin was the product of "our styleless age," in which all philosophical systems lay in ruins and individual freedom had triumphed to the detriment of cultural development.[81] If this decadent cult were not eradicated, Meier Graefe warned, Germany's potential cultural greatness would never be realized.

Meier Graefe's long polemic incited a bitter debate and inspired the publication of dozens of discussions of 'l'affaire Böcklin.' The Wagnerian Thode responded with eight public lectures on recent German painting, in which he attacked proponents of internationalism in art and identified a Berlin conspiracy which—for financial and ideological reasons—was attempting to foist 'un-German' impressionism on Germany.[82] Max Liebermann issued an

80. Alfred Julius Meier Graefe, *Der Fall Böcklin und die Lehre von den Einheiten* (Stuttgart, 1905), 78.

81. Ibid., 86, 248, 109–10.

82. Paret, *Berlin Secession,* 174–6.

angry reply to Thode, but there was no convincing the nationalist professor (who had married Wagner's daughter and who wrote regularly for the *Bayreuther Blätter*) that Böcklin was not the avatar of German modernism. Polemics continued for some years, but gradually left Böcklin behind; debates among connoisseurs increasingly focused on the technically more experimental expressionists. Younger German artists began to look elsewhere. By the spring of 1907, for example, August Macke had wholly abandoned his passion for Böcklin's paintings and could hardly believe he had loved them so much: "The images all seem to me so pathetic, so affected and bright, I can't look at them anymore." He now preferred Japanese woodcuts or the paintings of Manet, who, he wrote, "himself possessed so much poetry that he didn't need to make women into Naiads, his unpretentious and simple soul didn't need any symbols to paint the sea."[83] But for the German petit bourgeois, Böcklin's work continued to serve as a sort of 'pillars of Hercules' beyond which modern taste could not go. It is not accidental that Hitler and Goebbels regarded Böcklin as a great German artist, while Emil Nolde (a Nazi sympathizer), Macke (who died at the front in 1914), and of course Max Liebermann counted as 'decadent.'

Böcklin was not a decadent painter, either in terms of subject matter or technique. He did not evolve in the direction of abstraction, as did Gustav Moreau, Ferdinand Khnopff, or Gustav Klimt; nor do his canvases display the violent sexuality or antibourgeois blasphemy exemplified by Félicien Rops, Max Klinger, or Franz von Stuck. His decorative tendencies did inspire secessionist pioneers, but he himself did not 'secede.' He attempted to revitalize mythological landscapes, but he did not—in contrast to Max Ernst (born in 1891)—seek self-consciously "to become a magician and find the myth of his time."[84] Like the figure of Titian in the short play Hugo von Hofmannsthal revised for Böcklin's funeral, the artist was engaged primarily in the craft of producing paintings rather than the cerebral sport so despised by the vitalists—philosophical criticism.[85] He was fundamentally a respect-

83. Macke quoted in Elisabeth Erdmann-Macke, *Erinnerung an August Macke* (Stuttgart, 1962), 269, 270.

84. Ernst quoted in M. E. Warlick, *Max Ernst and Alchemy: A Magician in Search of Myth* (Austin, Tex., 2001), 34.

85. Hofmannsthal added a new preface to this play (originally written in 1892) so that it could be performed as part of the funerary rites for Böcklin in 1901. See "Der Tod des Tizian: Ein dramatisches Fragment," in *Hugo von Hofmannsthal, Sämtliche Werke III*, ed.

able, if playful, nineteenth-century pagan, a modernist who could not leave *Museumskultur* entirely behind. He may not have been a German painter, but neither could he speak the language of international modernism. Although considered a forerunner of the symbolists, it is by no means clear that his images perform a kind of synaesthesia; as Andrea Gottdang has argued, he used open mouths and harps simply to make ancient experience more immediate to modern viewers.[86] It appears that Böcklin was aware of the pervasive fin-de-siècle problem of the inability of language to communicate clear meanings. But unlike T. S. Eliot (for example), he did believe that mermaids—and paintings of mermaids—could sing to us, as long as we agree to look for meaning at an emotional and instinctive level, not at the level of consciously-articulated ideas.

Böcklin, then, was not quite a modernist—but his own, rather naïve revolt against neoclassicism undoubtedly set the scene for modernism and offered one important road into the (non-French) open. Using conventional terminology, his work is best characterized as transitional, linking late romanticism to early forms of modernism. He did not make the full break from history, tradition, and meaning as did the artists of the next generation—but can we be sure that his innovations were less important than those of the modernist painters who—as many of them admitted—had once stood on his shoulders? Unlike most of these card-carrying 'modernists,' Böcklin had a keen popular following, some of whom did him the disservice of stripping away his comedic, ironic side and suppressing his cosmopolitanism—just as was the case with his fellow Baseler Friedrich Nietzsche. We should not, in my view, dismiss Böcklin's popular, transitional art as merely a 'not yet' or worse, as 'kitsch.' Instead, his story may help us appreciate not only the hesitations and choices taken in the journey toward artistic modernism—the points at which travel speeds up and baggage must be thrown off the train—but also the creative power of the premodern generation, of long neglected figures like Adolph Menzel and Hans Makart.[87] Reclaiming this

---

Götz Eberhard Hübner, Klaus-Gerhard Pott, and Christoph Michel (Frankfurt, 1982), 221–35.

86. Andrea Gottdang, " 'Man muss sie singen hören': Bemerkung zur 'Musikalität' und 'Hörbarkeit' von Böcklins Bildern," in *Arnold Böcklin*, 131–7.

87. Paret makes this important point in two different ways in *German Encounters with Modernism*, 7–44, 119–32.

transitional moment may also serve to remind us of the long-lasting power that classical antiquity exerted over the European imagination. Having now lost the thread of the classical tradition, we may not be able to recognize the modernness of Böcklin's artistic vocabulary or appreciate the Dionysian transports to which his paintings gave rise. But we may yet conclude that the landscapes in which Böcklin's fauns and nymphs frolicked have much to tell us about the process by which 'German' art became modern and even the most ardent admirers of the classical world left the long tradition of *ut pictura poesis* behind.

Stefan George and Androgyny

ROBERT E. NORTON

Before Stefan George (1868–1933) became, in the last fifteen years of his life, a prophet and sage to an ever-growing number of Germans, before he had assumed the place of master and guide to a diverse group of talented intellectuals—philosophers, historians, artists, and poets—before he had even made a name for himself as one of the finest German-speaking poets of his day, he had already begun to regard poetry as an instrument of extraordinary, perhaps even singular, power. True poetry, the young George already believed, provided the blueprint for what would come later in reality. Poetry foretold, because it was the source for, what was to come. It literally engendered the future. Yet what is perhaps most remarkable is that George formulated this conception of poetry at the very moment his faith in it, and himself, was being challenged.

Ever since he had been to Paris in the summer of 1889, where the twenty-one-year-old Étienne George, as he was known then, met Stéphane Mallarmé and became acquainted with symbolist poetry, Stefan George—as he was henceforth known, partly in homage to his Parisian mentor—struggled with one of symbolism's central paradoxes: how to conquer nature in and through the poetic word and yet not to fall prey to sterility and thus death, or its poetic equivalent, silence. The figure of the androgyne or hermaphrodite, which was seen as representing both an affront to nature and a way to overcome its demands, seemed to offer a means to prevail over nature in both the poetic and personal spheres. What follows is a discussion of George's most sustained exploration of this possibility—and his realization of the failure of the androgyne to deliver what it appeared to promise—in his third book of poetry, which he published in 1892.

In the winter of the previous year, George had revealed to Hugo von Hofmannsthal that he was worried he did not know what to write "after

Halgabal."[1] *Algabal,* as the book was eventually called, does indeed have the feel of a conclusion, an absolute end, or at least as if some extreme limit had been reached. It is in its entirety an astonishing work, unprecedented in George's career and the first one that achieved a formal level that can be measured against his best verse. But Algabal is most remarkable not so much for what it positively says as for what it indirectly implies. Much later, when he no longer needed his former French friends and allies and could thus afford to forsake them, George himself said of that time, "In France I found people with whom I could live and whom I could like. Of course, they did not understand my true nature. Many think that there is only something artistic in my first books, not the will toward a new humanity. Totally wrong! *Algabal* is a revolutionary book."[2]

George left it to others to figure out what he meant by "revolutionary," but *Algabal* has always made people feel slightly uneasy. This was especially true of his later adherents, the members of his "circle," who were more than a little concerned that it might give his readers the wrong idea. Friedrich Gundolf, one of George's most gifted and most devoted followers, expended a good deal of energy insisting on what George was *not* doing in the book. "Neither the exotic nor the abnormal," Gundolf assured his readers in 1920, "neither vice nor riddle, neither psychology nor history attracted him"[3] in writing it. Similarly, George's appointed biographer, Friedrich Wolters, announced categorically a decade later that "*Algabal* has nothing of the unmistakable Parisian perfume of the Baudelaire poems, nothing of the particular odor of French decay." Wolters declared outright that "whether the historical image of the late Roman Emperor Elagabalus corresponds more or less, or not at all, to the poet's created symbol is of no importance."[4] Saying what George *was* up to in the book, however, proved to be rather more difficult. Gundolf and Wolters, as well as many others, largely took refuge in the safety of abstraction, providing generalizations about the book's aims and at best one-sided commentary on individual poems. In the face of their bullying

1. Stefan George and Hugo von Hofmannsthal, *Briefwechsel zwischen George und Hofmannsthal,* ed. Robert Boehringer (Munich, 1953), 12.

2. Ernst Robert Curtius, *Kritische Essays zur europäischen Literatur* (Bern, 1954), 112.

3. Friedrich Gundolf, *George* (Berlin, 1920), 80.

4. Friedrich Wolters, *Stefan George und die Blätter für die Kunst. Deutsche Geistesgeschichte seit 1890* (Berlin, 1930), 40, 38.

assertions, which were calculated to stifle and silence anyone impudent enough to object, an "official," sanitized, dehistoricized view of the book long prevailed. As a result, *Algabal* was often shorn of its real significance, both in terms of its historical and literary origins as well as its larger meaning for George's life.

Seen from a certain perspective, the fears of George's followers appear to have been wholly justified. *Algabal*'s subject matter tends to raise some questions—and not a few eyebrows even today. It was inspired by the life of the late Roman emperor Elagabalus, who assumed power in AD 218 at the tender age of fourteen and who was violently deposed and murdered only four years later. Elagabalus, or Heliogabalus as he was also known, is sometimes mentioned in the same breath with other, more famous Roman rulers such as Tiberius, Caligula, and Nero, who all presided over years of spectacular debauchery and inventive cruelty. But Elagabalus seems to have surpassed even these notorious reprobates in both the extent and sheer imaginativeness of his crimes. Elagabalus was in fact considered so detestable that after his assassination his body was mutilated and contemptuously tossed into the Tiber, all trace of his reign was expunged from senate records, and public monuments bearing his name were defaced or completely destroyed. The three main sources of information about the emperor—Cassius Dio, Herodian, and Lampridius—all vilify him, outdoing one another in painting a picture of unrelieved infamy and bestiality. Admittedly, each of these historians either had an ax to grind or interests to protect, or was simply motivated by the desire to curry favor with the reigning emperor by placing one of his predecessors in an unflattering light. But whatever George's own view of the reliability of these sources, he assiduously studied their works, and it was against their lurid and scabrous backdrop that he raised his own *Algabal*.

The salient details of Elagabalus's life are quickly told. Born in the Syrian city of Emesa in AD 204, raised by his mother and grandmother, he took his name from the sun god he had learned to worship there as a boy; once in Rome his Oriental name was modified to Invictus (or Deus) Sol Elagabalus. He was proclaimed emperor while still in Syria, and when he embarked on the arduous voyage to the imperial capital he took along an icon representing the deity, which he planned to install—along with his religion—in Rome. It was not a conventional, realistic statue, but an abstract, symbolic icon, a huge black stone (or betilos) in the shape of a massive cone that gradually tapered off at the top. The phallic connotations of the object were lost on no one, least of all the teenage emperor.

Once in Rome in 219, he immediately took a wife from one of the leading aristocratic families, but quickly tired of her and cast her off, forcing her to return, disgraced, to common life. He is also said to have robbed a vestal virgin from her temple, compelling her to break her sacred vow of chastity; he soon became bored with her as well and casually abandoned her to her fate. Another wife followed, and another, all of whom suffered the same treatment. But then Elagabalus began to demonstrate broader interests. We are told that he had always shown an inordinate taste for elaborate adornment and luxurious vestments. "He wore the most expensive clothes," Herodian chuffed, "woven of purple and gold, and adorned himself with necklaces and bangles. On his head he wore a crown in the shape of a tiara, glittering with gold and precious stones."[5] Shunning the wool and cotton clothes of ordinary Romans and Greeks, the Syrian emperor allowed nothing but the most costly garments to touch his body: "Only seric silk was good enough for him."[6] His shoes, also made of the choicest materials, were covered with gems, pearls, and silver or gold. Romans, however, "considered this kind of finery more appropriate for women than men."[7] The impression that Elagabalus was effeminate, or at least not unequivocally masculine, was strengthened by his habit of going "out with painted eyes and rouge on his cheeks."[8] Another historian mentioned that in the "public baths he always bathed with the women, and he even treated them himself with a depilatory ointment, which he applied also to his own beard."[9]

All this seemed bad enough. Most offensive to his later chroniclers, though, was the fact that the presumptive master of the Roman world assumed the role of a woman in sexual terms as well—or, as Edward Gibbon

5. *Herodian,* 2 vols., ed. and trans. C. R. Whittaker (Cambridge, Mass., 1969–70), 2:39.

6. Ibid., 41.

7. Ibid.

8. Ibid., 57.

9. Aelius Lampridius, "Antoninus Elagabalus," in *Scriptores Historiae Augustae,* trans. David Magie (London, 1924), 169.

gingerly phrased it, he "preferred the distaff to the sceptre."[10] It was noted—and deplored—that even during his long journey to Rome he had been "living in a depraved manner and indulging in unnatural vice with men."[11] Lampridius, who offered the most salacious version of the emperor's life and was the source George appears to have consulted most carefully,[12] went on to say that Elagabalus installed a public bath in the imperial palace so that "by this means he might get a supply of men with unusually large organs."[13] Couching his description in pseudo-evasive language, Lampridius suggested that the emperor also publicly engaged in sexually illicit behavior: "Such was his passion for Hierocles"—a former slave and palace favorite—"that he kissed him in a place which it is indecent even to mention, declaring that he was celebrating the festival of Flora."[14] Soon Hierocles was replaced by another paramour, a Greek athlete named Zoticus, and "with this man Elagabalus went through a nuptial ceremony and consummated a marriage, even having a bridal matron."[15] Dio tells us that, wanting to consummate the bond in every way, Elagabalus asked his physician to give him, by means of an anterior incision, an artificial vagina. Kissing his "husband" after the vows were exchanged, Elagabalus thereupon pronounced himself "empress."

For later observers and commentators, these were the most unwholesome but also the most characteristic aspects of Elagabalus's life and reign. Otherwise, his résumé reads like that of any other decadent emperor of the late Roman period. He is variously accused of performing ritual human sacrifices, of slicing open children to examine their entrails for useful portents, of harnessing naked women to a chariot and, while likewise naked, driving them about the imperial palace, and generally of engaging in a life oscillating between luxuriant profligacy and savage bestiality. It is said that he enjoyed having the path in front of him strewn with gold dust as he strolled about,

10. Edward Gibbon, *The Decline and Fall of the Roman Empire*, 7 vols., ed. J. B. Bury (London, 1897), 1:144.

11. Lampridius, "Antonius Elagabalus," 115.

12. On George's knowledge of the ancient sources, see Victor A. Oswald Jr., "The Historical Content of Stefan George's *Algabal*," *Germanic Review* 23 (1948): 193–205.

13. Lampridius, "Antonius Elagabalus," 123.

14. Ibid., 117.

15. Ibid., 127.

that he surrounded himself with exquisite scents and flowers (including roses, lilies, violets, hyacinths, and narcissus), that he had his dogs fed on goose livers and served himself and his guests rare and exotic aliments (such as camels' heels, tongues of peacocks and nightingales, flamingo brains, and partridge eggs). He is also supposed to have held extravagant banquets in which, to amuse himself, he would indulge in puerile pranks, such as inviting twelve people who were bald, or only those who were fat, or blind, and so on. Sometimes he would have his guests served not actual food, but elaborate imitations made of wood, marble, terra cotta, or glass. While the emperor complacently sampled the very real delicacies set before him, he would inquire with mock solicitousness about the meal and receive stammered assurances about the excellence of his kitchen from his bewildered and slightly frightened guests. Afterward, bloody contests were waged between gladiators and wild animals, while the bejeweled and painted adolescent emperor idly watched on, surrounded by his doting entourage of eunuchs, slaves, well-endowed athletes, and vacant-eyed prostitutes picked up from Rome's back alleys.

Although the name of Elagabalus has remained relatively obscure, it has never disappeared entirely. In modern France especially, the memory of his misdeeds has lived on, no doubt in part because of their appealingly subversive quality. Unsurprisingly, a century before *Algabal,* the Marquis de Sade had mentioned his name approvingly (alongside Nero and Tiberius) in *Justine et Juliette* (1797).[16] In the nineteenth century he even became something of a cult figure. The decisive impetus came from Théophile Gautier, whose novel *Mademoiselle de Maupin* (1834) inflamed generations of writers, not least of all the symbolists. Gautier was consumed by the notion that the culture of his own time, like that of the late Roman Empire, was corrupt, enervated, depleted, and generally on an inexorable path of decline and self-destruction. As a tonic to the pervasive sense of dreary sameness, to escape the numbing boredom with a world that no longer offered any surprises or enchantment, the characters in Gautier's works obsessively engage in a search for ever more bizarre forms of amusement. The protagonist of *Mademoiselle de Maupin,* Chevalier d'Albert, racked by ennui and yet still desiring

16. A. E. Carter, *The Idea of Decadence in French Literature, 1830–1900* (Toronto, 1958), 31.

new sensations and experiences, often fantasizes about what he calls "the impossible." "I am afflicted," he groans at one point, "by that illness that attacks powerful peoples and men during their old age." He soon reveals what this means concretely: "I have dreamt of igniting cities to illuminate my celebrations; I have wished to be a woman to taste new sensual pleasures . . . Nero . . . Heliogabalus."[17] This was, as one student of the time has observed, a veiled but reliably unsubtle way of signaling homosexual or "inverted" tendencies or desires. And indeed, in all of Gautier's works, homosexuality is a constant and central theme, along with the related phenomena of androgyny and hermaphroditism.[18]

For Gautier's numerous ardent admirers—most notably among them Baudelaire, for whom Gautier wrote a laudatory introduction to the *Fleurs du Mal,* and Joris-Karl Huysmans, a longtime friend of Gautier whose novel *Against the Grain (À Rebours)* of 1884 was hailed as the "breviary of the Decadence"—the name of Elagabalus thus became indelibly fixed with the association not just of excess and vice, but also specifically of sexual inversion (as it was then known). To be sure, it was not simply prurient interest or a private wish to confess secret longings that prompted all writers to dwell on the offenses attributed to Elagabalus or similar representatives of the "decadent" late Roman Empire. The predilection for topics deemed "unnatural" and "artificial"—which easily translated into associated notions of what was considered shocking, perverse, morbid, and evil—was only another expression of the greater effort in which all symbolists were engaged. It was a way of rejecting the values of the bourgeois society they uniformly loathed; it was seen as a generalized instrument of revolt, a convenient means of asserting their will over and against a world they perceived as adversarial or simply intransigent. As we know, this protest against nature was not solely, or even primarily, an artistic gesture, and its political undercurrents were well understood by those on both sides of the ideological divide. In yet another sign of the specific and enduring potency of this attack on bourgeois values, as many as forty years after George wrote *Algabal,* Antonin Artaud could still count on its resonance, titling his 1934 book *Heliogabalus, or the Anarchist Crowned.*[19]

17. Cited in ibid., 38.
18. See ibid., 39.
19. Antonin Artaud, *Héliogabale, ou l'anarchiste courroné* (Paris, 1934).

For George in 1892, the unification of aesthetic, political, and social subversion—which the figure of Elagabalus neatly synthesized to form a kind of symbolist, anarchic, and psychosexual amalgam—made the boy-emperor virtually irresistible. But it bears repeating, if only because his later exegetes labored so mightily to insist otherwise, that each one of these elements is an essential and very much a consciously chosen part of the whole. The attractions associated with Elagabalus were not merely abstract interests of recent vintage, but issues that had pursued George for most of his adult life.

It is principally the question of Elagabalus's sexuality, and its possible significance for the poet, that has remained hidden behind a veil of enforced secrecy and uncomfortable silence. It is surely no accident, however, that Karl Heinrich Ulrichs (1825–1895), one of the pioneers of nineteenth-century "scientific" attempts to account for homosexuality and a writer who openly identified himself as homosexual, also claimed Elagabalus as one of his own. As Ulrichs put it in 1862: "We are spiritually women, that is sexually, namely in the direction of our sexual love."[20] He remained convinced that "Uranier" or "Uranians"—the word "homosexual" was not coined until 1869, and Ulrichs always preferred his own term, "Uranian," derived from the mythological Greek figure Uranus who was castrated by Cronus—had the body of a male but the soul and sexual nature of a woman, representing a physical and spiritual "middle" or "third sex" that should be recognized and accepted as such. "The Uranian is a species of manwoman," Ulrichs proposed. "Uranism is an anomaly of nature, a game of nature of which we see a thousand examples throughout Creation."[21] He even thought that "Uranism is a species of hermaphroditism, or perhaps a coordinated variant of it."[22] For the rest of his public career, Ulrichs indefatigably sought to compile data attesting to the "presence of the female nature in Uranians,"[23] looking also to science, literature, and history for evidence to support his theory. It made perfect sense, then, that in his first publication (1864), Ulrichs singled out the precedent offered by the Roman emperor Heliogabalus as in-

20. Karl Heinrich Ulrichs, *Vier Briefe*, reprinted in *Documents of the Homosexual Rights Movement in Germany, 1836–1927* (New York, 1975), 47.
21. Ibid., 50.
22. Ibid.
23. Ibid., 51.

controvertible proof of his theory—and of the naturalness of the Uranian condition. For it was that emperor, Ulrichs reminded his readers with a little literary flourish, who had once enjoined to his beloved to "call me not Lord, but Lady."[24]

Whether George ever read Ulrichs is not known but quite likely. He was certainly aware of Ulrichs's work and was unquestionably interested in the subject. A few years after the publication of *Algabal*, Richard M. Meyer, a professor of literature in Berlin and the author of the first—and positive—critical evaluation of George's poetry to appear in Germany, reported back to George the results of some research he had conducted on the poet's behalf. "My informant," Meyer submitted, "writes the following: 'I personally know nothing about the publishing house *Kreisende Ringe,* but I hear from a well-informed (and I believe trustworthy) source the following: owner of the firm is Max Spohr, an extraordinarily wealthy man who is making an enormous profit with books on sexual matters of all kinds, who signs with *his* name, and on the side also publishes occult works, as well as novels, stories, etc.'" Meyer added that his "informant" further revealed that the "firm is quite respectable, it seems to me, but by virtue of the aforementioned main branch not first-class." Writing in his own words, Meyer concluded, "The assessment of this assessment I must now leave to you. As regards the 'aforementioned main branch' I would say: an author has no sexe [*sic*]!"[25]

The last phrase, in English in the original, is odd, but it appears to be a euphemistic reference to the "main branch" in which the publisher profiled himself. For Max Spohr, whose firm was based in Leipzig, did not merely publish books on sexual matters in general; he particularly specialized in works pertaining to the growing field of research into homosexuality. Spohr was also an activist in the nascent homosexual rights movement. On May 15, 1897, he founded the so-called *Wissenschaftlich-Humanitäres Komitee* with his friend and collaborator Magnus Hirschfeld and a ministerial official named Erich Oberg. The purpose of the committee was to work toward the

---

24. Hubert Kennedy, *Ulrichs: The Life and Works of Karl Heinrich Ulrichs, Pioneer of the Modern Gay Movement* (Boston, 1988), 59.

25. Richard M. Meyer to Stefan George, October 19, 1897, Stefan George–Archiv, Württembergische Landesbibliothek, Stuttgart.

abolishment of Paragraph 175 and public enlightenment about the nature of homosexuality.[26] In 1896, one year prior to Meyer's letter to George, Spohr had published *Sappho and Socrates: How Does One Explain the Love of Men and Women for Persons of the Same Sex?* by Hirschfeld, who was soon to become the most widely recognized—and controversial—researcher and advocate in the emerging field of sexology. In addition, Spohr published the influential *Yearbook for Intermediary Sexual Stages.* Edited by Hirschfeld from its inception in 1899 until the Nazis forced it to close down in 1933, its subtitle proclaimed that it gave "special consideration to homosexuality." And it was Spohr's firm that in 1898 published the collected works of Karl Heinrich Ulrichs, who had died three years earlier. Spohr's name occurs again in a letter to George from Alfred Schuler in 1899.[27] Finally, George possessed a scholarly article (by Max Kaufmann) about Heinrich Heine and August von Platen—in his *The Baths of Lucca,* Heine had viciously attacked Platen for his homosexuality—in which Ulrichs's works were extensively cited and discussed.[28] If George was ignorant of current research on homosexuality, it was not because of any lack of information or opportunity.

Ultimately, however, George did not have to know the work of Ulrichs to be aware of the intimate connection between the figure of Elagabalus and contemporary notions concerning the nature of homosexuality. It was so widely assumed among the French writers he admired, and it so permeated their works, that he could hardly have escaped its almost ubiquitous presence. One of the most impressive and widely noted retellings of the boy-emperor's story came in the form of a popular historical novel, *L'Agoni,*[29] published by Jean Lombard in 1888, the year before George first traveled to Paris. Set during the reign of Elagabalus and informed by extensive re-

26. James W. Jones, *"We of the Third Sex": Literary Representations of Homosexuality in Wilhelminian Germany* (Frankfurt am Main, 1990), 94–5. In 1871, the new German empire adopted the Prussion edict outlawing homosexuality into its penal code in paragraph 175. It stated, "Unnatural lewdness committed between persons of the male sex or by persons with animals is to be punished by prison. Loss of civil rights may also be imposed."

27. Alfred Schuler to Stefan George, November 3, 1899, Stefan George–Archiv.

28. Max Kaufmann, "Heine und Platen. Eine Revision ihrer literarischen Prozeßakten," *Zürcher Diskußionen* 2/16–17 (1899): 1–13.

29. Carter, *The Idea of Decadence,* 105–6.

search—most of Lombard's information about the emperor was gleaned from Dio and Lampridius—the novel is a not very thinly disguised portrait of the late nineteenth century dressed in Roman garb. The program, if one can call it that, of Lombard's work was the "révolution sexuelle" of the late Roman world, and its stated goal was to establish "l'universalisation de l'Amour Androgyne."[30] What this entailed is explained by one of the novel's central characters: the new cult imported to Rome by Elagabalus, he opines, based on the "relentless pursuit of the male sex by the male sex, would not need the female sex, or rather human bisexuality, and would aid in the creation of the ANDROGYNE, the being that is sufficient unto itself because it includes both sexes."[31] Like several other prominent figures of the Parisian avant-garde, Lombard was an autodidact with a checkered past—he had worked his way up from simple laborer to successful *littérateur* through hard work, perseverance, and guile—and he maintained strong anarchist sympathies. What set him apart from his like-minded contemporaries was his apparent belief that the path to salvation was paved by the elimination of sexual differences, or at least that, to his mind, the anarchic state was synonymous with an androgynist one.

While this may all sound like a self-serving plea for pederastic license, androgynism was a favorite and frequent subject in countless otherwise unrelated works of the time. Probably no one helped promote the popularity of androgynism with more success than the charismatic but outlandish figure of Joséphin Péladan, who adopted the royal Assyrian title "Sar," assumed the name of ancient Babylonian king Merodach Baladan, donned fanciful costumes consisting of heavy, dark robes and complicated hats, and espoused a promiscuous mélange of notions cobbled together from the occult teachings of Zoroaster, Pythagorus, Orpheus, the Knights Templar, and the Rosicrucians.[32] Péladan promulgated his bizarre vision in a series of enormously successful novels known collectively as *La Décadence latine,* which began to appear in 1884 (the same year in which Huysmans's *À Rebours* was

---

30. Ibid., 106.

31. Ibid. ["la poursuite acharnée du sexe mâle par le sexe mâle, inutiliserait le sexe femelle ou plutôt la bisexualité humaine, et aussi aiderait à la création . . . de l'ANDRÓGYNE, l'être qui se suffit à lui-même parce qu'il renferme les deux sexes."]

32. Raymond Rudorff, *The Belle Epoque: Paris in the Nineties* (New York, 1972), 188–9.

published). All the individual works in the *Décadence latine*—each one decked out in such lubricious titles as *Curieuse!* or *L'Androgyne,* as well as its transposition *Gynandre,* and so on—contain countless scenes of sexual aberrancy, with Péladan's interest predominantly fixed on androgynism. He pretended to deplore the symptoms of modern moral turpitude he described—it is not by accident that Max Nordau, that implacable critic of cultural decline and stout defender of middle-class values, quite liked Péladan—and the author of the *Décadence latine* insisted that the series was meant to serve as both a warning and preventive tonic. Whatever his intent, the number and vivacity of his detailed descriptions of all manners of sexual deviancy certainly did not hurt his sales. Ever resourceful, Péladan also presided over a succession of art exhibitions during the 1890s—grandiosely dubbed the Salons of the Rosy Cross—that drew huge crowds: the first salon, which opened on March 10, 1892, attracted over eleven thousand curious (or perhaps merely bemused) visitors.[33] George appears to have been fascinated for a time by this strange apparition, who combined in equal measure the role of magician, impresario, preacher, and confidence man. At the end of the following year, he made a point of going to one of Péladan's lectures in Brussels—where, as it happened, he also ran into Verlaine.[34]

When George said *Algabal* was a "revolutionary" book, then, he meant it in a way that encompassed but also went beyond Lombard's quasi-anarchic promotion of a "sexual revolution" as a means of hastening universal androgynism, not to speak of Péladan's disingenuous protestations that he was doing the opposite. Still, they and their renderings of the enterprising boy-emperor cannot have been very far from his mind when he sat down to create the comparably richer and darker figure of Algabal. In all probability, George simply took the associations linking Elagabalus and various permutations of an "unnatural" sexuality for granted, knowing that they would serve as a dependable and effective shorthand for one part of his overall design. Yet when his official biographer makes a point of saying that "the poet

33. Ibid.; see also Werner Paul Sohnle, ed., *Stefan George und der Symbolismus* (exhibition catalogue, Stuttgart, 1983), 103–4.

34. Ernst Morwitz, *Kommentar zu den Prosa- Drama- und Jugend-Dichtungen Stefan Georges* (Munich, 1962), 42; see also Sohnle, *George und der Symbolismus,* 117. Georg Fuchs also compared George to Péladan; cf. Fuchs, *Sturm und Drang in München um die Jahrhundertwende* (Munich, 1936), 132.

appears in *Algabal* only in a suprapersonal image of himself, in a symbolic figure,"[35] we should by all means take him at his word. Algabal obviously is not George, just as he is not identical with Elagabalus. But it is equally true that George poured his very being into his poetry, and to assert he strove for anything other than a total immersion of himself in his art would be a trivialization or a lie.

With a concerted intensity unmatched by his previous two books, *Algabal* marks out the outermost boundaries—and hidden dangers—of George's burgeoning conception of himself and his work. In fact, in an almost uncanny way, the "symbolic figure" he chose to represent his ambitions and fears encompasses an enormously wide range not just of his poetic aspirations, but also of his private experience. Unlike the earlier *Hymns* or the *Pilgrimages*, *Algabal* is a sustained, coherent exploration of a single image or symbol, rather than a series of thematically linked but ultimately disparate episodic portraits. Many of George's earlier concerns are operative here as well, but they are drawn together by a tauter, more unified organization and, above all, by the central, controlling presence of the titular character.

The book is divided into three main parts: "In the Lower Realm," "Days," and "Memories." The first section presents a magnificent fusion of the elements undergirding George's view of his poetic task. For the subterranean "realm" or "empire" it evokes (the German word "Reich," rich in connotations, repeatedly returns in varying contexts throughout George's career) is not simply one entirely of the emperor's making; it also is emphatically and flamboyantly contrived. Referring to the emperor for the moment in the third person as "he," George begins his narrative by informing his readers that "the landscape by the shore does not entice the master,"[36] who has instead built an alternative sanctuary according to his own plan, with "the houses and courtyards how he conceived them."[37] The underground grottos, hills, lakes, and fountains that make up this world are constructed not of natural materials, but of exquisite stones, precious gems, and choice woods—rubies, diamonds, crystal, pearls, alabaster, opals, topaz, ivory, cypress wood, and beaten gold comprise Algabal's building materials—and all

35. Wolters, *Stefan George und die Blätter für die Kunst*, 37.
36. Stefan George, *Gesamt-Ausgabe der Werke*, 18 vols. (Berlin, 1927–34), 2:90.
37. Ibid.

are illuminated by the flickering, artificial light of candles. In this, his private creation, "where no will governs apart from his own,"[38] and where he even "commands light and weather,"[39] Algabal has fashioned a self-made sphere that responds to, because it quite literally mirrors, his every wish.

There are several proximate literary models for this secret, buried domain, where the elaboration of an alternative reality acts as an antidote to or substitute for the less than perfect one we know.[40] Baudelaire's poem, "Le rêve Parisien" ("The Parisian Dream") in the *Fleurs du mal,* evokes a related world of hard, brilliant surfaces, dead and denatured vistas, and solipsistic silence. The tale "Duke of Portland," which Villiers de l'Isle-Adam included in the collection *Cruel Tales (Contes cruels)* of 1883, similarly describes a concealed dungeon—its vaults covered by Venetian glass, its floor tiled with marble and fantastic mosaics—where the story's protagonist, Lord Richard, lives in solitary splendor. The most famous of these reclusive master-builders is found in Huysmans's *À Rebours.* Its central character is Duc Jean des Esseintes, the overrefined scion of an ancient and noble family, educated by Jesuits, and a connoisseur of the Latin "decadent" period—he is, not incidentally, an avowed and knowledgeable admirer of Elagabalus. Des Esseintes is possessed of a complex, highly wrought sensibility; he locks himself away in his house, awakes only at sunset, and in lonely, midnight reveries he devotes himself to "extravagant caprices"[41] in rooms he has made to resemble ships' cabins, monastery cells, and torture chambers. Des Esseintes never travels—in fact he hardly goes out—"since he believed that the imagination could provide a more-than-adequate substitution for the vulgar reality of actual experience."[42] "Nature, he used to say, has had her day."[43]

These and other literary parallels are obvious enough not to require much interpretive massaging. The worlds they depict, like Algabal's underground realm, act as concrete images of rebellion. Yet this rebellion is not

38. Ibid., 91.

39. Ibid.

40. On the following and other literary influences, see H. J. Meesen, "Stefan George's *Algabal* und die französiche Décadence," *Monatshefte* 39 (1947): 304–21; Manfred Durzak, *Der junge Stefan George* (Munich, 1968); Claude David, *Stefan George. Sein dichterisches Werk* (Munich, 1967); Ernst Morwitz, *Die Dichtung Stefan Georges* (Berlin, 1934).

41. J.-K. Huysmans, *À Rebours* (Paris, 1977), 27.

42. Ibid., 35.

43. Ibid., 36.

simply against a particular time or place, but against Nature itself. The artificial realms contrived by the symbolists are meant to embody, in tangible form, their effort to subdue and overthrow the physical world; this they considered irretrievably debased, tawdry, and malignant—in short, too bourgeois—and they meant to install their own creation in its place. Ultimately, this conjuring of artificial worlds signifies an attempt to assume the role of God himself. In one of Des Esseintes's monologues, for instance, he flatly states that "man has done as well as the God in whom he believes."[44] As we know, this is a central tenet of the symbolist credo, and George subscribed to it as well. But the emperor Algabal is not just a kind of alter-ego, the fantasy fulfillment of his long-held wish-dream: an omnipotent ruler presiding unchallenged over a world beholden to him and him alone, because it is completely of his own manufacture. Algabal and the world he governs are also fairly transparent equivalents of his vision of the poet and his purpose.

But there was a problem. The heightened, vaguely sinister sheen of Algabal's underworld, with its petrified veneers and dampened, frigid glow, highlight its predominant feature: it is a dead zone. Apart from the emperor himself, this private reserve contains nothing living. At first, Algabal seems proud of this fact, as if it meant he had prevailed over life itself. But soon he realizes that this infertility will finally threaten his own sovereignty. In the concluding poem of the first section—perhaps the most monumental and finely chiseled of the entire book, and the first in which Algabal speaks in his own voice—this dilemma is directly addressed in the form of a dawning realization:

> Neither air nor warmth my garden needs •
> The garden that I built for myself
> And its lifeless swarms of birds
> Have never witnessed a spring.
>
> Of coal the trunks • Of coal the branches
> And dark fields against a darkening slope •
> The unbroken weights of eternal fruits
> Gleam like lava in the grove of pine.
>
> . . . .

44. Ibid., 38.

But how do I engender you in my sanctuary
—Thus did I ask when I traversed it deep in thought
And forgot my care in pondering bold constructions—
Great dark black flower?[45]

This image seems the perfect, if vaguely repellent, emblem of George's contradictory aims. The black flower that Algabal wants to cultivate has no equivalent in nature, but in conventional poetic iconography the flower is the symbol par excellence of a natural, benevolent fecundity, with no obvious purpose than to be beautiful. But the primary color of Algabal's underworld, with its landscape constructed of obsidian and coal is black, the shade of death (and, significantly, the color of ink as well). Algabal's black flower would thus be not merely one more addition to his subterranean realm. It would be its crowning achievement, the quintessential artifice: a man-made contrivance that is simultaneously vital, somehow both inanimate and patently inorganic yet also strangely alive. It represents a kind of botanical analog to the vampire or, perhaps better, to Frankenstein's monster. It would be the ultimate clone: not just creating life out of inert matter, it would fuse life and death itself.

Even the most chary of George's followers recognized that the black flower was also, as Gundolf put it in unusually direct terms, the "sensuous-dark symbol for the secret of procreation."[46] Somewhat more specifically, Ernst Morwitz, who was close to George for almost thirty years, understood the image within the context of a particular notion of sexuality. "Only softly does the wish for perpetuation and progeny assert itself in the 'Lower Realm,'" Morwitz suggested. "The emperor does not wish to be a father, he wants to give birth. Physical birth is not possible. Only the mind can shape the form of existence in reverse. Thus the emperor seeks to lead the life of a woman, as the history of Elagabalus reports."[47] But we can be more precise still. In one of the poems in the middle section of the book, Algabal recalls how he would shut himself away from the crowd and gaze at himself in a looking glass: "And the mirror returned to the viewer / The face almost of a

45. George, *Werke,* 2:96.
46. Gundolf, *George,* 86.
47. Morwitz, *Kommentar,* 37.

sister."[48] Elsewhere, Algabal is described celebrating in the temple he had built to house the towering black monolith representing his God. But in *Algabal*, in variance to what we know about his historical namesake, the massive idol does not possess only the stylized attributes of the male sex, but is explicitly said to have a "double form,"[49] which is to say it appears as an androgyne or hermaphrodite. The emperor, the high priest of the cult, seeks to model himself after his duoform God, to assume its multiple attributes, and even to take his place. Narcissus wants to become Salmacis, the dual-natured offspring of Hermes and Aphrodite, whose new name, merging those of both parents into a single term, symbolizes his/her double identity. And the black flower—that supreme hybrid, encompassing an even greater range of opposites than its maker—would be Algabal's signature creation.

At first glance, Algabal and his underworld appear to offer a symbolic fulfillment of George's long-cherished desire for absolute dominion in a realm entirely of his own making. Not only does the book adumbrate a counterreality that answers to Algabal's every wish, but, by uniting both sexes in himself and his works, the emperor seems to portend the divine ability to reproduce, to engender new life, to overcome even the death threatened by solipsistic asphyxiation. Yet the pall of sterility is merely held off, not permanently lifted. The hermaphrodite may solve certain problems, but it evades others. Like flowers, which frequently possess both the male and female reproductive organs—the stamens and the pistil—but are unable to pollinate themselves, so too the hermaphrodite enjoys an abundance of riches but is unable to bring forth life. Without external aid, both flowers and hermaphrodites are impotent and barren.

Significantly, the dominant temper throughout the rest of the book is not jubilation or even contentment, but a heavy dread. A pervasive atmosphere of violence infects many of the following poems, and Algabal himself seems indifferent, desensitized, cold in the face of death. A slave who inadvertently startles the emperor as Algabal walks by announces he will commit suicide for having unintentionally given his master alarm. Algabal accepts this self-sacrifice as a fitting tribute to his sovereignty: "A broad dagger already projected from his chest • / The green tile is tinged by the red pool. /

48. George, *Werke*, 2:107.
49. Ibid., 101.

The emperor recedes with a scornful gesture."[50] Likewise, in an episode based on the life of the historical Elagabalus, Algabal responds to his brother's attempt to usurp his power by arranging to have him murdered. As the emperor descends a marble staircase, he sees below: "A corpse without a head lying in the middle • / There seeps my dear, dear brother's blood • / I merely softly gather up my purple train."[51] In another scene—also handed down from the chronicles—guests at a banquet are asphyxiated under a mass of roses dropped from the ceiling. And Algabal's savagery is not confined to his immediate circle; it extends to the inhabitants of the entire empire. He admits to himself that in his darkest days he had often openly professed, "I want the people to die and groan / And anyone who laughs shall be nailed to the cross."[52] Eventually, Algabal begins to have premonitions of his own demise, but he announces his resolve to kill himself before giving anyone else the satisfaction of doing so. Yet the book ends uneventfully, not with an armed and angry uprising or grisly scenes of self-immolation, but with the emperor quietly indulging in private reminiscences about his childhood and his former glory—although this too represents yet another way of defying the power of the present.

Whether he realized it or not, George had reached a critical impasse. In practice, the promises held out by symbolist doctrine increasingly appeared to be partial, empty, or worse. The attempt to subsume—indeed, to replace—the world with the poet's word seemed to lead inexorably to precisely what the symbolists sought to escape: a kind of suffocating death, a silence imposed by a tacit acknowledgment of the futility (or impossibility) of the venture. Paradoxically, no matter how much the symbolists protested to the contrary, they at last fell into the same trap they thought the naturalists had blindly walked into. The endeavor to erase reality by means of language in fact gave language as much, and arguably more, power as did the allegedly naive faith in the ability of words to reproduce it. The symbolist poetic gospel, like the black flower, like Algabal himself, hubristically wanted to be everything to everyone all at once—man and woman, beginning and end, totality and nothingness, life and death—only to succumb in the end to its own self-administered poison.

50. Ibid., 99.
51. Ibid., 103.
52. Ibid., 107.

George's solution would be to leave the airless chambers of literature and move his operations out into life itself. But that solution would not come for another decade. Ultimately, the death of a young boy, Maximilian Kronberger, led George to the discovery of the neo-Platonic possibilities of what he called "spiritual marriage" and "supersexual love." But that is another story.

Death in Florence

Thomas Mann and the Ideologies of *Renaissancismus* at the Fin de Siècle

MARTIN A. RUEHL

In chapter 4 of Thomas Mann's early confessional novella *Tonio Kröger* (1903), the eponymous hero mounts a spirited defense of his residual bourgeois longings to a friend and fellow artist, Lisaweta. At the culmination of the exchange, Tonio declares that he "loves life" but immediately adds, in what seems to be a curious non sequitur: "Don't think of Cesare Borgia or some intoxicated philosophy that turns him into a hero. He means nothing to me, this Cesare Borgia, I don't think anything of him and I will never understand how one can venerate the extraordinary and the demonic as an ideal."[1] For Mann's contemporary readers, this reference to the ruthless quattrocento ruler was resonant enough. At the time of *Tonio Kröger*'s publication, Renaissance despots were omnipresent on the German stage as personifications of an amoral élan vital and a Nietzschean will to power. More than two hundred Renaissance plays appeared between 1880 and 1920. These were mostly popular, lowbrow productions,[2] but they also included works by Rainer Maria Rilke, Hugo Ball, Georg Heym, and Arthur Schnitzler.[3] In 1906, Richard Strauss—never one to ignore powerful cultural

---

1. Thomas Mann, *Tonio Kröger* (1903), in Thomas Mann, *Gesammelte Werke*, 13 vols. (Frankfurt am Main, 1974), 8:302. Hereafter cited as *GW*.

2. "Renaissance topics," Hugo von Hofmannsthal remarked in 1906, "seem to be destined to set in motion the brushes of the least delectable painters and the pens of the least fortunate poets." See *Richard Strauss–Hugo von Hofmannsthal: Briefwechsel*, ed. Franz and Alice Strauss (Zürich, 1952), 17.

3. See the comprehensive bibliography in Gerd Uekermann, *Renaissancismus und Fin de Siècle: Die italienische Renaissance in der deutschen Dramatik der letzten Jahrhundertwende* (Berlin, 1985), 293–314. Uekermann's is by far the most thorough and comprehensive treatment of the topic and part 2 of this essay relies partly on its rich excerpts from the (often obscure) primary material. On Renaissancismus, see also Michael T. O'Pecko, "Renaissancism and the German Drama, 1890–1910" (Ph.D. dissertation, Johns Hopkins University, 1976), and Lea Ritter-Santini, "Maniera Grande: Über italienische Renaissance

trends—asked Hugo von Hofmannsthal to supply him with a "nice Renais-sance theme" for a new opera: "A really wild Cesare Borgia or Savonarola would be the fulfilment of my desires."[4] Two years later, Robert Arnold noted that "no era of history stirs the fancy of today's playwrights as much as the Renaissance."[5] Another literary historian, Franz Baumgarten, eventually coined the term *Renaissancismus* to describe the obsession of German writ-ers with early modern Italy, particularly with the great demonic rulers of the fifteenth and sixteenth centuries.[6]

Renaissancismus, to be sure, transcended the generic boundaries of fin-de-siècle drama as much as the frontiers of the Second Empire. The old Reichstag building in Berlin (completed in 1894), Munich's Army Museum (opened in 1905), the paintings of Franz Stuck, Hans Makart, and Arnold Böcklin, and the interior decorations of Georg Hirth indicate the extent to which it affected other areas of Wilhelmine culture, while plays by Oscar Wilde, Gabriele d'Annunzio, and Maurice Maeterlinck illustrate its Euro-pean diffusion.[7] Yet nowhere did the fin-de-siècle fascination with Renais-sance Italy reach the heights (and depths) that it did in Germany. And nowhere was it more prominent than in the theater—the most vibrant, in-novative, and popular art form of the Wilhelmine era,[8] and one which re-mained, for twenty years, the true domain of Renaissancismus.[9]

With their glorification of unfettered subjectivity, the Renaissance plays

---

und deutsche Jahrhunderwende," in *Fin de Siècle: Zu Literatur und Kunst der Jahrhundert-wende,* ed. Roger Bauer et al. (Frankfurt am Main, 1974), 170–205.

4. *Strauss–Hofmannsthal Briefwechsel,* 15.

5. Robert Arnold, *Das moderne Drama* (Straßburg, 1908), 294.

6. See Franz F. Baumgarten, *Das Werk Conrad Ferdinand Meyers. Renaissance-Empfinden und Stilkunst* (Munich, 1917), 3–39.

7. See Wilde's *A Florentine Tragedy* (1906) and *Duchess of Padua* (1907); d'Annunzio's *Sogno d'un mattino di primavera* (1897), *Sogno d'un tramonto d'autunno* (1898), and *Francesca da Rimini* (1900); and Maeterlinck's *Monna Vanna* (1903).

8. See Wolfgang J. Mommsen, *Bürgerliche Kultur und künstlerische Avantgarde. Kultur und Politik im deutschen Kaiserreich, 1870–1918* (Frankfurt am Main, 1994), 43–6. See also Norbert Jansen et al., *Berlin-Theater der Jahrhundertwende. Bühnengeschichte der Reichshauptstadt im Spiegel der Kritik, 1889–1914* (Tübingen, 1986).

9. Compared to roughly 240 Renaissance plays, there were no more than 70 Renais-sance novels or novellas composed during the period 1890–1910. See Uekermann, *Renais-sancismus,* 321–6.

of the turn of the century signified a reaction against the historical dramas of the 1870s, which remained indebted to a state-sponsored neoclassicism and its Schillerian ideal of the poised, fully-rounded ethical self. The Renaissance plays also stood in opposition to the naturalist movement of the 1880s, which emphasized the social milieu's manifold pressures on the individual. Around 1900, the Renaissance became a rallying cry in the cultural revolt of a Nietzsche-inspired avant-garde against their *Gründerzeit* fathers.[10] Half *Übermensch*, half *Bürgerschreck* (bogeyman of the bourgeoisie), the tyrant embodied the antisocial, aristocratic individualism of a new literary bohemia.

Tonio's renunciation of Cesare Borgia in 1903 was a critical allusion to these "intoxicated" idealizations of the Renaissance at the fin de siècle. In *Gladius Dei*, published the previous year, Mann had already ridiculed the neo-Renaissance fashion of Munich's contemporary art scene.[11] He continued—and radicalized—his critique of Renaissancismus in the *Reflections of a Non-Political Man* (1918), where he lashed out repeatedly against the "puerile" followers of Nietzsche who venerated the "brutal and beautiful life" as an ideal embodied by Cesare Borgia (*das Cesare-Borgia-Leben*) and indulged in the un-German fashion of "Renaissance aestheticism."[12] Reviewing the various cultural roots of Nazism in *Doctor Faustus* (1947), Mann would again criticize the decadent literati of the turn of the century and wax ironic over their veneration of the Renaissance as an "age steaming with blood and beauty."[13]

In 1905, however, Mann himself published a piece of Renaissancismus, a three-act prose play entitled *Fiorenza*. The drama dealt with a notorious turning point in Florentine history: the decline of the Medici principate in the early 1490s and the rise to power of the Dominican friar Girolamo Savo-

10. See Torsten Bügner and Gerhard Wagner, "Die Alten und die Jungen im Deutschen Reich. Literatursoziologische Anmerkungen zum Verhältnis der Generationen 1871–1918," *Zeitschrift für Soziologie* 20 (1991): 177–90.

11. See Joachim Wich, "Thomas Manns 'Gladius Dei' als Parodie," *Germanisch-Romanische Monatsschrift* 53 (1972): 389–400, esp. 399.

12. Thomas Mann, *Betrachtungen eines Unpolitischen* (1918), GW, 12:538–41.

13. Thomas Mann, *Doktor Faustus. Das Leben des deutschen Tonsetzers Adrian Leverkühn erzählt von einem Freunde* (1947), GW, 6:382.

narola. Against the backdrop of these political events, Mann unfolded the essential conflict of his drama: the struggle of Savonarola's Christian spiritualism against the heathen aestheticism of Lorenzo de' Medici and his entourage. Mann had worked on *Fiorenza* since 1898 and regarded it, despite some doubts about its formal qualities,[14] as his "most important product of the years 1904–07."[15] He deemed its ending to be so accomplished that he transcribed it in his diary, using violet ink. The numerous references to the play in his correspondence with his brother Heinrich suggest his deep personal involvement in its content.[16] So do his frequent—and surprisingly contradictory—self-identifications with its dramatis personae. In his seventh notebook (1903), for instance, Mann referred to Savonarola as his "personal hero."[17] Later, in the *Reflections,* he observed again that his "secret spiritual sympathy" belonged "very much" to the friar (see Figures 11 and 12).[18] In a 1906 letter to Kurt Martens, however, he indicated that he had "given at least as much of his own character [*von Eigenem*]" to Lorenzo de' Medici as to Savonarola.[19]

Despite these authorial comments, critics either have tended to pass over *Fiorenza* as one of Mann's lesser early works—a failed and somewhat embarrassing excursion into the dramatic genre[20]—or have interpreted it as yet

14. See *Thomas Mann–Heinrich Mann: Briefwechsel, 1900–1949,* ed. Hans Wysling, 1st ed. (Frankfurt am Main, 1970), 35, 37.

15. Thomas Mann, "Preface" to *Stories from Three Decades* (1936), *GW,* 8:113.

16. See *Thomas Mann–Heinrich Mann: Briefwechsel,* 6, 8, 35, 37, 39, 44, 46.

17. Thomas Mann, *Notizbücher,* 2 vols., ed. Hans Wysling (Frankfurt am Main, 1991, 1992), 2:83.

18. Thomas Mann, *Betrachtungen, GW,* 8:93.

19. Thomas Mann to Kurt Martens, 28 March 1906, in *Thomas Mann: Briefe, 1889–1955,* 3 vols., ed. Erika Mann (Frankfurt am Main, 1961–1965), 3:64.

20. See Terence J. Reed, *Thomas Mann: The Uses of Tradition,* rev. ed. (Oxford, 1996), e.g., 94: "As a Renaissance drama . . . [*Fiorenza*] is hard to take seriously. Its plaster-statue figures, its melodramatic gestures, its stylised speeches and purple passages, with pentameters either creeping into or not wholly eradicated from the prose: all these things are barely credible from the author of, say, *Tristan.*" Significantly, the two major recent intellectual biographies of Mann make only a few passing references to *Fiorenza.* See Klaus Harpprecht, *Thomas Mann: Eine Biographie* (Hamburg, 1995), and Hermann Kurzke, *Thomas Mann: Das Leben als Kunstwerk* (Munich, 2001).

Figure 11. Thomas Mann in Munich, 1906. Note the oval portrait of Savonarola to the left of Mann's elbow. He kept this image on his desk while working on *Fiorenza*.
Thomas-Mann-Archiv, ETH Zürich.

another variation of the old Mannian theme of *Geist* (spirit) versus *Leben* (life).[21] As far as Mann's relation to Renaissancismus is concerned, they have generally followed Walter Rehm's judgment that *Fiorenza* represented a formidable critique of the genre, which effectively ended the cult of the Renaissance.[22]

This essay reassesses Mann's play as a much more complex—and important—work by approaching it as a self-reflexive and ambivalent intervention in Renaissancismus. Mann himself touched on this ambivalence when he defended his drama against the charge of anticlericalism put forth by a Catholic newspaper in 1908. He had written *Fiorenza,* he remarked in an open

21. See, e.g., Lothar Pikulik, "Thomas Mann und die Renaissance," in *Thomas Mann und die Tradition,* ed. Peter Pütz (Frankfurt am Main, 1971), 101–29. A noteworthy exception is Egon Eilers's excellent (but unpublished) Ph.D. dissertation, "Perspektiven und Montage: Studien zu Thomas Manns Schauspiel 'Fiorenza'" (Marburg an der Lahn, 1967).

22. See Walter Rehm, "Der Renaissancekult um 1900 und seine Überwindung," *Zeitschrift für deutsche Philologie* 14 (1929): 296–328.

Figure 12. Fra Bartolommeo's
1498 portrait of Savonarola was
both a visual source for *Fiorenza* and
a personal icon for Mann.

Thomas-Mann-Archiv, ETH Zürich.

letter, "from the first to the last word" as a "critic of the Renaissance"—but
as a critic who "has completely absorbed and comprehended" the object of
his criticism and "knows how to speak in its language."[23] An examination
of the particular ways in which Mann spoke and inflected the language of
Renaissancismus throws new light on his self-reinvention as a bourgeois in
the mid-1900s. But the political contours of this transformation only come
into focus if the play is set in the context of the fin-de-siècle controversies
over the Renaissance. Accordingly, this essay begins with a close look at Renaissancismus: its genealogy, its inner contradictions (modernist-reactionary,
vitalist-decadent, neopagan-*nationalprotestantisch*), and its eventual collapse

23. I am citing from the original manuscript version of the letter, preserved in the
Thomas-Mann-Archiv, Zürich (hereafter cited as TMA), Mp IX, 16, which differs slightly
from the published version in "Rede und Antwort," reprinted in *GW*, 11:560–3. See also
Thomas Mann's remark to Heinrich in 1905 that *Fiorenza* was "written as if it hailed from
one [of the artists] of Lorenzo's circle." *Thomas Mann–Heinrich Mann: Briefwechsel*, 37.

in the 1910s. It then turns to *Fiorenza* and investigates its peculiar 'Protestant' interpretation of the Renaissance. A concluding section offers a brief
survey of Mann's later revisions of this interpretation.

*Origins: The Birth of Renaissancismus from the Spirit of Burckhardt and
Nietzsche*

The cult of the Renaissance was deeply indebted to the writings of Jacob
Burckhardt and Friedrich Nietzsche. With some justification, Franz Baumgarten, writing in 1917, called Burckhardt the "historian" and Nietzsche the
"prophet" of Renaissancismus.[24] Published in 1860, Burckhardt's *Civilization of the Renaissance in Italy* soon became something like a textbook for
dramatists at the turn of the century.[25] Wilhelm Weigand and Adolf Bartels,
two of the most popular playwrights of the day, frequently consulted it while
drafting their respective Renaissance dramas.[26] So did Thomas Mann, who
thought that it provided "splendid material" for *Fiorenza*.[27] Burckhardt's
book, however, furnished the *Renaissancisten* not just with historical props,
but with a very distinctive interpretation of early modern Italy which cast a
particular spell on fin-de-siècle literati.

Though it is still frequently acclaimed as the foundational statement of
the modern conception of the Renaissance,[28] Burckhardt's *Civilization* is bet-

24. Baumgarten, *Das Werk Conrad Ferdinand Meyers*, 5.
25. The popularity of *Civilization of the Renaissance in Italy* coincided closely with the
vogue of Renaissancismus at the turn of the century: only three new editions of the book
appeared between 1860 and 1896, while the next twelve years saw twice as many. See
Evert M. Janssen, *Jacob Burckhardt und die Renaissance* (Assen, 1970), 249. In the 1890s,
Burckhardt's *Civilization* (as well as his *Cicerone*) all but replaced Goethe's *Italian Journey*
as the *vade mecum* of the *Bildungsbürger* on his grand tour through Italy. Significantly,
the tour ceased to be a quest for the traces of classical antiquity in the south and increasingly centered on Florence, with its riches of Renaissance art and architecture. See Bernd
Roeck, *Florenz 1900: Die Suche nach Arkadien* (Munich, 2001).
26. See Uekermann, *Renaissancismus*, 50–2.
27. Thomas Mann to Heinrich Mann, 25 November 1900, in *Thomas Mann–Heinrich
Mann: Briefwechsel*, 4: "The 'King of Florence' [Mann's working title for *Fiorenza*] has of
course been put on hold; but I have received the *Civilization of the Renaissance* and see
that the two volumes contain great material."
28. See, e.g., Richard Goldthwaite, *Wealth and the Demand for Art in Italy, 1300–1600*
(Baltimore, 1993), 5.

ter understood as a response to earlier histories—most notably Sismondi's *History of the Italian Republics* (1809–1818)—which hailed the communes of the trecento as the birthplace of a new individualist and 'civic' world view. It was an ambivalent response. On the one hand, Burckhardt viewed the Italian Renaissance, quite in accordance with Sismondi and other 'liberal' historians, as the "mother" of modernity, a dress rehearsal for the civil society of nineteenth-century Europe: a fiercely competitive, atomized world that was largely devoid of traditional religious and moral norms.[29] In this respect, his Renaissance men resembled the early capitalists described by Marx. Pioneering, self-made men, they demystified and eventually dismantled the old feudal relations of power with awe-inspiring irreverence. With their rational world view, their heightened subjectivity, and their strategies of cultural sublimation, they also revealed striking similarities to the seventeenth-century Puritans described in Max Weber's *Protestant Ethic and the Spirit of Capitalism* (1904–05).[30]

On the other hand, Burckhardt's *Civilization* was a forceful critique of Sismondi's emancipatory, progressivist interpretation of the Renaissance. This had a lot to do with Burckhardt's topical concerns about the social corollaries of modernization in the nineteenth century. Writing in the aftermath of 1848, he saw the culture of *Alteuropa* (old Europe)[31] as equally threatened by the revolutionary unrest and greedy materialism of the proletariat and by the bourgeoisie's complacent desire for *Sekurität*.[32] These anxi-

29. Jacob Burckhardt, *Die Kultur der Renaissance in Italien: Ein Versuch*, ed. K. Hoffmann (Stuttgart, 1988), 3.

30. Like Weber's Puritans, Burckhardt's Renaissance men are both ancestors of the modern *Bürger* and *mementi* from a more heroic 'early bourgeois' past. This parallel remains underexposed in Wolfgang Hardtwig's otherwise excellent "Jacob Burckhardts 'Kultur der Renaissance' und Max Webers 'Protestantische Ethik'. Ein Vergleich," in *Renaissance und Renaissancismus von Jacob Burckhardt bis Thomas Mann* (Tübingen, 1990), ed. August Buck, 13–23.

31. See Wolfgang Hardtwig, *Geschichtsschreibung zwischen Alteuropa und moderner Welt—Jacob Burckhardt in seiner Zeit* (Göttingen, 1974), and Friedrich Jaeger, *Bürgerliche Modernisierungskrise und historische Sinnbildung. Kulturgeschichte bei Droysen, Burckhardt und Max Weber* (Göttingen, 1994).

32. See Jacob Burckhardt, *Über das Studium der Geschichte. Der Text der 'Weltgeschichtlichen Betrachtungen' nach den Handschriften*, ed. Peter Ganz (Munich, 1982), 282–3, 236–7.

eties gave his account of the birth of modernity a strangely antimodern twist. Significantly, Burckhardt associated the new secular and individualist spirit of the Renaissance not so much with the humanists and merchants of the city-republics, but with reckless military leaders and despots (like Lodovico il Moro and Francesco Sforza), whose complete immoralism both fascinated and repelled him. With their radically "insecure" (*garantielos*) existence and their "objective" Machiavellian approach to politics, the tyrants, for Burckhardt, were the first modern men of Europe.[33] At the same time, they were the exact opposite of the modern bourgeois.

While tyrants were front and center in *Civilization*, they were hardly the only representatives of the Renaissance spirit. That they were eventually given such prominence in the pantheon of Renaissancismus was the work of Burckhardt's colleague and associate at the University of Basel, Friedrich Nietzsche. In the 1890s, as Nietzsche quickly descended into complete mental derangement, his popularity began to soar. For the next few decades, his philosophy affected Germany's cultural elites more than that of any other philosopher since Hegel.[34] One of the most potent symbols of fin-de-siècle Nietzscheanism—curiously ignored in Steven Aschheim's recent study[35]— was the Renaissance tyrant, whose outlines Nietzsche had drawn from Burckhardt's book.[36]

Nietzsche possessed two copies of Burckhardt's *Civilization*. His markings and marginal notes indicate that he was particularly absorbed by chapters 1 and 3, which dealt with the despots and the humanists respectively.[37] The *Birth of Tragedy* (1872), Nietzsche's first book, echoed Wagner's critique of the Renaissance as a shallow, artificial, 'Latin' attempt to revive the culture of classical antiquity. After his break with Wagner in the late 1870s, however,

33. See his assessment of the thirteenth-century emperor Frederick II as the "first modern man on the throne," in Burckhardt, *Kultur der Renaissance*, 4.

34. For the early Nietzsche reception in Germany, see Richard F. Krummel, *Nietzsche und der deutsche Geist*, 2 vols. (Berlin, 1983).

35. Steven Aschheim, *The Nietzsche Legacy in Germany, 1890–1990* (Berkeley, 1992).

36. On Nietzsche's indebtedness to Burckhardt in this respect, see L. Farulli, "Nietzsche und die Renaissance: Die Reflexion über 'Grenze' und 'Grenzüberschreitung,'" in *Renaissance und Renaissancismus*, ed. Buck, 54–70, esp. 54–8.

37. The copies are preserved in the Anna Amalia Bibliothek, Stiftung Weimarer Klassik, Weimar. For Nietzsche's markings, see Sign. C482a, esp. pp. 106–10.

Nietzsche began to reevaluate the legacy of the Renaissance. He praised its rational, secular ethos, which he saw as paving the way for the philosophy of the Enlightenment.[38] His later writings further emphasized these secular elements of Renaissance civilization, personified in his view by Frederick II, the great antagonist of successive popes, and the 'tropic beast of prey,' Cesare Borgia.[39]

In the *Antichrist* (1888), Nietzsche indulged at length in counterfactual speculations on the possible effects of Cesare Borgia's accession to the papal throne in the early 1500s. Such an attack on the Church from within, he mused, would have realized the true "meaning" of the Renaissance: a complete transvaluation of Christian slave morality. What cut this project short, Nietzsche believed, was not so much Borgia's premature death as the Protestant Reformation:

> There has never been a more critical question than that of the Renaissance—it is *my* question too. . . . To attack at the decisive place, at the seat of Christianity itself, and there to enthrone the noble values. . . . I see before me the *possibility* of a . . . heavenly . . . spectacle . . . *Cesare Borgia as pope!* . . . Am I understood? . . . Well then, that would have been the sort of victory that I alone desire today—: with that, Christianity would have been *abolished!*—What happened? A German monk, Luther, came to Rome. This monk, with all the vengeful instincts of a failed priest in him, rebelled *against* the Renaissance in Rome. . . . Luther saw the depravity of the papacy when in fact the opposite was becoming apparent: . . . Christianity no longer occupied the papal chair! Instead there was life! Instead there was the triumph of life! Instead there was the great yea to all lofty, beautiful and reckless things! . . . And Luther *restored the church:* he attacked it.[40]

Still, Borgia's *sceleratezza* (villainousness) had been a promising first awakening of a new type of virtue: "virtue in the Renaissance style, *virtù,* virtue

38. See Friedrich Nietzsche, *Menschliches, Allzumenschliches. Ein Buch für freie Geister* (1878), in *Sämtliche Werke. Kritische Studienausgabe,* 15 vols., ed. Giorgio Colli and Mazzino Montinari (Munich, 1986), 2:646. Hereafter cited as *KSA.*

39. Friedrich Nietzsche, *Jenseits von Gut und Böse. Vorspiel einer Philosophie der Zukunft* (1886), *KSA,* 5:117.

40. Friedrich Nietzsche, *Der Antichrist. Fluch auf das Christentum* (1888), *KSA,* 6:250–1.

free of moralistic acid [*moralinfreie Tugend*]."[41] In *Twilight of the Idols,* published the following year, Nietzsche invoked Borgia as a model of the superman, contrasting his consummate ruthlessness with the decadent sensitivity and "thickly cushioned humanitarianism" of the contemporary bourgeois.[42] This portrait of Cesare Borgia largely defined the image of the 'Renaissance man' in the German cultural imagination of the fin de siècle.

With its hero-worshiping representations of great individuals and its proudly proclaimed "aesthetic immoralism," Renaissancismus itself might be regarded as a Nietzschean product.[43] The tyrannical figures strutting across the stages of Wilhelmine Germany usually justified their transgressive actions by invoking a vulgarized version of the master morality. Thus Julius Riffert's Borgia announces that:

> There's but one way
> To be victorious in the struggle
> Between the beasts of prey called men:
> Lest you yourself want to go under in
> The stream of life, you have to be
> More forceful and more ruthless an oppressor
> Than everybody else. Victor or vanquished—
> That is the motto.[44]

In Rudolf Lothar's *Cesare Borgia's Downfall* (1893), the hero exonerates his crimes with the following reflections on might and right:

> There shan't be laws and duties betwixt Man and Man.
> Everyone should make his own laws and duties.
> The highest duty is the will of the strongest.[45]

It may have been this new cult of Renaissance ruthlessness that prompted the aging Burckhardt, in 1896, to dissociate himself explicitly from the early

41. Ibid., 170. See also *KSA,* 12:476, 478, 517 and 13:21, 52, 192, 480.

42. Friedrich Nietzsche, *Götzendämmerung oder Wie man mit dem Hammer philosophiert* (1889), *KSA,* 6:137.

43. See Walther Brecht, *Heinse und der ästhetische Immoralismus. Zur Geschichte der italienischen Renaissance in Deutschland* (Berlin, 1911).

44. Julius Riffert, *Alexander Borgia. Trauerspiel in fünf Akten* (Leipzig, 1889), 30.

45. Rudolf Lothar, *Cäsar Borgia's Ende. Trauerspiel in einem Akt* (Dresden, 1893), 26.

modern "men of force" (*Gewaltmenschen*) and "Outlaws" glorified by Nietzsche.[46] Unlike Nietzsche, Burckhardt never idealized the neopagan immorality of the tyrants. In light of their highly developed personalities, he remarked, it was hard to "pass moral judgment" on the despots.[47] Nonetheless, in the first section of *Civilization,* entitled "The State as a Work of Art," he identified a distinctive aesthetic quality in their violent political maneuvers and an elective affinity between them and the great artists they patronized, such as Leonardo and Raphael.[48] The "mysterious connection" that Nietzsche posited between "the artwork and the battlefield" in ancient Greece[49] also informed Burckhardt's interpretation of Renaissance culture. The fin-de-siècle playwrights studying *Civilization*—in many cases, no doubt, through a Nietzschean lens—were fascinated by this connection and turned it into a leitmotif of what Thomas Mann later mockingly called their cult of "blood and beauty" and their "aestheticism of ruthlessness."

Italian Despots and German Decadents: Renaissancismus and Its Discontents, 1890–1927

Literary as well as cultural historians of modern Germany have argued that in the heated ideological debates at the fin de siècle, reference to the Renaissance implied belief in the emancipatory mission of the bourgeoisie, political and social progress, and 'modernity.'[50] To be sure, the representatives of Re-

46. Burckhardt to Ludwig von Pastor, 19 November 1896: "I have never discoursed with him [Nietzsche] on the man of force; I don't even know if he already espoused this idea when I was still seeing him on a more regular basis. . . . For my part, I have never been an admirer of the men of force and outlaws in history. I rather regarded them as *flagella dei.*" Jacob Burckhardt, *Briefe,* 10 vols., ed. Max Burckhardt (Basel, 1949–1986), 10:263.

47. Burckhardt, *Kultur der Renaissance,* 13–4. See also 85, 157.

48. See, e.g., ibid., 85.

49. Friedrich Nietzsche, "Der griechische Staat" (1871), *KSA,* 1:772: "The mysterious connection between state and art . . . battlefield and work of art."

50. According to Rolf-Peter Janz and Klaus Laermann, the liberal-conservative *Bürger* of the 1890s and 1900s felt drawn to the quattrocento because this period "of relative bourgeois power in the city-republics" best served their "need for legitimisation vis-à-vis the aristocracy." Rolf-Peter Janz and Klaus Laermann, *Arthur Schnitzler: Zur Diagnose des Wiener Bürgertums im Fin de Siècle* (Stuttgart, 1977), 81. The editors of the catalogue for the 1974 exhibition 'Aspekte der Gründerzeit' at the Academy of Arts in Berlin similarly argue that the appropriation of quattrocento and cinquecento art was supposed to dem-

naissancismus generally had little time for the medievalizing nostalgia of neoromantic reactionaries and their obsession with a premodern 'community' (*Gemeinschaft*).[51] They hailed the Renaissance, after all, because it had exploded the corporate structures of the Holy Roman Empire with its new secular and individualistic ethos. Yet the idea of the Renaissance that they inherited from Burckhardt and Nietzsche was an ambivalent construct, one in which modern and antimodern elements were strangely intertwined. The connection that Burckhardt and Nietzsche established between the quattrocento and nineteenth-century Europe, as has been shown above, was tenuous. Both saw few similarities between the contemporary bourgeois *satisfait* and the tyrants living dangerous lives in the early modern *signorie*.

The playwrights of the fin de siècle similarly called into question the traditional liberal teleologies that posited Renaissance Italy as the cradle of bourgeois emancipation and the modern constitutional state. Significantly, the heroes of their dramas were hardly ever drawn from 'bourgeois' or 'protobourgeois' groups like the mercantile elites of Venice or Florence. Almost invariably, they were antibourgeois types: military leaders, princes, artists, clerics, noblewomen. As Robert Misch's Cesare Borgia reminds his sister in *Tiger-Borgia* (1905): "You are a Borgia, not a little bourgeois woman who can sigh and give her heart away as she pleases."[52] Rudolf Herzog's *Condottieri* (1905), one of the most popular Renaissance dramas of the time, shows Bartolomeo Colleoni as the representative of a new heroic breed of men "who live from day to day," worlds apart from the "miserly merchants" (*Krämerseelen*) of the Republic of Venice (see Figure 13).[53] Like so many tyrannical characters, Colleoni seems to be moving in a moral and religious void, where the will is the only measure.[54]

---

onstrate the "self-consciousness and prosperity of the liberal-conservative bourgeoisie." *Aspekte der Gründerzeit, 1870–1890,* ed. Peter Hahlbrock et al. (Berlin, 1974), 155.

51. An important exception is Adolf Bartels (1862–1945), who was a prominent spokesman of the so-called *Heimatkunstbewegung*. For the *völkisch* ideas permeating his literary productions, see Karl O. Conrady, "Vor Adolf Bartels wird gewarnt. Aus einem Kapitel mißverstandener Heimatliebe," in his *Literatur und Germanistik als Herausforderung* (Frankfurt am Main, 1974), 227–32.

52. Robert Misch, *Übermenschen* (Berlin, 1905), 26: "Du bist eine Borgia, keine kleine Bürgersfrau."

53. Rudolf Herzog, *Die Condottieri: Schauspiel in vier Akten* (Stuttgart, 1905), 79, 20.

54. Ibid., 19: "The will! It is precisely the will through which we live, no matter *how* we live. This is the motto of the strong."

Figure 13. Andrea del Verrocchio's equestrian statue of Bartolomeo
Colleoni (completed in 1496), the model for Rudolf Herzog's protagonist in his 1905 play *Condottieri*.

The despots of Renaissancismus were given ample opportunity by their
creators to manifest this will in a variety of misdeeds. Sexual transgression
was a common theme and often involved incest, rape, homosexuality, or
pedophilia. Oscar Panizza's *Council of Love* (1894) and Emil Ludwig's *The
Pope and the Adventurer* (1910) both offered vivid examples of papal debauchery in Renaissance Rome—so vivid, indeed, that their plays were
banned by the censors.[55] Political atrocities—from attempted poisoning to

55. On the scandal provoked by Panizza's *Liebeskonzil* in 1894, see Peter Jelavich, *Munich and Theatrical Modernism: Politics, Playwriting, and Performance, 1890–1914* (Cam-

mutilation, fratricide to patricide—were shown with an Ovidian love for detail. In his Borgia drama of 1910, Victor Hahn dedicated an entire majestic
scene to the execution of the rebellious condottieri of Sinigaglia at the hands
of Cesare Borgia.

Frequently, the staging of such tyrannical transgressions was little more
than *épater le bourgeois*: a taboo-breaking pose intended to shock the audience while playing to its voyeuristic impulses.[56] Sometimes, however, the tyrants served as a mouthpiece for the aestheticist's discontent, his longing for
liberation from the stifling corset of bourgeois morality. A number of fin-
de-siècle playwrights conceived their despots as artists, brilliant *Realpolitiker*
intent on recreating Italy in a new image. Bismarck might have been a model
here,[57] or Cavour, but the historiographical inspiration came from Jacob
Burckhardt. Alluding to the first section of *Civilization,* Herzog's Colleoni
calls Venice his "artistic creation" (*künstlerisches Gebilde*).[58] Hahn's Borgia
employs the same metaphor:

> Just as the master craftsman
> Needs dirty clay for his work,
> In front of which humanity sinks down, a-trembling,
> Thus the prince needs the people for his art.[59]

Despite such lofty declamations, the political creations of the fin-de-siècle
tyrants often turned out to be short-lived. At the end of Leo Greiner's play,
The Fall of Duke Boccanera (1908), the eponymous hero, contemplating his
untimely death, laments the fate which is about to take the chisel out of his
"sculptor's hands."[60] Weigand's Renaissance tetralogy concludes on a similarly melancholy note. Lorenzino, the princely protagonist of the final play,

bridge, Mass., 1985), 54–74. On the reception of Ludwig's *Der Papst und der Abenteurer*
(1910), see Uekermann, *Renaissancismus,* 246–8. In 1895, young Thomas Mann defended
Panizza's imprisonment for blasphemy in an article for the conservative newspaper *The
Twentieth Century.* See Kurzke, *Thomas Mann,* 96.

56. See Uekermann, *Renaissancismus,* 125–6.

57. Two of the most prominent representatives of Renaissancismus—Carl Bleibtreu
and Emil Ludwig—went on to write biographies of the Iron Chancellor.

58. Herzog, *Condottieri,* 35.

59. Victor Hahn, *Cesar Borgia. Die Tragödie der Renaissance* (Stuttgart, 1922), 108.

60. Leo Greiner, *Herzog Boccaneras Ende: Drama* (Berlin, 1908), 66.

feels that he lives in a "swamp whose every corner smells of death." "Sick, exhausted, and tired," he is unable to halt his own decline—or that of the Florentine Republic.[61] The sense of transitoriness, decline, and impending doom is particularly pronounced among the Viennese representatives of Renaissancismus. In Hofmannsthal's *Death of Titian* (1892), it was symbolized by the plague, which was also a popular motif in painterly representations of the Renaissance at the turn of the century (see Figure 14).[62] Paul Wertheimer saw a particular "shadow of resignation" hanging over the rebirth promised in Hermann Bahr's *Renaissance* (1897).[63] Bahr and the other members of the Young Vienna movement, according to Wertheimer, found the "historical counterpart" to their own time not in the quattrocento with its "strong emotions," but in the "melancholy" atmosphere of the "sinking Renaissance"[64] This melancholy mood is impressively captured in Böcklin's famous *Villa by the Sea* (see Figure 8 in Suzanne Marchand's essay, above).

Contemporary German dramatists such as Emil Ludwig likewise projected a topical "intimation of decadence" onto the late Renaissance.[65] "We are very ripe," Lorenzo remarks in Ludwig's Medici drama *A Decline* (1904), "and now we fall." A "free spirit [*Schöngeist*] of the first order," the Magnifico chooses to ignore the political threat of Savonarola and instead experiences his own decay as an aesthetic phenomenon: "What a delight to sense oneself at every moment and to relish the whole pleasure of slow decline!"[66] Reiterating a topos of fin-de-siècle aestheticism, Ludwig and the Young Viennese conceived the late Renaissance as an age of both decadence and heightened artistic refinement. The brilliant cultural achievements of Lorenzo's court in *A Decline* are the phosphorescent glow of a decaying body politic.

The Renaissance men of Renaissancismus were essentially Protean fig-

61. Wilhelm Weigand, *Die Renaissance. Ein Dramenzyklus* (Munich, 1899), 88, 83.

62. See Ritter-Santini, "Maniera Grande," 185–6.

63. Paul Wertheimer, "Hermann Bahrs *Renaissance*," *Die Gesellschaft* 13 (1897): 91–103, quoted in *Das Junge Wien: Österreichische Literatur- und Kunstkritik 1887–1902*, 2 vols., ed. Gotthart Wunbert (Tübingen, 1975), 2:780–90 (quotation, 783).

64. Ibid., 788, 790. See Karl Brandi, *Die Renaissance in Florenz und Rom* (Leipzig, 1899), 219: "More than anything else, it is the decline [*das Vergehen*] of the Renaissance that captivates us."

65. Emil Ludwig, *Geschenke des Lebens: Ein Rückblick* (Berlin, 1931), 158.

66. Emil Ludwig, *Ein Untergang. Drama in fünf Akten* (Berlin, 1904), 43.

Figure 14. Arnold Böcklin, *The Plague,* 1898.

Öffentliche Kunstsammlung Basel, Kunstmuseum. Permanent loan of the Gottfried Keller
Foundation, 1902. Photo: Öffentliche Kunstsammlung, Martin Bühler.

ures: reckless overreachers and heralds of a new age of 'noble values' in their
Nietzschean guises, feeble aesthetes and 'ripe' representatives of a corrupt
civilization in their decadent costume. They thus betray a peculiar tension
in the conception of early modern Italy underlying the cult of the Renaissance. This tension comes to the fore in another central motif of Renaissancismus: 'this-worldliness' (*Diesseitigkeit*).

A large majority of Renaissance dramatists followed Burckhardt's *Civilization* in emphasizing the neopagan character of the age. In Carl Bleibtreu's *Demon* (1887), Leonardo reduces the Christian cross to a "mere symbol" and proudly pronounces the "gospel of ancient beauty": "Long live the golden age of the great rebirth!"[67] Some playwrights gave this heathenism a more radical, Nietzschean twist. Berthold Weiß's Cesare Borgia, for example, upon hearing of Copernicus's astronomic findings, announces the death of God and describes the commandments of the Bible as the "inventions" of lesser men, designed to restrain greater ones like himself.[68] Yet very few dramatists joined in the anticlerical and anti-Latin polemics launched by Heinrich Treitschke and his followers during the 1870s. The worldly ways of the papacy under Alexander VI were sometimes the butt of satirical attacks, but these usually lacked the *kulturkämpferisch* bile of the *Gründerzeit*.

Not everyone bought into Burckhardt's disenchanted image of the Renaissance. Wilhelm Weigand reintroduced an explicitly Christian framework for the era in his *Belt of Venus* (1908), which ended with Pope Julius's "divine" judgment over the "dissipated" people of Perugia.[69] Victor Hahn concluded his Borgia drama on an equally apocalyptic note. Here it was young Martin Luther who condemned the corrupt Renaissance papacy.[70] A number of playwrights cast Savonarola as the scourge of clerical corruption—and as a harbinger of the Reformation.[71]

These Protestant, eschatological notes brought a strange dissonance into the otherwise confident and this-worldly music of Renaissancismus, revealing that by around 1900, Burckhardt's interpretation of the Renaissance no longer went unchallenged. The principal critique came from the Wagnerian camp. As early as 1885, the art historian Henry Thode—Cosima Wagner's son-in-law and a frequent contributor to the Bayreuth Circle's *völkisch* organ, the *Bayreuther Blätter*—called into question the secular, 'Latin' interpretation of the Renaissance in Burckhardt's *Civilization*. According to

67. Carl Bleibtreu, *Der Dämon: Tragödie in fünf Akten*, in C. Bleibtreu, *Vaterland: Drei Dramen* (Leipzig, 1887), 223–4.

68. Berthold Weiß, *Caesar Borgia: Schauspiel in vier Aufzügen* (Zürich, 1893), 34.

69. Wilhelm Weigand, *Der Gürtel der Venus. Eine Tragödie in fünf Akten* (Munich, 1908) 108.

70. Hahn, *Cesar Borgia*, 171.

71. See Alfred Teichmann, *Savonarola in der deutschen Dichtung* (Berlin, 1937), 11–31.

Thode, the Renaissance was a movement of spiritual renewal that began with St. Francis and concluded with Luther.[72]

Thode was seconded by Konrad Burdach, a prominent Germanist and also an associate of Bayreuth. More than anyone else, it was Burdach who shook Burckhardt's exclusive identification of Renaissance civilization with quattrocento Italy and traced its development north of the Alps, most notably to Bohemia.[73] According to Burdach, early Church reformers and mystics like Joachim of Fiore first had formulated the notion of *renovatio,* which represented the key concept of the Renaissance.[74] The various Renaissance movements of *renovatio* prepared the intellectual ground for the Protestant Reformation, which marked Europe's true moment of spiritual rebirth.[75] Burdach thus endowed the Renaissance with chiliastic and palingenetic ideas that resonated with particular fin-de-siècle discourses on life reform and national renewal.[76] At the same time, he restored the old *kulturprotestantisch*[77] credo (which dated back to Hegel) that Wittenberg—not Florence—had been the birthplace of modern subjectivity. With Burdach and Thode, the 'problem of the Renaissance', as Johan Huizinga called it, became a German problem.[78]

In 1899, yet another Wagnerian, Houston Stewart Chamberlain, tackled this problem from a decidedly *völkisch* angle.[79] Chamberlain's massive, ram-

72. See Henry Thode, *Franz von Assisi und die Anfänge der Kunst der Renaissance in Italien* (Berlin, 1885).

73. See Frank Borchardt, "Petrarch: The German Connection," in *Francis Petrarch Six Centuries Later: A Symposium,* ed. Aldo Scaglione, *Studies in Languages* 3 (1975): 427–31.

74. See Konrad Burdach, "Sinn und Ursprung der Worte Renaissance und Reformation," *Sitzungsberichte der preußischen Akademie der Wissenschaften* (Phil.-hist. Kl.) 32 (1910), 594–646.

75. See Burdach, *Deutsche Renaissance,* 2nd ed. (Berlin, 1917), 92.

76. See, e.g., Nicholas Goodrick-Clarke, *The Occult Roots of Nazism: Secret Aryan Cults and Their Influence on Nazi Ideology. The Ariosophists of Austria and Germany, 1890–1935* (New York, 1985), esp. ch. 7 ("The German Millenium").

77. See Gangolf Hübinger, *Kulturprotestantismus und Politik. Zum Verhältnis von Liberalismus und Protestantismus im wilhelminischen Deutschland* (Tübingen, 1994).

78. See Johan Huizinga, "The Problem of the Renaissance," in his *Men and Ideas* (Princeton, N.J., 1959), 243–88.

79. He was Wagner's son-in-law. On Chamberlain as an ideologist, see Geoffrey G. Field, *Evangelist of Race: The Germanic Vision of Houston Stewart Chamberlain* (New York, 1981).

bling, and best-selling *Foundations of the Nineteenth Century,* racist prophecy parading as 'universal history,' interpreted the Renaissance as the "rebirth of free Germanic individuality" and a "through and through Teutonic feat."[80] Chamberlain resolved the apparent paradox that this feat had occurred largely on Italian soil by identifying the major Renaissance artists as Lombards, Goths, and Franks—and hence of Germanic origin.[81] As the concentration of Germanic blood decreased in Italy, the Renaissance (Chamberlain in fact carefully avoided the term)[82] came to an early end. Teutonic types and "unconscious Protestants" like Savonarola and Michelangelo were extinguished by "Rome." The lasting renewal of European culture, according to Chamberlain, only came with Luther's Reformation.[83]

Six years later, Ludwig Woltmann, a social Darwinist and self-proclaimed historical anthropologist, tried to put Chamberlain's theories on a more scientific footing.[84] Like Chamberlain, Woltmann interpreted the Renaissance not as a rebirth of classical antiquity but as the emergence of a new, "independently creative" (*selbstschöpferische*) race on the stage of world history.[85] Drawing on a wide range of craniological measurements as well as comparative statistics of body height, complexion, and hair color, he concluded that "at least eighty-five to ninety percent of the Italian geniuses [of the Renaissance] belonged wholly or predominantly to the Germanic race."[86] This Germanization of the Renaissance reached its apogee during World War I, when Italy abandoned its former allies Austria and Germany to join the Entente's defense of what French war propaganda liked to call the Latin heritage of

80. Houston Stewart Chamberlain, *Die Grundlagen des neunzehnten Jahrhunderts,* 2 vols., 21st ed. (Munich, 1936), 2:828.

81. Ibid., 2:825–6.

82. See ibid., 2:848: "Perhaps there has never been a more pernicious concept introduced into historiography than that of the Renaissance. For it was associated with the phantasm of a rebirth of Latin and Greek culture, an idea worthy of the half-breed souls of degenerate southern Europe."

83. See ibid., 2:1009: "With this [his liberation from Rome] this man [Luther] became the hinge [*Angelpunkt*] of world history. . . . This hero emancipated the entire world."

84. Chamberlain obliged with a courteous cross-reference in a later edition of the *Grundlagen.* Ibid., 2:833 n. 1.

85. Ludwig Woltmann, *Die Germanen und die Renaissance in Italien* (Leipzig, 1905), 4.

86. Ibid., 145.

the West. On the other side of the Rhine, German intellectuals began to denounce the legacy of Italian humanism as the "doom of German culture,"
to quote the title of Richard Benz's popular pamphlet of 1915.[87] Against the
superficial art and learning of early modern Italy, they held up Albrecht
Dürer and Ulrich von Hutten as representatives of a specifically northern
Renaissance. Others called for a reappraisal of the Gothic style.[88]

Ironically enough, Renaissancismus had prepared the way for these anti-
Latin polemics. By emphasizing the immoral and decadent aspects of quattrocento civilization, the playwrights of the fin de siècle anticipated some of
the arguments put forth by the detractors of the Renaissance in the 1900s
and 1910s. Similarly, by depleting the humanist and rationalist aspects of
Burckhardt's conception of the Renaissance, they opened the door to neoromantic revisionists like Burdach and Thode. In this respect, they contributed to the rapid decline of Renaissancismus after World War I. During the
Weimar years, the idea of renewal became more or less monopolized by
the New Right. Renaissance now meant national rebirth, and members of
the Conservative Revolution began to herald a German 'Third Humanism.'

Published in 1927, Ernst Kantorowicz's biography of the thirteenth-
century emperor Frederick II, one of the most popular works of history in
the 1920s, reverberated with this notion of a German renaissance. A member
of the George circle and deeply influenced by its palingenetic nationalism,
Kantorowicz conceived Frederick as a Renaissance ruler, the "father of all
the fifteenth-century tyrants, the Scala, Visconti, [and] Borgia."[89] In the tradition of Nietzsche, he presented the emperor as a brilliant antagonist of the
papacy and ruthless autocrat beyond the claims of Christian morality. But
Kantorowicz also drew heavily on Burdach, portraying Frederick's reign as

87. Richard Benz, *Die Renaissance, das Verhängnis der deutschen Cultur* (Jena, 1915).

88. On the concept of a German Renaissance and its nationalist significance in the
fields of architectural and art history, see the astute remarks of Thomas Nipperdey,
Deutsche Geschichte 1866–1918, 2 vols., 3rd ed. (Munich, 1993), 1:720. As early as 1902,
Ferdinand Avenarius had founded a *Dürerbund;* see Fritz Stern, *The Politics of Cultural
Despair: A Study in the Rise of the Germanic Ideology*, 2nd ed. (Berkeley, Calif., 1974), 174.
On the new respectability of the Gothic, see Magdalena Bushart, *Der Geist der Gotik und
die expressionistische Kunst. Kunstgeschichte und Kunsttheorie, 1911–1925* (Munich, 1990),
esp. 8–129.

89. Ernst Kantorowicz, *Kaiser Friedrich der Zweite* (Berlin, 1927), 450.

a first age of *renovatio,* a quasi-apocalyptic time of spiritual and cultural renewal that prefigured the Reformation. His Hohenstaufen hero, moreover,
was a distinctly northern figure— "the most Germanic emperor" who ruled
like a scourge of God over the "dissipated" people of Italy.[90] The extraordinary success of *Emperor Frederick the Second* reveals the continuing appeal
of Renaissancismus twenty years after its heyday; but Kantorowicz's book
also points up the problematic ideological transformations it had undergone
since the fin de siècle.

Bellezza, Bürgertugend, and the Sword of God: Thomas Mann's Renaissance in 1905

In 1929, two years after the publication of *Emperor Frederick,* the prominent
literary historian Walter Rehm proclaimed the "overcoming" of the fin-de-
siècle cult of the Renaissance. According to Rehm, Thomas Mann's play *Fiorenza* had played a pivotal role in this process.[91] Rehm's judgment, which
influenced a number of subsequent literary and cultural histories, rests on a
reductionist reading of the Renaissance cult—and of Mann's play as well.
Mann's relationship to Renaissancismus, in fact, was much more ambivalent. While vehemently rejecting certain elements of it, he nonetheless drew
on some of its principal topoi. No doubt, *Fiorenza* was an attack on the "hysterical Renaissance" of the decadent movement, which included his brother
Heinrich; but it also represented Mann's attempt to positively reevaluate the
meaning of the age, as well as his own role as writer and Bürger.[92]

Since he first began to work on *Fiorenza* in 1898, Mann was almost permanently exposed to the Renaissance in one form or another. He spent two
years in northern Italy, including Florence, where he visited the Uffizi Gallery. He read the classics of Renaissancismus—Burckhardt and Nietzsche, as
well as Gobineau's *La Renaissance* (1877)—and studied a wealth of visual
material for his play, from the terra cotta bust of Lorenzo in the Royal Mu-

90. Ibid., 118. For Kantorowicz's Germanization of Frederick II, see Martin Ruehl,
" 'In this time without emperors': The Politics of Ernst Kantorowicz's *Kaiser Friedrich der
Zweite* Reconsidered," *Journal of the Warburg and Courtauld Institute* 63 (2000): 196–305.

91. Rehm, "Renaissancekult," 324–6.

92. For Mann's self-embourgeoisement around 1903, see Helmut Koopmann,
"Thomas Manns Bürgerlichkeit," in *Thomas Mann 1875–1975: Vorträge in München-
Zürich-Lübeck,* ed. Beatrix Bludau et al. (Frankfurt am Main, 1977), 39–60.

seum of Berlin to little reproductions of Ghirlandaio in the *Kunst-Kalender*. As a resident of Munich, the so-called 'Florence of the Isar,' he was surrounded by a cityscape filled with neo-Renaissance architecture.[93] One of the most prominent examples of this fin-de-siècle architectural style, favored by the German (in particular, the German-Jewish) upper middle class, was the Villa Pringsheim, on Arcisstraße 12, which was often referred to as a 'Renaissance palace' (see Figures 15 and 16).[94] Mann was first invited to the Pringsheims early in 1903 and immediately fell in love not just with the daughter of the house but also its interior decoration, above all the gobelin tapestries and the doorframe "in giallo antico."[95]

This was a kind of Renaissance quite different from that espoused by Mann's brother Heinrich. Heinrich's trilogy *The Goddesses* (1903) was a typical contribution to the fin-de-siècle cult of the Renaissance, a sometimes ironical, sometimes pompous paean to the ruthless, beautiful world of the quattrocento as reenacted by the novel's heroine, the duchess Violante of Assy. A great patroness, Violante, through a series of romantic adventures and sensual exploits, gradually turns her own life into a work of art. Thomas was especially appalled by what he called the novel's "sexualism," which he believed revealed an "utter ethical nonchalance." *The Goddesses* betrayed Heinrich not just as an immoral aestheticist and decadent dandy (see Figure 17);[96] it also articulated his newly found left-liberal *Weltanschauung*, which Thomas found equally distasteful.[97] The first part of the novel, entitled

93. See Heinrich Habel, *Münchener Fassaden. Bürgerhäuser des Historismus und des Jugendstils* (Munich, 1974).

94. See Hanno-Walter Kruft, "Renaissance und Renaissancismus bei Thomas Mann," in *Renaissance und Renaissancismus*, ed. Buck, 93–101.

95. *Thomas Mann–Heinrich Mann: Briefwechsel*, 26–7.

96. Thomas Mann to Heinrich Mann, 5 December 1903, in *Thomas Mann–Heinrich Mann: Briefwechsel, 1900–1949*, ed. Hans Wysling, 2nd ed. (Frankfurt am Main, 1984), 36. In this letter, Thomas subtly identified Heinrich's eroticism as a Latin, "un-German" trait (*außerhalb der deutschen Entwicklung*), while emphasizing his own "Germanness" (*daß ich dem deutschen Volksempfinden näher stände*).

97. See his letter to Heinrich Mann of 27 February 1904: "Much more remarkable, strangely interesting and in my eyes still a little implausible is the development of your world view towards liberalism. . . . This must give you an undreamt-of feeling of youth and power. . . . At the moment, 'liberty' means little to me. It is a purely mental-spiritual concept for me, equivalent with 'honesty'. . . . But I have no interest in political liberty." *Thomas Mann–Heinrich Mann Briefwechsel*, 1st ed., 25.

Figure 15. The neo-Renaissance façade of the Villa Pringsheim in Arcisstraße 12, Munich.

Thomas-Mann-Archiv, ETH Zurich.

Diana, was permeated with republican, emancipatory rhetoric—one of the heroes was modeled on Garibaldi—which anticipated Heinrich's later turn to the left and the biting social criticism of *Man of Straw* (1918). There can be little doubt that Mann's critique of the Renaissance artists in *Fiorenza* was aimed at least in part at his brother. In a letter of December 1903, he had already remarked that Heinrich's recent works reminded him of the "epic poets of the Quattrocento and Cinquecento" who were actually "no poets at all," but mere "artists": "What they wrote was an artistic literature of enter-

Figure 16. The Renaissance salon in the Villa Pringsheim, "with the Gobelins, the Lenbachs, and the door frame of *giallo antico*" (Thomas to Heinrich Mann, 27 February 1904).

Thomas-Mann-Archiv, ETH Zurich.

tainment [*künstlerische Unterhaltungslektüre*], a wild and colorful flight of risqué, impossible, and obscene diversions."[98]

If *Fiorenza* was conceived as a response to *The Goddesses,* it was also an exercise in self-criticism. The increasingly famous—and wealthy—author of *Buddenbrooks,* who had recently been introduced to Munich's haute bourgeoisie and had begun his courtship of one of the city's most eligible daughters, wanted to mark his distance from his own decadent beginnings and writings, such as *Little Herr Friedemann* (1898) and *Tristan* (1903), which had toyed with aestheticism.[99] *Buddenbrooks* itself, of course, had given a remarkably sympathetic portrait (as Mann acknowledged) of the "psychol-

98. Ibid., 37–8.
99. See Wolfdieterich Rasch, "Thomas Mann und die Décadence," in *Thomas Mann, 1875–1975,* 271–84, and Reinhild Schwede, *Wilhelminische Neuromantik. Flucht oder*

Figure 17. Heinrich Mann as *déca-dent:* a caricature by the *Simplicis-simus* illustrator Olaf Gulbransson.

Olaf-Gulbransson-Museum für Graphik & Karikatur, Tegernsee.

ogy of the spent life force and . . . the spiritual sophistication and aesthetic inspiration that accompany biological decay."[100] *Tonio Kröger* was a first reckoning, but in its ironic detachment, it still revealed a subtle ambivalence towards the aestheticist position. Such detachment was almost completely absent from *Fiorenza.*[101]

Zuflucht? Ästhetizistischer, exotistischer, und provinzialistischer Eskapismus im Werk Haupt-manns, Hesses und der Brüder Mann um 1900 (Frankfurt am Main, 1987).

100. Thomas Mann, "Zu einem Kapitel aus Buddenbrooks" (1949), *GW*, 554. See also Mann's retrospective, self-critical acknowledgment of his former aestheticism in a 1915 letter to Paul Amann: "I am partly of Latin-American blood . . . and have, at times, paid tribute in my works to the rhetoric of Latin aestheticism." Thomas Mann, *Briefe an Paul Amann, 1915–1952*, ed. Herbert Wegener (Lübeck, 1959), 33.

101. See Reed, *Thomas Mann*, 94: "[Fiorenza] is the Case of the Absent Ironist. The dramatic form excludes the sophisticated narrative voice and the array of syntactical means which would clear [Mann] of responsibility for the excesses of his figures. Without

Fiorenza employed the language of decadence in order to expose it. Its central topic—the decline of the Medici—was a classic motif of Renaissancismus,[102] but Mann approached it from a new angle. At first sight, he seems simply to be recapitulating standard decadent themes. Lorenzo's agony, even though it only moves to center stage in the final act, determines the atmosphere of the entire play. One of the first things we learn about him is that his "vital marrow" is "decomposing." He describes himself as standing "with one foot in Charon's boat" and "tired unto death." The visions that haunt him in his sleep recall Aschenbach's dreams of violence and decay in *Death in Venice.* In the context of Renaissancismus, there is little new here. Weigand, Ludwig, and Uhde depicted the fall of the Medici in a similar light.[103]

But insofar as he equates Lorenzo's decline with the decay of quattrocento art and learning Mann transcends the discursive boundaries of Renaissancismus. When Lorenzo descends into the sinner's grave, as Mann remarked in the *Reflections,* he takes his entire world of beauty and scholarship with him. In the plays of Ludwig and Hofmannsthal, political and economic deterioration is offset by a late flowering of culture. In *Fiorenza,* however, there is no such compensation. The sun setting over the Medici does not drench Florence in final, glorious burgundy. The arts and humanities at Lorenzo's court, as described by Mann, are as corrupt as their patron.

Mann's portrait of Renaissance art is particularly scathing and almost without equal in the literature of Renaissancismus. The group of sculptors, painters, architects, and goldsmiths around Lorenzo appear engaged in a frivolous worship of the "plasticity of the external world." Their repeated lip service to the aestheticist credo of art for art's sake barely conceals their base and materialist motives. Sycophantic courtiers and heathen hedonists, they lack any "ethical standards" (*Gesinnung*).[104] Lorenzo's son, Giovanni de' Me-

---

these, the characters must speak their own minds direct, and the ones who bear some intellectual message like Lorenzo and Savonarola, must do so with vehemence. If one cannot take the reconstructed Florence seriously, from the seriousness of the protagonists one cannot escape."

102. Uekermann, *Renaissancismus,* 148–56.

103. Mann, *Fiorenza,* in *GW,* 8:971, 1036, 1040.

104. Ibid., 8:1006. Mann's stage directions endow one of them with the "black eyes of an animal" (*schwarze Tieraugen*)—an echo of *Tonio Kröger* (*GW,* 8:305–6), where Tonio complains to Lisaweta: "By God, leave me alone with Italy. . . . Art, right? A velvet blue sky, racy wine and sweet sensuality. . . . In short, I don't like this. . . . All this *bellezza*

dici, has so fallen under the influence of their grotesque cult of beauty that he can no longer bear the sight of his suffering father.

The humanists do not fare much better in *Fiorenza*. Their lengthy arguments *in utramque partem* betray a similar lack of *Gesinnung*. Pico's defence of morality, for instance, rests on purely superficial, aesthetic grounds. Poliziano's neopagan scholarship seems even more shallow. His plea for the canonization of the "divine Plato" is rendered absurd by Ficino's inability to provide spiritual solace for the dying Lorenzo by invoking the philosophy of ideas. Purgatory, as the Magnifico wryly remarks, "is easier to understand than Plato." Mann's critique of the humanists turns into biting ridicule when Poliziano praises a well-known Florentine prostitute for her "great humanistic learning."[105] One of the marginal notes in Mann's copy of Burckhardt's *Civilization* brings home the point: "Humanism, classicism, art, beauty [are] the business of prostitutes [*Dirnen*]."[106] This comment suggests that Savonarola's assessment of the humanists and artists as "epicureans and pigs" might have been closer to Mann's own stance than some critics would have us think.[107]

Throughout the play, Mann sharply contrasts the sensuality and this-worldliness of humanists with the spirituality and ascetic moralism of Savonarola. Unlike other Renaissance dramatists, however, Mann does not present the friar as a mere zealot or fanatic. Savonarola sees the "need of the world" behind its "glistening surface." His call, "Long live Christ!" reverberates with compassion and an apocalyptic promise that contains potentially egalitarian elements.[108] Yet Mann's hero is not the democratic revolutionary that he had been in Carl Hepp's play of 1898.[109] The equality he promises is

---

makes me nervous. Moreover, I don't like all the terribly vibrant men down there with their black animal gaze [*mit dem schwarzen Tierblick*]. Latin people have no conscience in their eyes."

105. Mann, *Fiorenza, GW,* 8:986–7, 962, 1025, 968.

106. Mann's copy of Jacob Burckhardt, *Die Cultur der Renaissance in Italien,* vol. 1, 7th ed. (Leipzig, 1899) is preserved at the TMA. The marginalium in question is on 374.

107. Mann, *Fiorenza, GW,* 8:966. See, e.g., Pikulik, "Thomas Mann und die Renaissance." Pikulik regards Mann's critique of humanism in *Fiorenza* as essentially ambivalent.

108. Mann, *Fiorenza, GW,* 8:975, 1060, 1030, 1066.

109. See Carl Hepp, *Der Prior von San Marco. Ein Drama in fünf Aufzügen* (Leipzig, 1898).

essentially an equality before God and thus quite compatible with a theocratic dictatorship. His revolutionary pathos is very much that of a conservative revolution—and far removed from the republican rhetoric of the Marchese in Heinrich's *Goddesses*.

For all his iconoclastic animus against the heathen classicism of Lorenzo's artists, Savonarola is not an "enemy of beauty," as Poliziano wrongly believes. Mann makes much of the fact that Savonarola inspired Botticelli to abandon his classicizing projects and devote his art fully to the representation of religious themes. We also hear (from no other than Pico) that his theological writings are of great literary quality. For Mann, Savonarola is clearly more than just a critic of the dissolute hangers-on at Lorenzo's court. He also embodies a new artistic ideal: art as moral achievement and spiritual calling.[110]

At the same time, it would be wrong to read Mann's Savonarola as a representative of pure "spirit," opposed to Lorenzo, the incarnation of "life." A number of Renaissance plays had depicted the prior along these lines, as a pious idealist whose noble plans for religious reform were easily undermined by his wily papal opponents.[111] Mann's notes in the margins of Villari's *History of Savonarola*, the main source for his play, illustrate his strong disagreement with this interpretation. They show that Mann thought Villari's portrait of Savonarola as a Christian "lamb" was "profoundly misconceived" (*stark verrannt*); he insisted that the churchman, despite his own protestations to the contrary, was a "tyrant."[112] In *Fiorenza*, accordingly, Mann endowed Savonarola with a "wild, hard force" and a "demonic" will to rule, although these authoritarian features hardly seem to be negative attributes in the play. They form a necessary complement to the friar's spirituality and enable him to both "know and act." It is precisely this ability to know and act that allows Savonarola to become the "Christian judge of morals," the sword of God descending on the worldly city of Florence. Only insofar as he unites the realm of the spirit and the realm of power can he carry

110. Mann, *Fiorenza, GW*, 8:1030, 966, 969, 1005, 1034.

111. See Uekermann, *Renaissancismus*, 137–8.

112. Mann's copy of Pasquale Villari, *Geschichte Savonarola's und seiner Zeit*, 2 vols. (Leipzig, 1868) is preserved at the TMA. The marginalia in question can be found on 2:175, 194, 49.

out the work of destruction and purification that will lay the foundations for his great final achievement: "the miracle of a reborn naiveté."[113]

In terms of the play's dialectic, this miracle is ultimately predicated on Lorenzo's death. Though he draws the figure of the Magnifico with a considerable degree of sympathy—and perhaps even empathy—Mann rarely misses an opportunity to remind the audience of Lorenzo's sensuality and immorality. Like Ludwig, Weigand, and a number of other dramatists, he presents Lorenzo as a decadent and an aesthete. But unlike these avatars of Renaissancismus, he does not allow Lorenzo to aestheticize his own decline. *Fiorenza* shows the duke's agony through the merciless lens of Savonarola. In fact, the prior's moral perspective frames the entire play. This is Mann's first intervention in Renaissancismus: he replaces its aesthetic framework with a moral one.

If Mann returns his Renaissance men to a realm of good and evil, he also presents them as essentially bourgeois types. There is no room in *Fiorenza* for any declarations of the master morality. The stock character of Renaissancismus—the tyrant—is conspicuously absent from *Fiorenza*, appearing only in the bathetic guise of Piero de' Medici, a mere Fortinbras, "arrogant, loud, [and] haughty." Lorenzo says of himself that he is "no Malatesta, no Borgia," but a member of the "bourgeois estate" (*Bürgerstande*). One suspects that this is part of the reason for Mann's largely sympathetic treatment of Lorenzo. Mann emphasizes the Magnifico's former "civic virtue" (*Bürgertugend*), which he has squandered in a life of sensual excess. As a result, the true representative of *Bürgertugend* in the play is Savonarola, with his ascetic "ethics of achievement" (*Leistungsethik*). Significantly, Mann's monkish hero turns out to be yet another *Bürger* in disguise. As early as act one, Savonarola reveals that he stems from a "well-respected bourgeois family." His achievement, which makes him the hero of *Fiorenza,* is that he has overcome his own physical and moral frailty. His is a "heroism of weakness,"[114] wholly at odds with the reckless vitalism embodied by all the tyrannical characters of Renaissancismus.[115]

---

113. Mann, *Fiorenza, GW,* 8:984, 1064.

114. Mann adopted this expression from Carl Albrecht Bernoulli, *Nietzsche und Overbeck,* 2 vols. (Jena, 1908). He first used it in the *Betrachtungen, GW,* 8:453.

115. Mann, *Fiorenza, GW,* 8:1038, 964.

This is Mann's second intervention: he reinvents the Renaissance as a bourgeois age. Savonarola's spirituality and asceticism are held up as bourgeois virtues against the decadent aestheticism of the artists and the hollow ruthlessness of Piero. Almost simultaneously with Georges Sorel and Max Weber, Mann projected a "heroic" genealogy of the bourgeoisie, contrasting it sharply with the decadent forms of fin-de-siècle *Bürgerlichkeit*. A comment in the 1918 *Reflections* shows that Mann was quite aware of the parallels between his notion of an "ascetic" bourgeois heroism and the theories laid out in Weber's *Protestant Ethic and the Spirit of Capitalism*. The "main characters" of his play, Mann remarked, were "symbols" of the "ascetic idea of a professional calling" that had been described by Weber and also by Ernst Troeltsch.[116]

Curiously, Mann observed in the *Reflections* that it was Nietzsche who had opened his eyes to the "psychological" connection between Protestantism, heroism, and *Bürgerlichkeit*. He claimed that Nietzsche—despite his later polemics against Christianity in general and Luther in particular—was a deeply Protestant thinker and a "spokesperson of the middle class."[117] It was this reading of Nietzsche that informed *Fiorenza*. Indeed, Mann's Renaissance play can be read as a first pronouncement of this idiosyncratic interpretation of Nietzsche. In opposition to the playwrights of Renaissancismus who glorified the transvaluative theories of the *Genealogy of Morals* (1887) and the *Antichrist* (1888). Mann presented his hero as an incarnation of the pessimistic, Protestant, and Schopenhauerian thoughts of the *Birth of Tragedy*. The idea that a "glistening surface" hides the true nature of the world, which is "eternal struggle" and "suffering," the emphasis on renunciation and redemption, the *unio mystica* of compassion[118]—all these things reveal Mann's deep engagement with Schopenhauer's metaphysics in the years 1899–1901.[119] Whereas the late Nietzsche denounced "ascetic ideals"

116. Mann, *Betrachtungen, GW*, 8:145. On Weber and Mann, see Edith Weiller, *Max Weber und die literarische Moderne. Ambivalente Begegnungen zweier Kulturen* (Stuttgart, 1994) and Harvey Goldmann, *Politics, Death, and the Devil: Self and Power in Max Weber and Thomas Mann* (Berkeley, Calif., 1992).

117. Mann, *Betrachtungen, GW*, 8:146.

118. Mann, *Fiorenza, GW*, 8:1041, 1061.

119. This engagement is evidenced in notebooks 4 (1899) and 5 (1900–1901): see Mann, *Notizbücher*, vol. 1. Of all the commentators on the play, Eilers is the only one to

as self-contradictory and life-denying, Schopenhauer praised asceticism as the highest form of human existence. More importantly, Schopenhauer posited a strong affinity between the ascetic and the artist, who shared a 'purely objective' contemplation of the tragic nature of the world. Nietzsche reiterated some of these ideas in the *Birth of Tragedy*. Adopting Schopenhauer and the early Nietzsche as his philosophical models in *Fiorenza,* Mann marked his distance from the "puerile," "hysterical" Nietzscheanism of Renaissancismus.

Mann's fourth—and in many ways most significant—intervention in Renaissancismus concerns his representation of Florentine 'this-worldliness' and its spiritual transformation at the hands of Savonarola. Mann describes this transformation in decidedly Protestant terms. There are frequent references to Savonarola's inwardness—his "inner experience," his mystic visions, his "glowing originality"—as well as to his repudiation of the wealth and moral laxity of the Church.[120] The marginal notes in Mann's copy of Villari's *Savonarola* confirm that he regarded the friar as a kind of Luther avant la lettre. Savonarola's courage and moral independence strike Mann as "essentially Protestant";[121] Villari's claim that Savonarola's emphasis on faith as the only precondition for salvation should not be misread as an early version of *sola fide* provokes the following marginalium: "It is certainly justified to a great degree to call him [Savonarola] a Protestant. He was essentially un-Catholic . . . and born to protest."[122]

In the context of Renaissancismus, this association of Savonarola with the Reformation carried a particular political force. In the 1890s, as we have seen, Burckhardt's secular, southern interpretation of the Renaissance came under attack from nationalist scholars and literati, who contrasted the moral corruption of Renaissance Italy with the pure spirituality of the Lutheran Reformation. With *Fiorenza,* Mann joined the debate. His play was both a renunciation of the fin-de-siècle fascination with the decadent beauty of the south and the declaration of a specifically 'northern' moral asceticism. Savonarola's sword symbolized the severing of his old ties to the aestheticist

---

pick up on the Schopenhauerian traces in *Fiorenza*. See Eilers, "Perspektiven und Montage," 89–97.

120. Mann, *Fiorenza, GW,* 8:965, 968, 983,

121. See Mann's notes in his Villari, *Geschichte,* 42, TMA.

122. Ibid., 285.

movement—and his new will to a masculine *Leistungsethik*. The piece suggests that in the early 1900s, Mann shared in the general preoccupation with cultural decline and the hope for a comprehensive, cataclysmic, national renewal. In *Gladius Dei*, the apocalyptic vision of a great cultural *Kladderadatsch* was still ironically reflected. In *Fiorenza*, it was staged with a quite unambiguous force.

The play reveals *kulturpessimistisch* anxieties and a Protestant nationalism that are absent from Mann's earlier works and only resurface again in 1914.[123] Critics have rightly noted the palingenetic hopes underlying Mann's writings in the first years of the Great War, his "feverish expectation of a 'new age.'"[124] *Fiorenza* shows that these concerns with a new *saeculum* and the recuperation of an original 'naiveté' date back to the early 1900s.[125] It is no coincidence that Mann first used the expression 'the Third Empire' (*das Dritte Reich*), which was formulated by the twelfth-century apocalyptic thinker Joachim of Fiore, in an essay on *Fiorenza* in 1912, where he defined it as the "reconciliation of spirit and art, knowledge and creation, intellectualism and naiveté, reason and demonism, asceticism and beauty."[126] He invoked the vision of a Third Reich again in his *Thoughts in War* of August 1914, this time with reference to the coming victory of German arms, which would bring about a "synthesis of power and spirit" (*Macht und Geist*)— precisely the synthesis embodied by his monkish hero in *Fiorenza*. In his treatise on *Frederick and the Great Coalition*, Mann described the Prussian king as a latter-day Savonarola: "a monk in a . . . soldier's uniform," who possessed "an element of the demonic" and who was driven by an "ultimately nihilistic fanaticism of achievement" (*im Grunde nihilistischer Fanat-*

---

123. See Lothar Pikulik, "Die Politisierung des ästheten im Ersten Weltkrieg," in *Thomas Mann, 1875–1975*, 61–74.

124. See *Sinn und Form: Sonderheft Thomas Mann* (Berlin 1965), 328: "As is clear from the *Reflections* and the correspondence with Amann and Bertram from those years, Thomas Mann lived in the feverish expectation of a new age."

125. See Hermann Kurzke, *Auf der Suche nach der verlorenen Irrationalität: Thomas Mann und der Konservatismus* (Würzburg, 1980), 105–45.

126. Thomas Mann, "Über *Fiorenza*," *GW*, 11:564: "Die Versöhnung von Geist und Kunst, von Erkenntnis und Schöpfertum, Intellektualismus und Einfalt, Vernunft und Dämonie, Askese und Schönheit—das Dritte Reich."

ismus der Leistung).[127] According to Mann, Frederick's politics were deeply determined by his Protestant faith.

Similarly, the frequent and acerbic attacks on Western civilization during the First World War—on the grounds of its superficiality, its lack of moral earnestness, and, with reference to Gabriel d'Annunzio, its "lascivious aestheticism"[128]—developed ideas that Mann had first expressed in his critique of humanism in *Fiorenza.* The *Reflections of a Non-Political Man,* begun in 1915, continued and in some respects radicalized these *nationalprotestantisch,* anti-Latin themes. Denouncing the Italian Renaissance as un-German and ridiculing its fin-de-siècle admirers as "hysteric" sensualists, Mann held up Dürer's copperplate engraving *Knight, Death, and Devil* as a kind of personal counter-icon, a "symbol for an entire world, my world, a Nordic-moralistic-Protestant, that is, German world which is strictly opposed to that aestheticism of ruthlessness" (see Figure 18).[129] Though Dürer's engraving was executed as early as 1513, Mann interpreted it as a profoundly Protestant work. Like the Reformation itself, it symbolized a specifically German 'deed.' Luther and Dürer—as well as Nietzsche and Frederick the Great—stood for a "Nordic Christianity" (*nordisches Christentum*). Throughout the *Reflections,* Mann played off the Protestant ideal of "inwardness" against supposedly "Western" notions like democracy, the secular nation state, rationalism, and political involvement. In November 1918, as the German synthesis of *Geist* and *Macht* collapsed, he defiantly bought an iron bust of Luther.

Mann's enthusiastic reaction to World War I as a "purification" and "regeneration" of German culture surprised his contemporaries and continues

127. Quoted in Harpprecht, *Thomas Mann,* 384, 386.

128. *Briefe an Paul Amann,* 33.

129. Mann, *Betrachtungen, GW,* 12:541. Mann's interpretation of Dürer's engraving was indebted to Ernst Bertram, who employed *Knight, Death, and Devil* as an iconographic key to what he regarded as the essentially Lutheran, Nordic, and Faustian aspects of Nietzsche's character. See Ernst Bertram, *Nietzsche: Versuch einer Mythologie* (Berlin, 1918). In his Dürer essay of 1928, Mann still echoed Bertram—and his own *Reflections*—when he described Nietzsche's "emotional world" as a "Nordic-German, bourgeois-Dürerean-moralistic sphere," determined by "self-overcoming, self-discipline and self-crucifixion." *GW,* 10:231. The parallels to Savonarola are evident.

Figure 18. Albrecht Dürer, *Knight, Death, and Devil*, 1513. Art historians have pointed to Bartolomeo Colleoni and Girolamo Savonarola as possible models for Dürer's *Christian Knight*.

to puzzle his critics. What were the reasons, asks Hermann Kurzke, "for a *décadent* with refined manners to call something as uncivilized as war 'holy' and to fantasize about 'purification' and 'liberation'?" For Kurzke, this is "the question of all questions."[130] The contextualized reading of *Fiorenza* undertaken here offers some clues. The antihumanism, the palingenetic nationalism, the yearning for a new asceticism—these ideas did not emerge *ex nihilo*. Mann had formulated them as early as 1903 and 1904, when he began to dissociate himself more decisively from the aestheticists. With his critique of Renaissancismus in *Fiorenza,* he sought to refashion himself as a bourgeois *Leistungsethiker*. Read in conjunction with the heated debates about early modern Italy at the turn of the century, the play indicates how antibourgeois Mann's ascetic conception of *Bürgertugend* was—and how easily compatible with the *nationalprotestantisch* ideologies of the New Right. *Fiorenza* thus forms a discursive link between Mann's cultural despair at the fin de siècle and his militant outbursts of 1914 and 1915. More than any other of the early works, it makes the wartime writings, that great explanandum in his oeuvre, comprehensible.

Conclusion

In her seminal 1977 essay on Renaissancismus, Lea Ritter-Santini drew a trajectory between the fin-de-siècle fascination of the German middle class with the quattrocento tyrants and its susceptibility to the new breed of 'Gewaltmenschen' that took over power in 1933 and soon embarked on their own form of aestheticized politics. The fashion of *maniera grande* around 1900, according to Ritter-Santini, helped to prepare the way for the bombastic style in which the Nazis later staged their idea of national rebirth in front of the Feldherrnhalle, Munich's most famous neo-Renaissance building.[131] There are some instances in the *Rezeptionsgeschichte* of Renaissancismus that seem to lend credence to such claims. Kantorowicz's *Emperor Frederick the Second,* for instance, which rekindled the fin-de-siècle cult of the Renaissance tyrant, was a favorite of Göring and Himmler.[132] Dietrich Eckart, chief

130. Kurzke, *Thomas Mann,* 237.

131. See Ritter-Santini, "Maniera Grande," 193.

132. For the popularity of Kantorowicz's book among the higher Nazi echelons, see Ruehl, "Kaiser Friedrich," 187–8, 237–41.

editor of the *Völkischer Beobachter* and an early influence on Hitler, wrote a Renaissance play entitled *Lorenzacchio* (1918), which premiered in October 1933 to favorable reviews.[133] The Führer himself was a great admirer of Titian and Tiepolo and had the walls of the Reich chancellery decorated with massive Renaissance-style tapestries.[134] At his personal request, Mussolini confiscated Makart's triptych *The Plague in Florence* from its Italian owners and handed it over to the Reich so that it could be included in Hitler's pet project, the Linz Gallery. The overall picture, however, hardly bears out a connection between Nazism and *Renaissancismus*, whose 'southern' setting and decadent themes clashed with the *völkisch* values of the new regime. There was no renaissance of the Renaissance in the Third Reich.

If anything, Nazi ideology drew on the anti-Latin polemics of the *nationalprotestantisch* detractors of the Renaissance cult during the 1900s and 1910s. This nexus did not escape the author of *Fiorenza*. Mann's acceptance of the Weimar Republic and his fight against fascism went hand in hand with a positive revaluation of the Renaissance. *The Magic Mountain* (1924) represented a first step in this direction. One of the two characters fighting for Hans Castorp's soul in Mann's *Bildungsroman*, Settembrini, is clearly identified as a Latin humanist. Even though Settembrini shares some of the negative traits of the scholars in Mann's Renaissance play, it is he who eventually brings Castorp to embrace life and to renounce the nihilistic insinuations of his priestly antagonist Naphta, whose physiognomy is closely modeled, significantly, on Savonarola's. Twelve years later, Mann pleaded for a synthesis of Protestantism and humanism.[135] In his 1939 essay "Brother Hitler," he critically reexamined his own renunciation of Renaissance art and scholarship in 1905: "I was very young, when in *Fiorenza* I allowed the reign of beauty and *Bildung* to be thrown overboard by the social-religious fanaticism of the monk who announced 'the miracle of reborn naiveté' [*das Wunder der wiedergeborenen Unbefangenheit*]."[136]

By the end of World War Two, Mann's assessment of the Renaissance had come full circle. In his famous speech "Germany and the Germans"

133. See Uekermann, *Renaissancismus*, 169–70.
134. See Joachim C. Fest, *Hitler*, trans. R. and C. Winston (London 1974), 529–30.
135. See Thomas Mann, "Humaniora und Humanismus" (1936), *GW*, 12:635–640.
136. Thomas Mann, "Bruder Hitler" (1939), *GW*, 12:850.

(1945), he juxtaposed Erasmus and Pope Leo X on the one hand and Luther—"that gigantic incarnation of Germanness"—on the other. Luther's "separatist," "anti-Roman" attitude, Mann declared, "frightened" him: "I would not have liked to be Luther's dinner guest. I probably would have felt like [I was] dining with an ogre. I am convinced, however, that I would have found it much easier to get along with Leo . . . the pleasant humanist, whom Luther called 'the devil's sow, the pope.' "[137] Leo X, of course, was none other than Giovanni de' Medici, who originally appeared in *Fiorenza* as one of the "epicureans and pigs" around Pico and Poliziano. His metamorphosis from the shallow, hedonistic neopagan of 1905 to the preferred table companion of 1945 reflects Mann's own transformation since his first attack on Italian *bellezza* in *Tonio Kröger*.

137. Thomas Mann, *Essays*, 3 vols., ed. Hermann Kurzke (Frankfurt am Main, 1986), 2:286.

POPULAR CULTURE

DIVISIVE OR INTEGRATIVE?

"Am I Allowed to Amuse Myself Here?"

The German Bourgeoisie Confronts Early Film

PETER JELAVICH

Many Western philosophical traditions, from Aristotle to Hegel, argue that the essence of a phenomenon can be ascertained by examining how it came into being. Historians adopt this approach as well: for example, they might limn the distinctive features of bourgeois culture by studying its inception in the eighteenth century (or whenever). But the integral qualities of an entity also can be determined by analyzing its demise or its transformation into something essentially different. An examination of middle-class reactions to film, the paradigmatic mass medium of the twentieth century, allows us to highlight some of the characteristics as well as the limitations of bourgeois culture. Germany's *Bildungsbürger*—the university-trained bourgeoisie— initially regarded film as an absolute "other," as a pure expression of what their culture was not. But this opposition lasted only a few years, as the educated elite gradually joined the cinema-going public. The rise of a multiclass audience for film on the eve of World War I marked the beginning of the end of the domination of bourgeois culture and signaled the rise of mass-cultural forms of entertainment that would characterize the twentieth century. By examining how the *Bildungsbürger* of imperial Germany first resisted, then tolerated, and finally accepted film, one can perceive some of the contours of late bourgeois culture on the eve of this transformation.[1]

1. Though social historians of imperial Germany rarely have examined cinema, film historians have compiled several anthologies of primary sources that offer an entry into a number of issues discussed in this essay. See Ludwig Greve et al., *Hätte ich das Kino! Die Schriftsteller und der Stummfilm* (Marbach, 1976); Anton Kaes, ed., *Kino-Debatte: Texte zum Verhältnis von Literatur und Film 1909–1929* (Munich, 1978); Fritz Güttinger, ed., *Kein Tag ohne Kino: Schriftsteller über den Stummfilm* (Frankfurt am Main, 1984); Jörg Schweinitz, ed., *Prolog vor dem Film: Nachdenken über ein neues Medium* (Leipzig, 1992).

The author would like to thank the Alexander von Humboldt Foundation as well as the Arbeitsstelle für vergleichende Gesellschaftsgeschichte of the Freie Universität Berlin

Recent scholarly literature has criticized and modified the commonplace assertion that during its infancy, film attracted an exclusively working-class public.[2] Indeed, that view was challenged already in Emilie Altenloh's dissertation on cinema-goers in Mannheim in 1912, the sole sociological study of the film public conducted in Germany before the Great War. Altenloh reported that among men, unskilled young workers constituted the most avid film fans, and that frequency of attendance fell with rising age and in the higher social classes; consequently, "professions requiring an academic education (including students) comprised altogether the smallest percentage of filmgoers."[3] But Altenloh also noted that adult women of all social classes were to be found in cinemas—indeed, bourgeois women more than those of other classes: "For women of the upper strata, leaving aside a small intellectual elite, the same can be said as for . . . the young female shop assistants, except that the former attend films much more frequently than the latter, inasmuch as their time is not limited by having a job."[4] Newer studies have shown that the developments in Mannheim—where cinemas were opened first in working-class neighborhoods, then later in middle-class shopping and entertainment areas—could be reversed: in Köln, for example, cinemas were founded in working-class neighborhoods only after they had been established in the bourgeois center of the city.[5]

Corinna Müller has concluded that the "early film public was not prole-

---

for their generous support during the research and writing of the original, German-language version of this essay.

2. Important works among the ever-growing scholarly literature on film during the imperial era are: Heide Schlüpmann, *Unheimlichkeit des Blicks: Das Drama des frühen deutschen Kinos* (Basel, 1990); Paolo Cherchi Usai and Lorenzo Codelli, eds., *Before Caligari: German Cinema, 1895–1920 / Prima di Caligari: Cinema tesdesco, 1895–1920* (Pordenone, 1990); Sabine Hake, *The Cinema's Third Machine: Writing on Film in Germany, 1907–1933* (Lincoln, Neb., 1993), esp. part 1, "Writing on Cinema in Wilhelmine Germany, 1907–1918," 3–104; Corinna Müller, *Frühe deutsche Kinematographie: Formale, wirtschaftliche, und kulturelle Entwicklungen, 1907–1912* (Stuttgart, 1994); and Thomas Elsaesser, ed., *A Second Life: German Cinema's First Decades* (Amsterdam, 1996).

3. Emilie Altenloh, *Zur Soziologie des Kino: Die Kino-Unternehmung und die sozialen Schichten ihrer Besucher* (Jena, 1914), 92.

4. Ibid., 91.

5. Compare ibid., 50, with Bruno Fischli, ed., *Vom Sehen im Dunkeln: Kinogeschichten einer Stadt* (Cologne, 1990), 30.

tarian, but rather young" and included many children from middle-class families.[6] But from the very beginning, adult members of the lower middle and middle classes (though not the *Bildungsbürger*) also were acquainted with films, which were screened as the concluding numbers in variety shows for the first decade of their existence (1895–ca. 1905). If one looks at the production side of film—its entrepreneurs, directors, technicians, and performers—then it becomes even clearer that the new medium was a middle-class phenomenon (though in this respect too the university-trained bourgeoisie remained uninvolved). Heide Schlüpmann has provided what is perhaps the best summary of the situation: "Cinema and film production developed in Wilhelmine Germany largely independently from the *Bildungsbürgertum*. They were based on all of those middle-class elements that felt excluded from 'culture': the productive forces came from groups involved in technology, business, variety shows, and fairground displays, as well as actors, while the public consisted of women of diverse backgrounds, the 'little people,' the workers and salaried employees."[7]

The fight waged by the *Bildungsbürger* against film was largely a defensive war. During the Wilhelmine age, the university-trained bourgeoisie suffered a steady loss of importance. For much of the nineteenth century, that group had enjoyed a central, often hegemonic role in German society, owing to its prominence in the civil service, the judiciary, the legal and medical professions, journalism, politics, and not least of all the arts. But toward the end of the century, its dominance was being challenged not only by the persisting social prestige of the nobility and the increasing influence of the organized working classes, but also by a "shifting of forces within the bourgeoisie" in favor of the "rapidly ascending business-oriented elements of the bourgeois upper classes," as Hans-Ulrich Wehler has argued.[8] The *Bildungsbürger* continued to enjoy social prestige, but they could not have ignored the fact that classical culture and humanistic education were increasingly irrelevant in an age of rapid economic, technological, and scientific developments. Instead of adapting themselves to these new conditions, they clung to their old

6. Müller, *Frühe deutsche Kinematographie*, 194.

7. Schlüpmann, *Unheimlichkeit des Blicks*, 13.

8. Hans-Ulrich Wehler, *Deutsche Gesellschaftsgeschichte, Dritter Band: Von der "Deutschen Doppelrevolution" bis zum Beginn des Ersten Weltkrieges, 1849–1914* (Munich, 1995), 749.

ideals. In order to defend their position as intellectual and cultural leaders of the nation, they believed that they had to combat the "materialism" of the age. As part of that battle, they persistently criticized the increasingly commercialized "un-culture" of the "masses." They launched a litany of invective against "trashy" popular novels, "sensationalistic" tabloids and illustrated magazines, "obscene" postcards, and "kitschy" vaudeville and variety shows. By 1910, it was time to take on film as well.

This battle also was waged within the ranks of the middle classes. The *Bildungsbürger* considered it bad enough that workers and lower middle-class citizens wasted their time on uncivilized pursuits; they were downright appalled by the fact that the middling strata of the bourgeoisie became increasingly attracted to popular and commercialized entertainment. At first there were but few sites, such as the circus, where the middle classes congregated with the "lower" orders for purposes of amusement, but that changed with the rapid spread of variety shows after 1871. The reasons for this development became the subject of considerable debate. On the one hand, it seemed that variety shows functioned as a safety valve for stressed-out middle-class citizens, a place where they could lower their cultural guard and unwind, precisely because such venues offered "mindless" entertainment. On the other hand, some observers claimed that the fragmented form of vaudeville corresponded to the shattered psyche of citizens disoriented by the hectic nature of modern urban life.[9] Whatever the reasons, the booming variety business seemed to chip away at classicism's exemplary hold on bourgeois culture. Hence the 1890s saw a flood of outspoken attacks on vaudeville, which prefigured the antifilm discourse after 1910 (as well as the anti-television discourse since the 1950s): the fragmented structure of variety shows and their heterogeneous mixture of genres (song, dance, lyrics, comedy, acrobatics, magic, and stunts, to name only a few) were branded as "kitschy" and "uncivilized."

Not all representatives of elite culture, however, rejected the new aesthetic forms inherent in variety shows. Some even tried to rejuvenate middle-class theater by appropriating aspects of vaudeville, as a means of retaining or regaining middle-class viewers who were increasingly drawn to popular entertainment. After 1900, cabarets were founded as a means of "ennobling"

9. Peter Jelavich, *Berlin Cabaret* (Cambridge, Mass., 1993), 23–6.

variety shows, and vaudevillian elements were employed in plays (such as those of Frank Wedekind) and theater productions (like those of Max Reinhardt).[10] This division within the providers of bourgeois culture—a split between defenders of classical and literary drama and proponents of theatrical innovation under the aegis of vaudeville—can likewise be considered a forerunner of the so-called "cinema debate" (*Kinodebatte*). After 1912, playwrights, directors, and actors separated into two groups: those who wanted nothing to do with film and those who tried to "ennoble" it (via the so-called "authors' films") or even to learn from it.

In principle, the antifilm discourse could have arisen already at the turn of the century, in the context of the antivaudeville campaigns. But *Bildungsbürger* did not take note of film's existence until around 1910, after the first standing cinemas had been constructed and the genre of "film drama" (*Kinodrama*) had developed. The number of so-called *Kinematographentheater*—popularly called *Kintopp, Kientopp,* or simply *Kino*—grew rapidly: hundreds of shops, pubs, and vaudeville halls were transformed into cinemas. In 1910 there were 456 cinemas in 29 German cities; three years later, the number had swelled to 2,371. This breakneck speed of growth was viewed with great alarm by a number of groups. Obviously, protests were voiced by those who feared the commercial competition of film, such as vaudeville managers and pub owners. But the harshest critics of film were members of the university-trained bourgeoisie who belonged to the plethora of reform movements that thrived in the late imperial era: educators, professors, pastors, doctors, lawyers, judges, criminologists, and authors. Depending on their particular interests and attitudes, they considered film a threat to religious values, sexual mores, public health, political stability, or good taste. In the years before the Great War, they let loose a veritable flood of articles and pamphlets that expressed their concerns and fears.

Male *Bildungsbürger* who had the temerity to investigate film around 1910—whether out of genuine curiosity or to collect evidence to confirm their moralistic prejudices—were disoriented as soon as they walked into a cinema. Chances were good that they would enter during the middle of a

10. I have developed that argument in *Berlin Cabaret,* as well as in Peter Jelavich, *Munich and Theatrical Modernism: Politics, Playwriting, and Performance, 1890–1914* (Cambridge, Mass., 1985).

reel, since the average *Kintopp* had no fixed schedule; customers could stroll in at any time. This experience provided a first taste of the fractured, open-ended nature of early cinema, which directly contradicted bourgeois notions of aesthetic unity and coherence. If our observers were to have entered a working-class nickelodeon, they would have been disgusted by the physical ambience: three to four hundred people might have been packed into a narrow and poorly ventilated room. Indeed, early film journals were replete with advertisements for deodorants and air fresheners that cinema owners could spray in their theaters to make the experience somewhat more bearable.

What many middle-class male observers found most shocking of all was the darkness during screenings. That was troubling because it obscured the goings-on of an audience that consisted of the very groups most in need of observation and control, according to bourgeois attitudes of the day: youths, workers, and women. Michel Foucault has suggested that in the nineteenth century, many "panoptic" institutions were established to bring the anonymous masses into the light so that they could be better observed, recorded, and controlled.[11] If that was indeed the case, then cinema had the opposite effect: it was an antipanopticon that allowed the populace to plunge happily back into obscurity. There is little evidence to suggest that the type of sexual hanky-panky most feared by "reformers" actually occurred; young couples constituted a minority of film audiences. But cinema owners were well aware that their customers enjoyed the "lovely darkness."[12] In 1912, one enterprising manager in Mannheim stood in front of his theater and proclaimed, "Come right in, we have the darkest cinema in the entire town."[13]

The blackened cinemas of the prewar era nurtured a counter–public sphere in which values that were disparaged by *Bildungsbürger* could flourish. Many flicks—such as comedies, cartoons, or slapstick—wanted merely to entertain and sought only to provide amusement and diversion. This attitude negated bourgeois conceptions not only of art, but of leisure-time pursuits more generally: even in one's "free" time, one was supposed to engage

11. See Michel Foucault, *Discipline and Punish: The Birth of the Prison,* trans. Alan Sheridan (New York, 1977), 195–228, for his metaphor of the "panoptic" society.
12. Walter Serner, "Kino und Schaulust" (1913), in *Kino-Debatte,* ed. Kaes, 53.
13. Altenloh, *Soziologie des Kino,* 74.

in activities that contributed to one's intellectual or moral uplift. Would-be reformers of cinema called for more didactic films (e.g., ones dealing with the natural world), whereby entertainment could be tied to education. But this oft-repeated demand went unheeded, since every cinema owner knew that a program dominated by such reels would spell financial disaster. As Altenloh noted, "For the majority of cinema-goers, nature films are a boring transition to the ensuing works."[14]

Flicks that offered pure diversion were not, however, the main source of concern for bourgeois opponents of cinema. They were much more upset by works that had messages to convey: namely, the dramas that were preferred by women, as well as the "sensationalistic" strips full of adventure, sex, and crime. The high percentage of women in prewar cinema audiences has been highlighted in recent scholarship by feminist film historians (especially Heide Schlüpmann) in order to contend that early film was also thematically supportive of women. Already in 1912, Altenloh surmised that even though many cinema-goers did not really care what they saw, women constituted one group that had a "genuine interest in what was shown."[15] She noted that women were particularly interested in "social dramas," as they were called at the time: "These dramas mainly depict a woman's struggle between her natural, feminine-sensual instincts and the social conditions that stand against them. On the one hand she faces prostitution, on the other the option of marrying a man who usually belongs to either a significantly higher or lower social stratum."[16] The most popular films of this kind were those starring Asta Nielsen (see Figure 19).[17] To be sure, the radical potential of Nielsen's works was held in check because the women she portrayed onscreen ended either as wives, prostitutes, or corpses—in other words, marriage, prostitution, or death were the only imaginable (or rather, presentable) outcomes of a woman's desire for happiness in her private life. Nevertheless, Nielsen's talent as an actress was remarkable; she developed a

14. Ibid., 37.

15. Ibid., 94.

16. Ibid., 58.

17. Schlüpmann, *Unheimlichkeit des Blicks*, 98–106, passim. Schlüpmann summarizes some of the arguments of that book in her essay, "Cinema as Anti-Theater: Actresses and Female Audiences in Wilhelminian Germany," in *Silent Film*, ed. Richard Abel (New Brunswick, N.J., 1996), 125–41.

Figure 19. Asta Nielsen in 1912.

new vocabulary of gestures, facial expressions, and bodily movements that contradicted prevailing clichés of female self-presentation. Nielsen did not permit herself to be confined to any fixed image: her onscreen personae were sometimes feminine, sometimes masculine, and at times androgynous. Moreover, she not only acted youthful roles but depicted middle-aged and old women as well.

This thespian diversity was possible only in the early years of cinema, when performances were generally improvised during shoots. Later in life, Nielsen recalled that at the beginning of her career, "My scenes often were only hinted at" in the "sparse manuscripts. . . . I remember a particular scenario that stated: 'The child dies. Asta's big scene.' "[18] With such great leeway for interpretation, Nielsen herself could determine what her mainly adult female public would see onscreen. In this free space, the first (albeit short-lived) wave of "women's films" could develop. The fact that cinemas were filled by a female public watching films that sympathized with unconventional women was, of course, highly disconcerting to many male opponents of the medium. Indeed, perhaps unbeknownst to her, Altenloh's interest in film and its female spectators was regarded with disdain by her *Doktorvater,* the famous sociologist Alfred Weber. A litany of prejudices spilled out in a letter that he wrote in March 1912, where he referred to Altenloh as his "cinema-girl" (*Kinematographenmädel*), "that well-meaning, simple, steely-blue-eyed female student" (*jener braven biederen hartgesottenblauäugigen Studentin*). In order to understand what she was up to, Weber went to a cinema and reacted as a paradigmatic *Bildungsbürger,* complaining about everything from the lack of air to the kitschy quality of the films.[19] Whether she knew it or not, the attitudes of Altenloh's *Doktorvater* confirmed many of her contentions.

The most common targets of bourgeois ire were the so-called "sensationalistic films" (*Sensationsfilme*) that dealt with adventure, sexuality, and crime (which have remained the three major themes of commercial film production to this day). Sometimes nationalistic arguments were voiced in the assault. Before the Great War, only between 10 and 15 percent of all films screened in Germany were domestic products; most came from Denmark, France, the United States, or Italy. This led to chauvinistic and even racist comments, such as one that appeared in 1912 in the *Kunstwart,* a conservative arts magazine: "The films from abroad . . . often smuggle into our midst . . . bad alien habits, alien degeneracy, or even un-German looks and manners and make them appear to us as normal human or even German traits."[20] The nationalistic opponents of film invariably claimed that German

18. Asta Nielsen, *Die schweigende Muse* (Berlin, 1977), 140.

19. Unpublished letter to Else Jaffé cited in Schlüpmann, *Unheimlichkeit des Blicks,* 327.

20. Willy Rath, "Emporkömmling Kino" (1913), in *Prolog,* ed. Schweinitz, 78.

youth was being corrupted by "trashy" foreign films—a contention that neglected to note that "trashy" German films might have been numerically
fewer but not qualitatively better than their imported counterparts.

The most disturbing themes in the sensationalistic films were eroticism,
criminality, and social conflicts. Bourgeois opponents of film claimed that
depictions of erotic adventures corrupted the youths and women in the audience. They also attacked supposedly sympathetic dramatizations of criminality, or even socially critical renderings of poverty, fearing that such
themes would undermine the lower classes' subservience to the state and the
law. Robert Gaupp, a professor of psychology in Tübingen, summarized
these manifold concerns: "Distorted pictures of misery and hardship, poverty and disease, generate tormenting ideas about the injustice of the world
and destroy respect for law and state authority. In Germany our police generally keep sexual filth (*sexuelle Schweinereien*) within bounds, but a lascivious eroticism still manages to seep through. . . . I consider the gruesomely
graphic representations of criminal life even more dangerous. . . . The deterrent force of a moralistic ending counts for nothing against the profound
impressions that the heroic deeds of an audacious criminal leave on youthful
minds."[21] Gaupp was completely bewildered by socially critical films: "We
are shown that when a poor person steals, a rough hand shoves him into
jail, while a rich person who does the same is treated gingerly and buys his
way out of trouble. We adults know that here in Germany, such a tale is
absurd, because it slaps truth in the face!"[22]

Be that as it may, the professor from Tübingen certainly exaggerated the
radical nature of film, since the number of truly inflammatory works was
small. According to Altenloh, a worker in Mannheim even complained,
"Usually I'm disgusted by the shows, because they conform so little with the
facts, and because they usually have a tendency that's not to my taste, since
what's good for the ruling class always wins out."[23] But it also would be
wrong to consider early film as a tool of the "ruling class." Early cinema
conformed neither to bourgeois cultural ideals nor to the ideology of Social

21. Robert Gaupp, "Die Gefahren des Kino" (1912), in ibid., 67–8.
22. Robert Gaupp, "Der Kinematograph vom medizinischen und psychologischen
Standpunkt" (1912), cited in Schlüpmann, *Unheimlichkeit des Blicks*, 225.
23. Altenloh, *Soziologie des Kino*, 75.

Democracy; rather, it offered a free and uncontrolled space for expressing nonbourgeois values—adventure, frivolity, sensuality, letting-go—a space that occasionally questioned the justice of every social order.

While some of the themes of sensationalistic films seemed morally and politically offensive, the formal principles of early cinema challenged the aesthetic bases of bourgeois culture. *Bildungsbürger* often were completely disoriented by early films, which called into question logic, causality, the separation of artistic genres, and the priority of the word. With few exceptions, it was not until 1910 that audiences saw feature films consisting of several acts, i.e., multireel films that could run up to ninety minutes. Until then, film programs consisted of a motley variety of shorts, each of which lasted only three to fifteen minutes. As late as 1910, the *Lichtbildbühne,* a film trade journal, reported that a typical program might consist of the following parts: "1. Musical piece. 2. Current events. 3. Something humorous. 4. Drama. 5. Something comic. 6. Nature scenes. 7. Something comic. 8. The big attraction. 9. Something scientific. 10. Boisterous comedy."[24] Altenloh reported that the "normal program of a cinema" in Mannheim consisted of, "on average, three dramas, three comedies, and a nature film."[25] Thus, unlike a theatrical play or an opera, a film program did not consist of a single unified work; rather, it was like a variety show or a cabaret. Indeed, it offered an even greater diversity of genres and moods than the average vaudeville or cabaret program. Cinema presented a chaotic mixture of fact (documentary shots of current events) and fiction (short dramas), science (nature scenes) and nonsense (cartoons and slapstick), tragedy and comedy, moral and immoral tales. The clear separation of genres, moods, and spheres of knowledge that had characterized bourgeois culture since the Enlightenment dissolved in the hotchpotch of early film programs.

Film also offered new effects and experiences that had not been possible in earlier arts and media. An obvious example was the fact that a film could be run backwards, which provided a visual reversal of causal flow. As one author wrote in 1907, "The pleasure of suspending causality is especially refined. It's not easy to feel oneself into it, since our whole stupid intellect stands under the tyrannical influence of cause and effect. But along comes

24. Cited in Müller, *Frühe deutsche Kinematographie,* 12.
25. Altenloh, *Soziologie des Kino,* 23.

some flunky in a nickelodeon and sticks the film backwards into the projector. A small twist of the hand—and all of world history is turned around:
cause becomes effect, effect becomes cause."[26] Even during a normal screening, the viewer's sense of time was constantly undermined. Inasmuch as
early flicks were both filmed and projected by hand-cranked apparati, the
speed of actions onscreen could vary from that of real life. Sometimes slow-
or fast-motion was employed consciously for special effects, but most scenes
actually were projected somewhat more rapidly than normal, since that
shortened the length of programs and allowed cinema managers to pack in
more people over the course of a day.

Although there was no theory of film montage before the 1920s, bourgeois spectators also were disturbed by the editing of early films. They considered the constant switching among close-ups, medium shots, and long
shots to be annoying and unaesthetic. The curator of the royal print collection in Dresden—obviously a guardian of traditional aesthetics—wrote in
1913 regarding a film starring Albert Bassermann, one of the greatest actors
of the day:

> I cannot imagine anything more lacking in style and abhorrent to art
> than this perpetual jumping from image to image, this completely
> unjustified changing of scale, to which the eye must adjust at top
> speed. Bassermann, as the lawyer Hallers, sits drinking tea in the
> salon of councilor Arnoldy, when suddenly only his head appears, cut
> out of the same scene, six times larger than life. . . . Then a shadow,
> which cannot be explained by the lighting in the room, transforms
> his head into that of a Moor, but immediately thereafter it grimaces
> in full illumination. This constant changing of scale, of lighting, of
> tempo eventually drives the viewer to a state of nervous irritability.[27]

This visual confusion was exacerbated by the acoustic jumble of a program. "Silent" films never were silent, since they invariably were accompanied by music, and often by a narrator as well. Ideally the music would

26. Hanns Heinz Ewers, "Der Kientopp" (1907), in *Kein Tag ohne Kino*, ed. Güttinger,
13.

27. Max Lehrs, "Als ich zum ersten Mal im Kino war," in *Berliner Tageblatt*, 16 March
1913.

underscore the actions depicted onscreen, but that was not always the case. At times musicians would play against the mood of the film in order to amuse the audience: for example, when a gunned-down person fell to the ground, they would make a "thud" on a drum, or they would accompany a romantic scene of lovers kissing with a fanfare or a drum roll. One Berlin piano accompanist was fired after the following incident: "A gripping drama was unfolding onscreen, and when in the fourth act a tenement went up in flames and old people and children were trying to save themselves from the enveloping fire, the pianist played the tune 'Fritz, stay here, you can't forecast the weather!'" (*Fritz bleib hier, du weißt ja nicht wie's Wetter wird*).[28] Even when musicians did what they were supposed to do—namely, underscore the moods of a film—they would improvise a potpourri of folk tunes, current hit songs, marches, chorales, and opera and operetta arias. Such a melange massacred individual melodies by reducing them to short snippets, and the indiscriminate interweaving of "high" and "low" spheres of music punctured the aura of what bourgeois Germans considered the holiest of the arts.

Not just the music, but also the verbal commentary could contradict the content of a film. Of course, most narrators tried to provide the public with a reasonable explication of the scenes. This often was not an easy task, since many flicks, whether dramatic or humorous, suffered from bad editing, lousy acting, gaps in the reels, or grainy pictures. Just as musicians took liberties with the materials onscreen, the "talkers" could add sarcastic remarks. But bourgeois opponents of film were most appalled by those cases where the narrators made politically subversive comments. In 1912, a journalist filed the following report on a program in a working-class nickelodeon in Berlin:

> The film actually was terribly boring, the banal tale of a 'girl of the people,' dubbed the 'woman without a heart,' who is engaged to a

28. Reported in the *Deutsche Montags-Zeitung* of 25 May 1914, and cited in *Hätte ich das Kino*, 47. There were similar occurrences in the United States, such as in cinemas catering to African American audiences, where jazz musicians would provide an ironic commentary to Hollywood films. One observer in Chicago in 1927 noted, "During a death scene flashed on screen, you are likely to hear the orchestra jazzing away on 'Clap Hands, Here Comes Charlie.'" Cited in Mary Carbine, "'The Finest Outside the Loop':

distinguished young man, but her depraved character is revealed, so she flees to her lover from earlier years, a worker, but he disdains her and drives her away. Boring, no? But what did they do with it! The narrator steamed with pure moral outrage . . . and suddenly one was given to see: the woman without a heart, a victim of the upper classes; the poor worker, whom they consider good only for saving her from the gutter; the poor worker, a bulwark of proud honor, who casts the woman back up there to the murderers of human lives. . . . The announcer sobbed, the spectators clenched their fists, and a tragedy sped across the screen that was very, very different from the one envisioned by the film's producer.[29]

What might have been a sappy flick about a faithless woman who chooses money over love, only to get her just desserts in the end, was transformed into an indictment of the upper classes.

The outraged reporter assumed that the "film's producer" wanted to convey a clear and conscious message (otherwise he would not have asserted that a "very, very different film" than the one intended by the maker was seen by the public). But can one really speak of authorship and intentionality in early film? Cultural theorists like Roland Barthes, Jacques Derrida, and Michel Foucault have questioned the need (or even the possibility) of taking authorial intention into account when explicating a text. Such dicta are practically superfluous when dealing with early film, where no obvious source of intentionality can be located. As noted above, early films were usually products of a cooperative improvisation among actors and directors. It is hardly ever possible to interpret such works as the creative expressions of known individuals; indeed, the scriptwriters, directors, and even actors often were left unnamed. It was not until 1911 that Asta Nielsen became Central Europe's first film star, one whose name on billboards could attract large audiences. The anonymity of early cinema meant that a work could not be considered the inspired product of a single creative artist—which meant, once again, that film eluded bourgeois conceptions of art.

Motion Picture Exhibition in Chicago's Black Metropolis, 1905–1928," in *Silent Film,* ed. Abel, 254.

29. Ulrich Rauscher, "Die Welt im Film" (1912), in *Kein Tag ohne Kino,* ed. Güttinger, 135–6.

Film's greatest challenge to the culture of the *Bildungsbürgertum* resided in the fact that it was visual, not verbal. To be sure, words did have a role to play: one could hear the narrator (when there was one), one could read the intertitles, one could occasionally purchase a program booklet with a synopsis of the story. But the bottom line was that film tried to avoid words as much as possible. Georg Lukács wrote in 1913, "Whatever is important in the events presented is and must be expressed exclusively through actions and gestures; every appeal to words represents a falling out of this world, a destruction of its essential value."[30] The relative lack of words meant that *Bildungsbürger* often remained clueless vis-à-vis the plots of silent films. Altenloh reported, "It seems to be very difficult for intellectually highly educated people to immerse themselves in the story, which is often strung together in a disconnected manner. Various people who are used to comprehending things from a purely rational perspective said that they found it extraordinarily difficult to follow a film plot."[31] Instead of paying homage to the word, film fostered "visual pleasure" (*Schaulust*), as Walter Serner noted in 1913: "That is what pulls the populace like crazy into cinemas. . . . That is what made cinema win the battle without a fight: it devoted itself to the eye and to the pleasures of the eye."[32]

In sum, early cinema challenged bourgeois culture on a number of fronts: it was presented in crowded rooms under the veil of darkness; it catered to youths, workers, and adult women of all social classes; it offered social dramas about uppity women and sensationalistic films with sexual, criminal, or politically suspect themes, as well as flicks that wanted simply to entertain; and all of this occurred in an open form and a nonverbal medium that suspended the barriers between genres and moods, and that was devoid of conscious intentions and clear plot lines. To the *Bildungsbürger* of imperial Germany, film seemed a veritable chaos, and they tried to impose order on it in the years before World War I.

Censorship was one means of taming cinema. Films were routinely censored after 1906, at first by municipal police authorities. It soon became ap-

30. Georg Lukács, "Gedanken zu einer Ästhetik des 'Kino,'" in *Kino-Debatte*, ed. Kaes, 115.

31. Altenloh, *Soziologie des Kino*, 91.

32. Serner, "Kino und Schaulust," 54–5.

parent, however, that local police departments were overwhelmed by the dozens of shorts that they had to preview every week, especially in big cities, where numerous cinemas offered competing programs that changed twice weekly. This situation eventually led to a centralization of film censorship, so that by 1912 all films screened in Prussia required preapproval by the Berlin police, who employed four full-time officers for the job. Likewise, the police in Munich were responsible for films in Bavaria, those in Leipzig for Saxony, and so forth. Censorship was, however, a tricky business. On the one hand, there were the film fans, whose numbers increased steadily: by 1912, over a million Germans were attending cinemas every day. Hence excessive censorship would have been extremely unpopular. It also would have been unwise economically, since film had become an important sector of the entertainment business. On the other hand, there were many influential critics and opponents of film, who tried to persuade the local police, the interior ministers of the federal states, and members of state parliaments to tighten their oversight and censorship of film. There was hardly anyone from the bourgeoisie who supported a total suspension of film censorship; even Kurt Tucholsky, who became the outstanding satirist of the Weimar era and a vocal supporter of artistic freedom, approved of cinema censorship in 1913.[33] It was employed to attenuate or eradicate precisely those themes that most concerned bourgeois opponents of film: violence, sexuality, glorification of crime, and social and political radicalism, as well as scenes that touched on religious sensitivities.[34]

That did not mean, however, that the public was served bland fare. One ploy used by filmmakers entailed marketing sensationalistic flicks as historically informative works or as so-called "educational films" (*Aufklärungsfilme*). For example, it was possible to insert sadistic scenes into films about the persecution of Christians under Nero or the burning of witches in the Middle Ages. The first film of that ilk, entitled *A People's Court in the Middle Ages, or The Age of Terror and Dread*, was released in 1906 (at Christmas, no less). The posters, newspaper advertisements, and program booklets that

33. Kurt Tucholsky, "Verbotene Films" (1913), in *Prolog*, ed. Schweinitz, 214–9.
34. See Gary Stark, "Cinema, Society, and the State: Policing the Film Industry in Imperial Germany," in *Essays on Culture and Society in Modern Germany*, ed. Bede Karl Lackner and Gary Stark (College Station, Tex., 1982), 122–64.

touted such films claimed that they had great pedagogical value, e.g., for demonstrating the evils of religious intolerance.[35] In 1910 *The White Slave,* a Danish product, launched a series of "educational" films that supposedly warned young women about pimps and prostitution but in reality were vehicles for depicting sexual violence and bondage. Although such works were decried as trash and obscenity, they actually imitated a gimmick that had been long employed by bourgeois culture. Christians mauled in the Colosseum, nubile witches bound to stakes, manacled nude women in slave markets of antiquity or the modern "Orient"—such scenes regularly could be seen and bought in Berlin, Munich, Vienna, London, Rome, and every other city that hosted an annual salon of academic painting. The makers of sensationalistic films simply copied a common ploy of bourgeois culture, which tolerated (and financially rewarded) sexually explicit scenes as long as they were packaged in historical or exotic garb.

Filmmakers were well aware of bourgeois hypocrisy and even parodied it in a film comedy of 1912. *The Flicks Take Revenge* (*Wie sich der Kientopp rächt*) depicts a "Prof. Moralski," a member of the "Society to Fight Cinematography," who holds lectures attacking the new medium. The film industry strikes back by secretly filming scenes of his adulterous flirtation with an actress, which is edited into a "trashy" flick and smuggled into the projector during one of his talks against cinematic immorality. His own moral hypocrisy having been made public, he is pummeled by his wife and laughed out of the lecture hall.

Generally, however, the film industry believed that it would be better to woo the *Bildungsbürger* than to fight back. According to Altenloh, film's ultimate triumph was assured "when the sensationalistic dramas brought about a major change in film subjects and when cinemas moved from musty and narrow rooms into luxurious and comfortably appointed buildings. These two developments were decisive for allowing cinema to have the status that it does today."[36] The erection of "movie palaces" (*Lichtspielpaläste*) was a fundamental element in the industry's strategy of imitating highbrow aspects of bourgeois culture in order to defuse attacks by opponents of film and to gain the sympathy of *Bildungsbürger*. Paul Davidson, an entrepreneur

35. Müller, *Frühe deutsche Kinematographie,* 77.
36. Altenloh, *Soziologie des Kino,* 50.

Figure 20. The "Union-Theater" cinema in Berlin, 1909.

from Frankfurt, was the first to build spacious cinemas with comfortable seats and good ventilation. He opened his first upscale cinema in Mannheim in 1906, and his breakthrough came three years later with the "Union-Theater" on the Alexanderplatz in Berlin (see Figure 20).[37] By 1914 Davidson had over fifty cinemas in his "U.T." empire, and he headed a major production company as well. His success inspired other businessmen to found competing chains.

The relatively high prices charged by such movie palaces ensured that the middle classes could remain among themselves. One certainly got something for one's money. On the one hand, the classy foyers, plush chairs, coat-check rooms, and uniformed ushers—elements that copied upper-class theaters—provided a luxurious environment that was a far cry from the small, airless nickelodeons that had nourished film in its infancy. On the other hand, the disorder of popular cinema was tamed: the narrator was abolished, and the conductor of the ensemble ensured that the music would provide an appropriate accompaniment to the films. In such a setting, even the most exacting members of the bourgeoisie could begin to feel at ease. Already in 1912, Vic-

37. Michael Hanisch, *Auf den Spuren der Filmgeschichte: Berliner Schauplätze* (Berlin, 1991), 204–8.

tor Klemperer, at the time a graduate student and freelance author, could write, "The times when only the *Volk* sat in cinemas belong to the past. . . . In the ostentatious Mozartsaal in western Berlin, the soigné public sits with no less rapt attention than the proletarian clientele in a nickelodeon in the eastern Prinzenstrasse."[38]

While the social dramas appealed to middle-class women and the sensationalistic works attracted middle-class men, the content of film had to be "ennobled" to make it acceptable to diehard *Bildungsbürger*. A rather straightforward means of deflecting the attacks of nationalistic opponents of film was to gain the approval of the Kaiser. That proved an amazingly easy task. Wilhelm II soon became a film fan, especially when the films were newsreels with himself as the star attraction. Documentary footage of the Kaiser and his family, usually engaged in patriotic acts such as christening battleships, were regularly screened in both movie palaces and nickelodeons.[39] Whether they generated enthusiasm for the royal family is hard to ascertain. In 1913 a journalist describing "monarchist advertisement films" (*monarchistische Reklamefilms*) reported that at a screening in Berlin, "the public could not stop cheering the pictures of the crown prince."[40] But four years earlier, the author Alfred Döblin witnessed a very different reaction in a proletarian cinema in the north of Berlin: "No patriotism at the sight of the Kaiser and the army; just hateful staring."[41] Whatever the case, German producers could counter attacks by nationalistic opponents of film by flaunting the Kaiser's approval of cinema.

One of the most successful strategies employed by the silent film business was to adopt the attributes of bourgeois spoken theater, the genre that had occupied the highest rung of Germany's cultural hierarchy ever since the

38. Victor Klemperer, "Das Lichtspiel" (1912), in *Kein Tag ohne Kino*, ed. Güttinger, 77. Recently, Klemperer has gained posthumous renown for the diaries that he kept while living as a Jew in Dresden during the Third Reich. See Victor Klemperer, *I Shall Bear Witness: A Diary of the Nazi Years*, 2 vols., trans. Martin Chalmers (New York, 1998–99).

39. Martin Loiperdinger, "Der frühe Kino der Kaiserzeit: Wilhelm II und die 'Flegeljahre' des Films," in *Der deutsche Film: Aspekte seiner Geschichte von den Anfängen bis zur Gegenwart*, ed. Uli Jung (Trier, 1993), 21–50.

40. Ulrich Rauscher, "Kintopp" (1913), in *Kein Tag ohne Kino*, ed. Güttinger, 151.

41. Alfred Döblin, "Das Theater der kleinen Leute" (1909), in *Kino-Debatte*, ed. Kaes, 38.

days of Lessing, Goethe, and Schiller. Starting in 1912, famous stage actors, directors, and playwrights received lucrative offers from film companies. Max Reinhardt, Germany's most famous theater director, made two works for Davidson's production company, *Isle of the Blessed* and *A Night in Venice* (*Die Insel der Seligen* and *Eine Venezianische Nacht,* both 1913). A number of so-called authors' films (*Autorenfilme*) were produced, whose screenplays were scripted by well-known writers. The first such work, *The Other* (*Der Andere*), was penned by Paul Lindau and starred Albert Bassermann, considered Germany's greatest actor at the time (indeed, it was the film that the curator of Dresden's print gallery found so disconcerting). *The Other* dramatized the life of a schizophrenic man who is a respected lawyer by day and a criminal at night; the theme was chosen in part to counter arguments that silent film was incapable of portraying psychological complexity and depth. The premiere, which took place in January 1913, was reviewed in most of the prominent German newspapers and culture magazines, and it marked film's breakthrough to artistic respectability. The following two years saw the release of a number of other authors' films, such as Hugo von Hofmannsthal's *Das fremde Mädchen,* Gerhart Hauptmann's *Atlantis,* Arthur Schnitzler's *Liebelei,* and Hermann Sudermann's *Katzensteg.*[42]

Such works were welcomed by many *Bildungsbürger,* at least in principle. They provided cultural legitimacy to films, which began to receive regular reviews in major newspapers.[43] In particular, the employment of famous authors was lauded as a means of overcoming the initial anonymity of cinema. Herbert Tannenbaum, an early film theorist, believed that having a well-known author script the plot could stabilize the meaning of a work. It allowed one to speak of an author's intentions and to regard film as art, as the product of an artist in the conventional sense:

> To be sure, the actor in film is given much greater leeway for the individual characterization of his role than the actor in spoken theater, who largely is tied to the playwright and his intentions through the words of the text. Thus in a film (except in cases where the author himself directs) there appears to be a certain schism in the process of

42. Helmut H. Diederichs, "The Origins of the Autorenfilm," in *Before Caligari,* ed. Usai and Codelli, 380–401.
43. Helmut H. Diederichs, *Anfänge deutscher Filmkritik* (Stuttgart, 1986), 54–76.

production, one which contradicts the subjective-unitary process that is needed to create a work of art. Yet here too the author can and should present his intentions so unambiguously and comprehensively in the screenplay, so that the film actor (and here the director must be a skillful middleman) is able to perform according to the individual convictions of the film's author, so that the final product can be considered the expression of a singular artistic will.[44]

Despite the novel nature of the medium, Tannenbaum believed that film could be made to conform to traditional bourgeois aesthetics, which demanded clarity of authorial voice and rootedness in the written word.

Tannenbaum's goal could be achieved only partially, and in a way that he had not foreseen. To be sure, films were increasingly shaped by a singular vision, but it was that of the director, who did not allow himself to be degraded to the status of an author's "middleman." It soon became apparent that authors' films might have garnered the approval of some *Bildungsbürger,* but otherwise enjoyed only moderate success at the box office. As a short-term strategy, the film industry had found it worthwhile to employ well-known writers as a means of assuaging opponents of cinema. But in the long run, the concept of authors' films was misguided, since cinema was a nonverbal medium. It was the rise of prominent directors that gave film a point of stabilization, a source of intentionality, and a "singular artistic will" that accorded with bourgeois notions of art.

By 1914, it seemed that film already had been tamed in a variety of ways. The construction of movie palaces, the founding of large production companies and distribution networks, and the increasing dominance of directors (almost always male)—these were factors that promised to contain the potential anarchy of the cinematic medium. The film industry had made concessions to bourgeois culture, and many film fans thought that it had compromised itself in the process. In 1920, Carlo Mierendorff, an expressionist writer who soon would become a Social Democratic politician, wrote, "It is clear today how profoundly rotten cinema has become. It began when famous authors elbowed their way into the business, when Sudermann offered *Katzensteg* to the humblest viewer, when Paul Lindau tailored *The*

44. Herbert Tannenbaum, "Probleme des Kinodramas" (1913), in *Der Filmtheoretiker Herbert Tannenbaum,* ed. Helmut H. Diederichs (Frankfurt am Main, 1987), 54.

Other for Bassermann, when the whole rabble of bourgeois artists (sniffing money) threw themselves at film, when they chose to overlook its shady origins and declared it socially acceptable after unveiling it as an art—since then cinema simply mirrors the depths of bourgeois culture, pure, blunt, shameless, kitsch. The bourgeoisie made cinema into its own image."[45]

Be that as it may, the *Bildungsbürger* still did not feel completely at ease in the movie palaces. Altenloh captured their ambivalence in a number of ironic comments. While noting the "ever increasing attendance of the educated strata," she ascertained "a very curious ambiguity. . . . One goes there, but always with an uneasy and shameful feeling about oneself."[46] Altenloh's prewar comments retained their validity after the peace. In 1921 Hans Siemsen wrote:

> But the German! But the German professor and high school teacher! He doesn't ask: 'Am I having fun?' but: 'Am I allowed to amuse myself here?' Here, where there's no trace of Schopenhauer, nothing of Fichte, nothing by Goethe, not even a bit of psycho- or other logic, of grammar or orthography to be found—is the educated person allowed to amuse himself here? And after having amused himself, he goes home in a state of indignation. Or as a Herr Doktor who is very educated, very intelligent, and highly regarded in Berlin told me very innocently after a nice American Wild West film: 'That's of course more entertaining than the German films. But it doesn't have any intellectual value.'[47]

This ambivalence can be explained by the fact that film, despite Mierendorff's complaints, had made only superficial compromises with bourgeois culture. The pillars of the bourgeois value system—its orderly balancing between social obligations and individual cultivation, between work and private life, between reason and sentiment—found hardly any place in film, in an art that often served merely to entertain and that expressed itself through

---

45. Carlo Mierendorff, "Hätte ich das Kino!" (1920), in *Kein Tag ohne Kino,* ed. Güttinger, 387.

46. Altenloh, *Soziologie des Kino,* 55, 96.

47. Hans Siemsen, "Deutsch-amerikanischer Filmkrieg" (1921), in *Kein Tag ohne Kino,* ed. Güttinger, 435.

rapid, externalized images. Instead of advocating steady work, it reveled in boisterous action; in place of moderated feelings, it projected overt passions. Bourgeois culture paid homage to reason and the word; film, by contrast, was associative and visual. Granted, the film industry had to play the game called "culture" in order to attract the educated bourgeoisie. They found film palatable, even tasty, only after it had acquired some civilized coatings: nickelodeons evolved into movie palaces, and famous theater directors and playwrights added their names to the billboards. But after they swallowed the bait, the cultivated middle classes gradually became hooked on an art that provided visual pleasure and distraction. In the end, "tamed" film was a Trojan horse that smuggled nonbourgeois and antibourgeois values and modes of representation into the minds and hearts of the middle classes. Cinema's visual and spectacular qualities transformed the cultural landscape, and for the rest of the twentieth century, it remained central to a novel mass culture that all sectors of society could enjoy.

A World of Their Own?

Bourgeois Encounters in Berlin's *Jargon* Theaters, 1890–1920

MARLINE OTTE

Questions about German-Jewish identity and the integration of Jews into German society have not diminished in importance since Nazi Germany's near-destruction of European Jewry during the Second World War. Frequently, historians of German-Jewish history have considered the decades prior to 1933 as a mere prelude to the Holocaust—even, indeed, as a period of moral decay and social disintegration. They have denounced the contemporary notion of a German-Jewish "symbiosis" as false consciousness, leading to self-denial and over-assimilation. While this essay does not want to revive anachronistic notions of cultural harmony and an imaginary dialogue of equal minds, it does want to point to the inevitable dangers of a focus on high culture alone. The status of gentile-Jewish relations in modern Germany can only be truly assessed if we contrast and compare Jewish involvement in all public arenas. An analysis of live entertainment reveals the immense role that Jewish entertainers and entrepreneurs played in shaping these pursuits in fin-de-siècle Germany. Their success—as well as the diversity of their engagements—poses new challenges for our understanding of the integration and diversity of ethnic experiences in German society prior to 1933.

The history of Jewish entertainers is inseparable from the history of live popular entertainment in Germany prior to 1933.[1] In an unprecedented way, German-Jewish performers and theater directors understood and reflected the dreams and aspirations of mass audiences. As thousands found pleasure and distraction in Germany's amusement venues, popular entertainment created new spheres of sociability and enterprise. These gray areas

1. Peter Gay has made a similar argument for the relationship between the history of Germany's Jews and German history at large. Peter Gay, *Freud, Juden, und andere Deutsche* (Munich, 1989), 11.

of gentile-Jewish relations had the effect of blurring and redrawing the boundaries between insiders and outsiders. This essay attempts to explore this continuing negotiation, using German popular culture as the prism that refracts and redefines common assumptions about the ways gentiles and Jews interacted in twentieth-century Germany.

Prior to the First World War, countless Germans sought release from their regulated lives in what contemporaries commonly called *Jargon* theaters. To date, however, the subject of Jargon theaters has not received much scholarly attention, and the reception, artistic quality, and tradition of Jargon theaters in Berlin's drama scene remain contested.[2] Yet all interpretations agree that Jargon theater was not only a popular form of theater, but one that focused on "Jewish themes." They were the only theaters in Germany in which the majority of stage characters were of Jewish descent; in their performances, these characters celebrated and satirized their own Jewishness. Jargon theaters presented slapstick comedies and one-act shows, amusing hundreds of spectators every night. Between the 1890s and the 1920s, Jargon theaters flourished (especially in Berlin and its surrounding provinces), maintaining a prominent position in the expanding entertainment industry. Their ethnic humor, which ridiculed all segments of society, was appreciated as a unique contribution to Germany's rich popular entertainment scene. The most prominent Jargon theaters were the Gebrüder Herrnfeld Theater and the Folies Caprice, both of which will be discussed below.

Any discussion of Jargon theaters as an essential part of the ever-expanding milieu of popular entertainment has to start with a brief definition of this unique form of popular Jewish drama. The contemporary label "Jargon" carried a normative connotation. Jargon theaters clearly owed their name to the language employed by their actors. Contemporaries often used the word "Jargon" interchangeably with "Yiddish"—or, more properly, with Yiddish-inflected dialect. In the realm of theater, "Jargon" came to be applied almost exclusively to popular Jewish entertainment. "Jargon" held two

---

2. Like many other recent studies, Ruth Freydank's monograph, *Theater in Berlin: Von den Anfängen bis 1945* (Berlin, 1988), and her edited book, *Theater als Geschäft* (Berlin, 1995), do not even mention the Herrnfeld Theater. Peter Sprengel's recent monograph, *Populäres jüdisches Theater in Berlin von 1877 bis 1933* (Berlin, 1997), is a notable exception.

competing meanings: it was an ironic self-description employed by the performers, and it was simultaneously a denigrating ascription of Jewish dialect theater by its middle-class audiences. The often derogatory label "Jargon" originally had a more universal meaning that carried the stigma of linguistic impurity. The term was first and foremost meant to distinguish any dialect from *Hochdeutsch* (High German), the language of elite circles in German society. The distinction between Jargon and High German thus alluded to an ethnic, a geographic, or a class dimension. In a culture that heavily favored the written word, the term "Jargon" pointed to a purely oral language, thereby underscoring both its specificity to an identifiable milieu and the multiplicity of its cultural origins.

Previous scholars have falsely assumed that fin-de-siècle Jargon theaters were the direct descendants of Yiddish theaters. Jargon theaters in Berlin, such as the Gebrüder Herrnfeld Theater and the Folies Caprice, were by no means mere continuations of an older form of ghetto entertainment.[3] Instead, they represented more recent responses to Jewish emancipation and assimilation in Germany. These theaters did not stage Yiddish dramas, for the simple reason that their audiences would have been unable to follow the dialogues. Yiddish was not easily mastered by audiences of gentiles and assimilated Jews. Instead, Jargon theaters invented a language—a "Jargon"—of their own, a mixture of Yiddish, *Rotwelsch* (a secretive dialect spoken by outcasts and brigands), French, Bohemian, Russian, German, and whatever local dialect seemed to appear "authentic." Far from being sites of refuge from a hostile majority culture, they were both an integral part of a broadly engaging popular culture and a means of celebrating assimilated Jewish life in Central Europe—a life in which both Jews and gentiles participated on their own terms. Instead of being perishing anachronisms in a world of continuous marginalization, Jargon theaters reflected the self-confidence of an ethnic minority and its role in a modernizing and increasingly mobile society. Although Jargon theaters made reference to the aesthetics of traditional Yiddish theaters, they sharply differed from those theaters in atmosphere, intent, audiences and—most importantly—language.

3. Michael Brenner, *The Renaissance of Jewish Culture in Weimar Germany* (New Haven, Conn., 1996).

Actors and Audiences

Jargon theater in Berlin was inseparable from the lives and careers of individual performers and entrepreneurs. The brothers Anton and Donat Herrnfeld stood especially tall among the tightly-knit community of Jewish performers. Hungarian natives, stemming from a long lineage of comedians, the Herrnfelds introduced *Budapester Possentheater*—which soon became a synonym for Jargon theater—to fin-de-siècle Berlin. While they spent most of their childhood in Bavaria, the brothers carefully portrayed themselves as Hungarians in public, hoping that their references to Budapest would grant their shows just enough flair to appear exotic without alienating their Berlin audiences. According to family legend, Anton, the older brother, followed the example of his comedian forebears and began his professional career when he was only eight years old. Three years later, he and his siblings Donat (nine years old at the time), Käthe (seven), and Ella (five) started their first family production with a blackface masquerade (*Neger-Quartett*) in the popular Vienna Ringtheater.[4] From the outset, these entertainers created and reinvented their ethnic stage personae, whether black or Jewish, to please and tease their respective audiences. Far from being authentic Yiddish entertainers deeply rooted in an Eastern European *shtetl* culture, the Herrnfelds were experienced and worldly entertainers with an impressively cosmopolitan trajectory. They were well acquainted with international fads and fashions, and equipped with a keen eye and ear for regional, national, and ethnic differences in speech and gesture. Masters of several European languages, their linguistic expertise provided them not only with a rich and versatile command of dialects and postures, but with a knowledge of ethnic and religious stereotypes on which they could draw in their later careers.

The success of Jargon theater was thus inseparable from the development of mainstream drama in Germany. It was hardly the segregation from other trends in the performing arts that led to the success of Jargon theater in Berlin, but the latter's conscious embrace of and integration into precisely those trends. The Herrnfelds' productions amused their audiences not least because they mimicked "serious" plays, ridiculing their sincerity and didacticism. The timing of these parodies was crucial, since their punch lines

4. Egon Jameson, *Mein lustiges Spree-Athen* (Berlin, n.d.), 63.

rested upon the audiences' familiarity with the "classical cultural canon." Although traditional German drama and Jargon theater ranked quite differently in official esteem, they nevertheless drew similar crowds. To understand many of the jokes at the Herrnfeld theater, one had to be intimately acquainted with the content and protagonists of the "legitimate" theater scene. This congruence in spectatorship was certainly no coincidence. Jargon theaters were part of a middle-class subculture that continually imitated, challenged, and informed the hegemonic cultural canon in Germany.

Naturalism, with its passionate search for authenticity and its fascination with everyday life, was particularly critical in laying the foundations for Jargon theater. Naturalistic drama's claim to engage reality and truth was not least a political move against the hegemony of court theaters and their traditional aesthetics. It was meant to give voice to the growing demand among the German middle classes to have their lives and concerns resonate onstage. Although lacking the latter's relentless pathos, Jargon theater similarly sought the heroic in the profane, and it benefited from the innovations of naturalism, which made the use of local dialects and humble settings acceptable to and even desired by theater audiences.[5] Even more than the Deutsche Theater (the most important stage for serious drama in Germany), the Gebrüder Herrnfeld Theater came to approximate the *Volkstheater* called for by reformers of German drama.

The idea of creating a *Volkstheater* as a means for rejuvenating German drama had become immensely popular over the course of the nineteenth century. As national sentiments grew and began to find institutional expressions, middle-class interest in regional dialects and customs sparked the aestheticization of popular culture commonly referred to as *Volkskultur*.[6] This stylized folk culture appropriated regional histories and local traditions, rejecting most expressions of working-class culture as part of a potentially harmful mass culture.[7] *Volkskultur*, often created by provincial groups attempting to define and resuscitate their own cultural canons, also provided an unforeseen opportunity for former social and ethnic pariahs to partici-

5. Freydank, *Theater in Berlin*, 326–40.
6. Hermann Bausinger, "Bürgerlichkeit und Kultur," in *Bürger und Bürgerlichkeit im 19. Jahrhundert*, ed. Jürgen Kocka (Göttingen, 1987), 137.
7. Ibid.

pate in it.[8] Dialect theater, such as the Gebrüder Herrnfeld Theater, profited from the emerging interest in local and ethnic differences; although not party to this bourgeois cultivation of *Volkskultur* in the strict sense, it was nevertheless sanctioned—and, more importantly, frequented—by the middle classes.

As nationalist rhetoric increasingly became one of exclusion and discrimination against ethnic minorities, Jargon theaters were very careful to invoke a brand of nationalism that they found compatible with their specific notions of citizenship and community. Scriptwriters did not confine the setting of their plays to Germany alone, but they often remained vague about the specific locations of their plots. They projected a brand of nationalism that was based on the notion of a shared German culture, emphasizing the bonds of a common language, a shared understanding of history, and moral and political conservatism. In Jargon theaters, a belief in the centrality of the nation did not necessarily exclude a liberal agenda. Their implicit rejection of a *völkisch* nationalism is not surprising, for it secured Jews' inclusion into German society at large.

In the first decades of the twentieth century, Jargon theaters were far from being sites of anti-Semitism and Jewish denigration, as it has been argued; instead, they widened the range of material for Jewish dramatists. Unlike plays in most classical theaters, which simply inserted an occasional Jewish character in a drama for and by gentiles, plays in Jargon theaters were almost entirely populated by Jewish actors and stage characters, so that a Jew did not stick out by virtue of his or her ethnic identity. In addition, Jargon theaters provided Jewish characters with roles outside the limitations of traditional characters, such as Shylock, Nathan the Wise, Golem or Dybbuk. Male Jewish roles were consciously not confined to the haggling Jew (*Schacherjuden*) or money-grabbing father figures who inevitably drove their daughters into prostitution. Now the stage was populated by young Jewish lovers—a role absent in the classical tradition. The family enjoyed a central place in Jargon theater performances. Sketching Jewish family life in Germany and Austria-Hungary as loving, often sentimental, at times crude, and always comical, Jargon theaters provided a reference point for diverse audiences. Far from simply providing a negative contrast to the gentile hero,

8. Ibid., 139.

these new roles were invested with passions, desires, and convictions.[9] In short, Jargon theater depicted Jews as many things, but never simply as social pariahs.

Jargon theaters were folk theaters with a special flair. Marriages, adultery, and generational and gender conflicts formed the core of their plays. None of these topics were Jewish topics per se. The fact that they were set in Jewish families and homes suggested that themes discussed within Jewish families were simply a variation on those discussed in gentile families. At a time when regional identities were being rewritten in many folk theaters across Germany, ethnic difference thus was articulated without alienating a majority of the audience. In Jargon theaters in Berlin, Jews claimed their own dialect theater, thereby suggesting that theirs was yet another dialect—different but equal—among the many German dialects in Central Europe. Until the First World War, Jargon theaters seemed a symbol of the gradual, successful emancipation of Jews in imperial Germany. The extent and limitations of the integrative forces at work in this new public sphere only became apparent during the First World War.

Plays

Before the outbreak of the First World War, almost all plays at the Herrnfeld Theater and the Folies Caprice centered around one single leitmotif: the assimilation of German Jews. Themes such as mixed marriages, religious devotion, education, dietary laws, Jewish names, economic success, the stigma of the parvenu, and relationships with Germany's traditional elites were central to these plays. The Jewish family and its immediate environment provided the setting in which these issues were negotiated, ridiculed, and contested. Although the Folies Caprice was more direct in language and humor than the more tempered Herrnfeld theater, both shared the same concerns. One of the main assumptions of all the plays produced in these theaters before the war was that Jews represented a religious denomination, held together by a shared set of beliefs and practices, that did not conflict with their allegiance to the German nation. The Jews who were depicted on the stages of Jargon theaters were portrayed not simply as Jews but as German citizens of the Jewish faith (*deutsche Staatsbürger jüdischen Glaubens*).

9. See Hans-Joachim Neugebauer, *Judenfiguren: Drama und Theater im frühen 19. Jahrhundert* (Berlin, 1994).

The evidence suggests that Jewish performers in Jargon theaters took pride in their Germanness but had no illusions about the continuing discrimination against Jews in many spheres of public life. Jargon theaters problematized both the ability and willingness of German Jews to assimilate to middle-class norms and expectations, as well as the difficulties of the German gentile majority to accept them unconditionally. Jargon theaters were sensitive to current debates in the German press and streets. They recorded these debates by poking fun at all involved parties: Jews and anti-Semites, orthodox and reform Jews, men and women, young and old, rich and poor, rural and urban citizens. By not making any exceptions, they stressed equality as the ruling principle among the ordinary citizens in society—without, however, questioning the authority of the ruling regime and its elites.

The play *Nightshift* (*Nachtdienst,* 1902) serves as an example of the complex web of relations that the Herrnfeld siblings conveyed so masterfully to their audiences. This play was the first of its kind on several counts. For the first time, Berlin became the scene of action at the Herrnfeld Theater. Equally important was the introduction of intimate gentile-Jewish relations onstage, which went beyond the traditional realm of business relations. At a time when mixed marriages were not considered acceptable to either religious community, spectators witnessed the dilemma of a young Jew confronted with the supposedly immoral behavior of his gentile bride. Unlike dramas in many classical theaters, spectators here were not presented with allegorical plots but real-life situations. The Herrnfeld play capitalized on the familiarity of the audience with the dialects, location, and milieu in question.

The plot line of *Nightshift* is simple. The young gentile girl Else lives with her widowed father, Gottlieb Knolle; she is engaged to a poor Jewish student named Max. Max finds out that Else is a waitress in one of Berlin's many hostess bars (*Animierkneipen*) in the Friedrichstraße, one of Berlin's sleazier areas. Previously both Max and Else's father had thought that she was working night shifts as a phone operator. Everybody is shocked, since the wedding is imminent, and the fathers of groom and bride are old friends. To complicate matters, the fathers had previously decided to move in together, partly out of economic necessity and partly as an expression of their mutual affection. They had hoped that their camaraderie would eventually lead to the union of their children, who had been dear friends during childhood. Prior to the scandal, Gottlieb Knolle had overcome his friend Süssel Holzer's remaining reservations about the mixing of religious backgrounds, stressing the importance of religious tolerance and the merits of a middle-class work ethic: "Let the children do what they want, it's all destiny anyway! It's all right, he'll get an honest girl, and who cares that they have a different faith, so they'll have a civil wedding; and it also has happened before, that he has nothing and she hasn't either and they have achieved something anyway."[10] It turns out that Else, the daughter, lied to her loved ones only to earn money for her fiancé's education, so that he could pursue his studies and move out of the restricted circumstances into which they both were born. In this and other ways, the play appealed to its audiences not to pass judgment without first asking questions, since nothing is as clear-cut as it seems at first sight.

The following scene is a conversation between Else's father and a family friend, Rüdersberg. Knolle is outraged and disappointed after he discovers his daughter's alleged transgressions. He vents his anger to Rüdersberg, who points out the hastiness of his reaction (scene 13):

> RÜDERSBERG. [. . .] Do you know at all what motives tempted her to do this?
>
> KNOLLE. I didn't make her do it!
>
> RÜDERSBERG. I believe that, but just have a look (*spinning around*) at the splendid misery in this house—young blood—hedonism, keeping company with others who may have a bit more—good female friends—here a flounce on the skirt, silk petticoats, there another little lace-embroidered stockings; well, we can't even empathize with these things, that is exactly our social question—the spice of life, factory girl—has the desire to be someone at least once. . . .

---

10. "Denn las doch die Jöhren machen wat se wollen, det is allens Bestimmung! Dat is ja richtig, er kriegt ja nen braves Mädchen, und von wegen, des se beede verschiedenen Glauben haben, nan, da gibts ja ne civile Ehe, und solche Fälle waren ooch schon da, dat er nichts hat und sie nichts hatte, und sind doch zu wat gekommen." Landesarchiv Berlin, *Nachtdienst, Schauspiel aus dem Berliner Leben*, Gebrüder Herrnfeld Theater, Rep. 30c/a, Theater Z, Neuer Teil 2320.

KNOLLE. But the girl has nothing, she really has nothing!

RÜDERSBERG. You know, Gottlieb, at least you could have asked her why she has done it. . . .[11]

In the aftermath of this conversation, Knolle confronts his daughter and asks her what drove her into the scandalous milieu of the Friedrichstraße. He and Max are shocked when Else reveals her altruistic motives. Her unconditional feminine love is meant to touch the men onstage and the breathless spectator alike:

KNOLLE. Do you wanna tell me now, what possessed you? There she stands now—the missus with the obdurate face! I would have done anything for your mother—I would have stolen—if she had been wanting anything—I would have become a burglar—to help her!

ELSE. I haven't done anything worse! (*pointing at Max*) To help him—that money is from me![12]

This final twist to the drama left a deep impression on the audience and was the subject of heartfelt comments in Berlin's daily newspapers. The *Berliner Lokal-Anzeiger,* for example, asked who acted more immorally—the girls who tried to make a living in Berlin's amusement centers, or their clients who dragged the honor of their families through the mud. "Else has simply failed out of love for the penniless student, whose career she hoped to sup-

11. "RÜDERSBERG. [. . .] weißt du denn, welche Motive sie dazu verleitet haben? / KNOLLE. Ich hab se nicht dazu veranlaßt! / RÜDERSBERG. Das glaube ich, aber sieh mal (sich drehend) das glänzende Elend hier im Hause—junges Blut—Genußsucht, Umgang mit Anderen, die vielleicht ein bisschen mehr haben—gute Freundinnen—hier ein Volant am Rock, seidene Unterröcke, dort ein Spitzenchen mehr—tambourierte Strümpfchen, ja wir können uns da gar nicht reindenken, das ist eben unsere sociale Frage—der Reiz des Lebens, jedes Fabrikmädchen—hat den Wunsch einmal sich zu fühlen. . . . / KNOLLE. Aber det Mädchen hat doch nischt, se hat doch nischt! / RÜDERSBERG. Weisst du Gottlieb, du hättest sie doch wenigsten fragen sollen, warum sie es getan. . . ." Ibid.

12. "KNOLLE. Willst du mir nu sagen, wat dir bewogen hat da steht se nun—de Olle mit det verstockte Gesicht! Ich hätte für dein Mutter allens gethan—ich wäre Stehlen gegangen—wenn ihr wat gefehlt hätte—ich hätte eingebrochen, ich wäre zum Verbrecher geworden—um ihr zu helfen! / ELSE. Mehr hab ich ja auch nicht gethan! (*Auf Max deutend*) ihm zu helfen—dat Geld ist von mir!" Ibid.

port," the article concluded.[13] This commentary was all the more significant because at the time the issue of prostitution occupied the German public and was considered to be a major assault on the institutions of family and marriage. By working with the grain of these issues and simultaneously giving them a particular spin, the Herrnfelds secured the approval and engagement of their heterogeneous audiences.

Nightshift not only appealed to its audiences to support and accept mixed marriages between Jews and gentiles; it also pointed to the many achievements and merits of Jews as good and reliable citizens. One implicit argument was that the Jews' loyal service in the army provided the ultimate proof of their devotion to the nation. The playwrights took pains to establish Knolle's and Holzer's common experience as Prussian soldiers in the Franco-Prussian War. Their shared front experiences at Gravelotte, the site of German victory over the French army, serves as the foundation of their friendship and the basis of their equal status.[14] Against this backdrop, the anti-Semitism that costs Süssel Holzer his job stands as a form of injustice based on racial discrimination against which both veterans appear speechless, disappointed, and righteously angry. Indeed, the following scene reveals that although the main story line supposedly focuses on the complicated love affair of their children, the fathers turn out to be the real protagonists of the play (scene 5).

> KNOLLE. Yes—that's true, Süssel, your Max is a decent fellow!
> SÜSSEL. If all people were like this, like you, who looks at everyone the same way, no matter whether they are Jew or Christian—I would not have needed anything from Tuchel, but as it is—what an uproar! Suddenly Tuchel goes crazy—doesn't want Süssel Holzer any more! . . . Tuchel of all people. Now, did I do anything to anyone? Did not enough people live off me? Didn't I stand with you at Gravelotte? Would I not have just as willingly sacrificed my life for the father-

13. "Sehr hübsch ist in einer Scene auch die Frage aufgeworfen, wer verworfener ist: jene Mädchen oder aber die 'Cavaliere,' die die Ehre ihrer Familie dort in den Schmutz treten." Brandenburgisches Landeshauptarchiv, 30 Berlin C, Tit. 74, Th. 777, Akt. 124, *Berliner Lokal-Anzeiger*, November 21, 1902.

14. The victory of German troops in the battles of Gravelotte-Rezonsville (August 16, 1870) and Gravelotte-Saint Privat (August 18, 1870) in the Franco-Prussian War.

land—didn't I, just as you, have parents at home who wept for their child? Suddenly they change—Tuchel goes crazy!

KNOLLE. Yes, yes, pal, you won't change that, that's always a matter of perspective, one has to stay above that! Look, for example: today the *Staatsbürger* runs an article, a big story, well then, good God, I'll have a good day and the paper will sell; tomorrow the *Freisinnige* serves up a new sensation and I'll make a bundle again, everything has its audience, and the beauty of it is that those who buy the *Staatsbürger* also buy the *Freisinnige*—that's the kind of craziness we're dealing with! We are talking about delusions here, but because of it, old boy, the world stands, and both of us won't change it![15]

It should not be forgotten that this dialogue was part of a farce. It poked fun at the relativity of political leanings and sensationalism in the age of mass politics, and it urged the audience to display tolerance and acceptance of the "other." Forbearance, moderation, and pride were the principal attributes the two fathers conveyed to their spectators. As members of the older generation, they had experienced the passing of time and the transitory nature of political opinions. Politics is represented in this play as "theater," and Knolle and Holzer agree that it is best not to get involved. The Jew Holzer in particular, according to the *Berliner Lokal-Anzeiger*, was portrayed by Donat

15. "KNOLLE. Ja—das ist wahr Süssel, dein Max ist een anständiger Mensch! / SÜSSEL. Wenn alle Menschen so wären, wie du, dem jeder Mensch gleich is ob er Jud oder Christ—hätt ich nicht brauchen von Tuchel was aber so—e Gewalt! Mit e mal wird Tuchel verrückt—se woll's ka Süssel Holzer mehr! . . .—ausgerechnet Tuchel! Nu hab ich jemand was gethan? Haben nicht genug Menschen von mir gelebt? Bin ich nicht mit dir gestanden vor Gravelotte? Hätt ich nicht mein Leben ebenso gern fürs Vaterland geopfert—hab ich nicht ebenso gut wie du Eltern zu Hause gehabt, die geweint haben um ihr Kind? Mit e mal kriegen se e Ströhmung—Tuchel wird verrückt! / KNOLLE. Ja ja det, Mensch, wirst du nicht ändern, det is allens Ansichtssache, da muss man eben darüber erhaben sein! Sieh mal, bringt zum Beispiel heut de Staatsbürger eenen Artikel, so'ne grosse Sache, lieber Jott, denn habe ich nen guten Tag und das Blatt wird gekooft, morgen bringt de Freisinnige eene neue Sensation denn mach ick detselbe Bombengeschäft, es hat alles ein Publikum, und das Schönste, die die de Staatsbürger Zeitung koofen—koofen auch de Freisinnige, dat is nu mal so'n Theater! Des sind Einbildungen, aber deswegen oller Junge, die Welt steht und wir beede werden se nicht ändern." Landesarchiv Berlin, *Nachtdienst, Schauspiel aus dem Berliner Leben*, Gebrüder Herrnfeld Theater, Rep. 30c/a, Theater Z, Neuer Teil 2320.

Herrnfeld as "full of warm sensibilities, dedication, and sensitivity." In short, he represented a timeless and caring version of humanity in an age of hardship, injustice, and hasty judgments.[16]

Both fathers conversed in strong accents. While Gottlieb Knolle was what contemporaries might have called a real "*Berliner Schnauze,*" Süssel Holzer spoke with a strong Yiddish intonation, injecting into the conversation the occasional Yiddish word (many of which had entered Berlin Jargon long before). Instead of speaking in the Yiddish language, Holzer (or, more properly, Donat Herrnfeld) inverted his sentence structures to appear "authentic." By using verbs mostly as infinitives, separated from their subjects only by a negation, the actor imitated Yiddish grammatical structures.[17] In describing past events, he never used the simple past tense but always the present perfect, which required the auxiliary verbs *haben* or *sein*—a grammatical feature typical of Yiddish. At the same time, he did not use the Yiddish translations of these auxiliary verbs, *hobn* or *sain.* In addition, most verbs were used as reflexive verbs, preferably in connection to passive constructions. Knolle, in comparison, rambled more or less consistently in the well-known local dialect. He exchanged *Koofen* for *Kaufen, eenen* for *einen, det* for *das,* and *Jott* for *Gott.* He insulted friends and enemies alike as *die Olle* or *der olle Kerl,* belittling both in an agitated but amicable way. After all, this play was for Berliners, and Berliners had a reputation for being witty and direct. The hot-headed Knolle, with his quick temper and soft heart, succeeded in thoroughly captivating his audience.

In short, *Nightshift* addressed universal themes while paying particular attention to Jewish issues. The "fallen" daughter's relationship to her father and questions of sexual impropriety and moral corruption were bemoaned in the context of a positive treatment of mixed marriage and religious tolerance. The issues of poverty and class differences were introduced in connection with anti-Semitism. The Herrnfeld theater thus appealed to its audiences on many levels simultaneously. The spectator was addressed as

16. Brandenburgisches Landeshauptarchiv, 30 Berlin C, Tit. 74, Th. 777, Akt. 124, *Berliner Lokal-Anzeiger,* November 21, 1902.

17. For example: "Wenn alle Menschen so wären, wie du, dem jeder Mensch gleich is ob er Jud oder Christ—hätt ich nicht brauchen von Tuchel was. . . ."

father, daughter, or lover; as burgher, soldier, or German citizen; and as gentile or Jew. The play explored the intersection of all of these identities. No single identity was singled out as a mark of marginality. Even the daughter, at first sight the victim of her own desires, humbled the others. Her love for her Jewish fiancé was as pure as her desire to marry a learned man.

While *Nightshift* was moderate in tone and humor (not least in order to establish the Herrnfeld theater as a respectable house for the entire family), the drama *A Solomonic Judgment* (*Salomonisches Urteil*, 1908) was more representative of the theater's usual style. Not only did it exhibit the Herrnfelds' well-known verve; it also offered a rather crass depiction of factionalism within the Jewish community. The plot centered on the search for the father of an illegitimate child. The main theme of *Solomonic Judgment* thus remained true to the usual themes of contemporary bourgeois comedies (*bürgerliche Lustspiele*). The real attraction of the play, however, lay in the many humorous disputes between the fathers of a married couple, who disagree on their views of Jewish assimilation. One (Cohn) is a reputable businessman; the other (Abarbanell) is a former butcher who had become wealthy by his "invention" of white *Blutwurst*. These two men fight about how best to support their son/son-in-law, whom they suspect to be in financial difficulties due to the couple's lavish lifestyle. Cohn is outraged and feels estranged from his son and his in-laws, who he feels have ceased to respect Jewish traditions (including Jewish dietary laws). The following dialogue between Brünhilde, Abarbanell's wife, and Cohn establishes the leitmotif of the play (act 1, scene 3):

> BRÜNHILDE. But you must have received my invitation?
>
> COHN. Why must I have? I know nothing!
>
> BRÜNHILDE. You are only saying that to avoid at all costs having to eat something in your son's home!
>
> COHN. Here we go again! I certainly won't eat something that's not kosher!
>
> BRÜNHILDE. How can anyone hold such old-fashioned views?
>
> COHN. A cleverer man than me—the great King Frederick—once remarked quite fittingly: "Let all find happiness in their own fashion."
>
> BRÜNHILDE. Well, does it really make a difference whether the meat is purchased from Hefter or from Rosenthal?

COHN. Of course, it doesn't make a difference—why not buy from Rosenthal then!

BRÜNHILDE. Odd person.[18]

Brünhilde's name was a symbol of her clumsy over-assimilation. Classically Wagnerian and too pompous for a woman with little formal schooling and exposure to high culture, it was meant to ridicule her desire to become "teutonic." In Wagner's *Der Ring der Nibelungen*, the tragic goddess Brünhilde falls in love with Siegfried, a mortal hero who was seen by contemporaries as the archetypical German. Since Wagner's anti-Semitic tendencies were well known among contemporary gentiles and Jews, a name such as Brünhilde might well have signaled self-hatred. Cohn, by contrast, represented the ideal-typical name for a Jew. Often experienced as a stigma by many German Jews, the name "Cohn" is carried with pride in this play. Indeed, the character Cohn bemoans his son's attempt to shed his Jewish identity by buying a noble name. Quoting Frederick the Great, who was known for his religious tolerance, Cohn insists on his right to be different by obeying the dietary laws of the Jewish tradition, a position Brünhilde cannot grasp. Frederick's famous words, "Let all find happiness in their own fashion," becomes the motto of this play—a motto that encapsulates the defensive position of the Enlightenment in an era of neoromantic passions and delusions.

In *Solomonic Judgment,* the Herrnfelds spoke out against unconditional assimilation, which they believed would inevitably lead to the disappearance of a shared heritage. By making Cohn the play's most sympathetic character, they gave their audiences a clear message. They appealed for the acceptance of private difference, secured by the rights of the individual, in a society governed by a shared humanitarian consensus. Ridiculing Jews who desired to

18. "BRÜNHILDE. Sie müssen doch meine Einladung bekommen haben? / COHN. Warum muss ich? Ich weiss von nichts! / BRÜNHILDE. Das sagen Sie blos, um ja nicht im Hause ihres Sohnes etwas essen zu müssen! / COHN. Schon wieder die alte Leier! Ich ess doch kein Treifes! / BRÜNHILDE. Wie kann man nur solch veraltete Ansicht haben? / COHN. E klügerer Mann wie ich—der grosse König Friedrich—hat mal ganz treffend bemerkt: 'Lass Jeden selig werden nach seiner Facon.' / BRÜNHILDE. Bleibt sich das jetzt nicht gleich, ob das Fleisch von Hefter oder von Rosenthal gekauft wird? / COHN. Gewiss bleibt es sich gleich—warum kauft man da nicht von Rosenthal! / BRÜNHILDE. Komischer Mensch." Landesarchiv Berlin, *Salomonisches Urteil,* Gebrüder Herrnfeld Theater, Rep. 30 c/a, Theater Z, Neuer Teil 4030.

hide their ethnic identity behind antiquated titles and noble names, they portrayed most nobles as thoroughly snobbish and corrupt, living off their past glory, their vitality stifled by mindless rituals such as five o'clock teas. The following dialogue between Cohn and Abarbanell underscores the antagonism behind in their positions (scene 10):

> COHN. I always knew it was going to end like this—the thousand mark bills were just flying around! Why was it necessary for him to get a different name?
>
> ABARBANELL. You don't understand that!
>
> COHN. Well, that is quite the nasty trick by a healthy man, where the father will still live to be a hundred years old—to get himself adopted by a baron!—This adoption cost a fortune, you know!
>
> ABARBANELL. It wasn't that bad!
>
> COHN. He has to be called von Klamm-Cohn! Cohn by itself wasn't good enough for you!
>
> ABARBANELL. Cohn by itself is no longer a real name these days!
>
> COHN. (angry) There are millions of Cohns!
>
> ABARBANELL. That's not enough!
>
> COHN. Well, there you are!
>
> ABARBANELL. You are forgetting that your son has already attained an established position in society!
>
> COHN. This established position has broken his neck! He had to arrange Fife de Glockes—Fife de Glockes! I can't even pronounce it!
>
> ABARBANELL. Well, you are agitated now!
>
> COHN. And balloons rose up! Confetti thrown down on the people! Everywhere the mother-in-law was present—the old butcher's wife![19]

---

19. "COHN. Das Ende hab ich vorausgesehen—die Tausender sind nur so rumgeflogen! Zu was hat er nötig gehabt, sich e anderen Namen beizulegen? / ABARBANELL. Das verstehn Sie nicht! / COHN. Ja das e Streich von e gesunden Menschen, wo der Vater noch bis hundert Jahr lebt—sich von e Baron als Sohn adoptieren zu lassen!—diese Adoption hat doch e Vermögen gekostet! / ABARBANELL. Das war nicht so schlimm! / COHN. Er muss von Klamm-Cohn heissen! Cohn allein war euch nicht gut genug! / ABARBANELL. Cohn allen ist heut kein Name mehr! / COHN. (wütend) Millionen Cohns gibt's! / ABARBANELL. Das reicht nicht! / COHN. Na also! / ABARBANELL. Sie vergessen, dass Ihr Sohn in der G'sellschaft schon eine feste Position eingenommen hat! / COHN. Die feste Postition hat'n es Genick gebrochen! Fife de Glockes hat er arrangieren müssen—Fife de Glockes!

266 MARLINE OTTE

In the course of their conversations, Cohn incessantly appeals to his son "to stay true to himself" and not to deny his past.[20] More importantly, he claims a former Prussian king as his own cultural heritage, presenting it as compatible with his ethnicity. This play operates on many levels: while it seems to be about illegitimate parentage within a specific family, it really negotiates the Jews' position as the "stepchildren" of the nation. By claiming the national father—Frederick the Great—as his own, Cohn demands legitimacy for himself and his kin.

Aesthetics and the First World War

The outbreak of the First World War fundamentally altered the censorship policy of the Prussian authorities. The theater police moved quickly to ban musical comedies, operettas, farces, and variety shows; these genres, so beloved by Wilhelmine audiences, were now considered to be too frivolous or trashy for a nation at war.[21] When the war began, the Herrnfelds were presenting the play *Mandelbaum's Honeymoon*, a burlesque comedy about the Jew Mandelbaum who married out of financial greed and who desperately tried to escape his marriage after the "deal" did not turn out as favorably as he had hoped.[22] Reacting to the new laws with alacrity, the Herrnfelds sought to prevent the possible closure of their establishment by voluntarily changing the style of their performances. On August 24, 1914, they filed the following request to Berlin's theater police. Compared to earlier requests, which had been cheerful and assertive, the diplomatic and moderately submissive tone of this letter is striking:

> Since in the present serious times we do not deem it appropriate to put on stage our merry comedy *Mandelbaum's Honeymoon*, we have

---

Nicht mal ausprechen kann ich's! / ABARBANELL. Na ja—Sie sind's jetzt aufgeregt! / COHN. In de Luftbalons sind e hochgesteigen! auf de Leut Papierschnitzel runtergeschmissen! Überall war die Schwiegermama dabei—die alte Metzgerin!" Ibid.

20. Landesarchiv Berlin, *Salomonisches Urteil*, Gebrüder Herrnfeld Theater, Rep. 30 c/a, Theater Z, Neuer Teil 4030.

21. Gary D. Stark, "All Quiet on the Home Front," in *Authority, Identity, and the Social History of the Great War*, ed. Frans Coetzee and Marilyn Shevin-Coetzee (Princeton, N.J., 1999), 62–3.

22. Brandenburgisches Landeshauptarchiv, 30 Berlin C, Tit. 74, Th. 779, Akt. 219, *Berliner Börsen-Courier*, August 2, 1914.

adapted a patriotic play, *He Will Return* (*Er kommt wieder*), a war episode by Anton and Donat Herrnfeld. Enclosed we are submitting a copy in duplicate for your obliging censorship and approval, with the request kindly to grant the latter immediately.[23]

He Will Return was approved and became the first Herrnfeld play to be staged after the declaration of war. The new play captured the anxious desire of the Jewish community to belong to the "true" Germany as well as Anton and Donat Herrnfeld's attempt to meet the new censorship requirements, which demanded sincerity and national devotion—two very humorless mandates. It also captured the spirit of the first weeks of the summer of 1914, when enthusiasm for the war and righteous indignation were widespread among German citizens. A late August review of the play suggested that the Herrnfelds had struck a nerve:

> This too is a piece of Berlin: that the Herrnfeld brothers belong to the first ones who have the courage to open their theater again. They cannot cling to 'purity of style' but have to take into account the general mood. In particular, they do this with the patriotic-sentimental one-act play *He Will Return,* in which the playwrights, Anton and Donat Herrnfeld, effectively dramatize an incident at the German-Austrian border that occurred on the day of the declaration of war. The closing scene, when the "Wacht am Rhein" ("The Guard on the Rhine") is played onstage, turned into a powerful patriotic demonstration, as the entire audience joined in.[24]

In *He Will Return,* a mixed marriage between a Jewish man and Christian woman is again central to the plot. In a departure from previous Herrnfeld plays, the children do not consult their parents before exchanging vows. Whereas the Jewish horse dealer Moses (the father of the groom) is understanding and supportive of the young couple's choice, the gentile Joseph Grieshuber—a bailiff and the father of the bride—feels betrayed and disappointed. Moses appeals to Joseph to sanction the hurried wedding: "Bailiff, think about what you want to say. If two young people find and love each

23. Ibid., Akt. 227.
24. Ibid., Akt. 229, *Deutsche Monatszeitung,* August 31, 1914.

other, and believe they are meant for each other, then they should get married. That is my opinion. Come on, give me a hand, in these times of hardship, you can make two people happy."[25] Unlike the genial fathers of previous Herrnfeld dramas, Joseph reacts violently; he rejects not only his son-in-law but also his daughter, proclaiming, "It stays all as I have said before. . . . My child remains dead for me."[26] Much of the first half of the play consists of heated dialogue between the two fathers. Moses repeatedly beseeches Joseph to give his blessing to his daughter's choice:

MOSES. Joseph, I beg you once more, not for me, but for my son.—Look—my only son takes to the field today—and, and—with him thousands of our sons of all confessions, and they march side by side, shoulder to shoulder, without asking, "What is your religion?" They are going to war together in order to free their coreligionists from the Russian yoke, and the Jew will not ask: "Is that not a Catholic whom you have liberated?" The Catholic won't ask: "Is that a Muslim you have freed?"—No—they know not the difference in religion, because it's called justice to stand up for humanness. And you who stay home, you want to think otherwise? That is mean of you.

GRIESHUBER. (*excitedly*) You will never change my mind, despite all your smooth talking. If my daughter has acted against her father's will, then let her go on her own path alone.

MOSES. Why has she acted against her father's will? Because she wants to let the warrior take to the field with an easier heart. She has sacrificed herself for the fatherland. For the most sacred duty in war is—first your fatherland, then your family—and in the last place your faith—.[27]

25. Landesarchiv Berlin, *Er kommt wieder*, Gebrüder Herrnfeld Theater, Rep. 30 c/a, Theater Z, Neuer Teil 6015a.

26. Ibid.

27. "MOSES. Joseph ich bitte Dich noch einmal, nicht für mich, sondern für meinen Sohn.—Sieh—mein einziger Sohn geht heute ins Feld—und und—mit ihm tausende unserer Söhne aller Confessionen, und sie ziehen Seite and Seite, Schulter an Schulter in den Kampf, ohne zu fragen wie ist Deine Religion? Sie ziehen gemeinschaftlich in den Krieg um ihre Glaubensgenossen aus dem russischen Joch zu befreien, und der Jude wird nicht fragen, ist das nicht ein Katholik—den Du befreist? Der Katholik wird nicht fragen ist das nicht ein Mohamedaner, den Du befreist.—Nein—alle sie kennen keinen Unterschied in der Religion, weil es heisst für die Gerechtigkeit, für die Menschlichkeit einzutreten. Und

In this scene, Moses—the voice of the reason—tries to illuminate the clouded judgment of his friend and fellow citizen, Joseph. Moses uses universal and humanitarian concepts such as "human love," "justice," and the tolerance of other religious beliefs in an uneasy conjunction with particularistic concepts such as "fatherland," "duty," "battle," and "war." The defensive undertone of Moses's plea and the contradictory values in his system of morals reveal the uncomfortable situation of liberal and humanitarian thinkers, who were confronted with a war they did not want but which they had not helped to prevent. The Herrnfelds wanted to preserve their own voice without losing their foothold in the entertainment market. They felt compelled to follow the directives of the new order, which only tolerated that which furthered the war effort. Thus they appealed to their audiences with what they thought to be a suggestive combination of outdated rationalism and contemporary emotionality. Precarious though it was, this strategy seemed to work, at least as long as the *Burgfrieden* lasted.

He Will Return has a happy ending. After the groom Jacob proves himself to be a virtuous man of high morals, Joseph does accept him as his son-in-law, although not without making the inevitable reference to Holy Scripture. But here another wartime concession is evident. Joseph Grieshuber accepts his son-in-law not as his daughter's soulmate, but as her new guardian.[28] The new spirit of the time demanded clear-cut gender roles; men were warriors and providers, who guarded and protected subordinate women. Such an order was seen as ordained and sanctified by the Almighty himself. In earlier years of Jargon entertainment, as in so many of Shakespeare's dramas, men most often appeared as the intellectual inferiors of their wives. Driven by their desires into extramarital affairs, they were inevitably caught by their

---

Du der Du in der Stube hockst, Du willst anders denken? Das ist gemein von Dir. / GRIES-HUBER. (*aufbrausend*) Du kannst mich nicht durch Deine schön gefärbten Reden ja doch nicht umstimmen. Hat meine Tochter gegen den Willen Ihres Vaters gehandelt, so mag sie ihren Weg allein gehn. / MOSES. Warum hat sie gegen den Willen des Vaters gehandelt? Weil sie den Krieger leichteren Herzens in den Kampf ziehen lassen will. Sie hat sich für das Vaterland geopfert: Denn die heiligste Pflicht im Kriege gilt—zuerst Dein Vaterland, dann Deine Familie—und zuletzt erst Dein Glauben." Ibid.

28. "The wife should leave father and mother and follow the man. Love each other and pray to God that he returns healthy." ("Das Weib soll Vater und Mutter verlassen und dem Manne folgen—behaltet Euch lieb und betet zu Gott, dass er gesund wiederkehrt.") Ibid.

suspicious and strong-willed wives, who anticipated most of their strata-
gems. The audiences wanted and expected to see this pattern of unfaithful
husbands and domineering wives because it reflected—and inverted—ruling
gender stereotypes. Such a dramatic scheme allowed for many comical effects. In 1912, only two years prior to *He Will Return*, the *Vossische Zeitung*
had identified this pattern (with mixed feelings) as a leitmotif at the Herrnfeld theater: "Not that the playwrights digressed from their usual theme of
husbands whooping it up and their wives unerringly catching them, but they
know how to present the well-worn subject in constantly new ways, often
using surprising puns and indisputably hilarious situations to give the audience's laugh-muscles a workout."[29] After August 1914, the Herrnfeld theater
gave up these highly successful depictions of marital conflict in order to secure its continued existence. In this way, *He Will Return* represented a less
obvious, but nonetheless decisive, break from the comedic conventions of
the Wilhelmine Theater.

Other, perhaps less subtle, changes in style also followed the war's onset.
Before 1914, the Herrnfelds traditionally chose humorous and grotesque
names for their main characters. They named their Jewish stage characters
Blumentopf, Rosenblatt, Goldstücker, Morgenstern, or Perlmutter; unlike
other theaters, they found equally profane names for their gentile characters,
such as Wisskotschil, Knolle, Grieshuber, von Klamm, Neuendorf, Hansa,
Böhmer, or Nepomuk.[30] In the classical theater canon, the "Jewish" name
was meant to single out one individual in a potentially hostile environment; Jews were meant to personify alien souls living on the fringes of society. In Jargon theater, however, preposterous names were used on stage to
unify a community of individuals of divergent social standings and backgrounds. These theaters had thus suggested a normality in gentile-Jewish relations, which for at least some members of the audiences corresponded to

---

29. Brandenburgisches Landeshauptarchiv 30 Berlin C, Tit. 74, Th. 779, Akt. 140, *Vossische Zeitung*, October 6, 1912.

30. The origins of Jewish surnames in their great majority fell into four categories: "1.
names of origin (e.g., 'Berliner'), 2. patronymics ('Davidsohn'), 3. occupational names,
attributive names, nicknames ('Perlmann'), 4. arbitrary names ('Goldberg')." It is interesting to note that names employed by the Herrnfeld brother prior to 1914 always fell
into the last two categories. Dietz Bering, *The Stigma of Names: Antisemitism in German
Daily Life, 1812–1933*, trans. Neville Plaice (Ann Arbor, Mich., 1992), 17.

lived reality. The name of each Jargon theater character, although colorful and often ridiculous, was not meant to function as a stigma; it had lost its singularity.

Prior to the war, the traditional division of character roles between the Herrnfeld brothers had also allowed for a more balanced view of Germany's ethnic groups. In all their plays, Anton and Donat Herrnfeld operated as a comedy team with a very similar relationship: Donat impersonated a Jew, whereas Anton played a gentile. This division allowed them to poke equal fun at both sections of society without offending either group or focusing exclusively on Jewish types. Anton specialized in the character roles with Slavic names and origins—shrewd and canny, with an eye to personal advantage—while Donat, playing the Jews, was soft, agitated, and warm-hearted. Their types were well summarized in the following description by W. Fred, published in *Die Schaubühne* in 1912:

> Donat Herrnfeld shows the specifically Jewish manner of passing from controlled agitation into a fit of rage; Anton Herrnfeld portrays a naïve cleverness behind a mask of idiocy. The instruments of both actors are more gestures—something rhythmical, so to speak—than words per se. Both make you laugh because one gets less the feeling of "theater" than the recollection of having met people like that. And the amazement about the fact that there are such people among us, combined with the conviction that despite all external changes the essence of these archetypes are, if not eternal, at least persistent "for up to a hundred years," results in a powerful comical effect. There-fore, one feels closer to the Jew than to the Bohemian. One would like to see a master play with the Herrnfelds, Vienna's and Pest's Eisenback and Rott, who are really great character actors, with Schild-kraut and a Jewish Nestroy who writes a play for them: without superiority vis-à-vis the milieu and the jargon, robust and moving like the Jewish songs that unfortunately cannot be heard in these parts.[31]

After August 1914, the lightness, ease, and "normality" of gentile-Jewish relations among actors and in audiences suddenly became more complex.

31. W. Fred in *Die Schaubühne* 2 (1912): 420.

No careless or ambiguous jokes were cracked; sensibilities were no longer challenged, but instead were carefully respected. Characters' names, for example, became solemn and serious. In place of names like Isidor Blumentopf, Jewish protagonists now assumed biblical names, like Abraham or, as in the case of *He Will Return,* Moses and Jacob. By contrast, the substitution of Joseph Grieshuber for Gottlieb Knolle represented a much less conspicuous ennobling of the gentile characters. Biblical names put the Jewish stage characters beyond reproach and ridicule, turning them into heroes whose declarations were prophecies directed at their audiences. Yet these biblical names ironically enhanced the separateness of these Jews from their gentile counterparts. Now they were once again Jews in the diaspora, a community bound together by the threat of the "other." There were no intrafamily conflicts between fathers and sons; the crucial dividing line was now that which separated the Jew from the gentile. Full of conventional wisdom and very little humor, these new plays could only compensate for these deficiencies by incorporating what appears today to be dated sentimentality.

He Will Return was sufficiently successful among audiences and censors that the Herrnfelds soon produced a sequel, *This Is How We Live! (So leben wir!).*[32] The same little village on the Austrian border provided the setting for the play.[33] Taking up where *He Will Return* had ended, this sequel described the experiences of the first year of war on the home front, which were conveyed to the audience largely through press releases and occasional messages from soldiers. Jacob's letter from the trenches is a key example of Jargon theater's new tone during the war. On the surface, it describes trench experiences à la Ernst Jünger, experiences which shatter the comfort, security, and harmony of bourgeois homes. Jacob's letter arrives at a moment when everyone thinks he is already dead. His family therefore reads his lines as the last farewell of a heroic warrior:

> Indeed all seems lost for us—I can see how everyone is withdrawing; the only chance is to act quickly: "People, we must not abandon our comrades, if it must be like that, we'll all die!" With these words I storm to the front, my rifle high in the air. We hold out for a long time in the murderous fire—but no help arrives.—How shall this

32. Brandenburgisches Landeshauptarchiv, 30 Berlin C, Tit. 74, Th. 779, Akt. 232.
33. Ibid., Akt. 236, *Berliner Neueste Nachrichten,* November 1, 1914.

end?! . . . Don't be afraid, give my best to my Rosel, and let me embrace all of you affectionately,—and should I die—I'm dying for you—for my wife—and my fatherland—Yours, Jacob![34]

The Herrnfelds tried to bond with their audiences over the communal experience of a letter from a loved one. Since many families had sons at the front, spectators could identify with the anxieties and uncertainties presented onstage. Yet the Herrnfelds did not subscribe to the notion that war was a chivalrous game fought by gentlemen who were distinguished by their nobility and bravery. Their war was dirty and frenetic; it had to be survived day to day. By presenting this kind of war, the Herrnfelds offered a twin tribute: to naturalistic drama and to their Jewish roots. Although they singled out Jacob as someone whose courage in the end rescued others, it was not what he did alone but how he motivated others to work together that constituted his heroism. He was not a solitary fighter on a mission, but a responsible soldier who did not want to abandon his comrades (and who was later rescued by them). In the end, Jacob did not die, but the spectator was left wondering whether his survival was due to destiny or simply chance.

One of the most striking aesthetic departures evident in these wartime plays was the absence of ethnic or local dialects. Neither Jews nor gentiles spoke with heavy accents. In effect, Jargon theaters ceased to present Jargon of any kind. Whereas every intonation was indicated in the scripts of earlier plays, there is no sign that the actors were asked to perform in specific dialects or accents in *He Will Return* or *This Is How We Live!* Such linguistic distinctions automatically would have set individual actors apart, destroying the fragile sense of a national community. This was precisely the effect that Jargon theater directors now wanted to avoid. The virtuoso display of "authentic" accents and dialects apparently was a feature of public performance that neither the Herrnfelds nor their audiences thought appropriate or welcome in times of national crisis.

This Is How We Live! was not a great hit for the Herrnfeld theater. The longer the war lasted, the more German audiences' initial enthusiasm for patriotic plays diminished. Spectators wanted to be entertained and amused, but not tutored. Sensing this, the Herrnfeld brothers had tried to introduce

34. Landesarchiv Berlin, *Er kommt wieder,* Gebrüder Herrnfeld Theater, Rep. 30 c/a, Theater Z, Neuer Teil 6015a.

situational humor in *This Is How We Live!* whenever it was politically oppor-
tune. In November 1914, the press—and in particular the *Berliner Morgen-
post*—was positively impressed with their delicate balancing act, their careful
weighing of humor and patriotism:

> At the Herrnfelds' one does not only laugh, a considerable stream of
> tears also flows from beautiful eyes every evening. The two play-
> wright-directors Anton and Donat Herrnfeld have adopted a tone for
> their new work—*This Is How We Live!*, premiering last Saturday be-
> fore a full house—that is unusual for this temple. And one must ac-
> knowledge that the playwrights have molded with a sure eye for
> what's effective onstage, for a work that rises significantly above other
> more or less skillfully jumbled casual plays. Without any obtrusive
> jingoism, without kitschy sensationalism, they have shaped material
> that reveals that they have followed the events of these great times
> with open eyes and ears. Their characters are drawn in minutest, life-
> like detail; they grip all the more, because without exception they are
> splendidly portrayed. It's superfluous to mention that humor comes
> into play quite abundantly.[35]

The Folies Caprice

The Folies Caprice was an uncouth version of the Gebrüder Herrnfeld Theater. Whereas the Folies Caprice imitated and parodied classical theater in
the same manner as the Herrnfelds, it also exploited the successes of other
popular theaters, such as the Metropol Theater. In the first decade of the
new century, revue theater had become immensely popular among masses
and elites alike and had begun to replace more traditional variety and cabaret theaters. Revues habitually made reference to current scandals and
events, caricaturing famous personalities in politics and high society.
Whereas the Metropol Theater was known for its lavish, disciplined, and
fine-tuned revues, the Folies Caprice often presented a cruder, more openly
sexual version of the same genre. Provocative Jargon-jokes (*Anrühige Jargon-
Witze*) were the centerpiece of every performance, and they often risked censorship on account of their indecency. In contrast to the Herrnfeld theater,

35. Brandenburgisches Landeshauptarchiv, 30 Berlin C, Tit. 74, Th. 779, Akt. 235.

which had a reasonably strong plot line in each of its plays, the Folies Caprice typically presented a series of loosely connected sketches.[36]

In the early years of its existence, the Folies Caprice appeared to offer an even more "authentic" depiction of a specific Jewish milieu than the Herrnfeld theater.[37] By 1911, however, it seemed to have lost most of its artistic ambitions. *Third Class* (*III. Klasse*), for example, a play by Max Ernst and a spinoff of a famous satire by Emil Thoma, did not captivate its audience with its differentiated portrait of Jewish life in Germany. Without being particularly original, it nevertheless opens a window on the *Witzkultur* of the time.[38] Like many of the farces at the Folies Caprice, the entire action of *Third Class* was confined to one location—a train car on its way through Poznán. As passengers boarded and left the train, their conversations provided the plot for the play. The following scene is representative of such encounters. The main gentile character, Wallowitzer, is a witty, sharp-tongued, married man who is always ready for a little romantic encounter. Having managed to engage a young, attractive woman in a flirtatious conversation, his plans are upset by the arrival of a Jewish couple in his compartment. Their presence threatens to disturb his little tête-à-tête. Wallowitzer tries to discourage the couple from staying by insulting them:

> WALLOWITZER. Since we're sitting together so comfortably, allow me: Wallowitzer is my name.

36. Ibid., Th. 845, Akt. 241, *Vossische Zeitung,* December 21, 1907.

37. In 1906, the critic Walter Turszinsky praised the oeuvres of the Folies Caprice as "genuine, like Sabbath fish in butter sauce." Walter Turszinsky, "Jüdischen Theater" in *Die Schaubühne* 1 (1906): 446.

38. As one reviewer noted, "Yesterday (Friday) two comedies by Max Ernst premiered at the Theater Folies Caprice, both had everyone laughing. . . . The other one, *Third Class,* is a railway skit entirely in the tradition of the well-known farce à la Thoma; except that it was transplanted from the first into the third railway class and from the Bavarian highlands into the fields of the province of Posen. If thus the idea was not new, the execution of the satire was nevertheless exceptionally funny. The best actors, above all Messrs. Berisch and Müller, once again took the opportunity to showcase their performing abilities and dialectic talents. As the entire show was also rich in jokes and baffling, hilarious situations, the audience couldn't stop laughing and at the end applauded enthusiastically. Mr. Ignaz Wallowitzer's railway compartment adventures will likely dominate the program of the Theater Folies Caprice for some time." Brandenburgisches Landeshauptarchiv, 30 Berlin C, Tit. 74, Th. 847, Akt. 19, *Berliner Lokal-Anzeiger* April 22, 1911.

EICHKUTZ. Well, OK! Isedor Eichkutz, and my wife Sara.

WALLOWITZER. (*makes a bow*) Ach, Sara, the ancient biblical mother.

EICHKUTZ. Well, my wife isn't that old.

WALLOWITZER. Ach, what's a few days.

SARA. (*to Eichkutz*) Isedor, you let me be insulted like this?

EICHKUTZ. (*flying at Wallowitzer threateningly*) You! (*looking swiftly at Sara, in a calm voice*) Ach, what the heck, I guess you are right.[39]

In the course of the scene, the Jew Eichkutz and his perspectives on life become an endless source of conversation for Wallowitzer. A stream of loosely connected dialogues (such as the following), crowned by a more or less well-placed punch line at the end, was the typical format of most plays at the Folies Caprice:

WALLOWITZER. (*to Eichkutz*) What's the matter, Mr. Eichkutz, why are you wearing a black tie? Are you grieving?

EICHKUTZ. Sure, after all, Rothschild has died.

WALLOWITZER. Well, were you related to him?

EICHKUTZ. No that's exactly why I am grieving.[40]

Jokes about the Rothschilds and their extraordinary wealth were very common, especially among Germany's anti-Semites. Unlike most jokes of this kind, however, the author here chose to present the Jewish perspective: it is Eichkutz who completes the punch line and not Wallowitzer. Nor is Rothschild an object of ridicule or portrayed as the master of a Jewish world

39. "WALLOWITZER. Weil wir grad' so gemütlich beisammen sitzen, gestatten Sie, mein Name ist Wallowitzer. / EICHKUTZ. Na Also! Isedor Eichkutz, meine Frau Sara. / WALLOWITZER (macht ein Kompliment). Ah, Sara, die biblische Stammmutter. / EICHKUTZ. Na gar so alt ist meine Frau noch nicht. / WALLOWITZER. Na wegen die paar Tage. / SARA. (Zu Eichkutz) Isedor, Du lässt mich hier so beleidigen. / EICHKUTZ. (*fährt drohend auf Wallowitzer los*) Sie! (*Plötzlich mit einem Blick auf Sara in einem ruhigen Ton*) Sie haben doch nebbich recht." Landesarchiv Berlin, *III. Klasse,* Max Ernst, Folies Caprice, Rep. 30 c/a, Theater Z, Neuer Teil 5049.

40. "WALLOWITZER. (*Zu Eichkutz*) Was ist Herr Eichkutz, warum tragen sie schwarze Kravatten? Sind Sie in Trauer? / EICHKUTZ. Nu, Rothschild ist doch gestorben. / WALLOWITZER. Na, waren Sie denn verwandt mit ihm? / EICHKUTZ. Nein—deswegen trauere ich doch." Ibid.

conspiracy—a theme very common in German anti-Semitic discourse. The fool is not the greedy Jewish banker, but rather the petty-bourgeois Eichkutz, who envies his wealth.[41] This joke took the edge off these issues by focusing on the envious common man instead of the banker. It addressed one of the most critical arenas of gentile-Jewish encounters: moneylending and moneymaking. By emphasizing the universality—not the Jewish specificity—of the desire for wealth, the joke suggested to listeners that one might share interests even when one did not share identities.

The Jewish parvenu and his problematic encounters with Germany's aristocratic society played a central role in the Folies Caprice.[42] Unlike the Herrnfeld theater, which mostly focused on the bourgeois family, the Folies Caprice subjected to ridicule and laughter the parvenu's quest for respectability, distinctions, honors, and titles. It is often unclear whether the audiences laughed at or with the actors, since well-known stereotypes were often reproduced at the theater. Its actors, however, softened the effect by treating both gentiles and Jews to equally heavy doses of their acidic humor. Their jokes were Jewish jokes—but they were also German jokes. The imperial public was by no means as irritated by ethnic stereotypes as we are today. In German comedy, as in German folklore, sly Bohemians coexisted with infantile Czechs, stiff Prussians, and dumb Bavarians. Jewish stereotypes were no exception here.

Like other theaters, the Folies Caprice altered the content of its plays dramatically after the outbreak of the war. One drama—*Stand Firm and True . . . or Be Proud That You're a German*—offered everything its title promised. It was one of three new plays staged in 1914 that explicitly dealt with the war. According to the *Berliner Lokal-Anzeiger,* the tone of the play struck a responsive chord among the population, which was fascinated by the war's challenges. Even more than the Herrnfeld theater, the Folies Caprice tried to

41. This particular joke was very well known at the time and reemerged in various collections of Jewish humor. In 1922, more than ten years later, Alexander Moszkowski (1851–1934), one of the most famous humorists and journalists of his time, included a slightly altered variation in which he exchanged Bleichröder for Rothschild. Alexander Moszkowski, *Der jüdische Witz und seine Philosophie. 399 Juwelen echt gefaßt von Alexander Moszkowski* (Berlin, 1922), 74.

42. Brandenburgisches Landeshauptarchiv, 30 Berlin C, Tit. 74, Th. 847, Akt. 176, 1912.

blend its typical slapstick humor into its new patriotic sketches.[43] Whereas the Herrnfeld theater tried to preserve and integrate its philosophy on Jewish assimilation into its patriotic plays, the Folies Caprice did not focus on what the war would mean for Germany's Jews. Like the Herrnfeld theater, the Folies Caprice used conversations between members of different generations to explain contemporary events and outlooks. In *Stand Firm and True,* landowner Böhnke, while observing the marching troops, explained to his enthusiastic daughter Anna what the war was all about.[44] Although there was no identifiable Jewish character in this play, community and the nation were key concepts at work. Exclamations such as "And a people that is united, that united burns, lives, and strives for its fatherland, that people will not be conquered," or "We are German brothers, and the Kaiser has said, [we] no longer know parties" were woven into the play at every suitable occasion.[45] At the outset, it is not clear who is actually meant to be part of the German nation. As the story unfolds, however, it turns out that being German is a matter of self-perception, not of birth.

To make this message easily accessible to a wider audience, the Folies Caprice chose a classic scenario. Two young men, named Hermann and Charlé, are competing for Anna's love. Hermann, a farm laborer who was among the first recruits to volunteer for service at the front, is at first outdone by the slick Charlé, whose charms have blinded both father and daughter. The purifying effect of the military mobilization, however, brings the real nature of both rivals to light. Charlé, the son of French citizens who has lived as a German citizen in Germany his entire life, turns out to be a deceitful French nationalist. He has capitalized on the German fascination with French manners, fashion, and refinement. Hermann, by contrast, is a ponderous, uneducated farmer with upright morals, inflamed by his loyalty to Germany and his true love for Anna. In the end, the situation is resolved

43. Ibid., Th. 848, Akt. 54 RS, September 22, 1914, and Akt. 58, *Berliner Lokal-Anzeiger,* December 28, 1914.

44. Landesarchiv Berlin, *Fest steht und treu . . . oder sei stolz, daß du ein Deutscher bist,* Folies Caprice, Rep. 30 c/a, Theater Z, Neuer Teil 6043.

45. "Und ein Volk das einig ist, das einig für sein Vaterland glüht, lebt und strebt, das Volk wird nicht überwunden werden"; "Deutsche Brüder sind wir und unser Kaiser hat gesagt, ich kenne keine Parteien mehr." Landesarchiv Berlin, *Fest steht und treu . . . oder sei stolz, daß du ein Deutscher bist.* Ibid.

when Anna decides that she prefers the simple man with the "right" up-
bringing over the one who combines deceit with polished refinement. As
Germany goes to war, her initial infatuation with Charlé fades in favor of
Hermann.

The rivals carried names with similar national pathos; Hermann, hero of
the battle of Teutoburg Forest in AD 9, was presented as Charle(magne)'s
alter ego, as German culture's answer to Roman-French civilization. In a
shouting match, Hermann accuses Charlé of being a traitor:

> CHARLÉ. (*scandalized*) What? Me a traitor of the fatherland?
>
> HERMANN. That's precisely what you are, when you as a German
> take pleasure in fake news. Do you really believe I haven't heard what
> you whispered joyfully to old Marianne: "This time the Germans will
> likely have a bit of a tougher stand than in 1870." But one often mis-
> calculates, even the Grande Nation. We at least are considerate to the
> French gentlemen, and because we know they also like chocolates, we
> have presented them with a few 42 cm. chocolate truffles. Those
> things are hard to digest and you can easily upset your stomach on
> them. The Frenchmen who always march at the forefront of civiliza-
> tion, who believe in magnifying virtues only in the imagination and
> minimizing them in reality. Well, old Zeppelin with his airships,
> that's an invention, isn't it? And we merrily applaud the sight of such
> a mighty liverwurst and shout: "All that's good comes from above."
> And no matter whether we'll have more trouble this time than in
> 1870, I probably won't be able to discuss it with you, Mr. Charlé, after
> the Great War. My doctor has advised me that if I want to stay
> healthy I have to forget anything disagreeable, and do you know
> where I'll begin to forget first? With you, Mr. Charlé.[46]

46. "Charlé (empört). Was? Ich ein Vaterlandsverräter? / HERMANN. Jawohl, das sind
Sie, wenn Sie sich als Deutscher noch über falsche Nachrichten erfreuen. Glauben Sie
denn, ich habe nicht gehört, wie Sie der alten Marianne fast glückstrahlend zugeflüstert
haben, ja diesmal werden's die Deutschen wohl 'n bischen schwerer haben wie 1870. Aber
oft verrechnet man sich, vielleicht auch die grosse Nation. Wir sind aber immerhin auf-
merksam gegen die Herren Franzosen, und da wissen wir, dass sie auch gern Konfekt
essen, haben wir ihnen ein paar 42 cm. Pralinés offeriert. Die Dinger sind schwer zu ver-
dauen und da kann man sich den Magen einwenig daran verderben. Die Herren Franzosen, die immer an der Spitze der Zivilisation marschieren und glauben, alle Vorzüge nur
in der Einbildung vergrössert und in der Wirklichkeit veringgert. Ja, ja der alte Zeppelin

In the end, it is socialization and not birth that makes Hermann feel German and Charlé feel French. Hermann's family history is a complicated one, but it boils down to the fact that he had been born as a French citizen to French parents and had lost contact with his real family through fateful circumstance. He was adopted and raised by a Prussian officer. Faced with the calamity of war, he opts for Germany as his fatherland, even though he knows about his French origins. Hermann feels German and thus thinks himself to be German, a case that was not foreseen in Germany's citizenship law. Here, the Folies Caprice went against the grain of the contemporary legal framework, despite its need to conform on most political issues. It deliberately did not subscribe to racial thinking at a time when such opinions were increasingly common among the German public at large.

In Hermann's praise for the zeppelin, the Folies Caprice evoked a symbol that originally had carried two conflicting hopes: the transcendence of human boundaries and the desire for military and cultural superiority. In 1909–10, aviation still spurred the hope in some Germans that it would "bind nations together, and unify diverse people."[47] Just as humanitarian and international notions of justice and human love were used in the Gebrüder Herrnfeld Theater as a means of legitimizing Germany's wartime struggle against foreign enemies in 1914, a symbol of internationalism here was transformed into a vehicle to arouse chauvinistic sentiments.

In the monologue cited above, Hermann reveals himself to be a middle-class nationalist, identical in outlook and sentiments to the audiences of the Folies Caprice. The reference to the zeppelin was not accidental, since—despite the vain hope of pacifists—it was widely conceived as a powerful symbol of the superiority of Germany's cultural and technological superior-

---

mit seinen Luftequipagen ist eine Erfindung, nicht? Und wir klatschen vergnügt in die Hände beim Anblick einer so mächtigen Leberwurst und rufen: Aller Segen kommt von oben. Und ob es uns diesmal schwerer fallen wird als wie 1870, darüber werde ich mit Ihnen, Herr Charlé, nach dem grossen Krieg wohl nicht mehr sprechen können. Mir hat man ein Doktor gesagt, wenn ich gesund bleiben will, dann muss ich alles unangenehme vergessen, und wissen sie, wo ich anfangen werde zu vergessen, bei Ihnen, Herr Charlé." Ibid. [The 42 cm. chocolate truffles are a reference to the shells of the biggest Krupp howitzers (Big Berthas), which were 42 cm. in diameter. *Ed.*]

47. John H. Morrow Jr., "Knights of the Sky: The Rise of Military Aviation," in *Authority*, ed. Coetzee and Shevin-Coetzee, 307.

ity.[48] Although Hermann is neither eloquent nor insightful, the audience is asked to accept his implicit identification of his own status with the zeppelin, the "mighty liver sausage" that Germans considered slow but effective in warfare.[49] Even the food metaphor attacked French cuisine, which was still considered by many gourmands to be superior to the rather pedestrian German fare. Even without being born to German parents in Germany, Hermann turns out to be a true German patriot at heart. As such, he is a character with whom 'Germans' (whatever the accidental circumstances of their birth) could identify with their entire being—head, heart, and stomach.

Conclusion

Artistically rooted in many different entertainment genres, including variety theater, Yiddish theater, and classical theater, Jargon theaters were by definition a hybrid form of entertainment. They were arenas that blurred the boundary between the private and public spheres, allowing gentile and Jewish spectators to enjoy exceptional intimacy despite belonging to a society defined by rigid distinctions of class, gender, and ethnicity. While scholars such as David Sorkin, Marion Kaplan, and Shulamit Volkov agree that a "private Jewish culture" continued to exist in imperial Germany, they emphasize that Jews generally aspired to follow the formula of the Haskala: "Be a human being out of doors and a Jew at home."[50] Popular entertainment, however, permitted Jews to transcend this essential distinction. By focusing on the family, the most intimate sphere in which Jews experienced and defined themselves as Jews, Jargon theaters turned the private into a public affair. Onstage, where they were watched by hundreds of Jews and gentiles every night, Jews appeared to reaffirm their Jewishness in the intimacy of family life. In this private/public setting, they were human and Jewish at the

48. Morrow, "Knights of the Sky," 306. See also Peter Fritzsche, *A Nation of Fliers: German Aviation and the Popular Imagination* (Cambridge, Mass., 1992), 6–43.

49. "French accounts often depicted German aviators as fat, florid types in large slow planes, while claiming that the energy and initiative necessary to use airplanes accorded marvelous with Gaelic audacity." Morrow, "Knights of the Sky," 310.

50. Bering, *The Stigma of Names*, 21. See David Sorkin, *The Transformation of German Jewry 1780–1840* (New York, 1987); Marion Kaplan, *The Making of the Jewish Middle Class: Women, Family, and Identity in Imperial Germany* (New York, 1991); Shulamit Volkov, *Jüdisches Leben und Antisemitismus im 19. und 20. Jahrhundert* (Munich, 1990).

same time. It was precisely this dual quality that made them attractive to audiences, who sensed the more universal meaning in the endless stream of family comedies.

The First World War represented a great watershed for popular entertainment. It demanded changes in style, content, and—most importantly—type of humor. After 1916, it is uncertain whether one can really speak of the continuation of Jargon theater entertainment at all. As nationalist sentiments rose, it became increasingly difficult to maintain one of the main leitmotifs of Jargon theater. Community in diversity did not resonate for an audience that, by 1915, was confronted with chauvinistic war propaganda on all levels. Racist thinking pushed the Jewish community of Germany onto the defensive. Jokes about Jews became intolerable for a community that was not only under siege, but felt abandoned by its leaders. The rise of the Zionist movement—a product of the encounter of German Jews with Polish and Russian Jewish communities in the course of the First World War, as well as disillusionment with Jewish emancipation and assimilation in Central Europe—provided one of the most critical voices within Judaism against a theater that had embraced and envisioned a future for an assimilated Jewish community in Germany.

The early 1920s thus saw the end of a genre that had reflected the confidence and optimism of the German Jewish community earlier in the century. By the end of the war, Jews had ceased to define themselves as one of the German *Stämme,* equally distinct and as acceptable as the Bavarian or Bohemian "tribes." Although Jews moved into prominent positions in the realms of politics, the bureaucracy, and the military—spheres from which they had been largely excluded prior to 1914—their confidence in Jewish prospects for assimilation was shaken. Assimilation had not been rewarded with the benefits of social integration and acceptance. The anti-Jewish riots in Berlin's *Scheunenviertel* in 1923 represented the first climax of what was to be progressive social disintegration, expressed in a form of street violence that was reminiscent of traditional pogroms. As the Weimar years became conditioned by new sensibilities on every front, Jewish performers increasingly turned to other genres of entertainment.

We may conclude by noting the apparent ironies of gentile-Jewish relations in modern Germany. At a time when Germany was hardly known for its ethnic or religious tolerance, Jewish performers found a surprisingly sup-

portive audience among both gentile and Jewish Germans. Weimar, by contrast, despite its greater social mobility and receptivity to new ideas and
concepts, was surprisingly less inclined to support *Volkstheater* such as that
of the Herrnfelds. It seems as if a static social system might have sheltered a
highly dynamic entertainment industry from the limitations and restrictions
that ruled most of German society. By the end of the First World War, however, Jargon theaters found themselves caught between a rock and a hard
place. Their political conservatism did not endear them to the rising avant-
garde, while their ethnic distinctiveness excluded them from riding the
nationalist-völkisch tide that would sweep through German society during
and after the war years. Clearly, Jargon theater ceased to function as a bridge
between various worlds. Judged on the merits of their performances alone,
they quickly fell out of favor with their previously loyal following.

ANTIMODERN THOUGHT

PATHOLOGICAL OR PRESCIENT?

Two Antimodern Master Narratives

Jung and Heidegger

DAVID LINDENFELD

Introduction and Background

In *The Decline of the German Mandarins,* Fritz Ringer distinguishes between the "orthodox" and "modernist" variants of the mandarin type. The orthodox, he maintains, were uncompromisingly if not always coherently opposed to modernity, while the modernists, as the name implies, attempted to accommodate themselves to it. According to Ringer, the former were "generally the less articulate, politically unsophisticated, and intellectually less distinguished members of the German academic community," whereas the latter included more creative figures, such as Max Weber, Ferdinand Tönnies, Friedrich Meinecke, and Ernst Troeltsch, to name a few.[1] Ringer emphasizes that this second group were by no means enthusiastic fans of modernity as they saw it—their views on the contemporary scene could at times be quite pessimistic—but they were more or less resigned to its inevitability. This still set them apart from the orthodox, however, who remained unreconciled.

Nevertheless, it is intriguing to note that, although the mandarin elite might have declined in social and economic prestige over the course of the twentieth century, the general attitude of hostility to modernity that characterized the orthodox did not decline proportionately. To be sure, such hostility has never been a monopoly of the men of learning that the mandarin type denotes, either in Germany or elsewhere (one thinks of peasants and artisans, for example). And while the antimodernity of elites like the mandarins at the turn of the century might have been marked by a particular disdain of the masses and their culture, it overlapped with a number of other attitudes—distrust of reason and science, alienation from industrialization and urbanization—that were often shared by broader segments of the popu-

---

1. Fritz Ringer, *The Decline of the German Mandarins* (Cambridge, Mass., 1969), 130.

lation. More importantly, these attitudes have had remarkable staying power, surviving the upheavals of German and European history during the two World Wars to become staples of the culture of the second half of the century. There are multiple ironies here. For example, the student movements of the 1960s shared many attitudes with the ancestors of the professors against whom they rebelled. And many of these attitudes persisted among subsequent generations of academics as well, as is evident in their presence in postmodernism.[2]

My purpose in this essay is to suggest possible continuities between anti-modern attitudes at the fin de siècle and those later in the century. I do so by examining aspects of the work of two German-speaking intellectuals who, I believe, fit Ringer's description of "orthodox" mandarin, but who gained international recognition as highly creative figures later in the century: the psychologist Carl Gustav Jung (1875–1961) and the philosopher Martin Heidegger (1889–1976). One does not have to read far into their works to discover their intense dislike of modernity, evident in phrases like "our hypertrophic and hybristic modern consciousness," "the growing impoverishment of symbols," "the darkening of the world," "homelessness is coming to be the destiny of the world."[3] Both became involved with National Social-

2. On the terminological difficulties raised by the terms "modernity" and "modernism," see the introduction. On twentieth-century perspectives on the Enlightenment, see the anthology *What Is Enlightenment? Eighteenth-Century Answers and Twentieth-Century Questions*, ed. James Schmidt (Berkeley, Calif., 1996), which juxtaposes the eighteenth- and twentieth-century debates over the nature of the phenomenon.

Of course, we are already familiar with one critique of the Enlightenment which had at least some of its roots in the mandarin tradition, namely that of the Frankfurt School. But its members always maintained that they were critiquing the Enlightenment in the name of reason itself. This would put them closer to the "modernists" rather than the "orthodox" within the mandarin fold. On this issue, see Martin Jay, *The Dialectical Imagination* (Boston, 1973), 293–5.

3. Carl Jung, *Psychology and Religion* (1938) and "Archetypes of the Collective Unconscious" (1954), in *The Collected Works of Carl Jung*, 20 vols., ed. Herbert Read, Michael Fordham, and Gerhard Adler (Princeton, N.J., 1953–1979), 11.141, 9/1.28. Hereafter cited as *CW*. This edition is numbered by paragraph and will be so cited here. While I have not had access to the German version, I have relied heavily on the 11-volume edition published by Deutscher Taschenbuchverlag (München, 1990). Martin Heidegger, *Einführung in die Metaphysik* (1935), 4th ed. (Tübingen, 1976), 34; Heidegger, "Brief über den 'Hu-

ism in various ways and degrees and brought upon themselves a great deal of notoriety as a result. This did not prevent them, however, from attaining a wide following in the last half of the century that reached well beyond German borders.

Both Jung and Heidegger attempted to support and explain their distaste for modernity by providing their own master narratives of its genesis in the course of Western history. In Jung's case, this narrative is scattered throughout his various writings, but it is not difficult to reconstruct. In Heidegger's case, it is concentrated in a few specific works. Both of these narratives drew on the work of Nietzsche for inspiration, particularly his tracing of the roots of Western decline back to the ancient world in *Birth of Tragedy* and *Genealogy of Morals*.

Since neither Jung nor Heidegger (nor, for that matter, Nietzsche) were historians by training, it would be inappropriate to judge their grand historical vistas by the standards of academic scholarship. Neither could compare with such pessimistic students of modernity as Tönnies or Weber when it came to depth of analysis or subtlety of observation. Yet I would raise the question: did their peculiar psychological and philosophical perspectives yield distinctive and original insights into the features of modernity that they opposed—insights which might have eluded the "modernist" sociologists and which might help account for their long-term influence? In other words, do the cases of Jung and Heidegger point to the possibility that the "orthodox" mandarin position was not as intellectually impoverished as Ringer believed it to be?

Before examining these narratives themselves, a few preliminary questions are in order. First, do Jung and Heidegger deserve to be called German mandarins at all? In the case of Heidegger, the answer could hardly be clearer. He exemplified the qualities that Ringer attributed to the mandarin type in intensified, concentrated form. He was an academic who continually emphasized the superior insight of poets and thinkers and the cultural uniqueness of Germany; he disdained utilitarian knowledge and academic specialization. Heidegger's initial enthusiasm for National Socialism is well known. But some of his difficulties with the Nazis during and after his Frei-

---

manismus'" (1946), in *Martin Heidegger Gesamtausgabe* (Frankfurt am Main, 1976–), 9:339. Hereafter cited as *GA*.

burg rectorate stemmed from his opposition to scientific specialization and technical planning in the face of growing official favor of these activities.[4] There is no mistaking Heidegger for a "reactionary modernist."[5]

The case of Jung is more open to question, but a strong case can be made for his belonging to the mandarin fold, more because of his background than because of his later career. Although Jung was Swiss, his family background and early education was steeped in German learning, as Richard Noll has emphasized.[6] This permeated his written works as well. As a crude indicator, the index to his collected works lists four columns of references to Goethe's *Faust* and two and a half to Nietzsche. Nevertheless, Jung often wrote of Germany as an outside observer, not as a participant. He consistently referred to "we Swiss" when dealing with issues of nationality, on one occasion asserting that well-known Swiss traits of obstinacy and mistrustfulness helped immunize it from the mass enthusiasms that gripped Germany and Italy in the interwar period.[7]

Second, do Jung and Heidegger deserve to be lumped together at all? Their respective approaches were far apart, and to my knowledge, there is no record of either having had a direct influence on the other. Jung expressed a strong antipathy to Heidegger in his letters, and Heidegger was equally contemptuous of psychoanalysis.[8] They did, to be sure, have a common en-

4. Rüdiger Safranski, *Martin Heidegger between Good and Evil*, trans. Ewald Osers (Cambridge, Mass., 1998), 274–5, 289.

5. Cf. Jeffrey Herf, *Reactionary Modernism: Technology, Culture, and Politics in Weimar and the Third Reich* (Cambridge, 1984).

6. Richard Noll, *The Jung Cult* (Princeton, N.J., 1994), 20–2. Noll goes too far, however, in characterizing Jung's psychology as a whole, with its emphasis on the collective unconscious, as merely a version of Germanic *völkisch* thought. Jung's fascination with China, for example, is inexplicable on this interpretation.

7. E.g., Carl Jung, "The Swiss Line in the European Spectrum" (1928), *CW*, 10.903–24; Jung, "The Tavistock Lectures" (1935), *CW*, 11.278, 369; Jung, "Return to the Simple Life" (1941), ibid., 1352. On German-Swiss comparisons, see Jung, "Wotan" (1936), *CW*, 10.390; Jung, "After the Catastrophe" (1946), ibid., 412, where he warns the Swiss against becoming too complacent.

8. Carl Jung, *Letters*, 2 vols., ed. Gerhard Adler and Aniela Jaffé, trans. R. F. C. Hull (Princeton, N.J., 1973), 1:273, 330–2; Heidegger, *Die Grundbegriffe der Metaphysik* (1929–30), *GA*, 29/30:248.

There have been several explorations of the affinities between Jung and Heidegger, among them Richard M. Capobianco, "Heidegger and Jung: Dwelling Near the Source,"

thusiasm for the medieval German mystic Meister Eckhart; they also spent much time communing with nature on the shores of Lake Zürich and in the Black Forest respectively. There are two major factors in their background, however, which argue for their being viewed together.[9]

First, both grew up as outsiders to the German-speaking *Bildungsbürgertum* that is so often associated with mandarin values. Jung's relation to this class is admittedly complicated. Both of his grandfathers were illustrious men of learning and well known in Basel, a city which had a long tradition of hostility to the Enlightenment and had fostered such creative antimodernists as Böcklin, Burckhardt, and Nietzsche.[10] Jung's father had studied Hebrew and Arabic at Göttingen. But for financial reasons he was unable to continue an academic career and entered the Protestant clergy instead. The elder Jung's modest parish was located across the river from Basel, where Carl was able to commute to school and university on foot. The family's straitened financial circumstances helped set Jung apart from the more refined sons of the Basel patricians. More significantly, the son turned to the father for answers to questions about religion, but the father, who was himself undergoing a crisis of faith, merely told him to accept the church's teachings. At the same time, Jung was deeply influenced, on his mother's side and that of her family, by the occult; he developed an interest in it which, although not unusual in fin-de-siècle German culture, was probably less typical of its academic members.[11] Jung's involvement in his cousin's seances convinced him that there were aspects of mental life which Western science and learning had left unexamined. As a consequence, in later life

---

Existential Psychology and Psychiatry 21, no. 1 (1986): 50–9; Toshio Kawai, *Bild und Sprache und ihre Bedeutung zur Welt* (Würzburg, 1988); and Roger Brooke, ed., *Pathways into the Jungian World: Phenomenology and Analytical Psychology* (London, 2000).

9. On this and the following, see Gerhard Wehr, *Jung: A Biography*, trans. David M. Weeks (Boston, 1987), chs. 2, 5; Paul J. Stern, *C. G. Jung: The Haunted Prophet* (New York, 1976), chs. 1–4; Safranski, *Martin Heidegger*, chs. 1–3, 5.

10. On the intellectual milieu of Basel, see Carl Schorske, "History as Vocation in Burckhardt's Basel," in *Thinking with History* (Princeton, N.J., 1998), 56–70; Thomas Albert Howard, *Religion and the Rise of Historicism* (Cambridge, 2000), 112–7. Howard notes that Burkhardt's pessimistic view of history, based on the ineradicability of evil within the human psyche, bears strong affinities to Jung's view (ibid., 160).

11. Ronald Haymon, *A Life of Jung* (New York, 1999), chs. 3–5.

Jung could never accept the purely secular or material emphases of the world around him.

Heidegger, born fourteen years after Jung in a village in the Black Forest—just across the German border from Basel—was more genuinely rural in background. His father was a master cooper and Catholic church sexton, and his ancestors were peasants and craftsmen, far removed from the mandarin world. His father, moreover, had defended orthodox Roman Catholicism against the so-called *Altkatholiken*, who wanted to accommodate Catholic doctrine to modern Germany—a controversy which had divided the village. Heidegger initially aspired to be a Jesuit priest, then a Catholic theologian, and he retained his allegiance to Catholic antimodernism before World War I. All of this was quite atypical for the German *Bildungsbürgertum*, and Heidegger, like Jung, became aware at an early age of the social gap that divided him from this class.

A second underlying similarity between Jung and Heidegger as young men lay in the way they coped intellectually with the challenges of modernity. Both had to deal with conflicting aspects of their intellectual environments: a commitment to "scientific" standards of rigor and precision on one hand, and the need to acknowledge a spiritual dimension on the other. Certainly neither were isolated cases in this respect. The biologist Ernst Haeckel's doctrine of monism had a wide appeal and functioned as an ersatz religion; other natural scientists and psychologists embraced various forms of holism in the years before the war.[12] Jung and Heidegger saw, in their different ways, that the solution to the conflict was not to side with one aspect or the other, but to find a means of transcending the dichotomy.

Jung's way of resolving this dilemma was his decision in 1900 to pursue psychiatry, which enabled him to commit himself to medical science and still pursue the occult phenomena that fascinated him.[13] His dissertation was based in part on observations of his cousin's seances. Jung also brought together psychiatry and experimental psychology by employing word-association tech-

12. On monism, see Gangolf Hübinger, "Die monistische Bewegung. Sozialingenieure und Kulturprediger," in *Kultur und Kulturwissenschaften um 1900*, 2 vols., ed. Gangolf Hübinger, Rüdiger vom Bruch, and Friedrich Wilhelm Graf (Stuttgart, 1997), 2:246–59; on holism, see Anne Harrington, *Reenchanted Science* (Princeton, N.J., 1996).

13. Carl Jung, *Memories, Dreams, Reflections*, ed. Aniela Jaffé, trans. Richard and Clara Winston (New York, 1989), 72, 108–9.

niques in his research on mental patients. As is well known, he broke with Freud in 1913, claiming that Freud's explanation of unconscious patterns in terms of sexuality was too narrow.

As for Heidegger, the young theology student sought to defend his Catholic faith with the tools of logic—an enterprise which drew him to Neo-Scholasticism and a *Habilitationschrift* on Duns Scotus. He drew heavily at first on the Neo-Kantianism of Heinrich Rickert, which sought to draw a clear line between logic and the temporal flux of the experiential world. Consistent with this division, he inveighed in a student essay in 1910 against the "modern sense of life guided by the continually shifting stimulus of the moment."[14] Yet at the same time, Heidegger read voraciously in contemporary thought and poetry, and he soon found that logic was an insufficient insulator from the questions about temporal flux raised by people like Dilthey and Nietzsche. This eventually led to his decision in 1919 to break with Catholicism; around the same time he embraced phenomenology and became Edmund Husserl's assistant. Husserl's method proved to be a more satisfactory means of dealing rigorously with spirituality without sacrificing its temporal dimension. Whatever might be doubtful about the claims of religion from an empirical scientist's perspective, there was no doubt that these claims existed as contents of one's conscious life—in other words, as phenomena rather than noumena. Husserl's call for a mapping of such contents—finding the *logos* of phenomena—provided for Heidegger a means of preserving spirituality against both the skeptical implications of empiricism and the irrational excesses of *Lebensphilosophie.*

Jung's Master Narrative

Let us now turn to the role which historical narrative played in Jung and Heidegger's work. To begin with Jung, it is fairly clear that he turned to historical research in order to find some basis in reality for his experiences with the occult. He turned first to the Hellenistic mystery cults such as Mithraism, which had existed contemporaneously with early Christianity. In this interest he was by no means alone; thus he was able to draw on the work of classical philologists such as Albrecht Dieterich and the Belgian scholar

---

14. Quoted in John Van Buren, *The Young Heidegger* (Bloomington, Ind., 1994), 124. Chs. 3–6 treat his early development.

Franz Cumont.[15] These themes played a large role in the work which precipi-
tated the break with Freud, *Wandlungen und Symbole der Libido* (1912). This
work already contains the plot of Jung's master narrative. He distinguished
between two types of thinking: "directed thought," which typically worked
through language and was directed to external reality, and "dreaming or fan-
tasizing," in which inner mental states were projected onto reality. The latter, Jung claimed, played a much greater role in earlier civilizations. Jung
treated animistic religions as a manifestation of the second type. Quoting
Cumont on Mithraism, Jung wrote, "The gods were everywhere and mixed
themselves in all processes of daily life."[16] In the first century AD, when the
Roman world was ripe for a new religion, Mithraism competed with Christianity, which initially unleashed similar intense feelings of salvation while
also seeking to tame the moral excesses of pagan religion. Over time, however, Christianity became less magical and more philosophical: God became
accessible primarily through creed and theology rather than through direct
experience. This had the result of fostering directed thinking, thereby laying
the foundation for modern science and technology. Jung's later research into
Gnosticism and alchemy as suppressed alternatives within the Christian tradition were driven in part by the need to find confirmation of a magical view
of the world. In the 1920s, Jung reformulated his initial distinction of directed versus fantastical thinking into that of extraverted versus introverted
thinking. These terms continued to have epistemological as well as socio-
psychological connotations for Jung: extraversion was turned outward
towards objects, while introversion was turned inward towards the powers
of the mind. According to Jung, Judeo-Christian culture and its modern secular descendent clearly favors the extraverted type.[17] Thus Jung's master nar-

15. Richard Noll, *The Aryan Christ* (New York, 1997), 127–8. These two sources are
cited more often in the *Wandlungen* than the others Noll mentions: Friedrich Creuzer,
Richard Reizenstein, and K. H. E. DeJong.

16. Carl Jung, *Wandlungen und Symbole der Libido: Beiträge zur Entwicklungsgeschichte
des Denkens* (Munich, 1991), 82; see also 33–4, 78–83. This is a reprint of the original
1912 version rather than the revised edition that appeared in the *Collected Works* as vol.
5. The 1912 edition has since been issued as Supplement B (1991) of the latter, under the
title *Psychology of the Unconscious*.

17. Carl Jung, *Psychological Types* (1921), *CW*, 6.577–78. Jung deliberately spelled "extraverted" with an "a" to distinguish his use of it from the common meaning of the term.

rative is one of movement away from animism, a story of the removal of magic from the world.

The distinction between introverted and extraverted orientations formed an important part of Jung's new model of psychotherapy, which emerged from his period of intense personal crisis and near-insanity during the First World War and which served as a basis for many of his later reflections on culture and history. According to Jung, no one person is entirely introverted or extraverted; rather, these qualities are part of a complex pattern of characteristics—familiar to many through the Myers-Briggs psychological test—whereby certain dominant, conscious traits are compensated for by other, unconscious ones.[18] In normal times, these different aspects are more or less in equilibrium. But in periods of crisis, equilibrium breaks down and one comes under the sway of unconscious archetypes. In such states, one could experience intense visions and feelings of God-likeness—as did Jung himself in the years after his break with Freud. He later called such states *enantio-dromia,* the running to opposites, a term he derived from Heraclitus. This was obviously similar to Freud's notion of the return of the repressed, except that it did not depend exclusively on the Oedipal conflict or repressed sexuality. Such crisis periods can be fruitful and even necessary as a means to achieving greater personal integration: only by acknowledging and coming to terms with the irrational and morally proscribed aspects of one's personality—what Jung called the shadow—can one genuinely grow. This was in marked contrast to Freud's program of strengthening the ego at the expense of the id.[19]

Jung applied the same dynamic to society. A predominately extraverted culture, such as that of the West, risked ignoring its introverted side. In giving examples, Jung made extensive use of the notion of projection, which he defined as the displacement of a psychic content onto an object.[20] In ani-

18. Mary H. McCaulley, "Jung's Theory of Psychological Types and the Myers-Briggs Type Indicator" in *Advances in Psychological Assessment,* 6 vols., ed. Paul McReynolds (San Francisco, 1981), 5:294–352. The origins of the test go back to the 1920s, when Katherine C. Briggs became convinced of the value of Jung's theory and taught it to her daughter, Isabel Myers, who developed the questions which comprised the initial test between 1942 and 1957.

19. On the shadow, see Jung, "Archetypes of the Collective Unconscious," *CW,* 9/1.43–45.

20. Jung, *Psychological Types, CW,* 6.783.

mism, fantastical thinking worked primarily through projection, as in the personification of natural forces in the form of gods and goddesses. The shift to directed thinking could be described as a "withdrawal of projections."[21] In antiquity, this was already marked by the shift from polytheism to monotheism. During the Reformation, the Protestant disdain for religious imagery represented another step in the process. From here it was but a short step to the Enlightenment and the replacement of superstition by reason.[22] Still, Jung was under no illusions that projections had disappeared entirely. They gave voice to the unconscious, introverted orientations of modern civilization. These remaining projections were all the more intense for being unacknowledged:

> After it became impossible for the demons to inhabit the rocks, woods, mountains, and rivers, they used human beings as much more dangerous dwelling places. . . . A man does not notice it when he is governed by a demon; he puts all his skill and cunning at the service of his unconscious master, thereby heightening its power a thousandfold.[23]

"Our fearsome gods," he wrote, "have only changed their names. They now rhyme with—*ism*."[24] Jung's narrative is thus a powerful critique of modernity: the removal of magic is bound to fail.

All of this bears comparison to Max Weber, who coined the term "disenchantment" (*Entzauberung*, literally removal of magic). As is well known, Weber was likewise concerned with the long-term process of modernization, in which disenchantment played a crucial role.[25] Weber used similar words

21. Jung, *Psychology and Religion, CW*, 11.140.

22. On Protestantism, see ibid., 82–5; Jung, "Archetypes of the Collective Unconscious," *CW*, 9/1.22–4. On Enlightenment, see Carl Jung, *Two Essays on Analytical Psychology* (1943, 1945), *CW*, 7.150.

23. Carl Jung, *Marginalia on Contemporary Events* (1945), *CW*, 16.1365.

24. Jung, *Two Essays, CW*, 7.326.

25. For reconstructions and interpretations of Weber's historical overview, which he never expounded in narrative form, see Wolfgang Schluchter, *The Rise of Western Rationalism*, trans. Guenther Roth (Berkeley, Calif., 1981), esp. 136–8; Lawrence Scaff, "Weber on the Cultural Situation of the Modern Age," in *The Cambridge Companion to Weber*, ed. Stephen P. Turner (Cambridge, 2000), 110.

to Jung's when describing the precariousness of this process. "Many old gods," he wrote, "ascend from their graves . . . [and] take the form of impersonal forces."[26] Furthermore, Weber's notion of charismatic authority served the same irrational function of transgressing social and political boundaries and rules in his schema as did the collective archetypes in Jung's. Nevertheless, the socio-psychological process of Weber's disenchantment was somewhat different from Jung's. The key mechanism for Weber was asceticism, derived from the Protestant ethic—namely, denying oneself the sensual pleasures of life in the name of the pursuit of a calling. In other words, rather than demonic energy being withdrawn into the unconscious and projected outward, it is channeled—in good extraverted fashion—into the transformation of the world via capitalism and instrumental rationality. As Weber presented it, the main problematical consequence of this transformation was a kind of cultural entropy: the loss of unity and the pluralization of values, the fragmentation of the true, the good, and the beautiful.[27] The incompatibility of a modern political career with an ethics of ultimate ends, or of a scientific career with value-prescriptions, are cases in point.

Weber's response to this dilemma remained within the bounds of his asceticism: choose, as honestly as possible, a central value-orientation that fits your personality, being aware of the limitations it imposes and the sacrifices it entails.[28] To be sure, this did not mean becoming a monolithic personality; Weber's portraits of the ideal politician and the ideal scientist reveal a balancing of opposing forces and a sense of proportion. Even the Machiavellian should know when to say, "Here I stand"; the value-free scholar could at least clarify the meaning of ultimate concerns even while abstaining from passing judgment on them. But, as Weber's own personal commitments reveal, the boundaries between what one does within one's calling and what one does outside it should remain firm and fast, with as little seepage as possible.[29]

26. Max Weber, "Science as a Vocation," in *From Max Weber: Essays in Sociology*, trans. and ed. H. H. Gerth and C. Wright Mills (New York, 1958), 149.

27. Ibid., 147–8.

28. Rogers Brubaker, *The Limits of Rationality: An Essay on the Social and Moral Thought of Max Weber* (London, 1984), 68, 96–7.

29. See David Lindenfeld, *The Practical Imagination: The German Sciences of State in the Nineteenth Century* (Chicago, 1997), 317.

It is on this last point that Jung would have found Weber's response to be psychologically untenable.[30] The vicissitudes of life, whether at the personal or the social level, simply do not allow the compartmentalization of attitudes and activities to remain fixed and rigid. Crisis is bound to occur, and the dark side of one's personality or culture must be integrated, lest it rage out of control.

Jung interpreted the traumatic events of the twentieth century in just these terms. He wrote of World War I, "This war has pitilessly revealed to the civilized man that he is still a barbarian, and has at the same time shown what an iron scourge lies in store for him if ever again he should be tempted to make his neighbor responsible for his own evil qualities."[31] At the war's end, he was by no means convinced that the danger had passed, particularly in Germany. In 1918, he wrote of that country, "As the Christian view of the world loses its authority, the more menacingly will the 'blond beast' be heard prowling about in its underground prison, ready at any moment to burst out with devastating consequences."[32] By the late 1920s, he had recovered a certain optimism: the extremity of disenchantment was sparking a compensatory movement in the direction of introversion and spirituality, as shown in the increased interest in psychology and Eastern religions, not to mention movements like theosophy and anthroposophy. In 1933, he wrote, "The sickness of dissociation in our world is at the same time a process of recovery, or rather the climax of a period of pregnancy which heralds the throes of birth."[33]

This mood of expectation influenced his attitude towards Nazism. He saw the Germans as under the sway of an archetype, and he claimed that this explained more of what was taking place in Germany than any "reasonable" account (such as an economic or political explanation).[34] He identified the

30. On Weber's attempt to bracket the psychological dimension of action and its shortcomings, see Jon Elster, "Rationality, Economy, and Society," in *Cambridge Companion to Weber*, 24–5.

31. Carl Jung, preface to first edition of "Psychology of the Unconscious" (1916), in *Two Essays, CW*, 7, p. 4; cf. Carl Jung, "Role of the Unconscious" (1918), *CW*, 10.45.

32. Jung, "Role of the Unconscious," *CW*, 10.17.

33. Carl Jung, "Meaning of Psychology for Modern Man" (1933), *CW*, 10.293; Carl Jung, "The Spiritual Problem of Modern Man" (1928), ibid., 148–96.

34. Jung, "Wotan," *CW*, 10.385.

archetype as the Germanic god Wotan, a hunter of men who took possession of them, bringing out the "blond beast." Given his view that such encounters with archetypes were part of a constructive growth process, it is hardly surprising that Jung initially failed to condemn National Socialism outright and was willing to cooperate with certain Nazi-sponsored organizations—particularly if it meant furthering his brand of psychology at the expense of Freud's. All of this later did tremendous damage to his reputation.[35] In marked contrast to Heidegger, however, he did admit in 1945 that he had made a mistake and unequivocally condemned the regime.[36] None of this altered his fundamental diagnosis of modernity: the same dissociative combination of self-righteousness and barbarism, under the aegis of the increasingly powerful state, was just as characteristic of the cold war as it had been of World Wars I and II.[37] If anything, the shadow, that symbol of ineradicable evil, assumed a greater role in his writings during these years. As he wrote in 1950, "Light and shadow are so evenly distributed in man's nature that his psychic totality appears . . . in a somewhat murky light."[38]

Nevertheless, in his later years Jung did alter his master narrative in one large and crucial respect—by enframing it, so to speak, in a broader and even more speculative schema. This was the result of two interrelated developments in his thought. First, his ongoing researches in Gnosticism and alchemy led him to work out an elaborate mapping of religious and astrological symbols, which provided a context for his later thinking about Christianity. Second, he became less inhibited in giving voice to his mystical inclinations, which found expression in part in his famous notion of "synchronicity"—the idea that meaningful simultaneous events were not merely coincidental. It seemed that the career of psychiatry was no longer able to contain those speculative impulses which had long occupied him.

This change led him in the 1950s to a new concept of historical epochs,

35. See Aryeh Maidenbaum and Stephen A. Martin, eds., *Lingering Shadows: Jungians, Freudians, and Anti-Semitism* (Boston, 1991); Wehr, Jung, 315–26; Aniela Jaffé, *From the Life and Work of C. G. Jung*, trans. R. F. C. Hull and Murray Stein, 2nd ed. (Einsiedeln, 1989), 86; Andrew Samuels, "Jung, Anti-Semitism, and the Nazis," in *The Political Psyche* (London, 1993), 297–305.

36. Jung, "After the Catastrophe," *CW*, 10.400–443.

37. Carl Jung, "The Undiscovered Self" (1957), *CW*, 10.588, 499–504, 510–6, 544.

38. Carl Jung, *Aion* (1950), *CW*, 9/2.76.

in which he synthesized Christian and astrological schemata. Jung explored the fish symbolism in early Christianity and remarked on the synchronicity of the birth of Christ with the onset of the astrological "aeon," when the equinox passes through the constellation of Pisces. He further ascertained that the sun's path intersected with the second of the two fish within that constellation in the sixteenth century, just as Christianity was beginning to unravel and give way to secularism—which, according to ancient Christian beliefs, could be interpreted as the era of the Antichrist. Finally, the path would enter the constellation of Aquarius in the third millennium, ushering in a new age—a prophecy which has since generated a popular folklore of its own.[39] Thus Jung's gloom in surveying the present was offset by an optimism regarding the future.

Heidegger's Master Narrative

Turning now to Heidegger, a comparison with Jung immediately suggests itself. Heidegger's starting point, phenomenology, was based on the notion of intentionality, which had been formulated by Husserl's teacher, Franz Brentano. "Every psychic phenomenon," Brentano claimed, "is characterized by that which the scholastics of the Middle Ages called the intentional . . . inexistence of an object, and which we would call . . . the relation to a content, the direction to an object."[40] In other words, all consciousness is consciousness of something. This may be fairly viewed as the philosophical articulation of directed or extraverted thinking in Jung's sense. Whereas Brentano himself developed the psychological implications of this proposition, his students Edmund Husserl and Alexius Meinong developed the notion of what it meant to be a content and object. Heidegger's contribution was to focus on the middle: the "being directed to," the relations between subject and object. But it must be added that—thanks to his readings of Christian thinkers such as Paul, Augustine, and Luther—for Heidegger, "being directed to" was not a one-way street from consciousness to object, but a two-way thoroughfare via which transcendent objects were directed to

39. Ibid., 148–9.

40. Franz Brentano, *Psychologie vom Empirischen Standpunkt,* ed. Oskar Kraus (Hamburg, 1955), 1:124. For Heidegger's comments on Brentano and intentionality, see his *Prolegomena zur Geschichte des Zeitbegriffs* (1925), *GA,* 20:23–8, 35–40.

subjects as well. Heidegger's ability to develop a philosophy based on relatedness, evident in such terms as "being in the world," "care," "resolve," "boredom," "illumination," "concealedness," "disclosure," and ultimately "Being" itself, constitutes his great original contribution to modern philosophy and is the source of much of his international reputation and influence. This focus also helps explain the convolutedness of Heidegger's language as he attempted to fit relatedness into the Procrustean bed of Western grammar, with its atomic structure of subject-predicate-object.[41] Much of Heidegger's thought plays on the distinction between the relational term *Sein* and the object-term *Seiendes,* translated here as "Being" and "entity." Entities are commonsensical things, like persons, buildings, and institutions, which are accessible to the senses and localizable in space and time. The Being of such entities is not accessible and localizable in the same way. Heidegger's exploration of Being served as a new means to express his earlier theological concerns. This relational perspective also helps to explain Heidegger's disdain for theories built on subjectivity, which of course included psychoanalysis.[42]

How does a master narrative fit into this approach? Certainly Heidegger had a lively interest in history from his earliest years as a lecturer (he had already read and critiqued Spengler's *Decline of the West* by 1920–21). Yet for much of his philosophical career, he was quite hostile to conventional narrative and academic history, which he felt instilled a false sense of complacency in human affairs by explaining too much.[43] The famous analysis of historicity in *Being and Time* was designed to undercut such complacency. The fundamental contingency of human relatedness was revealed in the experience of extremity, such as "being unto death." Such experiences were

41. Heidegger admits as much in *Sein und Zeit,* 11th ed. (Tübingen, 1967), 38–9.

42. See n. 8 above.

43. Heidegger, *Phänomenlogie des Religiösen Lebens* (1920–21), *GA,* 60:33; "Die Zeit des Weltbildes" (1938), in *Holzwege* (Frankfurt am Main, 1950), 76. For a relatively lucid treatment of his views on history, see *Logik als die Frage nach dem Wesen der Sprache* (1934), *GA,* 39:79–116. This text is of extraordinary interest: it is based on the notes of students who heard these lectures (given when Heidegger was still an enthusiastic Nazi) rather than on Heidegger's own notes, which were lost. He thus was unable to alter them later. For an analysis of Heidegger's views on history that concentrates on his early works, see Jeffrey Andrew Barash, *Martin Heidegger and the Problem of Historical Meaning* (The Hague, 1988).

concentrated in decisive moments, in which past, present, and future were knitted together. In such situations, the past did not function as a narrative explanation of how the moment came to be, but rather as inspiration, as a set of traditionally handed-down possibilities which could serve as a basis for a present resolve that is oriented towards the future. In other words, as we are contingent entities, our decisions are constrained by our particular handed-down pasts, which Heidegger calls our destiny.[44] But we are not entirely bound by these constraints. The past should rather serve to energize us into action than lull us into acceptance that comes with a surfeit of understanding and explanation. The influence of Nietzsche's *Use and Abuse of History* is evident here, and Heidegger mentioned it specifically in his analysis in *Being and Time*.[45] Commentators have also pointed out the Christian inspiration of this view—the notion of *kairos*, a pivotal moment in time when God enters into human history, as found in Paul and revived in the 1920s by Paul Tillich.[46] Heidegger's thought thus reflected the sense that the crisis situation in which Europe found itself after World War I could only be a sign that a decisive moment of history was at hand.[47]

Heidegger's outline for the projected treatise of which *Being and Time* was but a fragment indicates that he had already conceived a sweeping critique—his own word was *Destruktion*—of the history of Western philosophy, which he believed to have focused excessively on entities (subjects and

---

44. Heidegger, *Sein und Zeit*, 385–6. On Heidegger's notion of possibility, see Werner Marx, *Heidegger and the Tradition*, trans. Theodore Kisiel and Murray Greene (Evanston, Ill., 1971), 111. This book presents a useful guide to Heidegger's interpretation of Greek terms that play a key role in his philosophy. On Heidegger's anti-narrative stance, see Paul Ricoeur, *Time and Narrative*, 3 vols., trans. Kathleen Blamey and David Pellauer (Chicago, 1988), 3:60–96, 120–6.

45. Heidegger, *Sein und Zeit*, 396.

46. Michael Allen Gillespie, *Hegel, Heidegger, and the Ground of History* (Chicago, 1984), 153; Charles R. Bambach, *Heidegger, Dilthey, and the Crisis of Historicism* (Ithaca, N.Y., 1995), 214; Michael Zimmerman, *Heidegger's Confrontation with Modernity* (Bloomington, Ind., 1990), 53. On Tillich's use, see John Powell Clayton, "Tillich and the Art of Theology," in *The Thought of Paul Tillich*, ed. James Luther Adams et al. (San Francisco, 1985), 279–82. Clayton quotes Tillich's original use of the term in 1922, which differs significantly from his later uses of it in the 1940s and 50s.

47. Jung also made similar statements in the late 1920s. See "The Spiritual Problem of Modern Man," *CW*, 10.195–196.

objects) rather than on Being. This critique was not to be cast in narrative form, but rather as a series of steps leading backward from Kant to Descartes to Aristotle.[48]

How then did Heidegger come to reverse these steps and write a master narrative? The change was part of the "turning" in Heidegger's thought that began after the publication of *Being and Time*. As Heidegger himself later described it, he was unable to find the language which would link his analysis of historicity back to Being.[49] In addition, the reception of *Being and Time* indicated that many critics had understood it as philosophical anthropology, i.e., philosophy from a human, subject-centered—and hence entity-centered—perspective, which was far from the relational one that Heidegger was striving to convey.[50] The "turning," then, was to distance himself still further from anthropomorphic language and to adopt a more impersonal form of expression—which involved his taking leave of phenomenology.[51] Instead of focusing on relations whose rootedness in human experiences could be intuitively grasped, Heidegger's language became even more abstract and abstruse. Now two relations would take center stage in his writing: the simultaneous "concealment" and "unconcealment" of truth. Linked to this, the term "essence" (*Wesen*) suddenly loomed large in his vocabulary—which unavoidably entailed a shift of emphasis from relatedness to penetrating the underlying "whatness" of Being, however much Heidegger resisted this connotation.[52]

A part of this shift was also an increasing appropriation of the vocabulary of holism. Being-in-the-world now presupposed a world view (*Weltanschauung*), a grasp of the world as a whole.[53] Heidegger was aware of the affinities of his view with the holistic biology of Jakob von Uexküll and mentioned it

48. Heidegger, *Sein und Zeit*, 19–27, 39–40.

49. Martin Heidegger, "Brief über den 'Humanismus,' 9:327–8.

50. Barash, *Heidegger and the Problem of Historical Meaning*, 245–8.

51. Otto Pöggeler, *Martin Heidegger's Path of Thinking*, trans. Daniel Magurshak and Sigmund Barber (Atlantic Highlands, N.J., 1987), 60.

52. Martin Heidegger, "Vom Wesen des Grundes" (1929) and "Vom Wesen der Wahrheit" (1930), both in *Wegmarken*, *GA*, 9:123–202. On "whatness," see ibid., 201. Here Heidegger begins to use "Wesen" not only as a noun but also as a verb. The contrast to Heidegger's earlier discussion of truth in his lectures on Plato in 1924–25 is striking: the term "Wesen" does not appear. See Martin Heidegger, *Platon: Sophistes*, *GA*, 19:15–9.

53. Heidegger, "Vom Wesen des Grundes," ibid., 139, 155–6.

in his lectures of 1929–30.[54] This is connected to Heidegger's opposition to the fragmentation of modern learning—a constant theme in his work.

Heidegger applied these new ways of expressing himself to the temporal dimension as well: his master narrative of Western thought emerged as the result of his newfound desire to view history as a whole. In the 1929–30 lectures he again discussed Spengler and other grand syntheses of Ludwig Klages and Max Scheler. He soon came to advocate a similar overview. The "history of Being" was the way to penetrate to the hidden essence of truth. "The question of the essence of truth is the question of the essential history of man, and vice versa," Heidegger affirmed in his lectures of 1931–32.[55] By expounding a master narrative of Western history, Heidegger hoped to uncover the roots of the anthropocentric perspective that he was trying to explode.

These lectures, which center on Plato's simile of the cave and the image of the philosopher-hero contained therein, also include the elements which explain Heidegger's embrace of Nazism: the belief that a new era of human existence is just beginning, that truth is won through struggle, and that the lonely philosophers and poets play a mediumistic role in bringing about this new era. Heidegger was soon to act out these interrelated convictions as the self-appointed Führer of German learning.[56] As rector of Freiburg University, Heidegger resolved to create a model of higher education that would be stripped of bourgeois trappings and would serve the nation, extending even to paramilitary drill and labor service. Here was a case of Jungian *enantiodromia* if ever there was one! By 1935, Heidegger had incorporated the language of German idealism into his metaphysics: that of *Geist* and its decline, and of Germany as the "most metaphysical of nations," caught in the pincers of the modern superpowers, America and Russia.[57]

Heidegger unfolded his master narrative in his series of lectures on

54. Harrington, *Reenchanted Science*, 53–4 (see n. 12).

55. Heidegger, *Vom Wesen der Wahrheit: zu Platons Höhlengleichnis und Theätet* (1931–32), *GA*, 34:115. On Heidegger's discussion of Spengler, Klages, and Scheler, see Zimmerman, *Heidegger's Confrontation*, 26–31.

56. Zimmerman, *Heidegger's Confrontation*, 86, 125, 324. See also Safranski, *Martin Heidegger*, 214–24, ch. 13.

57. Heidegger, *Einführung in die Metaphysik*, 28–9, 34–8.

Nietzsche between 1936 and 1941, which he later published in book form.[58] These were years when Heidegger became disillusioned with aspects of Nazism. Although he remained loyal to the regime to the end, he could not deny that the technological planners were interfering with his vision of Germany's spiritual reawakening and that his call for the latter had been premature.[59] Heidegger's work is ambitious: to portray Nietzsche's philosophy of the will to power as the end of Western metaphysics. To my mind, the Nietzsche lectures play a similar role in Heidegger's oeuvre to that of *Capital* in Marx's. Just as Marx began by portraying capitalism in all its power and then proceeded to show how it undermined itself by its own logic, so Heidegger performed a similar operation on Nietzsche's will-to-power, which for him represented the final stage in the history of Being—that of nihilism.

The process may be broken down roughly into three stages, with several substages within them.[60] For the Greeks, the predominant mode of being was "presence" (*Anwesenheit*), which emanated out from entities and which still left room for a certain amount of wonder on the part of perceiving subjects. Much of this was snuffed out, however, by Plato with his theory of ideal forms. In Roman times, presence gave way to "actuality" (*Wirklichkeit*, containing the verb *wirken*, to have an effect), thus highlighting causality. This gave primacy to human agency in the deeds of the Roman republic and empire. During the Christian era, causal agency was transferred to God the Creator. There is a similarity to Jung's narrative here, in that God gradually distances himself from humankind and becomes more intellectualized over the course of the Middle Ages. In the modern period, which was ushered in by Descartes, the mode of Being becomes representation (*vorstellen*), in

58. Heidegger, *Nietzsche*. 2 vols. (Pfullingen, 1961). For an accounts of another version, see John Caputo, "Demythologizing Heidegger: *Aletheia* and the History of Being," *Review of Metaphysics* 41 (March 1988): 519–46.

It is noteworthy that Jung also turned to the study of Nietzsche during the Nazi years; his seminars in Zürich concentrated on *Zarathustra* largely as a key to understanding Nietzsche's personality and his failure to attain equilibrium. See Jung, *Jung's Seminar on Nietzsche's Zarathustra*, ed. and abr. James L. Jarrett (Princeton, N.J., 1998).

59. Safranski, *Martin Heidegger*, 293–4.

60. Heidegger, *Nietzsche* 2:390–420, also 220, 254, 309. For secondary accounts, see Zimmerman, *Heidegger's Confrontation*, ch. 11, or Gillespie, *Hegel, Heidegger*, 134–49.

which Being emanates from the subject (*cogito ergo sum*). Re-presentation is an active process on the part of the subject (*vor-stellen*, putting forth), which eventually leads to Being's final incarnation as will, the subject's imposition of forms onto the world—which is, in turn, the key to modern technology. The end result is the will to power and the current struggle for world-conquest (as well as phenomena such as racial breeding).

As with Jung, this story is an indictment of modernity, because of the constant thread that connects these different epochs and renders it a master narrative. Heidegger calls this thread the abandonment of Being itself. This is the concealment of truth which, Heidegger claims, is indissolubly linked to a mode of disclosure of truth. But he sees this concealment as having a cumulative effect in Western philosophy, resulting in an ever more anthropomorphic and anthropocentric view of things—of which Nietzsche's vision of the overman is the ultimate expression.[61]

Heidegger worked out his master narrative during the Second World War, which he viewed as confirming his conviction that he lived at a turning point in history. In his lectures, he was not above altering the details of his narrative to fit the changing fortunes of the *Wehrmacht*.[62] As the magnitude of Germany's loss became clear, however, Heidegger returned to the kairetic perspective he had embraced in the late 1920s: the very destruction of Europe could undermine illusions about the technical way of life and thereby ready people for a new arrival of Being.[63] He invoked the term "eschatology" in a 1946 essay, but without providing any concrete indication of what the new arrival would look like.[64]

61. Heidegger, *Nietzsche*, 1:469–70, 654–7, 2:20–4, 355.

62. Thus in 1940, when the Germans were winning, nihilism was destined for a sort of *Aufhebung*, giving birth to a "new freedom" based on human subjectivity and the ability of technology to dominate the world. One must simply pursue the will to power to its violent conclusion, rather than stopping at half-measures (such as communism). See Heidegger, *Nietzsche* 2:279–80, 319–22, 333. This comes out even more strongly in the original lectures on nihilism, published as *GA*, 48, which contain many passages that were excised in the 1961 book on Nietzsche. See Domenico Losurdo, "Heidegger and Hitler's War," in *The Heidegger Case*, ed. Tom Rockmore and Joseph Margolis (Philadelphia, 1992), 141–64.

63. Heidegger, *Nietzsche*, 2:391.

64. Martin Heidegger, "Der Spruch des Anaximander" (1946), *Holzwege*, 301–2; Marx, *Heidegger and the Tradition*, 165–6.

The collapse of Germany and the Allied victory coincided with the exhaustion of the master-narrative approach in Heidegger's thinking; from this point on, he no longer invoked it. Instead, he returned to the view of temporality as manifest in momentary situations, as in *Being and Time*, albeit with different language. In fact, he had been working out such an approach in an unpublished manuscript from 1936 onwards, the very years that he was lecturing on Nietzsche.[65] Here the emphasis is not on the whole of history but on the "event" (*Ereignis*). Heidegger's customary use of wordplay links this term to "*eigen*" (own), thus giving it an overtone of "appropriation"—making an event one's own.[66] By a similar word-association, history (*Geschichte*) is once again linked to destiny (*Geschick*).[67] And there is no longer an inclination to treat the different historical manifestations of being as a patterned sequence.[68] Instead, Heidegger turned increasingly to spatial metaphors ("neighborhood," "clearing," "arrival," "lodging") rather than temporal symmetries to express himself, bringing him closer to the imagery of the ecological movement.[69]

During these years, Heidegger also became more open to the possibilities of psychology, thanks to the initiative of Medard Boss. Boss was a Swiss psychiatrist who had studied with Jung but became disillusioned with him; he had subsequently developed a therapy based on the ideas of *Being and Time*.[70] Although Heidegger participated in Boss's seminars between 1959 and 1969, his approach remained antipsychoanalytic, stressing relations be-

---

65. Heidegger, *Beiträge zur Philosophie (Vom Ereignis)*, now available in *GA*, 65. Otto Pöggeler considers it to be his main work. See Pöggeler, "Heidegger's Political Self-Understanding," in *The Heidegger Controversy*, ed. Richard Wolin (Cambridge, Mass., 1991), 224.

66. Martin Heidegger, *Identität und Differenz* (Pfullingen, 1957), 28.

67. Martin Heidegger, "Die Frage nach der Technik" (1953), *GA*, 7:25.

68. Heidegger, *Identität und Differenz*, 64.

69. There is an interesting parallel between the late Heidegger and Jung on the matter of spatial symmetries. Heidegger develops the notion of the "fourfold" of earth, heaven, gods, and mortals as embodied in objects. Jung's discussion of alchemical symbols also led him to postulate a quaternity—rather than a trinity—as an optimal classification. Cf. Martin Heidegger, "Einblick in Das was Ist" (1949), *GA*, 79:11–2; Carl Jung, *Psychology and Alchemy* (1944), *CW*, 12.26, 31, 167–9, 209–11, 327.

70. Brooke, *Pathways into the Jungian World*, 2 (see n. 8); Safranski, *Martin Heidegger*, 404–5; Stern, *Jung*, 224–6 (see n. 9).

tween subjects and the world, and he was inclined to see the pathology of psychiatric patients as part of the pathology of technological society itself.[71]

In an interview with *Der Spiegel* in 1966, Heidegger admitted that the "traditional metaphysical mode of thinking, which terminated with Nietzsche, no longer offers any possibility for experiencing in a thoughtful way the fundamental traits of the technological age, an age which is just beginning."[72] True to his impersonal perspective, he denied the abilities of human effort to initiate a spiritual transformation of the world; but he was in the end willing to utilize religious language and invoke "a god" as the agent of such a future transformation.[73]

In this respect, the trajectory of Heidegger's later thought was the reverse of Jung's. Whereas the elder Jung was willing to go further out on a prophetic limb, the elder Heidegger became more cautious, moving closer to Weber's position of abstention from ultimate meaning. Yet Heidegger never gave up on the possibility of a new manifestation of Being that would be appropriate to a technological age. As he reiterated in the *Spiegel* interview, it was the task of the poets and thinkers to be in "readiness" for such a manifestation—or its absence.[74]

Conclusions

What final comparisons between the two master narratives suggest themselves? Both Jung and Heidegger viewed the story of modernity as one of withdrawal or abandonment, although they would have disagreed about what was withdrawn or abandoned. For Jung, it was projections; for Heidegger, it was what cannot be projected, namely Being itself. A further similarity is encapsulated in an image they both used: that of the shadow. For Jung, the shadow was an often unacknowledged but ineradicable side of one's personality or of a culture, a function of the fact that dominant, consciously cultivated traits leave other traits underdeveloped and festering in the unconscious. For Heidegger, it was the concealment that accompanies every

71. Safranski, *Martin Heidegger*, 406. See, for example, his critique of projection in Heidegger, *Zollikoner Seminare*, ed. Medard Boss (Frankfurt am Main, 1987), 208–9.

72. Heidegger, "Only a God Can Save Us," in *The Heidegger Controversy*, 109.

73. Ibid., 107.

74. Ibid., 107, 108, 110.

disclosure in our relations to objects—as in his reading of Plato's simile of the cave. For both, the shadow expresses the constant interplay of darkness and light in human affairs, a counter-image to the Enlightenment view of progress from one to the other. Whatever the differences of perspective, then, the two can be said to be telling similar tales.

How may these tales, and the tales of the two men who fashioned them, be viewed as illuminating the fin-de-siècle in relation to what followed? Recall that both came from religious backgrounds; their intellectual journeys started out by seeking a method of harmonizing their own spiritual longings with "modern" precision of thought. Jung attempted to do this through psychiatry, especially psychoanalysis, and Heidegger did so through phenomenology. In later life, each found this harmony to be precarious and their approaches to be inadequate. Indeed, the trajectories of the two men in terms of their personal biographies show remarkable parallels. Jung was thirty-one years old when he began corresponding with Freud in 1906; Heidegger embraced phenomenology and became Husserl's assistant in 1918, at age twenty-nine. At age thirty-eight in 1913, Jung broke with Freudian psychoanalysis and entered an extended period of personal crisis during which he nearly went mad, experiencing the *enantiodromia* and ego-inflation that he later incorporated into his theories. At age forty in 1929, Heidegger became Husserl's successor at Freiburg and distanced himself from phenomenology; in the following years, he experienced the delusions of grandeur that led him to see himself as the Führer of German learning. At the same time, both of their midlife crises coincided with and were amplified by the social, economic, and political crises of Germany. And for both Jung and Heidegger, the combined result of these personal and societal upheavals was their embrace to a greater degree of the irrational and mystical aspects of their beliefs—a development which, however morally perilous during the years 1933–45, accounted in no small degree for their remarkable staying power thereafter.[75]

This brings us to an important difference between them. Jung's critique of Western modernity as excessively extraverted drove him to explore alter-

---

75. Albeit in different circles: Heidegger had an immense influence on academic philosophy in Germany and the rest of continental Europe, while Jung's influence, aside from his professed disciples, was more at the level of popular culture.

natives among non-Western cultures that were more introverted and that might play a role in redeeming the West. He devoted much of his life to this quest, although he tended to prefer those non-Western traditions that had a strong visual element (such as Hinduism and Taoism) and to neglect those that did not (such as Sufism). Jung eventually came to the conclusion, however, that rejection of Western traditions was not the cure for the ills of modernity—simply to embrace Eastern religion was a case of *enantiodromia*. Yet there is no doubt that Jung's own non-Western explorations influenced his late views as to how Christianity might redeem itself in the New Age. By contrast, Heidegger's critique of modernity as the abandonment of Being remained within the Western extraverted conceptual framework of relational thinking, and his attitude towards non-Western thought was more provincial. To be sure, he showed a passing interest in Taoism as early as 1930 and was drawn to Zen Buddhism in the late '30s. At the time of his personal collapse in 1946, Heidegger did turn to a Chinese scholar to collaborate on a translation of the *Tao Tê Ching,* but the project was never completed.[76] Hans-Georg Gadamer once suggested that scholars of Heidegger's generation were incapable of going beyond their linguistic competence to deal with texts which they could not read in the original language.[77] In any case, Heidegger also maintained in his *Spiegel* interview that the source of redemption was only to be found within the traditions of the West, rather than in reaching to "Eastern experiences."[78] But his interpretation of "East" marked an act of concealment: by identifying the "East" with Asia, and by identifying his beloved Greeks with the history of Europe, he missed their "near Eastern" connections to Hellenistic civilization and the alternate avenues to Being which this opened up—the kind of connections at which Jung, with his studies of Mithraism and Gnosticism, excelled.

This brings us back to the question with which we began: does the resolute antimodernity of these narratives add anything new to our understanding of the twentieth century in ways that the "modernists" among the German mandarins did not grasp?

76. Graham Parkes, ed., *Heidegger and Asian Thought* (Honolulu, 1987), 6–7, 10, 51–2, 93–101.

77. Ibid., 7.

78. Heidegger, "Only a God Can Save Us," 113.

In the final analysis, both Jung and Heidegger affirmed the indispensability of a religious perspective. The fragmentation of values that a secular world view offered them was inadequate, and the price required by mere accommodation to modernity was too high. Certainly the events of the last quarter of the twentieth century—i.e., since the appearance of *Decline of the German Mandarins*—have undermined the self-confidence of the West as a predominately secular culture. Could this then be the legacy of "orthodox" antimodernity to the postmodern world?

CONTRIBUTORS

ANN TAYLOR ALLEN is professor of history at the University of Louisville in Kentucky. Her publications include *Satire and Society in Wilhelmine Germany: Simplicissimus and Kladderadatsch, 1890–1914* (Lexington, Ky., 1984) and *Feminism and Motherhood in Germany, 1800–1914* (New Brunswick, N.J., 1991). In addition, she has published many articles on the history of German women's movements, some of which have a comparative dimension. She is at work on a book tentatively entitled *The Maternal Dilemma: Feminism and Motherhood in Western Europe, 1890–1965,* which considers the development of the maternal role in several Western European countries.

PETER JELAVICH teaches modern European cultural and intellectual history at The Johns Hopkins University. His publications include *Munich and Theatrical Modernism: Politics, Playwriting, and Performance, 1890–1914* (Cambridge, Mass., 1985) and *Berlin Cabaret* (Cambridge, Mass., 1993).

DAVID LINDENFELD teaches at Louisiana State University in Baton Rouge. He is the author of *The Transformation of Positivism: Alexius Meinong and European Thought, 1880–1920* (Berkeley, Calif., 1980) and *The Practical Imagination: The German Sciences of State in the Nineteenth Century* (Chicago, 1997) as well as articles in *History and Theory, Central European History,* and the *German Studies Review.*

SUZANNE MARCHAND teaches German and European intellectual history at Louisiana State University in Baton Rouge. She is the author of *Down from Olympus: Philhellenism and Archaeology in Germany, 1750–1970* (Princeton, N.J., 1996) and numerous other essays on the history of anthropology, art history, and classical scholarship. She is now writing a history of German 'orientalism.'

ROBERT E. NORTON teaches in the Department of German and Russian Languages and Literatures at the University of Notre Dame. His books include *The Beautiful Soul: Aesthetic Morality in the Eighteenth Century* (Ithaca, N.Y., 1995) and *Secret Germany: Stefan George and His Circle* (Ithaca, N.Y., 2002).

MARLINE OTTE teaches German and European history at Tulane University. She has completed a book manuscript entitled *Walking the Tightrope: Performing Jewish Identities in German Popular Entertainment, 1890s–1920s.* She is currently working on a study of amateur photography in the two Germanies from 1949 to 1989.

KEVIN REPP is associate professor of history at Yale University, where he teaches intellectual and cultural history of European modernism. He is the author of *Reformers, Critics, and the Paths of German Modernity: Anti-Politics and the Search for Alternatives, 1890–1914* (Cambridge, Mass., 2000). He is currently finishing another book, *Berlin Moderns: Art, Politics, and Commercial Culture in Fin-de-Siècle Berlin.*

FRITZ K. RINGER'S distinguished career has taken him from Harvard University to Indiana University, Boston University, and the University of Pittsburgh. He is currently adjunct professor of German and European studies at Georgetown University. He is the author of numerous important books and essays, among them *The Decline of the German Mandarins: The German Academic Community, 1890–1933* (Cambridge, Mass., 1969), *Education and Society in Modern Europe* (Bloomington, Ind., 1979), *Fields of Knowledge: French Academic Culture in Comparative Perspective, 1890–1920* (New York, 1992), and *Max Weber's Methodology: The Unification of the Cultural and Social Sciences* (Cambridge, Mass., 1997). He has recently completed a new book, *Max Weber: An Intellectual Biography* (Chicago, 2004).

MARTIN A. RUEHL is assistant lecturer in intellectual history at the University of Cambridge and director of studies in history at Sidney Sussex College. He has researched and written on Nietzsche, Wagner, and the George Circle, and co-edited (with Ingo Gildenhard) *Out of Arcadia: Classics and Politics in Germany in the Age of Burckhardt, Nietzsche, and Wilamowitz*

(London, 2003). Ruehl is currently working on a 'history of cultural history' from Winckelmann to Burckhardt.

RICHARD WETZELL is a research fellow of the German Historical Institute in Washington, D.C. He earned his Ph.D. from Stanford University and was a postdoctoral fellow at Harvard. His research focuses on law, science, and deviance in modern Germany. He is the author of *Inventing the Criminal: A History of German Criminology, 1880–1945* (Chapel Hill, N.C., 2000) and co-editor (with Peter Becker) of *Criminals and Their Scientists: The History of Criminology in International Perspective* (Cambridge, 2004). He is currently completing a legal and political history of penal reform in Germany from 1870 to 1945.

INDEX

World War I (*continued*)
295, 298; trauma caused by, 98; and zeppelin, 279–81; and Zionism, 282
World War II, 28, 30, 250, 299, 306–7, 306n62
Wundt, Wilhelm, 84, 96

Yearbook for Intermediary Sexual Stages (Hirschfeld), 176
Yiddish theaters, 252, 281
Young Vienna movement, 201

Younger German Historical School of Economics, 44

Zelger, Franz, 137
Zemstvo liberalism, 38–40
Zen Buddhism, 310
Zeppelin, 279–81
Zetkin, Klara, 85
Zionism, 3n2, 28, 282
Die Zukunft (journal), 121